# DISTINGUISHED AFRICAN AMERICANS IN AVIATION AND SPACE SCIENCE

**Recent Titles in the
Distinguished African Americans Series**

Distinguished African American Scientists of the 20th Century
*James H. Kessler, J. S. Kidd, Renee A. Kidd, and Katherine A. Morin*

Distinguished African American Political and Governmental Leaders
*James. Haskins*

# DISTINGUISHED AFRICAN AMERICANS IN AVIATION AND SPACE SCIENCE

Betty Kaplan Gubert, Miriam Sawyer, and Caroline M. Fannin

*Distinguished African Americans Series*

ORYX PRESS

Westport, Connecticut • London

*The rare Arabian Oryx is believed to have inspired the myth of the unicorn. This desert antelope became virtually extinct in the early 1960s. At that time several groups of international conservationists arranged to have 9 animals sent to the Phoenix Zoo to be the nucleus of a captive breeding herd. Today the Oryx population is over 1,000 and nearly 500 have been returned to reserves in the Middle East.*

**Library of Congress Cataloging-in-Publication Data**

Gubert, Betty Kaplan, 1934–
    Distinguished African Americans in aviation and space science / Betty Kaplan Gubert, Miriam Sawyer, and Caroline M. Fannin.
        p. cm.   (Distinguished African Americans Series)
    Includes bibliographical references and index.
    ISBN 1–57356–246–7 (alk. paper)
    1. African American air pilots—Biography.   2. African American astronauts—Biography   I. Sawyer, Miriam.   II. Fannin, Caroline M.   III. Title.
    TL539 .G83   2002
    629.13'092'273—dc21        2001034821

British Library Cataloguing in Publication Data is available.

Library of Congress Catalog Card Number: 2001034821
ISBN: 1–57356–246–7

First published in 2002

Oryx Press, 88 Post Road West, Westport, CT 06881
An imprint of Greenwood Publishing Group, Inc.
www.oryxpress.com

Printed in the United States of America

The paper used in this book complies with the Permanent Paper Standard issued by the National Information Standards Organization (Z39.48–1984).

10 9 8 7 6 5 4 3 2 1

Photograph on cover: (*first row, l to r*), Guion S. Bluford Jr., Charles F. Bolden Jr., Yvonne Cagle; (*second row, l to r*), Marcellite J. Harris, Mae C. Jemison; (*third row, l to r*), Robert W. Deiz, Frederick Drew Gregory Sr., Lemuel R. Custis.

To my dear granddaughters, Alexandra, Victoria, and Daniela D'Acunto.
BKG

To the memory of my mother, Goldie Kanter Mayer, a woman of valor, and to my grandson,
Benjamin Sawyer.
MS

To Alfred Bruce Brown Jr., Marjorie Burns Brown, and John Paul Fannin, who have been
my support and inspiration—on and off the ground.
CMF

# Contents

Contents

# Preface

This volume consists of biographical sketches, arranged alphabetically, of 80 African American men and 20 African American women who have had successful careers in aviation or space science. Photographs accompany about two-thirds of the sketches. To augment the sparse information available for most of these figures in the standard sources, we have tried, in every case, to provide as many details of a subject's life as possible. We also wanted to bring knowledge of these people to a wider audience. Most are little-known, lacking the celebrity of sports figures and entertainers, but each is a person who achieved his or her dreams against formidable obstacles and thus deserving of greater attention. Their lives are set in the context of the social and economic conditions of their times, such as segregation, racism, the Great Depression, and World War II. High school students, college students, and the general public will find inspiration in these stories of courage, perseverance, and outstanding ability played out against America's social history.

Each essay begins with a brief listing of salient facts: full name at birth; birth and death dates; educational institutions attended with location, degree, and date; positions held with title, employer, and date; awards and honors; and a short summary that describes the individual's contribution to aviation, space science, or other fields. The narrative is then divided into three sections. The first, "Early Years," concerns the subject's family and childhood through high school. Information for this section was often obtained from personal interviews with the individuals themselves, or with their relatives. The next section, "Higher Education," deals with their college and university training, and, in some cases, with their mentors. For pilots, their licenses and the dates they were obtained are included here. The third section, "Career Highlights," relates the positions held by the subject. Details of marriage and children are mentioned here, with the narration of the essays proceeding in chronological progression. Memberships in professional and fraternal associations, volunteer work, and hobbies are included if known. Whenever dates or other facts are in doubt, they are enclosed by brackets.

Each profile concludes with "Sources," a list of the articles, books, correspondence, and interviews that were used to compile the entries. If the reader wishes to undertake further research, most of the published sources are available in libraries. A selected list of 44 books and videos found at the end of this volume provides a general bibliography. Almost all these titles were published between 1990 and 2000. The authors hope these additional references will spur readers to add to current knowledge of the African American contribution to aviation and aeronautics with articles and books of their own.

A number of deserving individuals were not included in this biographical dictionary, even though they too were war heroes or pioneers in the field of aviation. Information about them in reference sources was sparse, and we were unable to locate addresses or telephone numbers for some of these individuals and so could not contact them directly. In some cases, letters went unanswered. As the deadline neared, we concentrated on those people for whom we could prepare in-depth profiles. When more information becomes available, as we expect it will, we hope to include these individuals, as well as others, in a second edition of this book.

Information may be found on some of the following pilots and astronauts in the books listed in the bibliography, and we very much regret their omission in this work.

*Early Pilots*: Marie Dickerson, Harold Hurd, Lola Jackson, Lola Jones Peppers, Doris K. Murphy, Billie Renfroe, Earl W. Renfroe, Marie St. Clair, and Dale L. White.

*Tuskegee Airmen*: Robert Ashby, William Campbell, Herbert E. Carter, Hannibal M. Cox, George G. Daniel, Joseph D. Elsberry, Charles R. Foxx, Willie Fuller, Edward C. Gleed, Vernon V. Haywood, Jack D. Holsclaw, Freddie Hutchins, Clarence C. Jamison, Elmore M. Kennedy, Herman A. Lawson, Armour G. McDaniel, Norman McDaniel, Charles E. McGee, Alfred McKenzie, Luther H. Smith, Edward Toppins, Spann Watson, and James T. Wiley.

*Astronauts*: Joan E. Higginbotham and Winston Scott.

*Others*: Theresa Claiborne, Marvin Perry Jones, Theresa Deborah Newsome, Melissa (or M'lis) Ward, and Otis B. Young.

# Acknowledgments

First and foremost, our deepest-felt thanks go to those subjects of the profiles, and to their families, who so generously answered the telephone calls and letters of researchers unknown to them. They well understood how hard it is to find information about their accomplishments, and sometimes, it is nearly impossible. They shared their stories, their photographs and archives, and in some cases, the hospitality of their homes. They are: F. Carl Barnett, Charles F. Bolden Jr., Ethel Bolden, Ruby L. Bostic, Isham A. "Rusty" Burns, Khephra Burns, Lemuel R. Custis, Christine M. Darden, A. Portia Davis King and Edward W. King III, Carl H. Deiz, Ruby Deiz, Aprille Ericsson-Jackson, Jean R. Esquerre, Louis L. Freeman, Joseph P. Gomer, Bernard A. Harris Jr., Wesley L. Harris, Frances Haynes, the late Joseph H. Haynes, Fred Hutcherson III, Melva Jackman, Ester LaGrone, Barbara Lawrence, Clare Loving, Dianne McIntyre, Dorothy Layne McIntyre, Marcella A. Ng., Chauncey and Anne Spencer, Carol Taylor, Barbara Watson, Craig Watson, George Watson Sr., Marc C. Watson, Edmund L. Wilkinson, O.S. Williams, and Shakeh Young.

We owe gratitude as well to librarians all over the country who provided articles and obituaries, and who smoothed our paths through the thickets of regulations, and in one case, led us to the daughter of A. Porter Davis, an early aviator, about whom there was only a brief mention here and there. They are: Alice Adamczyk, Kristine Anthony, Ernest Blackwell, Donna Burgess, David Burgevin, James P. Danky, Anne DeAttley, Bryan Estabrooks, Diane Johnston, James Hibbard, Sharon M. Howard, Katherine Igoe, Marianne A. Kane, Ellen M. Kovarik, Suzanne Levy, Clinton Lowell, Genette McLaurin, Brian Nicklas, Betty Odabashian, Michael Roudette, Georgia Slaughter, Tracy-ann Suleiman, Melanie Sze, Douglas Thar, and Antony Toussaint.

Other people helped us by listening, suggesting, sending clippings, inspiring, and with their computer expertise and patience. They are: Kim Brackeen, Alice Bradshaw, Randall K. Burkett, Joseph S. Cooper, Al D'Acunto, Mary D'Acunto, Rachel Carter Ellis, John Paul Fannin, William T. Fischer, Emily Gubert, Erminio Gubert, George and Karen Gubert, Von

Hardesty, Julia Hotton, Leon Joy Gurley Jennings, Vivian Mendelsohn, William Miles, Joan Miller, Anne M. Morey, Richard Newman, Donna Sanzone, Fay Stetner, Andrew Mark Wentink, and Wilhelmina Wynn.

To them all, we say thank you for your kind helpfulness.

# Introduction

*D*istinguished African Americans in Aviation and Space Science is the first biographical dictionary of its kind. The entries sketch the lives of 100 African American pilots, astronauts, engineers, scientists, and flight attendants, and of the Tuskegee Airmen of World War II. Twenty of the sketches are of women. The time span ranges over more than the last 80 years of the twentieth century. Because this topic has not been covered before with such depth, most of our research is primary and original, often dependent on the subjects themselves or their relatives.

When we told colleagues that we were writing a biographical dictionary about African Americans in aviation and aeronautics, responses were often, "I didn't know there were any," or "Are there enough for a book?" Some had heard of the black flyers in World War II, thanks to a 1995 cable television program about the Tuskegee Airmen. To be fair, information about African American pilots, astronauts, aerospace engineers, and other scientists engaged in space research is neither plentiful nor readily available. What little has been published is sparse and scattered, often targeted to specific audiences. Because of the paucity of information found in standard reference sources, the essays in this book necessarily vary in length and detail.

Because the books that do exist have been published during the last 15 years by scholarly or small presses or have even been self-published, they are difficult to find. Articles appear in obscure journals or in small-town newspapers. Articles usually contain little or even inexact information about the major dates of the subject's life, family background, schooling, or any information other than the one major accomplishment for which he or she is known. These capsule accounts leave out the textures of lives that were rich in adventure, achievement, and determination.

The profiles in this book show the vibrancy of men and women who insisted on doing what others said they could not do, who knew that someday they would fly. They understood, in the words of Reeve Lindbergh's 1996 children's book about Bessie Coleman, the first black woman to become a pilot, that "nobody owns the sky." To gather information, we contacted libraries all over the country. We conducted interviews in person, by telephone, by mail, and by e-mail to fill in the gaps of the limited printed material, check facts, acquire photographs, and bring the trajectory of their lives up-to-date.

We have used our subjects' own words, whenever we could, gleaned from personal interviews as well as from published sources. We contacted as many subjects and their families as we could locate through friends and the Internet. One of the more unusual responses came from General Charles F. Bolden Jr., a former astronaut, who, on Christmas Eve in Japan, e-mailed us detailed stories of his childhood. Another unexpected response came from Shirley Tyus, a former flight attendant and now a pilot, who telephoned us from her plane.

Almost all the people in this book have been "firsts" or "onlys." While these titles mark impressive accomplishments against odds, they leave a bittersweet taste at the start of the twenty-first century because there is still room for "firsts." As far back as 1976, General Daniel James Jr., the first black four-star general, recalled his mother telling him that "there are two Negroes we can do without: the first one and the only one. . . . I'm looking forward to the day when so many black people will be doing so many things that are noteworthy that it will no longer be newsworthy."

The history of blacks in aviation is fascinating. The earliest pilots include Eugene J. Bullard, who flew for the French in 1917, and A. Porter Davis and J. Herman Banning, who both obtained licenses in the late 1920s. In 1932, Banning and Thomas C. Allen made the first transcontinental flight by African Americans from Los Angeles to New York. The following year, C. Alfred Anderson and Albert E. Forsythe were the first African Americans to make a round-trip cross-country flight from New Jersey to Los Angeles and back.

In Chicago, Cornelius Coffey and Willa Brown founded an aviation school and trained many of the pilots who later went to Tuskegee. In 1937, they also co-founded the National Airmen's Association of America, with Chauncey Spencer and Grover C. Nash among the charter members. Other Chicago flyers were John C. Robinson, active in the Italo-Ethiopian war, and Janet Harmon Waterford Bragg. William J. Powell made his mark as a pioneer aviation educator in Los Angeles.

On March 7, 1942, the first five African American men ever to become pilots in the U.S. military received their wings at Tuskegee Army Air Field in Alabama. General George E. Stratemeyer, Army chief of air staff, said at their graduation, "I am sure that everyone present, as well as the vast unseen audience of your well-wishers, senses that this graduation is a historic moment filled with portent of great good. Future graduates of this school will look up to you as Old Pilots. They will be influenced profoundly by the examples you set." The five men were Lemuel R. Custis, Benjamin O. Davis Jr., Charles H. DeBow Jr., George S. Roberts Sr., and Mac Ross.

Nearly 950 others followed them, including Lee A. Archer Jr.; Roscoe C. Brown Jr.; Isham A. "Rusty" Burns, who opened a flying school and service; Woodrow W. Crockett; Robert W. Deiz; Elwood T. Driver; Jean R. Esquerre, who in 1973 became the first African American elected to the board of directors of Grumman Corporation; Charles B. Hall, first to down an enemy plane; Vance H. Marchbanks Jr., a specialist in aviation medicine who monitored John Glenn's 1962 Earth orbit; and James B. Knighten, who went from lieutenant colonel to stand-up comedian in Las Vegas. Fred Hutcherson Jr., flying for the Royal Canadian Air Force during World War II, was the first man of color to fly across the Atlantic Ocean.

Other military personnel include Jesse Leroy Brown, who in 1948 became the first African American aviator in the U.S. Navy, and Frank E. Petersen Jr., who became the Marine Corps's first black aviator in 1952 and the first general in the corps in 1979. Among women in the military who achieved firsts, there are Marcella A. Ng, pilot in the Air Force, 1979; Brenda E. Robinson, pilot in the Navy, 1980; and Marcelite J. Harris, who in 1990 became a general in the Air Force.

Perry H. Young Jr. and Carol Taylor were among the first African Americans to be employed by commercial airlines. Young became chief pilot for New York Airways, a helicopter service, soon after he was hired in December 1956. Carol Taylor was hired as a stewardess by Mohawk Air in December 1957.

It required a decision by the U.S. Supreme Court in 1963 to open commercial aviation to more African Americans. Among the first pilots to be hired by major airlines were David E. Harris, American Airlines, December 1964; Leslie A. Morris, Eastern Airlines, 1965; William R. Norwood, United Airlines, 1965; and Marlon D. Green, the plaintiff in the seven-year court case that went to the Supreme Court, Continental Airlines, 1965. Southwest Airlines hired its first black pilot, Louis L. Freeman, in 1980. Women pilots arrived in commercial aviation some years later. United Airlines hired its first black female pilot, Shirley Tyus, in 1987, and in 1994, Patrice Clarke Washington was named the first black woman captain of United Parcel Service. Warren H. Wheeler and Michael R. Hollis founded their own airlines—Wheeler Airlines in 1976 and Air Atlanta in 1984, respectively.

The first black aeronautical engineers were Douglas C. Watson and O.S. Williams Jr., graduating in 1941 and 1942. Even though they finished tops in their classes and the country was at war, finding employment was difficult due to racial discrimination. After the war, Williams was confronted by an unusually creative reason for his not being hired. The company, the personnel officer explained, hired college graduates from west-

ern colleges in odd years, and from eastern colleges in even years. Williams, with a degree from New York University, and the year being 1949, was ineligible. African American scientists working in aeronautics include George R. Carruthers, Patricia S. Cowings, Christine Mann Darden, Aprille Ericsson-Jackson, and Isaac T. Gillam IV at NASA, and Wesley L. Harris, an educator and researcher at both NASA and MIT.

After astronaut designees Edward J. Dwight Jr. resigned in 1966 and Robert H. Lawrence Jr. died in an accident in 1967, the American space program had no black astronauts until 1978, when Guion S. Bluford Jr., Frederick Drew Gregory, and Ronald E. McNair were selected. In 1983 Bluford became the first African American to fly in space. McNair died in the *Challenger* explosion of 1986. In 1992, Mae C. Jemison became the first black woman to go into space and in 1995, Bernard A. Harris Jr. became the first African American to walk in space. Other black astronauts include Yvonne Cagle and Robert L. Curbeam Jr.

We believe the lives of these men and women need to be known, that their remarkable achievements need to be acknowledged, and that their stories need to be included in standard histories and school textbooks. African Americans have struggled against racism, segregation, ignorance, and indifference to be included in every aspect of American life. The field of aviation, both commercial and military, is no exception. In writing this book we were impressed over and over again by the talent, the persistence, and the courage of people who never stopped believing that "nobody owns the sky."

Betty Kaplan Gubert
New York

# Profiles

# A

## George W. Allen

**Born:** About 1910, Tyrone, Pennsylvania

**Education:** Private pilot's license, commercial and instructor ratings, Carroll School of Aviation, Latrobe airport, Pennsylvania, 1930s.

**Positions Held:** Drummer in dance bands; instructor, chief instructor of pilot cadets, Tuskegee Army Air Field, Alabama, 1941–1945; chief pilot, Carroll School of Aviation.

**Summary:** George W. Allen learned to fly some years after the transatlantic flight of Charles A. Lindbergh in 1927. In 1941, he became the chief instructor of pilot cadets at Tuskegee Army Air Field, when C. Alfred Anderson advanced to the position of chief of primary instruction of pilots.

### Early Years

The news of Lindbergh's spectacular flight electrified the world. It clinched Allen's interest in aviation, which had already been piqued by watching the planes take off and land at his hometown airport when he was 15 years old.

### Higher Education

Around 1933, Allen moved to Latrobe, Pennsylvania, because he had heard the airport there had a busy schedule of classes and welcomed new pilots. To earn money for flying lessons, Allen held numerous jobs. He played drums five or six days a week with dance bands, using the musical training he had all through his childhood. A respected pilot and instructor, Lloyd Santmyer, gave him lessons at the Carroll School of Aviation, located at the Latrobe airport. After he had made his solo flight, Allen sold his car to buy his own plane. It was an Eagle Rock, a used plane that needed repairs before the Civil Aeronautics Authority could certify it as air worthy. Allen, with the help of two aviation mechanics, spent a winter restoring it. Allen then used it to fly more than 400 hours, and to earn his private license and his limited commercial, commercial, and instructor ratings.

### Career Highlights

In addition to his musical gigs, Allen also worked for the Pittsburgh financier, J.H. Rogers, possibly as a chauffeur. Frank Carlson, also of Pittsburgh, hired him to fly passengers and cargo from the New Alexandria strip along the William Penn Highway. C.B. (Charlie) Carroll, the operator of the aviation school at Latrobe, also employed him in that capacity, as well as for general maintenance and as a flight instructor.

Allen, known for his competence as a flyer and an instructor, made several lengthy flights. One was from Pittsburgh to Toronto, Canada, in a Piper Cub; another was to New York in a B-5 Kenner Bird. In 1939 he flew to Chicago for the August 25–27 air meet that was sponsored by the National Airmen's Association of America (NAAA), a two-year-old organization of black pilots.

Soon after, in 1941, he went to the Tuskegee Institute as an instructor of pilot cadets. Allen was one of three black instructors of a total of seven working for the federally funded Civilian Pilot Training Program (CPTP) in mid-1941, before the United States went to war. The other two African American instructors were Lewis A. Jackson and C. Alfred Anderson. Allen was promoted to chief instructor when Anderson moved to the higher position of chief of all pilot training at Tuskegee. Their students ultimately became the core of the 99th Pursuit Squadron and other fighter groups—the first black pilots ever to fly for the U.S. military.

Allen chose Tuskegee over other venues that had recruited him, such as West Virginia State College and the Casey Jones School of Aeronautics, a white school in Chicago. More than 50 years later, on May 29, 1992, Allen wrote to his friend, Chauncey Spencer, a founding member of the NAAA, informing him of the death of "our good friend Pete Geff. . . . As you know, color didn't mean a thing to him. He recommended me to Tuskegee and West Virginia State College." Allen wrote in his letter of some health problems, "but everything seems OK now. . . . Hoping to play summer bookings with the band."

At the end of the war, Allen returned to Pennsylvania, to the Carroll School of Aeronautics. He was the chief pilot there, su-

pervising four instructors. Among his students was Fred Rogers, host of the long-running children's television program, *Mister Rogers' Neighborhood*. In 1992, Allen and his wife were living in Toledo, Ohio, but it could not be determined when they moved there, or for what reason.

### Sources

Allen, George W., Toledo, Ohio, to Chauncey Spencer, Lynchburg, Virginia, May 29, 1992.

Barbour, George Edward. "Early Black Flyers of Western Pennsylvania, 1906–1945." *Western Pennsylvania Historical Magazine* (April 1986): 95–119.

Jakeman, Robert J. *The Divided Skies: Establishing Segregated Flight Training at Tuskegee, Alabama, 1934–1942.* Tuscaloosa: University of Alabama Press, 1992.

"Those Who Fly." *Chicago Defender* (July 15, 1939): 24.

## Thomas C. Allen

Thomas C. Allen. Courtesy of National Air and Space Museum, Smithsonian Institution (SI Neg. No. 99-15421).

**Full Name at Birth:** Thomas Cox Allen

**Born:** April 2, 1907, Quitman, Wood County, Texas

**Died:** September 11, 1989, Oklahoma City, Oklahoma

**Positions Held:** Mechanic and pilot, 1920s to 1940s; founder, Thomas C. Allen Aviation School, Inc., Los Angeles, California, 1939; ferried airplanes for Douglas Aircraft, early 1940s to 1960s; full-time volunteer for Oklahoma Air and Space Museum, Oklahoma City, late 1980s.

**Awards, Honors:** Honored as a pioneer at the "Black Wings" exhibition, National Air and Space Museum, 1982; Inductee, Oklahoma Air and Space Museum Hall of Fame, 1992.

**Summary:** With James Herman Banning, Allen completed the first transcontinental flight made by African Americans, September 18–October 9, 1932.

## Early Years

Thomas Allen was the youngest of three children, whose parents both taught at Negro schools in Wood County, Texas. Allen's father, who was originally from Louisiana, died only three months after Thomas was born.

"I got the flying bug when I was a little boy in east Texas," Allen later said. "We had a farm there with about 50 acres of grass and one day an airplane made a forced landing. I'd never seen an airplane on the ground before . . . people by the hundreds came out to get a look at it. The pilots said they'd pay us to stay with the airplane and watch it. . . . [T]hose early airplanes were made of something that a cow reacted to like . . . a salt block. Leave an airplane in a pasture overnight and the cows would eat it." When the pilots left, Allen told one, " 'I'm going to fly an airplane some day.' He said, 'You just keep that on your mind and someday you will.' "

Allen's mother, who came from Arkansas, moved the family to Oklahoma City and began teaching at the Douglas Negro school complex there. For years, Allen bicycled to a nearby "landing field" whenever he could. "I just hung around and learned all I could about it. One day I asked the man what he'd take to teach me to fly. He said $300. He gave me $100 in trade for a saxophone I had and let me work out the rest." After five months of helping repair airplanes, Allen, now in his late teens, had earned about an hour of flying time. There were no instruments in a plane except the oil gauge. Everything else was measured by memory or landmarks. Allen's lessons continued intermittently for months.

After five hours in the air, Allen had not yet soloed. He could not afford the $500 bond to fly alone; his mother's monthly salary was $80. One day when Allen was about seventeen, while the instructor was in town, the crew at the flying field got drunk on home brew and dared Allen to fly solo. The only operable plane on the field was the instructor's, so Allen got in it and took off. The instructor looked up, saw his plane and guessed what was happening. He returned to the field in a rage, just as Allen was landing. "[B]ut the others were telling him, if he could teach me to fly he could anyone. So he billed himself that way—'If I could teach a Negro boy to fly I could teach you.' People came from everywhere to learn—because of that."

## Career Highlights

Allen decided it was time to move on. With $9.88 in his pocket, he headed for San Antonio. He pictured himself as an army aviator. Quickly he learned that the Army was not interested in accepting African Americans as aviation cadets.

He became a general handyman and mechanic's helper at Stinson Field, earning $7.00/week and learning all he could about planes and instruments. He went from there to work in an airplane salvage warehouse at Kelly Field, and there had the chance to observe most of the existing types of airplanes. He held other aviation-related jobs in Texas and Kansas, including a stint for Braniff Airline, then in its infancy.

In 1929, Allen married; he and his wife, Celine, would have a son, Orrin. In Oklahoma City that year, Allen met several of the organizers of the Bessie Coleman Aero Club, over a disabled car. Instrumental in getting their car repaired and back on the road, Allen persuaded the organizers to let him into the Club as an airplane mechanic. He quit his job in Oklahoma City and headed for Los Angeles to join the struggling group. There he discovered that the group did not yet have a plane and, despite his years in aviation, when he took the examination for a mechanic's license, he failed "terribly." These disappointments led him to consider returning to Oklahoma City, but a letter arrived from his mother, telling him not to come back until he had done something worthwhile.

For the next year, he attended every air show in the area and studied all he could about new inventions and airplane mechanisms. In 1931, he returned full-time to aviation, as a mechanic. His relations with the Bessie Coleman Aero Club during this period were somewhat tempestuous: emotions ran high, and Allen often was at odds with other members, particularly William Powell and J. Herman Banning, who he felt undervalued his potential.

In the late 1920s and early 1930s, a number of pilots were attempting to find financial backing for transcontinental flights. Corporate backing for long-distance flights was far more easily garnered by white pilots, although it was said that someone was offering a $1,000 prize to the first black pilots who flew cross-country. Several pilots talked of making the trip, but by the summer of 1932, none had yet done so.

Late that summer, Allen was approached by J. Herman Banning. Banning, who had a four year old plane with a 14-year-old motor, planned to fly cross-country, but he needed a mechanic—and he needed one who could also provide a needed additional investment of about $125 for fuel to get started. Allen agreed.

With barely $100 left between them, Banning and Allen left Los Angeles on September 18, 1932. They became known as "The Flying Hoboes," since they planned to "hobo" across the country, stopping in towns where they knew people, staying with friends when they could, and, they hoped, picking up enough additional money on the way to reach the next stop. They flew a southern route, over Arizona, New Mexico, Texas, and Oklahoma. Old friends and new along the way assisted with meals, beds, and repairs. In return, the Flying Hoboes asked them to sign their "Gold Book" on the lower left wing tip, which became a record of all those who helped along the way.

As they inched their way east, the press picked up the story. The pair stopped in both El Reno and Oklahoma City, homecomings for them both. It was Allen's first return since receiving his mother's letter in 1929; he was accomplishing something worthwhile. In Tulsa, Oklahoma, they persuaded oil company owner William Skully, an aviation enthusiast, to arrange for them to buy oil and gas on credit from Tulsa to St. Louis, Missouri. In St. Louis, trade school students helped them correct the engine trouble that had caused a forced landing there. When they reached Pittsburgh, Pennsylvania, they met a worker for Franklin Delano Roosevelt's presidential campaign. Robert Vann arranged for the Flying Hoboes to drop 15,000 Roosevelt campaign flyers en route from Pittsburgh to New York. In return, the Democratic Party would finance that part of the flight.

On the morning of October 9, 1932, the Flying Hoboes landed their Eagle Rock at Curtiss Airport in Valley Stream, Long Island, three weeks after they left California. Their actual flying time was less than 42 hours.

They were given the keys to the city of New York by Mayor Jimmy Walker, and fêted by the Harlem supper clubs. The Democratic Party completely rebuilt the plane for them—but they never found the person who had offered the $1,000 prize to the first black pilots to cross the country.

Their return flight ended not far from Pittsburgh. In a forced landing in a snowstorm, they crashed into a pasture fence near Blairsville, Pennsylvania, and broke a wing tip. The *Pittsburgh Courier* paid for bus tickets to Los Angeles. As they crossed the country from east to west, they made a number of public speeches, usually for African American groups in community halls and churches. They never revealed that they had left the plane in a pasture in Pennsylvania.

Allen and Banning broke up their partnership in January 1933, a few short weeks before Banning's death in a crash at an air show on February 5.

Allen continued to work in aviation. In autumn 1939, the Thomas C. Allen Aviation School was incorporated in Los Angeles, with plans to open in early January 1940. Plans called for instruction to be provided by licensed experts in airplane and engine mechanics, blueprint reading, riveting, welding, and metal work. Each student would be required to complete nine months of actual experience with airplanes before allowed to qualify for flying time, and would not be allowed in the air until they had completed a year of training. No student planes of the school would be allowed in the air until after the school had been in existence for two years. Allen had spent several years studying methods of teaching aviation as applied by other aviation schools, and told a reporter that the majority of aviation school failures were caused by accidents. The school would be open to all, regardless of "race, creed, or color." Allen also said, "There has been much talk about aviation and the Negro, yet there has been little done about placing or training Negroes for any openings that may eventually appear. . . . If the Negro is to be fitted in to the future of the airplane industry, he should get his training NOW."

In 1941, the El Capitan Aircraft Corpo-ration, of Los Angeles, was granted a charter and permission to sell stock. Thomas C. Allen was mentioned in a press release as the man behind the corporation.

Shortly thereafter, America entered World War II, and Allen began ferrying bombers overseas for Douglas Aircraft. In 1949, still resident in Alhambra, California, he announced plans to become the first African American to make a round-the-world flight, announcing the venture as "the People's Project," without any commercial promoters. He planned "to drop off letters from the United States to people of other nations."

He continued to ferry airplanes for Douglas for 20 years, retiring from that company in the 1960s. In his seventies, he returned to Oklahoma City, and in his 80s he still volunteered full-time at the Air and Space Museum there.

In 1992, three years after his death, Thomas Cox Allen was inducted into the Hall of Fame of the Kirkpatrick Air and Space Museum, which honors Oklahomans who have made significant contributions to aviation.

## Sources

Carter, Sharon. "Aviation pioneer Thomas Allen dies." *General Aviation News* (November 6, 1989): 7, 19.

Fentress, J. Cullen. "1st Negro Cross Country Flier Plans to Open School" (October 28, 1939). [Claude A. Barnett Papers, Chicago Historical Society].

"First Negro Transcontinental Flyer to Fly around the World" (May 8, 1939). [Associated Negro Press (ANP) release, Claude Barnett Papers, Chicago Historical Society].

Hart, Philip S. *Flying Free: America's First Black Aviators.* Minneapolis, MN: Lerner Publications, 1992; 35–39.

Lynn, Jack. *The Hallelujah Flight.* New York: St. Martin's Press, 1989. A fictionalized version of Allen and Banning's 1932 cross-country flight.

"Oklahoma has long been known for making history in aviation." Untitled manuscript, possibly 1970s.

Powell, William J. *Black Aviator: The Story of William J. Powell.* Washington, DC: Smithsonian Institution Press, 1994. A new edition of Powell's *Black Wings*, first published in 1934.

# C. Alfred Anderson

C. Alfred Anderson. Courtesy of National Air and Space Museum, Smithsonian Institution (SI Neg. No. 90-7010).

**Full Name at Birth:** Charles Alfred Anderson

**Born:** February 9, 1907, Bridgeport, Pennsylvania

**Died:** April 13, 1996, Tuskegee, Alabama

**Education:** Lower Merion High School, Ardmore, Pennsylvania; Drexel Institute, Philadelphia, Pennsylvania; Petz Aviation School, Philadelphia, Pennsylvania; commercial pilot's license No. 7638, 1932; advanced training, Chicago School of Aeronautics, Chicago, Illinois; cross-country training, Boston School of Aeronautics, Boston, Massachusetts.

**Awards, Honors:** Chevalier, Legion of Honor, Haiti; Certificate of proficiency, Southeast Air Corps Training Center, 1941; the "Winky" fix, located on the VOR-A instrument approach to Moton Airport, Tuskegee, Alabama, was renamed the "Ander" fix in his honor, 1981; honored as a pioneer at the "Black Wings" exhibition, National Air and Space Museum, 1982; Frank G. Brewer Trophy, given by the National Aeronautic Association for significant contributions of enduring value to aerospace education, 1985; Elder Statesman of Aviation Award, National Aeronautic Association, 1992.

**Summary:** C. Alfred Anderson has been called the father of black aviation. A pioneer who had to overcome severe obstacles merely to learn to fly, Anderson made history in three flights with his colleague, Dr. Albert Forsythe, most notably the first cross-country round trip by African Americans. He was the chief instructor of the Tuskegee Airmen, as well as of many other African American pilots.

### Early Years

Charles Alfred Anderson was born on February 9, 1907, in Bridgeport, to Iverson and Janie Anderson. During his early years, Alf, as he was then called, lived for a time with his grandmother in Virginia, where he began his lifelong fascination with flying. Anderson is quoted in an article in the *Chicago Tribune*, "It started prior to the time I was eight years old. . . . Whenever I heard there was an airplane in the vicinity, I'd run away and try to find it. . . . I remember hearing people say, 'That boy's crazy.'"

He was sent back to live with his parents in Pennsylvania where his father was a caretaker of a large estate used as a private school and owned by a wealthy woman, Mrs. Wright. Receiving his driver's license at the age of 14, Anderson worked for Mrs. Wright as a chauffeur to save money for flying lessons.

## Higher Education

In 1920, Anderson applied to the Drexel Institute Aviation School, in Philadelphia, but was denied admission because of his race. He also attempted to join the United States Army, but was rejected, again because of race. The army did not allow black men to become military pilots until the U.S. became involved in World War II, in 1941.

Anderson persisted. He found an aviation school that gave him mechanical and ground work training but no flight training. Having learned these rudiments, he persuaded a small Pennsylvania flying school to give him tips on takeoffs and landings with the condition he provide his own plane.

Anderson used his savings, together with donations from the black community and a loan from his father's employer, to purchase a Velie Monocoupe. In this plane, he attempted to teach himself to fly. His first venture in the air found him crash landing into a tree. Despite this setback, which left him with a scar on his forehead, Anderson managed to learn to fly competently enough to earn his pilot's license in 1929.

In 1930, Anderson decided to obtain a commercial license, but needed further instruction to qualify. After many instructors turned him down, he found Ernest Buehl, a naturalized American who had been a German combat pilot in World War I. Buehl agreed to instruct Anderson in navigation and aeronautics, and in 1932, Anderson at last earned his commercial pilot's license.

## Career Highlights

In the meantime, Anderson's father had died, and the young man had taken over his father's job. The sympathetic Mrs. Wright had also died, and her daughter-in-law, heir to the estate, fired him when she learned of his acquisition of a transport license, telling him to use his license to earn his living.

This was more easily said than done. It was the height of the Great Depression; jobs were scarce or nonexistent. Anderson, who had married Gertrude Nelson in 1932 and was the father of two children, Alfred and Charles, needed work to support his family. He went to work for the Works Progress Administration (WPA), a federal agency which placed unemployed people in public service jobs. Anderson was employed in laying sewage pipes.

Sometime in the early 1930s, Anderson met Dr. Albert Forsythe, a young physician from Atlantic City, New Jersey, who was also one of Buehl's pupils. The friendship was to be a close and productive one. Forsythe, a successful physician, was prosperous enough to purchase an airplane. Telling Anderson that his present employment was not suitable for a young pilot, Forsythe persuaded the other man to join him in several historic flights.

The two men were determined to show the world that black pilots could do anything white pilots could do. To prove their point, they planned three daring long-distance flights, to be known as "good will" flights: one from Atlantic City to Los Angeles, a second from Atlantic City to Montreal, and a third from Miami to the West Indies and South America. The purpose of these trips was to show the world that African American men could fly airplanes—the generally accepted wisdom being that African Americans were inferior and incapable of flying. Forsythe and Anderson planned their trips for maximum publicity, to let the world know that black people could indeed pilot aircraft.

Their first trip was to be a cross-country flight from coast to coast and back. According to Forsythe, "The trip was purposely made to be hazardous and rough, because if it had been an ordinary flight, we wouldn't have attracted attention." In July, 1933, the "good will" pilots started for California to the roar of cheering crowds. Their Fairchild monoplane, *The Pride of Atlantic City*, was equipped only with a compass and an altimeter. They had no radio, lights, or parachutes. They used a Rand McNally road map to chart their course—until it blew out of Forsythe's hands on their return flight. Nevertheless, despite heavy rain and strong winds, they made it to Los Angeles and back, making history as the first round-trip transcontinental flight made by black pilots.

Their second trip, from Atlantic City to Montreal, Canada, was just as successful and set another record, making them the first black pilots to fly over an international border.

Their third and last good will trip took them to the Caribbean and Latin America where they were to land in 25 different countries, bearing a scroll to be signed by government officials in each. For this journey, they purchased a Lambert Monocoupe plane in St. Louis, Missouri. In the course of negotiating the purchase, they met Charles Lindbergh, who attempted to discourage their plans; it was Lindbergh's belief that only white men could fly. The two refused to be discouraged. With the support of the International Goodwill Aviation Committee (IGAC), an Atlantic City group that provided publicity and financial backing, the two proceeded with their plans.

The plane was christened the *Spirit of Booker T. Washington* in a ceremony at the Tuskegee Institute. Nettie H. Washington, Booker T. Washington's granddaughter, was among the hundreds of enthusiastic students, faculty, and members of the general public in attendance at the ceremony. The two men embarked on their trip on November 8, 1934.

The Caribbean flight was the most difficult of all. In many places there were no runways or landing fields and the men were often forced to land on a city street or a playing field. In Nassau, where they arrived at night after an unexpected delay, cars surrounded the runway, their headlights on to illuminate the plane's landing.

Contemporary newspaper accounts show the pair being enthusiastically greeted at every port of call. The first leg of their trip was to Nassau, Bahamas. "There wasn't any landing strip or airport in those days," Dr. Forsythe is quoted as saying, "but our friends in my home town . . . had cut down brush and . . . moved all the telephone poles in the area and shifted their wires." They again made history by landing in Nassau—only seaplanes had ever landed there before.

The governor greeted them ceremoniously in the presence of a large crowd numbering 5,000 persons, including the United States consul and other government officials. This was a great triumph for Dr. Forsythe, who was a native of the Bahamas. Dr. Forsythe presented the governor with a scroll conveying a greeting from the people of the United States. Forsythe's parents were among the honored guests who welcomed the two men.

Their next stop was in Kingston, and on the way there, they circled Port Antonio, Forsythe's home town, where a waiting crowd gave them a big ovation. On the way to Cuba, their next stop, the tropical rain was so hard, it "peeled the paint off the struts," as Anderson recalled in a 1988 interview with *People* magazine.

In Havana, Cuba, they were also received by the officals of that island; they then proceeded to Santiago, Cuba, where several receptions were held in their honor.

They never reached South America. As they left Trinidad, strong tailwinds forced them off course and they crash landed, seriously damaging the plane. The remainder of the trip was canceled. From a public relations standpoint, however, the flight had been a huge success. Despite this forcible shortening of their tour, the two were honored when they returned to New Jersey and a parade was held in Newark, in September 1935.

During the 1930s, Anderson introduced ground school training in black high schools in Washington, D.C., and trained pilots in land and amphibious aircraft at Hybla Valley, Washington, D.C.

Meanwhile, events in Europe were worsening. The rise of Hitler and Mussolini and their aggression toward other countries convinced President Roosevelt and his advisors that war was inevitable. Pilots would be needed if war broke out, and there was a shortage of pilots. To remedy this, a plan, called the Civilian Pilot Training Program (CPTP) was established to train young American men to fly. The program was intended only for white men.

After much lobbying and pressure from civil rights organizations, prominent African Americans, and the black press, the administration agreed that young African American men could participate in the program. An all-black segregated site at the Tuskegee Institute, a black institution in Tuskegee, Alabama, was chosen. C. Alfred Anderson was to be chief pilot instructor. It was here that he received the soubriquet "Chief," by which he was thereafter affectionately known.

"Chief" Anderson came to Tuskegee in July 1940. Sometime that summer, he was sent to Curtis Reynolds Airport, near Chicago, to complete a secondary training course for flight instructors. The Stearman PT-13, which were used for training, had a front and rear seat. Anderson, as the trainee, was seated in the front seat. He seemed to be having trouble executing slow rolls, which were necessary to pass the course. Anderson, sensing sabotage, insisted on flying in the rear seat, from which position he executed the rolls flawlessly. He subsequently found that the front seat controls had been rigged to prevent him from passing.

While teaching at the civilian flight school, Anderson was visited by Eleanor Roosevelt, the wife of the president, who was a trustee of the Rosenwald Fund. As Anderson later recalled: "Mrs. Roosevelt asked me to take her for a flight over the area against the tremendous opposition of her entourage. Mrs. Roosevelt was willing to risk her life with one of us because she saw no reason why blacks could not fly." This incident received nationwide publicity, featuring photographs of Mrs. Roosevelt in Anderson's plane.

On December 7, 1941, the Japanese bombed Pearl Harbor in a surprise attack. The United States Congress declared war the next day against Japan, Germany, and Italy. At that period, the military establishment did not believe African Americans capable of flying. Such African Americans as were permitted in the services served in segregated units. Now the Army brass were being asked to allow African American men to participate in the Air Corps. Under great pressure, they grudgingly agreed to what was to be called "the Tuskegee Experiment." Moton Field at the Tuskegee Institute, which had been the site of the civilian training program for African Americans, was now converted to a training site for Army Primary Training Cadets under the U.S. Army Air Corps (now the Air Force). Anderson continued as chief flight instructor, his job changing from training civilians to training military pilots.

Anderson successfully trained more than a thousand black pilots. The men he trained were to become the nucleus of the famed 99th Pursuit Squadron, which distinguished itself in the European theater of the war. General Benjamin O. Davis Jr. and General Daniel (Chappie) James Jr. are two of his better known students.

But in the early years of the war, the Tuskegee Airmen were kept in Alabama, many in menial jobs. At last, in April 1943, they were sent to North Africa and then to Italy. At Anzio, the 99th had a chance to prove itself, and did, shooting down eight planes in one day and seventeen during the course of the campaign.

The 99th was joined with three other black squadrons—all trained at Tuskegee—to form the 332nd Fighter Group, which escorted heavy bombers over Europe, never losing one to enemy aircraft.

The war ended in 1945, but Anderson continued to train pilots, providing both ground school and flight training to students of all races. In 1951, he began a flight training program at Moton Field for private students as well as Army and Air Force ROTC (Reserve Officers Training Corps) cadets.

Anderson's devotion to flight training continued. In 1991, he donated a Cessna 172 worth $34,000 to the Tuskegee University Aero Club. He was a founding member of the Tuskegee Airmen, Inc. (TAI) and of Negro Airmen International (NAI) and remained active in these organizations. One of the chief activities of the NAI (Negro Airmen International) was to sponsor the NAI Summer Flight Academy, which provided opportunities for African American youth to train for aviation careers.

Anderson continued flying regularly three or four times a week until he was well into his eighties. He retired from the Moton Field training site in 1984, but remained active and interested in aviation. In 1991, Anderson recreated the Caribbean good will trip of 59 years before as a birthday present to himself.

"Chief" Anderson died of cancer on April 13, 1996, in Tuskegee, Alabama.

## Sources

*Alfred "Chief" Anderson: The Most Famous Black Aviator in America.* Http://www.coax.net/people/lwf/chief.htm. Accessed December 15, 1999.

"Bizplane People." *Aviation International News* (Midland Park, NJ) (May 1, 1985): 157.

"Black Pilot Is Honored As Pioneer." *USA Today* (October 16, 1986).

Brock, Pope. "Chief Anderson." *People* (November 28, 1988): 149+.

"Chief Anderson Receives Brewer Trophy." *Aviation International News* (Midland Park, NJ) (November 1, 1986): 116.

Coax-Net People Links, Lest We Forget Page, C. Alfred "Chief" Anderson. Http://www.coax.net/people/lwf/anderson.htm. Accessed December 15, 1999.

"Four Added to Aviation Hall of Fame." *NJ Historical Commission Newsletter* (April 1985): 2.

Hunt, Rufus. "Among the First Black Aviation Pioneers." *Chicago Defender* (August 18, 1981): 6.

"Nassau Welcomes Goodwill Fliers." *Nassau Daily Tribune* (Bahamas) (November 10, 1934).

"Transport License Given Negro Pilot." *Washington Post* (February 28, 1932).

White, John C. "Father of Black Aviation Still Flying, Teaching at 75." *Chicago Tribune* (May 23, 1982): sec. 3, 13.

# Lee A. Archer Jr.

Lee A. Archer Jr. Courtesy of U.S. Air Force.

**Full Name at Birth:** Lee Andrew Archer Jr.

**Born:** September 6, 1919, New York, New York

**Education:** DeWitt Clinton High School, New York; New York University, studies in international relations, 1940(?)–1941; Advanced Flying School, U.S. Army Air Corps, Tuskegee, Alabama, July 28, 1943; University of California at Los Angeles, bachelor's degree, 1949; New York University, master's degree; Air Force Command and Staff College, USAF Air University, 1956.

**Positions Held:** enlisted ranks, U.S. Army, November 1941–December 1942; U.S. Army Air Corps, 1943–1948, including combat pilot, 332nd Fighter Group, 302nd Squadron, 1943–1945; Chief of the Instrument Instructors School, Tuskegee Army Air Field, 1945; base operations officer, Lockbourne AFB, Columbus, Ohio, 1946–1947; U.S. Air Force, 1948–1970, including assignments as Chief of Protocol for the French Liaison Office-SHAPE; White House Air Force-France Project Officer; Chief, Latin American Postal Region; Chief and Executive Officer of the SHAPE-Liaison Office, the 36th NORAD Division and HQ USAF Southern Command-Panama; General Foods Corporation, 1970–1984(?), including director of corporate equal opportunity affairs, 1970; president, later chairman/CEO, Vanguard Capital Corporation, a General Foods minority enterprise small business investment company (MESBIC); chairman, North Street Capital Corporation, 1973; corporate vice president of urban affairs; board member, Beatrice International Foods Corporation, the Institute for American Business, Atlanta University, Hofstra University School of Business, the International Amateur Athletic Association; Boys' Clubs of America, Tuskegee Airmen Commission; founding member, Negro Airmen International, Tuskegee Airmen International.

**Awards, Honors:** Distinguished Flying Cross; Air Medal with 18 oak leaf clusters; Distinguished Unit Citation, Legion of Merit.

**Summary:** One of the outstanding World War II combat pilots commissioned at Tuskegee, Archer saw action with the 332nd Fighter Group in the Mediterranean and was credited with four and a half air victories, although he was unofficially said to be the only African American ace pilot of World War II. Archer retired from military service in 1970 at the rank of lieutenant colonel and subsequently had a distinguished career in the private sector.

## Early Years

Born on September 6, 1919, in New York City, Lee A. Archer Jr. was the son of Lee A. and Mae Piper Archer. By the time he was a teenager, Archer was "a rabid fan of flying." While living in Saratoga Springs, New York, he spent much of his time at the nearby airport. He "did the usual things in keeping with being a flying buff," reading aviation magazines and building model aircraft.

While a student at De Witt Clinton High School in the Bronx, New York, Archer repeatedly attempted to become an aviation cadet and twice passed the competitive test. However, the Army Air Corps did not accept African Americans and Archer was never called.

## Higher Education

After his graduation from high school, Archer entered New York University to study international relations. But, Archer said in a video interview many years later, "we knew the war was coming . . . [and] that sooner or later we'd be in it. I thought that Hitler and Germany were a greater risk to us as black people . . . than the racism in America; [it was] a very virulent type [of racism]. I was very, very set on doing anything I could to stop it." So he volunteered for the Army, entering as a private in late November 1941, days before the attack on Pearl Harbor.

After basic training he was assigned to Macon, Georgia, and trained as a radio telegraphy network technician. Later he became an instructor in radio communications, with the rank of acting sergeant.

In May 1942, Archer reapplied to the U.S. Army Air Corps, once he learned that African American pilot candidates were being accepted. He reported to the U.S. Army Air Corps flying school at Tuskegee, Alabama, in December 1942. Recalling his arrival there, Archer said, "The town of Tuskegee was probably one of the strictest segregationist towns. . . . I find on the base that it is a segregated base, a beautiful little base, but—places for colored and places for white, white fountains, colored fountains; all this was a complete shock to me."

Training at Tuskegee included several months each of pre flight, primary flying, basic flying, advanced flying, and gunnery school. Of his fellow cadets, Archer later said, "They were uniformly arrogant, self-confident. Generally they were a different type of people, as I was different from the little group I left in New York City; I ended up in a group that were just like me. If there was a modest, shy and retiring man there, I didn't meet him."

Archer graduated first in his class on July 28, 1943.

## Career Highlights

Commissioned as a second lieutenant in the U.S. Army Air Corps, Archer was assigned to the 332nd Fighter Group, stationed at Selfridge Air Base, Michigan. With Wendell Pruitt and others, Archer gained a reputation for imaginative flying. "At one time [Colonel] Davis was going to court martial four of us because . . . we were trying to fly acrobatics in formation, and that was not done. He thought it was a risk we should not be taking. If something happened, it would reflect badly on the Group." Once overseas, Archer and Pruitt became known in the squadron as the "gruesome twosome" and flew together every chance they could.

The 332nd conducted fighter training at Selfridge until they were transferred to the Mediterranean theater in December 1943. Throughout the spring of 1944, the group was assigned to coastal patrol and the support of ground troops, dive-bombing, and strafing. At the end of May, the 332nd was transferred to the 15th Strategic Air Force and assigned to bomber escort duty, using new P-47 Thunderbolt fighter planes.

In late June 1944, the 332nd was assigned P-51 Mustang fighters, faster and more powerful than the P-47s. As was the custom with many pilots, Archer named his P-51 for his future wife, "Ina the Macon Belle."

Archer's first air victory occurred on July 18, 1944, during an air war over Memmingen, Germany, in which the 332nd destroyed 12 enemy fighter planes. Two days later, the 332nd moved on a group of enemy fighters attacking their bombers northeast of Venice, over the Udine area. Lieutenant Charles Bussey drove an enemy plane across Archer's path. Archer also gave chase, and, the enemy, hit with a volley from Archer's guns, crashed into the side of a mountain. Recollections varied, however, as to what had taken place. "The Air Corps—the powers that be—didn't know to whom to credit the kill. . . . there was no conscious decision, 'No, he isn't going to be made an ace.' They had no idea there would be any more."

On October 12, 1944, during an air battle near Lake Balaton, Hungary, the 332nd shot down nine enemy aircraft and destroyed 26 more on the ground. Archer received credit for three victories that day, and he later described the battle:

> Just after we had destroyed our first plane Pruitt noticed the formation of enemy planes coming directly toward us. Instead of avoiding them, Pruitt flew directly into the formation with his guns blazing. As we passed through the formation the planes scattered. We were now flying side by side with the enemy planes going in the opposite direction. We made a tight turn and fell in behind three enemy aircraft. After getting within shooting distance I fired a couple of short bursts at one of the planes. My fire was accurate and I tore off the wing of the plane. It tumbled down to earth. Then I slid my plane down below Pruitt's plane, which was now on the tail of a second plane. However, before I could fire, Pruitt's shots hit the target. The plane burst into flame. At this time an [enemy fighter] came in from the left and slid in behind Pruitt, who was now on the tail of a third enemy plane. I immediately pulled up behind him, and gave a few short bursts, the plane exploded, throwing the pilot out of the cockpit, and then fell to the ground. Pruitt was

still chasing the plane he had lined up. However, on his third burst his guns jammed. As I pulled beside him I could see him fiddling with his controls trying to start his guns. Seeing that Pruitt wasn't getting any results I told him to move over and let a man shoot who could shoot. He pulled over and I eased my plane into his position. I gave the enemy plane a long burst. Then [it] went into a dive for a runway that I observed below. Seemingly, he had decided to land. I gave him another long burst and he crashed on the runway. The German ground crew opened with all their guns. Lights were blinking at me from all directions. For a few seconds I had to dodge flak and small arms fire that burst all around my ship. But I was lucky and managed to wiggle out.

that other passengers could not see them. Years later, Archer commented on his military experience:

> We talk about special missions: the invasion of southern France, . . . Anzio beach. . . . But what we talk about most is how we were treated! We conformed to the Army Air Corps and the expectations placed upon us, but we were segregated on Tuskegee Army Air Field! . . . When I'm asked "Why did you do it?" I can't fully explain why; but it is my country. My grandfather was born here. Under a system that I consider reprehensible, I flew 159 combat missions and then turned around and went to Korea. It is my country and I will fight for it.

In the fracas Archer's propeller was hit. Pruitt flew beside him across the Alps, to make sure that Archer safely reached the emergency landing field on an island in Yugoslavia.

Archer flew 159 combat missions and was then reassigned to the United States as chief of the Instrument Instructors School at Tuskegee Army Air Field. "I did feel that it was ironic that we were fighting a Fascist country for a country that was in our estimation almost as bad, especially in some sections of the country. You wondered sometimes whether it was worth while to do it—but it was always in the back of your mind that, ok, when this is over, *they'll change*."

Archer married Ina Dodson Burdell of Philadelphia, Pennsylvania and Macon, Georgia, in 1945. Over the years she accompanied him to military assignments in France, Guam, Canada, and Panama. They had three sons and a daughter, Lee A. III, Raymond, Roy, and Ina Diane.

However, as the newly married Archers traveled by train to Archer's next duty assignment in 1945, it was apparent that the United States had not, as yet, changed; they were allocated a table in the far corner of the dining car, with a curtain drawn around it so

Selected for a regular commission in the U.S. Army Air Corps, Archer was sent to complete his bachelor's degree at the University of California at Los Angeles, and then saw active duty in Korea. After the Korean War, Archer attended the USAF Air Command and Staff College of the Air University, graduating in 1956, and also graduate school at New York University, where he was awarded a master's degree. In the late 1950s, Major Archer was chief of protocol for the French Liaison Office-SHAPE, stationed at Orly Field, near Paris.

Achieving the rank of lieutenant colonel, Archer held several high-level command positions during his later Air Force service, including chief and executive officer of the SHAPE-Liaison Office, the 36th NORAD Division, and headquarters of the Southern Command, based in Panama. He retired from the air force in 1970, after 29 years of military service.

The Archers moved to New Rochelle, New York, and Archer joined the General Foods Corporation as a vice president, assisting General Foods with the development of Beatrice Foods International and working to break down discriminatory barriers in the higher echelons of corporate America. "No, things aren't perfect,"Archer would later say, "but you can help make them so."

Archer was a founding member of Negro Airmen International and of the Tuskegee Airmen International. After his retirement from General Foods, Archer continued to be active on many civilian and educational boards and in appearances at military and public affairs events.

Ina Archer died on October 6, 1996, and is buried at Arlington National Cemetery.

In 1997, Archer and 17 others were appointed by Alabama governor Fob James to the Tuskegee Airmen Commission, with the purpose of establishing a memorial to the 332nd Fighter Group. In 2000, Archer was the first recipient of the Dr. Roscoe Brown Jr. Award, presented by the Sports Foundation, a Bronx-based organization that builds social responsibility through sports, providing positive alternatives to violent behavior and substance use or abuse for individuals of all ages.

More than forty years after his World War II combat experience, Archer would recount, "I was offered an opportunity to review the records and almost guaranteed that I would get [Ace status]. I refused that offer. It had been too many years in which they hadn't given it to me and that was that. I have been content."

## Sources

"Archer Leads All U.S. Negro Airmen." *New York Sun* (January 29, 1945).

Cooper, Charlie, and Ann Cooper. *Tuskegee's Heroes: Featuring the Aviation Art of Roy La Grone.* Osceola, WI: Motorbooks International, 1996; 66–67.

Francis, Charles E. *The Tuskegee Airmen: The Men Who Changed a Nation.* 4th ed., revised and updated by Adolph Caso. Boston, MA: Branden Publishing Co., 1997.

*Nightfighters: The True Story of the 332nd Fighter Group, The Tuskegee Airmen.* Produced by Fulmar Television and Film. Videocassette. Xenon Entertainment Group, 1994. Includes interview clips with Archer and others.

Sandler, Stanley. *Segregated Skies: All-Black Combat Squadrons of World War II.* Washington, DC: Smithsonian Institution Press, 1992; 110–111.

*Who's Who in Colored America.* New York: Christian E. Burckel & Associates, 1950; 585.

*Who's Who among Black Americans, 1992–1993.* Detroit: Gale Research, 1992; 40.

# B

## J. Herman Banning

J. Herman Banning. Courtesy of National Air and Space Museum, Smithsonian Institution (SI Neg. No. 83-99).

**Full Name at Birth:** James Herman Banning

**Born:** November 5, 1900, Canton, Oklahoma

**Died:** February 5, 1933, San Diego, California

**Education:** Faver High School, Guthrie, Oklahoma, 1918; studied engineering, Iowa State College, Ames, Iowa, 1919–1921; received aviation license #1324, U.S. Department of Commerce, 1926.

**Positions Held:** owner, J.H. Banning's Auto Repair, Ames, Iowa, 1921–1925; pilot, 1926–1933, experience included barnstorming, passenger, mail and cargo carrying; chief pilot, Bessie Coleman Aero Club, Los Angeles, California, 1929–1933(?).

**Summary:** Banning was the first African American aviator to be licensed by the U.S. Department of Commerce. With Thomas C. Allen, Banning completed the first transcontinental flight made by African Americans, September 18–October 9, 1932.

### Early Years

As many black freedmen did after the Civil War, James Herman Banning's parents, Riley and Cora Banning, moved to Oklahoma in the 1880s as homesteaders; that is, to acquire land under the federal Homestead Act by settling on a piece of land for a certain number of years. The Bannings homesteaded near Kingfisher, Oklahoma. They built a small school building on their land, where the pupils were their own four children and neighboring black and Indian children.

James Herman Banning started school in 1907 and showed an early aptitude for mathematics, reading, and anything mechanical. Even as a young boy, he enjoyed repairing farm machinery. In 1916, as a student at Faver High School in Guthrie, east of Kingfisher, he continued to develop his mathematical and mechanical interests. By his senior year in high school, Banning was a competent automobile mechanic.

In Europe, World War I was raging, and Banning was transfixed by newsreel footage of the nascent air forces in combat. He began to read anything he could find about aviation. With good grades in mathematics and his obvious mechanical talent, he planned to go on to college to study engineering. First, however, he spent a year helping on his family's farm and saving money from mechanic jobs.

## Higher Education

In spring 1919, Banning considered his options for higher education. Both Langston College in Oklahoma and Tuskegee Institute in Alabama were all-black institutions with strong engineering programs. Iowa State College, in Ames, also had an excellent engineering program and was located in a "hotbed of aviation activity." Banning was surprised and pleased when the predominantly white institution accepted his application. His parents rented their farm and moved to Iowa with him.

Many barnstormers and air circuses performed around the state, and in the spring of 1920 Banning paid five dollars for a 45-minute flight in Stanley M. Doyle's Canuck biplane at an air circus in Ames. He landed safely, brimming with aviation questions that Doyle could not answer.

In addition to studying, Banning set up a

mechanic's shop in his parents' garage, and soon was so successful a mechanic that his grades were suffering. He left college in 1921, to open J.H. Banning's Auto Repair on West Second Street in Ames.

## Career Highlights

As the business expanded, Banning moved to larger quarters on Fourth Street. Over the next several years, he read all he could about aviation and attended many of the air circuses that came to the Ames area, sometimes going for a ride with one of the pilots.

By 1924, Banning's interest in airplanes had overtaken his interest in automobiles. After rejections by aviation schools in four cities because of his race, he at last found a flight instructor in Des Moines, a World War I veteran named Lieutenant Raymond C. Fisher, who taught him to fly in an old Hummingbird biplane. Years later, in an article for the *Pittsburgh Courier*, Banning recalled,

> after three hours and forty-five minutes of training, and this stretched over a period of five months' time, I approached that stage of the game wherein the instructor permits the student to glide toward the landing field—if he can find it—and attempt a landing. Every movement, of course, is closely supervised by the instructor. This very day that the pilot complimented me on my progress to that date, five minutes later he took a new student up in the same ship and was killed in a crash. Lt. Fisher was a very good pilot, but made the fatal mistake of allowing a rank novice to attempt to fly the ship at too low an altitude. This was a sad blow to me.

Although the airplane was wrecked, Banning found that the motor was only slightly damaged. He bought it and moved it to his Ames repair shop. He watched the ads for war-surplus planes, and finally bought an old fuselage, body, and wings. In the help of "several white, mechanically inclined friends and the aid of an instruction book purchased from the Curtis Airplane Company," he built his first airplane.

Having never flown a plane alone, he asked other, experienced pilots to test the completed plane for him. But every one he asked knew that he was using the motor from Lieutenant Fisher's fatal crash, and refused to fly it. He recalled, "Each day I would . . . start the motor, climb in the seat and . . . slowly roll along the ground. . . . Finally this became the town joke—Banning and his ground plane." One day he taxied to the end of the field, intending to allow the plane to leave the ground for a few feet but to come to a stop before reaching the far side of the field.

> [T]o my . . . intense discomfiture the full power blast of the motor carried me down the field far faster than I had expected and there was a very substantial fence dead ahead. Instinctively I yanked backward on the stick and there I was—in the air alone—forced by accident to solo in a ship which had never been flown before. To my general astonishment, I found myself calm and collected. I immediately became self-reliant. I felt as only one who flies can feel—that here at last, I have conquered a new world, have moved into a new sphere. I had sprouted wings, a rhapsody in air, but the stark realization came to me that I had yet a landing to make!
>
> . . . Well, the ship flew level and straight almost of its own accord; perfect job of rigging. I circled the field three times . . . and started down in an erratic glide. . . . A minute later the machine settled on the ground with the gracefulness of a bird, rolling only a few feet before stopping. I had made it! I breathed a long sigh of relief and clambered from the ship to the ground, and, immediately, . . . a great change occurred. My head erect, eyes to the front, shoulders squared, I was a different man. A full-fledged pilot.

Banning named his plane *Miss Ames.*

In 1926, when the U.S. Department of Commerce instituted aviation licensing laws, Banning was the first African American pilot to be licensed in the United States, receiving license number 1,324.

Banning became an experienced barnstormer, logging more than 250 hours of flying time over the next three years. In 1929, in response to a news release issued by William Powell and his fledgling Bessie Coleman Aero Club, based in Los Angeles, Banning moved to the West Coast. The most experienced black pilot in the country, Banning was designated the Aero Club's chief pilot, with the responsibility of training others in the club.

Powell and Banning flew several promotional flights on behalf of the club, and talked of being the first black pilots to fly nonstop from Los Angeles to Chicago. While attempting to fly from Los Angeles to Jackson, Mississippi, for an exhibition at the Mississippi State Fair in the fall of 1929, they lost their bearings—not uncommon for flyers then. Far off course, they landed near the Gulf of California, 300 miles south of the Mexican border. They walked north along the coast for four days, with little water and no food, before they reached a town.

The following summer Banning and Powell went on a barnstorming tour of Texas, although negative press reports spread by rivals in Los Angeles kept them from raising any money to support the Aero Club. The tour ended at last when the plane was wrecked in attempting to take off from a tight field in Jacksonville, Texas. Powell returned at once to Los Angeles. Banning remained in Texas; while in Dallas, he fell in love with and married Mable Norford.

On Labor Day, 1931, the Bessie Coleman Aero Clubs staged the first All-Negro Air Show in Los Angeles; Banning returned from Texas in time to take part in the show, which was a great success. In the second show, that December, Powell decided to feature Colonel Hubert Julian, with Powell's

Five Blackbirds. Banning, feeling that he and not Julian should be featured, refused to take part.

In the late 1920s and early 1930s, a number of pilots were attempting to find financial backing for transcontinental flights. Corporate backing for long-distance flights was far more easily garnered by white pilots, although it was said that someone was offering a $1,000 prize to the first black pilots who flew cross-country. Julian talked of making the trip, but by the summer of 1932, had yet to do so, while Powell and Irvin Wells planned to enter the National Air Races to Cleveland at the end of that summer.

By this time Banning had logged nearly 800 miles in the air, more than half with the Bessie Coleman Aero Club. With Hensley, a mechanic, Banning overhauled an Eagle Rock, a World War I surplus plane, for $450, planning to fly to New York. Once the plane was ready, however, neither of them had additional funds, and Banning turned from Hensley to Thomas C. Allen, another Oklahoman associated with the Bessie Coleman Aero Club, who was also a mechanic and who was willing to provide fuel money, provided he could also make the trip.

Announcing that the team would be called the "Flying Hoboes," Banning left Los Angeles with Allen on September 18, 1932. They planned to "hobo" across the country, stopping in towns where they knew people, staying with friends when they could, and, they hoped, picking up enough additional money on the way to reach the next stop. They flew a southern route, over Arizona, New Mexico, Texas, and Oklahoma. Old friends and new along the way assisted with meals, beds, and repairs. In return, the "Flying Hoboes" asked them to sign their "Gold Book" on the lower left wing tip, which became a record of all who helped along the way.

As they inched their way east, the press picked up the story, and soon whites as well as African Americans were lending assistance. In Tulsa, Oklahoma, they persuaded

oil company owner William Skully, an aviation enthusiast, to arrange for them to buy oil and gas on credit from Tulsa to St. Louis, Missouri. In St. Louis, trade school students helped them correct the engine trouble that had caused a forced landing there. When they reached Pittsburgh, Pennsylvania, they met a worker for Franklin Delano Roosevelt's presidential campaign. Robert Vann arranged for the Flying Hoboes to drop 15,000 Roosevelt campaign flyers en route from Pittsburgh to New York. In return, the Democratic Party would finance that part of the flight.

On the morning of October 9, 1932, Banning and Allen landed their Eagle Rock at Curtiss Airport in Valley Stream, Long Island, three weeks after they left California. Their actual flying time was less than 42 hours.

They were given the keys to the city of New York by Mayor Jimmy Walker, and fêted by the Harlem supper clubs. The Democratic Party completely rebuilt the plane for them—but they never found the person who had offered the $1,000 prize to the first black pilots to cross the country.

Their return flight ended not far from Pittsburgh. In a forced landing in a snowstorm, they crashed into a pasture fence near Blairsville, Pennsylvania, and broke a wing tip. The *Pittsburgh Courier* paid for bus tickets to Los Angeles. As they crossed the country from east to west, they made a number of public speeches, usually for African American groups in community halls and churches. They never revealed that they had left the plane in a pasture in Pennsylvania.

"The successful man," Banning wrote in a *Courier* article a month later, "must make the most of time in order to survive and surpass. . . . In America we have twelve million colored people. Out of this grand total we can boast to date of only ten licensed airplane pilots. One pilot for about every one million people. Do you believe that this is our just representation? Do you believe that in this great country we can continue to compete with every other race under the sun on an equal economic basis and be practically unrepresented in the major fields of endeavor?" He went on to exhort African Americans to "go ahead and prove that you stand for progress."

Four months after the historic flight, Banning was killed in a crash at an air show near San Diego. The Traveler two-seater was piloted by Albert Burghardt, a white machinist mate second class, from San Diego Air Station. Reports differed as to whether the machinist had simply offered to fly Banning over the field "to see how the crowd was coming" while his own plane was being readied for the air show, or whether in fact an instructor at the Airtech Flying School had refused Banning permission to fly the plane himself, claiming that he did not believe that Banning was a capable pilot.

Investigations by aviation experts indicated that Burghardt was responsible for the accident. Press reports expressed outrage, claiming that "Banning's expert knowledge of aviation would probably have averted the accident if he had been at the controls." But unlike some two-seater models, the plane had only one set of controls, and was flying too close to the ground for a parachute to have been effective.

The air show had been intended to raise funds for Banning to return east to retrieve the plane forced down near Blairsville.

## Sources

Banning, J. Herman. "The Negro and the Airplane." *Pittsburgh Courier* (November 23, 1932).

———. "Pilot's Biggest Thrill Is First Time He Gets a Chance to Fly Solo." *Pittsburgh Courier* (December 17, 1932).

"Famous Coast-to-Coast Trail Blazer Killed As Plane Crashes in West." *Pittsburgh Courier* (February 11, 1933): 1, 4.

Hart, Philip S. *Flying Free: America's First Black Aviators.* Minneapolis, MN: Lerner Publications, 1992; 28–39. (Hart is Banning's great-nephew.)

Powell, William J. *Black Aviator: The Story of William J. Powell.* Washington, DC: Smithsonian Institution Press, 1994. A new edition of Powell's *Black Wings*, first published in 1934.

"Two Negro Pilots Forced Down in Lower California." *Los Angeles Times* (November 2, 1929): sec. 2, 10.

# Earsly Barnett

Earsly Barnett. Courtesy of Fred Wilmot. Appeared in the Jamaica Defence Force Air Wing magazine, *The Altimeter*.

**Full Name at Birth:** Cora Earsly Taylor

**Born:** February 1, 1913, Vicksburg, Mississippi

**Died:** March 22, 1975, Kingston, Jamaica

**Education:** Eastern High School, Detroit, Michigan [1931]; Private pilot's license, June 15, 1948; Commercial pilot's license (U.S.F.A.A.), September 10, 1954.

**Positions Held:** Bookkeeper at a gas station until 1946; Co-owner, Wayne Aircraft Company, 1941–1944; Co-founder and manager, Wayne School of Aeronautics, Detroit City

Airport, 1946–1951; Co-founder and manager, Barnett Aviation, Jamaica, 1954–1959; Co-founder and manager, Wings Ltd., 1959, changed name in 1972 to Wings Jamaica Ltd., Jamaica, 1959-March 21, 1975.

**Summary:** Holder of the first commercial pilot's license in Jamaica, Earsly Taylor Barnett launched more people on aviation careers than anyone else in Jamaica, West Indies. From 1952 until 1975, through training, publicity, and managing an air charter service, the American-born pilot became known as the mother of the Jamaican flying community. Many of her students became pilots in the Jamaica Defence Force. She had an international impact as well when her flight students obtained positions with international carriers such as Sabena and Aer Lingus, the airlines of Belgium and Ireland, respectively.

## Early Years

Born on February 1, 1913 in Vicksburg, Mississippi, to Tamotheus Amour and DeMoss Taylor, a carpenter, Cora Earsly Taylor was the third of their five children. The two oldest were Rudy and Henrene, and the younger children were Walter and Sam. Taylor moved with her family to Detroit, Michigan, in 1918. They moved north, along with thousands of other African Americans who were leaving a southern environment that provided no economic opportunity or physical safety for them. The Taylor family had witnessed a particularly humiliating form of southern rural atrocity—the tarring and feathering of one of their close friends.

Taylor was interested in aviation from an early age and her parents supported her interest. From 1933 she was associated with Neal V. Loving (1916–1998), another aviation enthusiast, who in his autobiography, recalled their meeting. It was February 1933, and Loving attended his first meeting of the Ace Flying Club. The secretary was Earsly Taylor, "a tall and slender young woman

with gray eyes and reddish-blond hair. Her devotion to aviation was on a par with mine. It was the beginning of a lifelong friendship and shared aviation careers."

## Career Highlights

In 1941, Taylor and Loving became partners in a manufacturing venture, the Wayne Aircraft Company. The company was established to design and build gliders for the Army Air Corps to use in training programs. Not only was Taylor responsible for managing the office, but she also became a specialist on the small-component fabrication and assembly of wing ribs and stability control surfaces. Her expertise included the sewing, fitting, and doping (varnish for waterproofing or strengthening) of the fabric used to cover their gliders, and for the award-winning midget racer, *Loving's Love*. Taylor's brother Rudy also joined them at Wayne, the first black aircraft factory. The company closed in 1944, after Loving lost both his legs in a glider crash.

In December 1941, the U.S. Army Air Corps formed the Civilian Air Patrol (CAP) to provide premilitary training for young men and women. Airplane owners were needed because they could be trained for air-sea rescues. Taylor, a licensed pilot and part owner of both a Waco plane and a glider, applied for membership six months later. White squadrons would not accept her application, forcing her and Loving to request permission to form an all-black squadron. Permission was granted and Earsly was appointed commanding officer of Squadron 639–5, the group that resulted. Everything was taught, from military courtesy to flight theory, and real aircraft were used for training. Parachute jumping became a specialty of Squadron 639–5, and it became known as the Parachute Squadron. Taylor, with the rank of Captain, was the lead instructor.

After Loving had recovered from his accident, he and Taylor established the Wayne

School of Aeronautics in 1946. The management at the Detroit city airport threw up many roadblocks, and incorporation of the school required pressure from civil rights groups such as the NAACP and the Urban League, as well as from the Detroit Common Council and the Michigan Civil Air Patrol. Many of their students were black war veterans who were using their GI Bill benefits to learn to fly. Excluded from white flying schools, the veterans and others saw Taylor's school as a boon to them. She served as office manager after quitting her job as the bookkeeper at a local gas station.

By the middle of 1951, *Ebony* reported that the school had five planes, in addition to the midget racer, *Loving's Love*. Both white and Negro instructors were employed by the school. They trained over 200 pilots, about 30 of them white. One of the students, Carl Barnett of Kingston, Jamaica, had come to the University of Detroit to study engineering. He too had a lifelong interest in aviation, and the three soon became fast friends. Taylor and Barnett were married in April 1951, and they had two sons, Mark and Christian. Born on January 16, 1960, Mark Barnett is employed by the Marriott hotel chain in Atlanta, Georgia. Christian Barnett, born on December 25, 1962, holds a commercial pilot's license, with multiengine, instrument, and instructor's ratings. He leases two of the three aircraft he owns to Wings Jamaica.

The couple set about rebuilding one of the school's Piper J-3 Cubs, planning to fly it to their new home in Jamaica. They also hoped to use it as a trainer in the flight school Carl Barnett wanted to establish. After all the export requirements were received and the plane was registered in Jamaica as VP-JAZ, they set off on July 9, 1952. Earsly Barnett nicknamed the plane the "Jamerican." After visits to relatives in Baltimore, New York, and Pittsburgh, they reached Jamaica's Palisadoes International Airport. Their flight included a brief stay in a jail in Santa Clara, Cuba, because they had failed to obtain the required military clearance to fly over Cuban territory.

The Barnetts joined the Jamaica Flying Club, a small group of aviation enthusiasts. Many were former RAF pilots whose interests were more social than professional. Carl and Earsly Barnett, in 1954, returned to Detroit and earned commercial pilot's licenses from the American FAA. She then flew their second plane, a Stinson Voyager N8607K, to Jamaica the following month. Earsly Taylor Barnett was now the first certified flight instructor in Jamaica, the holder of its commercial pilot's license no. 1. Carl Barnett holds license no. 2. They were now ready to create a vital flight training operation in Jamaica.

She managed Barnett Aviation, a flight training and air charter operation, from 1954 to 1959. In that year, the Barnetts and others founded Wings Ltd. In 1972 the name was changed to Wings Jamaica Ltd. This service includes local and overseas charter flights, sightseeing tours, and an air ambulance, as well as flight training. Wings Ltd. was the first commercial flying school in the British West Indies, offering courses leading to the private pilot's license, night ratings, instructor's rating, and commercial pilot's license. Sectors of the public—industry, agriculture, military—were recognizing aviation's time-saving benefits and the demand for trained pilots began to grow.

Earsly Barnett specialized in flight training, achieving the status of Jamaican Flight Examiner. She combined rigorous training methods with warm personal regard for her students. Barnett managed Wings Jamaica from its inception in 1954 until March 21, 1975, the day before her death from a cerebral hemorrhage.

## Sources

Barnett, F. Carl, Kingston, Jamaica, e-mail message to Betty K. Gubert, New York, July 4, 2000. Personal interview, plus 15 pages of handwritten notes, Bronx, New York, July 17, 2000.

"Legless Pilot." *Ebony* (May 1951): 43–44, 47–48.
Loving, Neal V. *Loving's Love.* Washington, DC: Smithsonian Institution Press, 1994.

# F. Carl Barnett

F. Carl Barnett. Courtesy of Major F. Carl Barnett.

**Full Name at Birth:** Frederick Carl Barnett

**Born:** March 22, 1924, Port Antonio, Jamaica

**Education:** St. George's College (high school), Kingston, Jamaica, [1942]; Wayne School of Aeronautics, private pilot's license, 1949; B.S., Civil Engineering, University of Detroit, June 1950; M.S., Civil Engineering, University of Michigan, June 1951, commercial pilot's license, 1954.

**Positions Held:** Meteorological assistant, British Admiralty Meteorological Department, Palisadoes Airport, 1944–1945; instructor, civil engineering, University of Detroit, 1949–1950; engineer, Jamaica Public Service Company, 1952–1959; field engineer, Sprostons Jamaica Ltd., 1959–1962; Raymond International, 1959–1960; Caribbean Cement Company (CCC), 1962–1963; chief engineer, later, plant superintendent, CCC, 1963–1970; managing director, specialist construction services, Jamaica Reinforcement Company, 1970–1975; co-owner and founder, Barnett Aviation, Jamaica, 1954–1959; co-founder and manager, Wings Ltd., 1959, later Wings Jamaica Ltd., 1972– .

**Summary:** F. Carl Barnett co-founded Wings Ltd. in 1959, after also establishing Barnett Aviation in 1954. Changing its name to Wings Jamaica Ltd. in 1972, it was the first flight training school in the British West Indies. These two operations offered flight training and air charters, and expanded and enhanced Jamaica's fledgling aviation community into an active and vibrant venture of national and international significance.

## Early Years

F. Carl Barnett, born on March 22, 1924, was the second child of Leslie Arthur Barnett and Jeanne Alexandria Hannah Stuart Barnett. His older sister, Clare Thérèse, born in 1922, and his younger brother, Felix, completed the family. Leslie Barnett was the superintendent of two hydroelectric stations administered by Jamaica Public Service. Living in the town of Lodge, near one of the stations situated on the White River, the family had a comfortable life. They kept cows on their land, and were able to employ a cook, laundress, and gardener. Mrs. Barnett was born in Freetown, Sierra Leone, and she met her husband, an engineer for the Jamaica Railway Company, when he traveled to Sierra Leone. He was part of a team that assisted in the construction of a railroad in the West African country, then a British colony. Mrs. Barnett designed custom-made clothing, and created a garden known for its variety of flowers.

Barnett's first sight of an airplane, when he was four years old, a yellow biplane against a blue sky, made a deep impression on him, and led to his lifelong interest. He built model planes from plans in *Popular Me-*

*chanics*. An early model plane "ran into every obstacle in the yard, animal, vegetable, or mineral. But it never left the ground," Barnett wrote many years later. Barnett made other crafts projects: a movie projector that worked and a steam engine that didn't. He completed a crystal short-wave radio just in time to hear the first boxing match between Joe Louis and Max Schmeling in June 1936. His hand-launched model glider earned him the all-time endurance record of the Model Airplane Club, when "it joined a flock of crows and flew out of sight."

Barnett also ran track in high school, St. George's College, finishing second in the 1942 All Island Championship. He graduated that year, and soon after won a scholarship to the University of Detroit.

## Higher Education

Barnett's adviser at the University of Detroit counseled him to rethink his planned major of aeronautical engineering. Knowing that Barnett wanted to return to Jamaica after his studies were completed, and that Jamaica had no aviation industry, he suggested civil engineering instead. Barnett thought the suggestion was a good one, and that he would learn to fly "when the opportunity presented itself." He earned his bachelor's degree in June 1950.

While at college, Barnett was a member of the track team, and he attempted to join the University of Detroit Flying Club, but the club refused his application. In his senior year, Barnett attended a lecture given by Neal V. Loving, the co-owner of the Wayne School of Aeronautics at Detroit City Airport, and an African American. As "opportunity presenting itself," Loving invited him to take flight instruction there. Loving thought Barnett had "the natural skills and coordination of a born pilot," and in 1949, he earned his private pilot's license.

Barnett went on to the University of Michigan to earn a master's degree in civil

engineering in June 1951. In 1954, the Barnetts returned to Detroit, Michigan, to become FAA-certified commercial pilots. Carl Barnett holds Jamaica's commercial pilot's license no. 2, while his wife Earsly earned license no. 1.

## Career Highlights

Just out of high school, Barnett worked as a clerk for Jamaica Rums Ltd., 1942–1943, and in the Collector's General Office, 1943–1944. He then became an assistant at the British Admiralty Meteorological Department, at Palisadoes Airport, from 1944–1945. In his last two years at the University of Detroit, Barnett was an instructor at the school's Civil Engineering College. After his marriage to Earsly Taylor, a pilot as well as Neal Loving's partner, in April 1951, Carl Barnett began enacting his plan to return to Jamaica. The couple set about rebuilding one of the school's Piper J-3 Cubs, planning to fly it to their new Kingston home, which Barnett had designed while still a college student. After all the export requirements were received and the plane was registered in Jamaica as VP-JAZ, they set off on July 9, 1952. They visited family members in Baltimore, New York, and Pittsburgh, before they reached Jamaica on July 19. Their flight included a brief stay in a jail in Santa Clara, Cuba, because they failed to obtain the required military clearance to fly over Cuban territory.

The Barnetts joined the Jamaica Flying Club, a group of aviation enthusiasts, and involved themselves deeply in the creation of a flight training school. He became a designated flight test examiner in the civil aviation department in 1955, a position he still holds. For almost all of his professional life, Barnett has been employed as an engineer. He worked for both government agencies and private companies, including: Jamaica Public Services Company from 1952 to 1959; Sprostons Jamaica Ltd., 1959–1962; and as a field engineer for Raymond International. In this position he was involved in road and bridge construction at Negril, Jamaica, and in numerous projects at Palisadoes International Airport, such as the construction of the airport's apron and hardstands. From 1962 until well into the 1990s, Barnett was associated with the Caribbean Cement Company. He was chief engineer, and later plant superintendent from 1963 until 1970. Moving to Jamaica Reinforcement Company in that year as the managing director of specialist construction services, he remained until 1975. In March of that year his wife Earsly died suddenly. Barnett then chose to devote himself full time, as managing director, to Wings Jamaica, the flight school and charter service they had founded together in 1959.

The first flight training school in the British West Indies, Wings Jamaica has started 4,000 student pilots. Well over 1,000 students have succeeded in earning their wings as private or commercial pilots. Night ratings and instructor's ratings are offered. Graduates of the school fly for the Jamaica Defence Force, Air Jamaica, and for such international carriers as Sabena (Belgium) and Aer Lingus (Ireland). Ground and flight instructors regularly participate in educational career days. Charter flights on both the island and throughout the Caribbean serve both the business community and vacationers. Mercy flights, or ambulance service, have carried stretcher cases to the southern part of the United States and to South America.

From 1989 until 1999 Barnett was a member of the board of directors of the Caribbean Cement Company. In addition, Barnett uses his expertise in aviation to contribute to the development of Jamaica's young people, as well as to the country's safety and well-being. He serves as the commanding officer of the air section of the Jamaica Combined Cadet Force of the Jamaica Defence Force. Holding the rank of major, Barnett has been a member since 1956. He has held the offices of both secretary and director of the international service organization, the Rotary Club

(Kingston), since 1986. Also a member of the Kingston advisory board of the Salvation Army, Barnett has served on its disaster preparedness committee, among others.

The Barnetts had two sons, Mark, born on January 16, 1960, and Christian, on December 25, 1962. Mark Barnett is employed by the Marriott hotel chain in Atlanta, Georgia. Christian Barnett holds a commercial pilot's license, with multiengine, instrument, and instructor's ratings. He leases two of the three aircraft he owns to Wings Jamaica.

### Sources

Barnett, F. Carl, Kingston, Jamaica, e-mail messages to Betty K. Gubert, New York, July 4, 19, 2000. Personal interview, July 17, 2000, plus 15 pages of handwritten notes.

Loving, Neal V. *Loving's Love*. Washington, DC: Smithsonian Institution Press, 1994.

# Guion S. Bluford Jr.

Guion S. Bluford Jr. Courtesy of NASA.

**Full Name at Birth:** Guion Stewart Bluford Jr.

**Born:** November 22, 1942, Philadelphia, Pennsylvania

**Education:** Pennsylvania State University, B.S. in Aerospace Engineering, 1964; Air Force Institute of Technology, Ohio, M.S., 1974, Ph.D., 1978; M.B.A., University of Houston, Texas, 1987.

**Positions Held:** Branch Chief of the Aerodynamics and Airframe Branch of the Air Force Flight Dynamics Laboratory, 1974–1978; astronaut, NASA, 1979–1993; vice president and general manager, science and engineering group, Federal Data Corporation (FDC), Bethesda, Maryland.

**Awards, Honors:** Leadership Award of Phi Delta Kappa, 1962; National Defense Service Medal, 1965; Vietnam Campaign Medal, 1967; Vietnam Cross of Gallantry with Palms, Vietnam Service Medal, 10 Air Force Air Medals, 1967; three Air Force Outstanding Unit Awards, 1967, 1970, 1972; Air Force Commendation Medal, 1972; Air Force Institute of Technology, Marvin E. Gross Award, 1974; Air Force Meritorious Service Award, 1978; National Society of Black Engineers Distinguished National Scientist Award, 1979; three NASA Group Achievement Awards, 1980, 1981, 1989; NASA Space Flight Medal, 1983, 1985, 1991, and 1992; Ebony Black Achievement Award, NAACP Image Award, 1983; Black Engineer of the Year Award, 1991; NASA Exceptional Service Award; Legion of Merit; honorary doctorate degrees from at least 11 universities.

**Summary:** A U.S. Air Force pilot since 1965, with a doctorate in aerospace engineering earned in 1978, Guion S. Bluford Jr. became an astronaut in 1979. He became the first African American to ride into space on the eighth shuttle mission, on August 30, 1983, and he remained an astronaut until 1993.

## Early Years

Guy Bluford, as he likes to be called, is the oldest of three sons born to Guion Bluford Sr. and Lolita Harriet Brice Bluford. The parents, a mechanical engineer and inventor, and a special education teacher, raised their children to seek academic and professional success. Both sides of the family boasted several examples of the excellence the Bluford parents hoped their sons would achieve. They included Lucille Bluford, the editor of the *Kansas City Call*, a black newspaper in Missouri; F.D. Bluford, president of the Agricultural and Technical State University in Greensboro, North Carolina; contralto Carol Brice; pianist Jonathan Brice; and Charlotte Hawkins Brown, the founder of Palmer Memorial Institute in North Carolina.

Nicknamed Bunny as a child, Bluford grew up in a middle-class, racially mixed neighborhood, whose life reflected elements considered "all-American." He had a paper route, made model planes, played chess and ping-pong, worked crossword puzzles, and excelled in the Boy Scouts, eventually achieving the rank of Eagle Scout. Bluford was strongly influenced by his parents and their work ethic. Watching his father leave for work every day made him think, he later said, that "if engineers enjoy work that much, it must be a good thing to get into." Of the other Bluford children, Eugene became a computer programmer and Kenneth, a teacher. Both hold doctoral degrees in their fields.

Bluford's father, suffering from epilepsy, retired early. His joblessness and subsequent illness forced Mrs. Bluford to take another job to support the family; it also made a strong impression on the children. According to Bluford's brother Kenny, their father was "the closest thing my brother ever had to a hero. Bunny was always quiet and serious. But he got more so after that." He was a loner, never one for socializing. This in itself was not unusual among his family; Christian Scientists, the Blufords were known for their reserve and conservatism. Though he had been interested in math and science since early childhood, Bluford was not a strong student. He, however, was captain of the chess team and a member of the science club, and he also worked on the school yearbook. He was considered such a lackluster scholar that Overbrook High School sent a counselor to the Bluford household to tell his parents that young Guion wasn't college material, and that he ought to consider learning a trade. Given the family's attitude toward education, that was not an option.

## Higher Education

After graduating from Overbrook in 1960, Bluford enrolled in Pennsylvania State University, majoring in aerospace engineering. His professors there remember him as a quiet, studious young man. As one of them later told a reporter, Bluford was not "the sort you would expect to be interviewed about 20 years later." Perhaps the one thing that set Bluford apart from his fellow aerospace engineering students was that he was the only African American in the program. But if this racial isolation had any effect on him—or if he ever found himself facing racism—Bluford has not publicly complained. "I can't really say I had any obstacles," he told a reporter before his first space flight. "If I had any obstacles, they were self-made."

Slowly but surely, the average high school student transformed himself into an ambitious, hardworking, and ultimately outstanding collegian. Joining a local Christian Science church as well as the Air Force ROTC program, Bluford was honored with a Phi Delta Kappa leadership award in 1962 and graduated with distinction in 1964. He married Linda Tull, a fellow student, who became an accountant. They are the parents of two sons, Guion S. Bluford III, born June 12, 1964, and James Trevor, born October 25, 1965.

After graduation from Pennsylvania State, Bluford continued his aeronautical training at Williams Air Force Base in Arizona. He was awarded his wings in 1965, and then continued flight instruction in Florida to pre-

pare himself for combat duty. In 1967 Bluford left for Vietnam where he was assigned to the 557th Tactical Fighter Squadron. Based in Cam Ranh Bay, Bluford flew F-4C jet fighters in 144 combat missions, 65 of them over North Vietnam. For these missions Bluford won the Vietnam Service Medal, Vietnam Campaign Medal, Vietnam Cross of Gallantry with Palm, and 10 Air Force Air Medals in 1967. In addition, he received the first of three Air Force Outstanding Unit Awards. The other two were awarded to him in 1970 and in 1972.

Returning to the United States, Bluford taught flying at Sheppard AFB in Texas, instructing other pilots in the operation of the T38A fighter. He also continued his training, graduating from Squadron Officers School in 1971. The following year Bluford started graduate school at the Air Force Institute of Technology at Wright-Patterson Air Force Base in Ohio. While a student there, the young veteran worked as an engineer in the school's flight dynamics laboratory, eventually becoming chief for the aerodynamics division. He achieved his master's degree, with distinction, in 1974. After writing his dissertation on the design of airplane wings, Bluford received his Ph.D. in aerospace engineering, with a minor in laser physics, in 1978.

## Career Highlights

Although Bluford had been flying professionally for more than a decade by now, his career as an astronaut did not begin until 1978, when he applied to the astronaut program at the National Aeronautics and Space Administration (NASA). As one of 10,000 applicants, the odds of being accepted were so long Bluford told no one he had applied. To his surprise NASA chose him as one of 35 new astronauts. Among the others were Sally K. Ride, the first American woman in space, and two other African American men, Frederick Drew Gregory and Ronald E.

McNair. Asked about the prospect of being the first black American in space, Bluford characteristically downplayed race, talking instead about the assignment itself. "It gives me a chance to use all my skills and do something that is pretty exciting," he said. "The job is so fantastic, you don't need a hobby." He went on to say that he thought "it might be better to be second or third because then you can enjoy it and disappear—return to the society you came out of without someone always poking you in the side and saying you were first."

For the next year Bluford trained to be an astronaut, pursuing advanced study in engineering, mechanics, navigation, geology, oceanography, and other scientific specialties as well as intense physical conditioning and flight training. At the end of the year, in August 1979, Bluford was qualified to serve as mission specialist on the space shuttle program. His turn came in 1982, when NASA chose Bluford to join the crew, as a mission specialist, for the shuttle's eighth flight mission. He became the first black American to fly in space. (A black Cuban, Arnaldo Tamayo Mendez, had flown on the Russian spaceship, *Soyez 38*, in 1980.) NASA had already made history in the seventh shuttle mission, on which Sally Ride became the first American woman to fly on the shuttle. Although that decision had been criticized by the NAACP and other African American groups, Bluford was pleased. "She can carry the spear and get the attention," he told reporters, relieved at not having to bear the burden of the first to break into NASA's historically all-white male club.

Still, Bluford's presence on the shuttle brought unprecedented media attention and great pride within the black community. The dramatic nighttime launch took place on August 30, 1983, at 2:32 A.M., at the Kennedy Space Center in Florida. The event was attended by distinguished black congressmen, educators, civil rights activists, and figures from the entertainment and sports worlds. Once aloft, all went well on the eighth shuttle flight (STS-8). The mission had multiple goals, including launching a communication and weather satellite over India, testing the shuttle's remote manipulator arm, and conducting medical experiments. After completing 98 orbits of the earth, the shuttle touched down on September 5, after midnight, at Edwards AFB, California. Characteristically modest and inclusive, Bluford said he was "humbled" by the reception. "I feel very proud to be a member of this team," he told the crowd, "and I think we have a tremendous future with the space shuttle—I mean *all* of us."

In great demand as a speaker following his first shuttle mission, Bluford told audiences about the value of setting high goals and working hard to get them. "I want you to be the future astronauts flying in space with me," he told a group of students in Harlem. The year following his historic space flight Bluford was honored with many awards, including the Ebony Black Achievement Award and the NAACP Image Award.

Bluford's second shuttle mission (STS-61A) was launched on October 30, 1985. The German D-1 spacelab mission carried eight crew members—the largest shuttle crew to date—including three European astronauts. Duties included the deployment of a communication satellite and 76 different scientific experiments concerning physics, biology, navigation, and materials processing. In addition to working as an astronaut, Bluford took a Masters in Business Administration degree from the University of Houston in 1987. The third mission (STS-39) Bluford flew with NASA came on April 28, 1991, when he joined the crew of the *Orbiter Discovery*, which gathered data from outer space and performed valuable satellite work. Bluford's last space flight (STS-53) came a year later, on December 2, 1992, when he and four other astronauts deployed a classified Department of Defense payload and conducted various NASA experiments. By the time Bluford retired from NASA in 1993, he had logged more than 688 hours in space. In the same year he retired from the U.S. Air Force with the rank of colonel.

Bluford then went to work in private industry, first as vice president and general manager for engineering services at NYMA, Inc., in Greenbelt, Maryland, then for the Federal Data Corporation (FDC), an information technology and engineering services company. As vice president and general manager, Bluford manages a workforce of 400 scientists and engineers for FDC, which is based in Bethesda, Maryland. FDC is a supplier of information technology services, focused on the federal government market. They work "on everything from desk top outsourcing to space shuttle payloads."

At various times in his life, Bluford has relaxed by jogging and playing racquetball, handball, and tennis. He enjoys reading and photography. He is a member of the American Institute of Aeronautics and Astronautics, the Air Force Association, and the Tau Beta Pi fraternity.

## Sources

The Astronaut Connection. Www.nauts.com/bios/nasa/bluford.html. Accessed February 15, 2000.

"Astronaut Guion Bluford Jr. Resigns from NASA to Join Engineering and Computer Firm." *Jet* (July 5, 1993): 32.

"Bluford, Guion S(tewart), Jr." *Current Biography* (September 1984): 3–6.

Broad, William J. "First U.S. Black in Space." *New York Times* (August 31, 1983): B6.

Leavy, Walter. "A Historic Step into Outer Space." *Ebony* (November 1983): 162–164, 166, 168, 170.

Phelps, J. Albert. *They Had a Dream: The Story of African-American Astronauts.* Novato, CA: Presidio Press, 1994; 77–99.

Prochnau, Bill. "Guy Bluford: NASA's Reluctant Hero." *Washington Post* (August 21, 1983): A1, 8–9.

# Charles F. Bolden Jr.

Charles F. Bolden Jr. Courtesy of NASA.

**Full Name at Birth:** Charles Frank Bolden Jr.

**Born:** August 19, 1946, Columbia, South Carolina

**Education:** C.A. Johnson High School, 1964; B.S. in electrical science, United States Naval Academy, 1968; M.S. in systems management, University of Southern California, 1978; graduated from the U.S. Naval Test Pilot School, Patuxent, Maryland, 1979.

**Positions Held:** Commissioned as second lieutenant, U.S. Marine Corps, 1968; became a naval aviator in 1970; VMA (AW)-533, Thailand, June 1972–June 1973; selection and recruiting officer and other assignments, Marine Corps Air Station, El Toro, California; test pilot, Naval Air Test Center, June 1979–August 1981; joined astronaut program, 1981; pilot, STS-61C (Columbia), STS-31 (Discovery) in 1990 and mission commander on STS-45 (Atlantis) in 1992;

commander, STS-45, the first Spacelab mission dedicated to NASA's Mission to Planet Earth; assistant deputy administrator, NASA headquarters, Washington, DC 1992–1994; deputy commandant, U.S. Naval Academy, 1994–1995; assistant wing commander, Third Marine Aircraft Wing, Miramar, California, 1995–1997; deputy commanding general, First Marine Expeditionary Forces Pacific, 1997–   .

**Awards, Honors:** Two Legion of Merit Awards, Distinguished Flying Cross, Air Medal; inducted into the National Aeronautics and Space Administration's Space Hall of Fame, 1997; South Carolina Hall of Fame, 1998.

**Summary:** Charles F. Bolden is an Annapolis graduate and naval pilot who fulfilled his lifelong dream to be an astronaut, and rose to become the highest ranking African American in the Marine Corps.

## Early Years

Charles Frank Bolden Jr. was born in Columbia, South Carolina, on August 19, 1946. He was the first child of Ethel Martin Bolden, a librarian, and Charles F. Bolden Sr., a social studies teacher and athletic coach. He had a younger brother named Warren Maurice.

As a boy, Bolden was athletic, excelling in many sports. From an early age, he had an interest in science and math and enjoyed doing science projects in school. His parents encouraged his interests. Hardworking and determined, Bolden did well in school. His mother remembers him as daring and adventurous, eager to try new things and to test himself. General Bolden disagreed with his mother in an e-mail interview: "While some may have considered me daring . . . I think I was just a normal kid growing up. . . . Perhaps the single most frightening incident for my mom (after the fact) was a day when my first cousin, several of our friends, and I were playing on the Broad River and I decided to cross the river on one of its intermediate dams. . . . We encountered significant slippery patches of moss that caused us to begin losing our footing. Although we almost lost some of our gang, . . . we managed to . . . complete the trek undaunted. When my mom later found out, she was quite upset."

The first Apollo and Gemini space shots took place when he was a boy, and he remembers being very excited by these historic events. In an interview in *Marines* in 1994, Bolden is quoted as saying, "I was interested in being an astronaut when I was young, but I didn't think it was possible. I . . . put it out of my mind."

According to Bolden, "While there were distinct disadvantages to attending schools that were not as well funded or equipped as the white schools, we were blessed with superbly dedicated teachers. . . . I learned in that environment that I could be as good as I believed I was and that I could accomplish almost any goal were I willing to invest the time in study, hard work, and a belief in what others said could not be done." When Bolden was in junior high, two of his teachers, Mr. Jeffcoat and Mr. Neil, fostered his interest in science and math by assigning him outside study in the two subjects and encouraging him to participate in science and math fairs.

His interest in math and science continued in high school. His grades were excellent, and he excelled in sports as well. He was a good swimmer; his team, the Drew Park Sharks, won many awards in the 1950s and 1960s. He went out for football and was a mediocre but eager player. His football coach was his father. Perhaps as a result of this, father and son had a very close relationship. Charles Bolden Jr.'s great opportunity came when he replaced the injured starting quarterback, leading his team to the 1963 championship. When football season ended, he played percussion instruments in the high school band.

## Higher Education

Bolden was eager to attend the U.S. Naval Academy. While still in high school, he wrote to his senators and his congressman, as well as to then-vice president Lyndon B. Johnson. Johnson answered the young man and asked Bolden to get in touch with him when the time came to apply to the Academy. During his senior year, when it became clear that neither the senators nor the congressman would appoint him, he wrote to Johnson, who was then president, reminding him of his promise and asking for his help. Johnson arranged for Bolden to be appointed by an Illinois congressman, and upon graduation from high school, Bolden enrolled at the U.S. Naval Academy in Annapolis, Maryland.

His ambition at the time was to be a frogman, a branch of the Navy that engages in underwater military maneuvers. He found his first year at the academy rough going, but he managed to stay the course. John Riley Love, Bolden's first company officer, was impressed by the young man's intelligence and character: "[H]e established himself as a 'non-color person' who did not use the color of his skin or his race as a crutch when something went wrong." In his senior year at the academy, he took his commission in the Marine Corps, largely as a result of Major Love's influence.

Immediately after graduating from the academy, on June 8, 1968, Bolden married his childhood sweetheart, Alexis Walker, at the academy chapel. After completing basic training, he decided to become a pilot. It was while attending flight school at Meridian, Mississippi, that he again entertained the idea of being an astronaut, but he made no attempt to do so, thinking, "that just . . . wasn't in the cards for me." He graduated from flight school and has been flying since 1970.

## Career Highlights

During the Vietnam War, he was stationed in Thailand, where he flew 100 sorties into Vietnam, Laos, and Cambodia. After the war, Bolden applied to the elite U.S. Naval Test Pilot School at Patuxent, Maryland. Although he had been rejected four times, his fifth application was accepted, and he graduated from this institution in 1979. He was an engineering test pilot at the Naval Air Test Center from June 1979 to August 1981.

During this period, he applied to the astronaut program. In January 1980, he was notified that he was one of five Marine Corps nominees for the shuttle program and was told to report to Houston for interviews. As part of the interview process, he was asked to complete an essay on "Why I Want to Be a Shuttle Pilot."

In an interview with *Eagle & Swan*, Bolden revealed what he had written in his essay: "I sat down and wrote a letter to my mother. . . . My mother had not been overjoyed with my decision to become a pilot. . . . The second least happy moment [for his mother] was when I went to [Test Pilot School] and this was the third least happy moment. . . . I said that I wanted to be in the program because space was the new frontier, a new challenge. . . . Also my Dad, who passed away last October, had said . . . that he would be so very proud if I were selected." He made copies of this letter and gave them to the selection panel.

He was chosen for the program in 1980, and in August 1981 he became the fourth African American astronaut. As an astronaut, he served as a pilot aboard the Columbia mission and on the *Discovery*, which launched the Hubble Space Telescope, and as mission commander on the *Atlantis*. He commanded a crew of seven on the historic first Spacelab mission. It was he who delivered the eulogy at the NASA memorial service for the victims of the *Challenger* disaster in 1986.

In an interview for *EM*, Bolden, then a colonel, spoke of the value of the space program for young people: "I think every kid has an interest in space. . . . it makes kids want to study; excites them, gives them desire to be somebody . . . and that's something no other program can do . . . if we want to look to the future, space is it. . . . And that excites people from kindergarten through college; it excites me. It tends to draw people together."

In 1992, Bolden was appointed assistant deputy administrator of NASA. He was responsible for monitoring the agency for efficiency and cost-effectiveness and for reporting to Congress. In 1994, he became deputy commandant at the U.S. Naval Academy. His task while there was to help restore the integrity of the institution, which had been rocked by cheating scandals. In 1995, he became assistant wing commander, Third Marine Aircraft Wing, Miramar, California.

While serving at Miramar, Bolden was appointed major general and became the highest ranking black man in the Marine Corps. He was then reassigned to his present position, as deputy commanding general, First Marine Expeditionary Forces Pacific. He is stationed at Yokota Air Base, outside of Tokyo, Japan.

Bolden's favorite sports are racquetball, soccer, and golf: "Both my soccer and golf are pretty bad, but I enjoy them nonetheless." Bolden and his wife are avid sports fans; their favorite spectator sport in Japan is sumo wrestling.

Major General Bolden and his wife Alexis (who prefers to be known as Jackie) have two grown children, Anthony Che, born June 9, 1971, who followed his father into the military, and Kelly Michelle, born March 17, 1976, who plans to become a physician.

## Sources

"After the Cheating: Astronaut Charles Bolden Has a New and Daunting Mission—Helping Restore Integrity at the U.S. Naval Academy." *Charlotte Observer* (May 1, 1994): 7.

Bolden, Charles F. Japan, e-mail correspondence to Miriam Sawyer, New Jersey, April 12, April 13, December 24, 1999.

"Bolden Slated for Promotion to Marines Major General." *Jet* (February 24, 1997): 9.

"Charles Bolden Jr.: He Gives Stargazing a Different Meaning." *EM (Ebony Man)* (August 1990): 20, 22–23.

Charles F. Bolden, Jr., http://observe.ivv.nasa.gov/nasa/ootw/1998/ootw_980211/bio_3.html. Accessed May 2, 2001.

"The Crew of the Atlantis: 7 in the 46th Shuttle Flight." *New York Times* (March 25, 1992): A20.

"Ex-Astronaut Becomes Senior Black Marine," *New York Times* (July 5, 1997): 9.

Larson, Craig. "Perchance to Dream: Marine Astronaut Makes Fourth Flight into Space." *Marines* (April 1994): 9.

"Major Bolden Joins NASA Space Shuttle Project." *Eagle & Swan* (September 1980): 42.

"Marine Col. Bolden Pilots Hubble Telescope Shuttle." *New York Amsterdam News* (April 14, 1990): 4.

"NASA Extends Shuttle's Flight by One Day." *New York Times* (March 30, 1992): A8.

Wilford, John Noble. "Shuttle Lifts Off to Study Atmosphere." *New York Times* (March 25, 1992): A8.

# Ruby L. Bostic

Ruby L. Bostic. Courtesy of Ruby L. Bostic.

**Full Name at Birth:** Ruby Lee Campbell

**Born:** August 5, 1933, Chadbourn, North Carolina

**Education:** Chadbourn High School, 1951; B.S. in business administration and economics, St. Augustine's College, Raleigh, North Carolina, 1955; Master of Social Work, Adelphi University, Garden City, New York, 1975; private pilot's license, 1978.

**Positions Held:** Social worker, New York City Department of Human Resources, 1961–1992; Queens Borough Director for Group and Family Services, 1989–1992.

**Awards, Honors:** *Guinness Book of World Records*, 1985; Mme C.J. Walker/Villa Lewaro Foundation (Queens, N.Y.) award for outstanding service, 1999.

**Summary:** Ruby L. Bostic and her friend Melva Jackman became the first two African American women to fly from New York to Trinidad in a single engine plane in February 1985. This feat gained them entrance into the *Guinness Book of World Records*. Since getting her pilot's license in 1978, Bostic has worked tirelessly within African American organizations to introduce youngsters to the opportunities that are available in the aviation industry.

## Early Years

Ruby L. Bostic was born to Lonzay and Mary Campbell on August 5, 1933, in Chadbourn, North Carolina. She was the fourth of seven children, and came to be known as "the sandwich child." The three older children were Margaret, Johnnie James, and Helen Eloise; the younger three, Nancy Louise, Bertha Mae, and Lonzay Jr. The Campbells were farmers and harvested extensive crops of strawberries, corn, beans, and tobacco. As the children grew older, they all helped with the harvests. Their other chores were feeding and watering the livestock, which included horses, cows, pigs, and chickens. In high school, Bostic particularly enjoyed French and home economics, and she played basketball.

## Higher Education

Bostic attended St. Augustine's College in Raleigh, North Carolina, and graduated in 1955 with a Bachelor of Science in business administration and economics. She joined the Alpha Kappa Alpha sorority, and she is still a member. One of the few students to own a typewriter, Bostic typed the papers of other students. Her enterprise was so successful that teachers borrowed money from her. In 1978, Bostic earned a Master's in Social Work (MSW) from Adelphi University, Garden City, New York. She received her private pilot's license in 1978.

## Career Highlights

After her marriage to Joney Williams in 1955, the year of her college graduation, the couple moved to Long Island, New York. Her husband was co-owner and vice president of W. Williams Moving and Storage Company. They soon had two children, Joney Randolph, born in 1958, and Philip Jonathan, born in 1961. Home alone with her little boys, Ruby Bostic couldn't help but see and hear planes flying overhead. They took off almost hourly from nearby Mitchell Field in Hempstead. The contrast of the flying planes above and Bostic's literal groundedness (her husband took the family car to work) kept alive her dream of flying one day. Bostic said, "I wanted to go everywhere and I wanted to get there now." Her dream started to become reality when Willie Valentine, a colleague of her husband's, offered to take her up in his plane. Bostic found that first ride "thrilling." While watching Valentine work the controls she thought, "If he can do this, then I can too." She then began flying lessons, and after

100 hours of flight training, received her private pilot's license on July 30, 1978.

During this time, Bostic pursued her career as a social worker for the New York City Department of Human Resources, which she began in 1961. During her tenure, which ended with her retirement in December 1992, she taught parenting skills and held various positions of increasing responsibility. She became a supervisor of child welfare in the Group and Family Services. In 1989, she was appointed Queens borough director of that group, and she remained director until her retirement.

Joney Williams died in a car accident on April 18, 1969, leaving Bostic a working, single mother. In 1973 she married Carl Bostic, a salesman for IBM, and was widowed again when he died on August 5, 1996.

Once Bostic got her license, she began flying in the New York metropolitan area, the Caribbean, and over the African plains. On a vacation to Puerto Rico in 1980 Bostic met some pilots at the Isla Grande airport, and she soon had a job from January to April as the co-pilot on planes delivering produce to neighboring islands. Her most challenging flight, the one that entered the *Guinness Book of World Records*, occurred in 1985.

On February 10, 1985, Bostic and her friend and fellow pilot, Melva Jackman, took off from Republic Airport in Farmingdale, New York, bound for Trinidad and Tobago, a trip of 5,600 miles, mostly over water. Jackman's single engine plane, a Piper Cherokee Arrow, held only enough fuel for five hours. Among the stops they made for refueling were Myrtle Beach, South Carolina; Ft. Lauderdale, Florida; Grand Exhuma Island, Bahamas; Dominican Republic; Puerto Rico; Antigua; St. Lucia; and Grenada. They reached Trinidad on February 14, just in time for Carnival. They became the first black women to pilot a single engine plane from New York to Trinidad. They did not know they had set a record, nor was that their intent. Their idea was to commemorate the 1934 Goodwill Flight of C.A. "Chief" Anderson and Dr. Albert E. Forsythe, which covered some of the same route. At all their stops, "People couldn't believe that two women were flying an airplane by themselves," Bostic recalled. After five days in Trinidad, the pair returned home on February 23, making refueling stops at Guadeloupe, Puerto Rico, Grand Turks and Caicos Islands, Nassau, and Palm Beach, Florida.

On earlier trips abroad, Bostic flew in Senegal and The Gambia (1980), Egypt (1981), and Kenya and Tanzania (1982). Sometimes she was accompanied by her friends and fellow pilots, Melva Jackman and Steve Young. In 1986, while on a trip to Europe, she flew in Italy, France, and other countries.

Bostic is a member of many organizations and holds office in some of them. She is a life member of the Claude B. Govan Tristate Chapter of the Tuskegee Airmen, Inc. (secretary); NAACP; National Council of Negro Women; Rockaway Golden K Kiwanis Club (president), among others. She also belongs to the Ninety-Nines, a group of women pilots; the Falcon Squadron of the Civil Air Patrol, in which she is a captain; and she serves as treasurer for Black Pilots of New York, a branch of Negro Airmen International (NAI). This group has an active program to interest youngsters in careers in aviation, and they operate a school and a summer camp.

Bostic has many interests, including the study of calligraphy and American sign language (to qualify as an interpreter for the deaf). She teaches defensive driving as a volunteer, and she works part time in real estate and the travel industry. She is in demand as a lecturer to youth groups, both locally and nationally. Her real love is flying, and she still pilots her own plane, a Cessna single engine. Bostic has said, "Flying is a sensation you can't describe. It's very tranquil . . . and yet you feel a great sense of power. You have such a feeling of achievement and accomplishment . . . look at me, I'm here!"

## Sources

Alexander, Cinde. "She Goes through Life with the Greatest of Ease." *Winterset* (Iowa) *City Limit News* (November 27, 1998): 20.

Bostic, Ruby L., Jamaica, New York, to Betty K. Gubert, New York, telephone and personal interviews, correspondence, clippings, November 1998–July 1999.

Drew, Carol. "People and Places." *New York Voice* (March 1985).

Hawkins, Shirley. "Community Profile: Ruby Bostic." *Our Times* (March 1–14, 1995): 3, 15.

# Janet Harmon Waterford Bragg

**Full Name at Birth:** Janet Harmon

**Born:** March 24, 1907, Griffin, Georgia

**Died:** April 11, 1993, Blue Island, Illinois

**Education:** Educated at public school, St. Stephen's Episcopal School, Griffin, Georgia, and Fort Valley Episcopal High School, Fort Valley, Georgia; RN, Spelman Seminary (now Spelman College), Atlanta, Georgia, 1929; graduate work in public health administration, Loyola University, Chicago, and in pediatric nursing at Cook County Hospital School of Nursing, Chicago.

**Positions Held:** Health inspector, Metropolitan Burial Insurance Company, 1941–1951; registered nurse; operated several nursing homes in Chicago; wrote a weekly column, "Negro Aviation," in the *Chicago Defender* in the 1930s under the byline Janet Waterford.

**Awards, Honors:** Outstanding Citizen Award, Tucson, Arizona, 1981; Inducted into the International Forest of Friendship, sponsored by the Ninety-Nines, an organization of women pilots, 1982; honored as a pioneer at the "Black Wings" exhibition, National Air and Space Museum, 1982; honored by the Civil Rights Division of the Federal Aviation Administration (FAA) as a pioneer aviator, commending her efforts to encourage African Americans to enter the field of aviation, 1984. Bishop Wright Air Industry Award for outstanding contributions to aviation, 1985.

**Summary:** Janet Harmon Waterford Bragg, a registered nurse, was a pioneer in black aviation and one of the founding members of the Challenger Aero Club, an organization that gave African Americans in Chicago the chance to band together for flying opportunities. Together with other members of the club, she helped build the first airstrip open to African Americans in the all-black town of Robbins, Illinois. She was one of the first African American women to obtain a commercial pilot's license. In addition, she later owned and operated several nursing homes.

## Early Years

Janet Harmon was born in Griffin, Georgia, on March 24, 1907, the youngest of seven children of Cordia Batts Harmon and Samuel Harmon. She and all her siblings were born in a house that her grandfather had built, the same house where her mother was born. Her maternal grandfather was a freed slave of Spanish descent; her maternal grandmother was a Cherokee. She remembered her childhood as a happy one. Though far from well-off, her parents were able to provide the necessities and educate all the children. A tomboy as a child, her favorite companion was her brother Pat. One of her father's favorite sayings was, "If Jack can do it, so can Jill"—a statement that made a deep impression on the young Janet, leading her to the conviction that "I could do anything I set my sights on."

The family encouraged independence in the children. Unusual for that time and place, they allowed the young people to attend any church they chose, as long as they attended regularly. Although her siblings chose other churches, Janet and her brother Pat attended the Episcopal Church, which their parents had helped to build. Janet transferred to St. Stephen's Episcopal School from public school, and when the time came for high school, she went to an Episcopal boarding school. She excelled in math and science and was an outstanding athlete.

## Higher Education

Harmon attended Spelman College in Atlanta. During her first year, she majored in home economics, but switched to nursing during her second year. Spelman's nursing program was very rigorous. Bragg was one of two—out of a class of 12—to survive the six-month probationary period. As there were no interns, the students took over the duties of interns, assisting in operations. She received her registered nurse (RN) degree in 1929.

## Career Highlights

Bragg worked as a nurse in a segregated department of a Griffin hospital, but left after a month because of the inferior care offered to black patients. She then moved to Rockford, Illinois, to live with a sister. While there, she passed the Illinois test for her nurse's license. Unable to find work in her profession in Rockford, she moved to Chicago, where she became a nurse at Wilson Hospital. While working at Wilson she met her first husband, Evans Waterford, who was visiting a patient there. The marriage lasted only two years, but she kept the name of Waterford.

After her divorce and the death of her father, Waterford had to support her mother and two nieces, who joined her in Chicago. She left the hospital for a more lucrative nursing job in the office of three practitioners, two doctors and a dentist. Still seeking advancement, she took graduate courses at Loyola University, earning a graduate certificate in public health administration. She also did graduate work in pediatric nursing at the Cook County School of Nursing. On the strength of these educational attain-

ments, she became a health inspector for the Metropolitan Burial Insurance Company where she worked for 10 years. During this period, Waterford became determined to fly. In her words, "I saw a billboard with a bird . . . nurturing her young fledglings into the flying world. It read, 'Birds Learn to Fly. Why Can't You?' That did it." The sign evoked memories of watching birds fly as a child and longing to emulate them. She began to look for a school where she could learn to fly.

She enrolled in Aeronautical University ground school, where she learned what she needed to know to fly and to maintain airplanes, under the tutelage of black aviation pioneers John C. Robinson and Cornelius Coffey. However, the school owned no airplanes, so she did not receive actual flight instruction. Waterford, not to be deterred, purchased her own plane, the first of three she was to own. The plane cost $600. In order to be able to fly it, it was first necessary to build an airfield because black people were not allowed to fly out of airports used by whites. In order to build this facility, the whole class at the ground school, with the aid of Robinson and Coffey, formed the Challenger Aero Club. They secured land and built an airfield with their own hands. In the spring of 1934, in her own plane and from the airfield she had helped build, Bragg learned to fly. After 35 solo hours, she passed the test for the private pilot's license.

In 1939, the federal government announced the Civilian Pilot Training Program (CPTP); it specifically excluded African Americans. To combat this discrimination, and to interest young black men and women in careers in aviation, the black pilots, who were members of the National Airmen's Association of America, lobbied to have this restriction removed. Their lobbying efforts proved successful, thanks in part to Senator Harry S Truman, who interceded with President Roosevelt to allow African American pilots to receive training, at certain designated schools, from the agency.

The United States entered World War II

in December 1941 after the bombing of Pearl Harbor. In 1943, Waterford and several other black women applied for appointments with the Women's Auxiliary Service Pilots (WASPs). Her application was regarded favorably, but when she showed up for an in-person interview, the interviewer told her she did not know what she would do with a black woman. Waterford appealed to higher-ups unsuccessfully and so was refused the opportunity to serve her country. She then applied for the military nurse corps, but she was informed that the quota for black nurses was filled.

Stymied in this direction, Waterford decided to go to Tuskegee, Alabama, where there was a CPTP school, and obtain her commercial pilot's license. She completed her written work flawlessly. She took and passed her flight test, but she was denied a license by a bigoted instructor who refused to give a commercial license to a "colored girl." Back in Chicago, she passed the test with ease, making her one of the first black women to achieve this advanced license.

Although she still flew as a hobby, she continued as a health inspector. Much of her work at Metropolitan involved making home visits. In the course of these visits, she noticed how poorly many of the indigent elderly fared, without proper food, care, or medical attention. This, together with the suggestion of a friend and the acquisition of a suitable property, led her into the nursing home business. After her marriage to Sumner Bragg, late in 1951, he joined her in running the business. They operated several nursing homes successfully until their joint retirement in 1972.

She also had time to befriend several Ethiopian students while they were studying in the United States, traveling with them and showing them the country. For her helpfulness, she was invited to Ethiopia to meet Emperor Haile Selassie in 1955. In the 1970s she traveled widely in Africa, leading tour groups. In 1986, after the death of Sumner Bragg, she moved permanently to Arizona, where the Braggs had spent winters for a number of years.

In her later years, Bragg's achievements were recognized, she was invited to appear and lecture at many aviation events around the country, and she received many awards and honors. She was also active in such civic organizations as the Tucson, Arizona, Urban League, Habitat for Humanity, and the Adopt-a-Scholar Program at Pima College, in Tucson. She died on April 11, 1993, at Blue Island, Illinois, a suburb of Chicago.

## Sources

"African Americans in Aviation in Arizona." *African American History Internship Project*. Puma, Arizona, 1989.

Bragg, Janet Harmon. *Soaring above Setbacks: The Autobiography of Janet Harmon Bragg, African American Aviator*. Washington, DC: Smithsonian Institution Press, 1996.

Hine, Darlene Clark, ed., *Black Women in America*. Brooklyn: Carlson Publishing, 1993.

Holden, Henry M., and Captain Lori Griffith. *Ladybirds II*. Mount Freedom, NJ: Black Hawk Press, 1993.

Hunt, Rufus. "A Page from Chicago's Aviation History." *Chicago Defender* (May 2, 1981): 10.

"Janet H. Bragg, Pioneer Black Aviatrix, Succumbs at Age 86." *Jet* (May 5, 1993): 36.

"Rites Set for Bragg; Nurse, Pilot." *Chicago Defender* (April 15, 1993): 26.

Young, A.S. (Doc). "She's Mother to Ethiopians." *Chicago Defender*, n.d.

# Jesse Leroy Brown

**Full Name at Birth:** Jesse Leroy Brown

**Born:** October 13, 1926, in Hattiesburg, Mississippi

**Died:** December 4, 1950, North Korea

**Education:** Attended Ohio State University, September 1944–March 1947, engineering.

**Awards, Honors:** Distinguished Flying Cross, Purple Heart, and Air Medal, all awarded posthumously.

Jesse Leroy Brown. Courtesy of National Archives and Records Administration (NARA).

**Summary:** Jesse Leroy Brown made civil rights history when he became the first black naval aviator on October 21, 1948. He died in action.

### Early Years

Jesse Leroy Brown was born in Hatties-burg, Mississippi, on October 13, 1926, one of six children of John and Julia Lindsey Brown. John Brown worked in a grocery warehouse and Julia Brown had been a schoolteacher. Brown had four brothers, Marvin, William, Fletcher, and Lura, and a sister, Johnny. The family lived in a house without central heat, water, or indoor plumbing. A fireplace provided warmth on chilly days. Brown's brother William was se-verely burned when he fell into the fireplace as a small child.

When John Brown lost his job in the early years of the Great Depression, the family re-located to Palmer's Crossing, where he found employment in a turpentine factory. In 1938, having lost this job, John Brown moved to a sharecropper farm in Lux, Mississippi. The family lived a spartan existence in Lux. The young Brown shared a bed with his older brother Marvin until Marvin went off to col-lege, and the children had to walk three miles to attend a one-room school. Never-theless, the parents had high standards for their children. They were strict about school attendance and homework. The family were dedicated Baptists, attending church faith-fully. Jesse, William, and Julia Brown sang in the choir, and John Brown was a deacon.

When Brown was six years old, his father took him to an air show, awakening an in-terest in flying that continued for the rest of his life. As a boy, he was drawn to a dirt airfield where the white mechanic who was in charge repeatedly chased him away. Brown nevertheless returned when he could.

At the age of 13, Brown got a job selling the *Pittsburgh Courier* in his area. One benefit of the job was that he was entitled to a free copy. The *Courier* was a prominent African American newspaper of the day, and in its pages Brown read of the exploits of the early black aviators—C. Alfred Anderson, Eugene Jacques Bullard, and Bessie Coleman, among them. Reading this convinced the youth that he, too, could be a pilot.

Brown went to live with his aunt in order to attend Eureka High School, a segregated high school in Hattiesburg, which was su-perior to the local high school where his family lived. He excelled in both academics and athletics. He played basketball and foot-ball and was a member of the track team. He graduated as salutatorian of his high school class.

### Higher Education

During his last year in high school, Brown was eager to go to college up North, to Ohio State University. His boyhood hero, Jesse Owens, the famed Olympic track star, had attended this well-known midwestern university. He consulted the principal of his high school, Nathaniel Burger, who advised him to attend one of the historically black colleges, as his brother Marvin had done. Burger pointed out that only seven African Americans had graduated from Ohio State the previous year. Brown felt he could compete with white students, and that at a black college, "I'd breeze through."

Brown had worked to save money for college and had managed to put by $600. Among his jobs was waiting tables at the Holmes Club, a saloon for white soldiers, where he had learned to take verbal abuse and keep his mouth shut. He knew he would have to work to pay his living expenses while he attended Ohio State. He would be in unfamiliar surroundings, among strangers, many of whom would not wish him well. He was prepared for that. He wanted his chance to make the best he could of himself.

In September 1944, Brown matriculated at Ohio State University. He had arranged to stay at a campus rooming house run by a black woman, Mrs. Jenkins. He had planned to major in architectural engineering, but in the back of his mind he knew that what he really wanted to do was fly. He applied and was refused admittance to the aeronautics program on the basis of his race.

Brown went out for track and wrestling, but he was soon forced to drop out of both sports because of the necessity of making money to stay in college. After a stint as a janitor in a local department store, he found employment with the Pennsylvania Railroad, loading boxcars from 3:30 P.M. to midnight. The work was rigorous. "I seldom pick up anything weighing less than 80 pounds," he wrote to his future wife, Daisy Pearl Nix, whom he had met in high school.

Back in Columbus for his second year of college, Brown learned of a new aviation program, the V-5 program, that was recruiting college students to be naval aviators. Although he met stiff resistance from navy recruiters, Brown insisted that he was quali-

fied and demanded to be allowed to take the test for the program.

In a letter to Nix, he wrote, "the test is very hard, I'm told. That's all the more reason I have to take it. It's a challenge and I will always regret it if I don't. I'm not sure I told you that the lieutenant is a pilot and I think he resents the idea that a black man could become a carrier pilot."

He passed the test and was admitted to the program. This made him an apprentice seaman in the navy. One welcome result of his admission to the program was a stipend of $50 a month, which allowed him to quit his job loading boxcars and concentrate on his studies. In March 1947, Brown reported to Glenview, Illinois, for selective flight training. For the first time, he was in a totally white world—the only black man in the barracks. The only black faces he saw belonged to the stewards in the mess hall where the group took their meals. Though Brown was prepared for rejection by his fellow trainees, he was met with some friendliness and very little overt racism.

Brown was fortunate in his flight instructor, Lieutenant Christenson, who accepted and encouraged him. The program was rigorous; almost every day one of the men flunked out, to be replaced immediately by someone else. The process was designed to weed out all but the best. Brown stayed the course, completed the program successfully, and he was transferred to Ottumwa, Iowa, for the next phase of his training.

The weeding process was far from over, but Brown had gotten over the first hurdle. At Ottumwa Naval Air Station, Naval Academy rules applied, and training concentrated on fitness and technical training.

"We march or trot everywhere," Brown wrote in a letter to Nix. "I pity my white classmates who didn't grow up walking five miles to school." Many, he continued, would wash out because of lack of physical coordination, and by the end of the program "a lot of faces will be gone. . . . Not mine, I hope."

Brown successfully completed this phase of

the program, and it was on to Pensacola, Florida, to the Naval Air Station there. During his stay in Pensacola, Brown and Daisy Pearl Nix secretly married. The marriage had to be kept a secret from his superiors, as naval aviators were not permitted to marry until their training was over, on pain of dismissal. Nix took a room in Pensacola, and the two were together on weekends.

At Pensacola, Brown encountered serious and open racism from an instructor. But he also found his flying lessons difficult and stressful. He came close to washing out, but stuck with it and successfully completed the program in August 1947. Out of 66 candidates, 36 had made it.

Brown was excited about his future. In a letter to Christensen, dated June 12, 1948, he wrote: "I hope to qualify aboard a carrier about Thursday of next week. So within the next 10 days I should be on my way to Jacksonville. . . . I've requested fighters, either the Hellcat or the Corsair."

Landing an airplane on an aircraft carrier is dangerous and demands a high degree of skill and nerve. The ability to land safely on a moving carrier requires rigorous preparation, split-second timing, and ability to coordinate actions with the crew who guide pilots safely to landing. The risks are enormous—few pilots survive carrier crashes.

Brown successfully qualified for carrier landing, and he was sent to Jacksonville, Florida, for advanced training. Completing all his training successfully, Brown received his gold wings, qualifying as the first African American naval aviator, on October 21, 1948. On December 22 of the same year, his daughter, Pamela Elise, was born.

On April 26, 1949, Brown was sworn in as an ensign. At last, he could reveal his long-concealed marriage and the existence of his daughter without fear of dismissal. His wife and baby soon joined him at Quonset, Rhode Island, where he was stationed.

In January 1949, Brown joined Fighter Squadron 32. On June 25, 1950, North Korean troops invaded South Korea. In response, all naval forces were placed on alert, including the carrier on which Brown was serving, the *Leyte*.

Brown flew 20 missions after being sent to Korea in October 1950. On December 4, his squadron flew in support of a marine contingent that was trapped by Chinese soldiers. Shortly after launch, Brown's plane was struck by enemy fire and crashed, trapping him inside the burning aircraft. Lieutenant Thomas Hudner Jr. saw Brown waving and went to his aid. The temperature was subzero, and Brown had stripped off his helmet and gloves in an effort to free himself from the fuselage that was crushing his leg and keeping him pinned to the plane.

After a futile attempt to rescue Brown, Hudner radioed for help, and a rescue helicopter was sent, but the two men working together could not free Brown. Brown was obviously in great pain but did not complain. He instructed Hudner to "tell Daisy I love her." Shortly afterward, he died. Hudner received the Medal of Honor from President Truman for his failed rescue attempt. Despite the shortness of his life, Brown's heroism was an inspiration to others. In California, seaman Frank E. Petersen Jr., a young black recruit, heard of his death, and, though saddened by the loss, determined that he too could aspire to be a naval aviator. In a memorial printed in his ship's newspaper, his shipmates honored him as "a Christian soldier, a gentleman, shipmate, and friend. . . . His courage and faith . . . shone like a beacon for all to see."

On February 17, 1973, a destroyer escort, the USS *Jesse L. Brown*, the first American naval vessel to be named in honor of an African American, was christened at a ceremony in Boston. Daisy Brown Thorne, Brown's widow, who had remarried, and Pamela Brown were present; Lieutenant Hudner spoke these words: "[Brown] died in the wreckage of his airplane with courage and unfathomable dignity. He willingly gave his life to tear down barriers to freedom of others."

On July 27, 1994, the Navy decommissioned the ship bearing Brown's name. The vessel was taken out of service at Pensacola, Florida, and sold to Egypt.

### Sources

Christman, T.J. "We All Shared a Common Bond." *Navy Times* (December 16, 1985): 71.

"Ens. Brown, Navy Pilot, Dies a Hero." *Journal and Guide* (Norfolk, Virginia) (December 12, 1950): 1, 2.

Greene, Robert. E. *Black Defenders of America: A Reference and Pictorial History*. Chicago: Johnson Publishing Co., 1974.

"The Last Days of a Naval Pilot." *Ebony* (April 1951): 15–24.

Lee, George L. *Interesting People: Black History Makers in the United States, 1750–1984*. Jefferson, NC: McFarland, 1991.

"Ship Is Losing Name of Black Navy Hero." *New York Times* (July 26, 1994): A13.

Taylor, Theodore. *The Flight of Jesse Leroy Brown*. New York: Avon Books, 1998.

Jill E. Brown. Courtesy of National Air and Space Museum, Smithsonian Institution (SI Neg. No. 2001-1898).

# Jill E. Brown

**Full Name at Birth:** Jill Elaine Brown

**Born:** 1950, Baltimore, Maryland

**Education:** Arundel High School, B.S. in home economics, University of Maryland.

**Positions Held:** Home economics teacher, Massachusetts, and Baltimore, Maryland; United States Navy, 1974; pilot, Wheeler Airlines, 1976–1978; Texas International Airlines, 1978; cargo pilot, Zantop International Airlines, 1978–mid-1980s.

**Summary:** Jill Brown made aviation history as the first African American woman to be chosen by the United States for training as a military pilot and also the first to serve as a pilot for a major U.S. airline.

### Early Years

Jill Brown was born in 1950 in Baltimore, Maryland, the only child of Gilbert and Elaine Brown. Gilbert Brown owned a construction company. Elaine Brown was an art resource teacher in the Baltimore school system. The family also owned a farm in West Virginia, where they spent summers and weekends when Brown was a child. Though the family was comfortably well off, Brown was not coddled or babied, but was expected to pitch in and work. Her father enjoyed training her to perform jobs that were considered "men's work." At the age of nine, she worked on the farm, learning to operate a tractor and perform other farm chores.

Throughout her adolescence, every summer found her hard at work. When she was 15, the young woman began to sell vegetables she had grown on the farm on the streets of Baltimore, earning her own pocket money. At 16, she became a painting contractor for her father's company, painting both interiors and exteriors of houses. Brown spent her 17th summer as an assistant playground director.

It was when she was 17 that the whole family took up flying. According to an interview in *Ebony*: "Daddy was tired of getting speeding tickets, and one day, while they were driving past a small airport, they saw a plane landing. Daddy decided that was for us." Brown soon learned to fly, soloing in a Piper J-3 Cub. The family acquired their own plane, a single engine Piper Cherokee 180D, christened the *Little Golden Hawk*. "Every weekend became a potential holiday. I'd take my friends flying to dinner dates, or we'd fly to our farm in West Virginia. We started calling ourselves BUA—Brown's United Airline."

## Higher Education

"While my father was teaching me that I could do traditional men's work, my mother was stressing femininity. . . . My mother is a teacher and thinks it's the ideal profession for a woman. . . . I was always kind of handy in the kitchen, so I chose home economics."

Brown attended the University of Maryland, majoring in home economics. Upon graduation, she accepted a teaching job in Massachusetts. However, she was disappointed by the realities of teaching home economics. Most of her students were not interested in home economics but took it to avoid studying more rigorous subjects. She found herself turning back to her first love, flying. Spending her spare time and money on flying lessons, Brown managed to earn her instrument, commercial, and instructor's ratings. Her eventual goal was to become a commercial airline pilot, but the goal was continually frustrated by lack of money and time.

## Career Highlights

Brown had previously tried to enroll in the military. In 1969, when she was 19, she asked the recruiter at the Air Division at Fort Meade when they expected to enroll women and was dismissed with a laugh. By 1974, the military was no longer laughing, and Brown was able to sign up for flight training in the U.S. Navy.

Her admission to the naval air training program was a historic event; she was the first black woman to be admitted to the program. Brown was featured prominently in a number of newspapers and magazine articles. Her swearing in by Spann Watson, one of the original pilots of the illustrious 99th Fighter Squadron, made headlines in the African American press. Her hitch with the Navy was to last only six months, however. According to Brown, "My every move was watched. . . . And I made some mistakes, some really bad ones." One of her worst mistakes, she felt, was "Not being able to keep my mouth shut."

Brown and the Navy parted company by mutual consent. "After six months, the Navy and I decided I'd just take my honorable discharge and leave." Although she spoke of her experience with disparaging humor, it was a heavy blow to Brown. "It was humiliating. I honestly couldn't face people. It was a long time before I'd even go out of the house."

Nevertheless, she did muster up courage to resume flight training, earning the advance rating and a multiengine rating. To earn her living, she went back to teaching, this time teaching inner-city children in her hometown of Baltimore. By chance, Brown happened upon an article in *Ebony* about Warren H. Wheeler, an African American who owned and operated a small airline in Raleigh, North Carolina. She immediately telephoned Wheeler, and flew down for an interview. Wheeler, after taking her for a check-out flight, admitted she was qualified to fly, but had no immediate openings for a pilot. He told her he would inform her when he was able to add another pilot to his staff.

Brown was unwilling to wait. "I'll fly for nothing. . . . Find me a ground job just to make enough to live on, and I'll fly right now—with or without pay." She was hired as a ticket seller for $300 a month. But the opportunities to fly were plentiful, and eventually she was made resident co-pilot.

The work was rigorous. As she tells it, "I was up every morning and at the airport before six A.M. for preflight. . . . I had to check the oil and hook up battery carts. Then I took reservations and wrote up the tickets. After that I loaded the passengers' baggage—by myself." After completing these chores, she supervised the passengers' boarding of the aircraft. Once they were all settled in their seats, she climbed into the cockpit and flew the plane to its destination.

Brown remained at Wheeler Airlines until she had logged 800 hours in the Beechcraft. These hours, added to 400 she already had, qualified her for employment as a pilot for a major airline. She left Wheeler for Texas International Airlines in 1978.

Brown suspected that Texas Airlines had hired her as a token African American woman. Despite her protests, special ceremonies were planned when she received her wings. She felt that she was being used by the airline to boost their own image. After six months, she left Texas International.

She was then employed as a co-pilot by Zantop International Airlines, a cargo carrier based in Michigan. In this capacity, she was responsible for flying materials for the automotive industry and was based in Detroit, Michigan. The work was strenuous: cargo pilots were on call for 24 hours a day, except for one free weekend a month. They had to be ready to take to the air at two hours' notice. Schedules frequently changed and itineraries were unpredictable. Brown remained with Zantop until some time in the mid-1980s.

## Sources

"Blacks in Aviation—1994." Commemorative Brochure. Miami, Florida: Miami-Dade Aviation Department.

Burgen, Michele. "Winging It at 25,000 Feet." *Ebony* (August 1978): 58–60, 62.

"Jill Brown May Be First Black Woman Pilot." *Jet* (October 24, 1974): 19.

Smith, Elizabeth Simpson. *Breakthrough: Women in Aviation.* New York: Walker and Co., 1981; 38–51.

"Working World. Flying High: Jill Brown, Pilot." *Essence* (December 1979): 28, 30, 34.

# Roscoe C. Brown Jr.

**Full Name at Birth:** Roscoe Conkling Brown Jr.

**Born:** March 9, 1922, Washington, D.C.

**Education:** Dunbar High School, Washington, D.C., graduated 1939; B.S., Springfield College, Springfield, Massachusetts, 1943; M.A., Ph.D., New York University (NYU), 1951.

**Positions Held:** Professor, West Virginia State College, New York University; editor, *Negro Almanac*, 1967; director, Institute of Afro-American Affairs, New York University 1964–1977; radio and television host, 1973; president, Bronx Community College, City University of New York (CUNY), 1977–1993; director, Center for Urban Education Policy, Graduate Center, CUNY, 1993–    .

**Awards, Honors:** Distinguished Flying Cross, Air Medal, 1945; Distinguished Alumni Award, Springfield College, 1973; Distinguished Alumni Award, New York University, 1973; Emmy Award, 1973; Bronx Museum's Education Award, 1990.

**Summary:** Roscoe C. Brown was one of the Tuskegee Airmen, the first group of African American pilots ever to serve in the U.S. military. After serving in World War II, he went on to become a college president, radio and television host, and influential African American leader.

## Early Years

Roscoe C. Brown Jr. was born in Washington, D.C., on March 9, 1922. His father, Roscoe Conkling Brown Sr., was a pioneer in the field of public health, particularly as it affected African Americans. The elder Brown was a dentist, but he gave up his practice in order to serve in the U.S. Public Health Service. A respected figure on the national scene, he was a member of President Franklin D. Roosevelt's informal black cabinet.

The younger Brown conceived his desire to fly when, as a child, his father took him to airports to visit the sightseeing airplanes. The young man built airplane models from kits and followed aviation news in such magazines as *Air Trails* and *Flying Aces*, which were popular periodicals of the day. In these publications and in daily newspapers, he followed the exploits of famous aviators. He also loved to visit the Smithsonian Institution to look at the airplane exhibits.

At the time, black people were not permitted to take the airplane rides that others were enjoying. But, according to his later reminiscences, "I'd always bug [his father] for a ride. . . . My dad told me what the realities were. . . . I didn't want to know about it and kept bugging him and finally he came up with an idea. He's a light-skinned man so he told them we were the children of a French diplomat. . . . We kept our mouths shut until we were up in the air. That's how I got my plane ride."

## Higher Education

After graduation from Dunbar High School, Brown attended Springfield College, in Springfield, Massachusetts, an integrated school from which he graduated as valedictorian in 1943. He participated in many intercollegiate sports in college. He did not encounter much racism when playing other local New England colleges, but when the lacrosse team played Army at West Point: "one well known All-American football player . . . called me a 'nigger' and chased me all around the place with his stick. He finally cracked me on the head. My white teammates . . . practically caused a riot there at West Point."

Brown schooled himself to ignore the racist taunts and catcalls he encountered: "You just can't let yourself get into something like that. You'd just play a good game and when you came off the field, your head was held high."

## Career Highlights

It was while he was still attending college that war began to loom. The Axis powers, Germany, Japan, and Italy, were starting to overrun Europe and Asia, causing President Roosevelt and his advisers to prepare the U.S. military for a world war. It was only now, at the beginning of World War II, that black men were allowed to be airplane pilots. Due to the racism prevalent at the time, African American pilots were trained separately and served in segregated units. Nevertheless, the fact that they were given the chance to fly was cause for optimism and hope for the future in some quarters.

Brown had not lost his ambition to be a pilot, and the war offered him an opportunity. After graduation from college, in March 1943, Brown was called to active duty. He went through basic training: "We went to Keesler Field in the heart of Mississippi and marched in the mud for a couple of months and took a lot of tests. . . . We did very well on the tests, much better than I think they expected blacks to do. . . . The drill instructors were black and the supervising officers were white. The drill instructors were tough regular army men, and they were there to break in the recruits, especially 'smart niggers' from the North who'd been to college. . . . We took everything they dished out and gave them a little back."

Those men who passed the tests, Brown among them, were sent to Tuskegee Institute in Tuskegee, Alabama, for preflight orientation. The instructors were civilian pilots, most of them black. C. Alfred "Chief" Anderson, one of the first African Americans to get a pilot's license, was in charge of instructors.

The whole operation at Tuskegee was led by Colonel Noel Parrish. Fortunately, though a southern white man, he was not a racist and treated everyone decently. "In fact, Parrish fought hard to see that the group was able to stay intact and to make sure we were treated fairly . . . if he had been hostile and racist, he could have made it really rough on us. They called it the Tuskegee Experiment because they expected it to fail, but Parrish helped it succeed."

After getting their wings, the group was sent to Waldenborough, South Carolina. The group had their first experience of hardcore southern racism there. Attempting to attend a segregated movie theater, the men sat in the "white" section. When asked to move, they said, "We're officers and we're not leaving." The colonel in charge attempted to enforce the segregation rules, but the men were adamant. They won their point, and the theater was integrated.

They were next shipped to Italy, where the group were assigned to escort bombers on their missions, under the command of Lieutenant Colonel Benjamin O. Davis Jr. Their superb teamwork and discipline caused them to excel in this function, and the group could boast that they never lost a bomber to enemy fire. Brown distinguished himself as the first African American pilot to engage and destroy an enemy jet plane. He was named in field dispatches, to the great pride of his then-wife, Laura Jones Brown. Mrs. Brown, in an interview with the *New York Herald-Tribune*, was happy in the realization that Brown's heroic action provided "a further rebuke to those who would take away from the Negro's courage as a combat soldier."

Brown was promoted to captain, commanding the 100th Fighter Squadron of the 332nd Fighter Group by the war's end. This escalation of rank did not prevent the men of the 332nd from being treated as second-class citizens. They had to eat in segregated dining halls, and had to suffer the humiliation of observing German prisoners of war being fed in white dining halls. Nor did his promotion or his record of heroism persuade Eastern Airlines to hire him as a civilian pilot at the war's end.

After a stint as a social welfare investigator for the New York City Department of Welfare, Brown entered the education field. He was a coach at West Virginia State University from 1945–1947. He developed an interest in what was then called exercise psychology, and he undertook research in the qualities that made for a good combat pilot. Returning to New York City, he attended New York University, where he received his M.A. and Ph.D. degrees. He then became a full-time professor at the same institution's School of Education.

Brown developed a wide range of interests; in addition to his interest in physical fitness, a field in which he published many articles in leading periodicals, he became a respected authority on African American history and urban policy. In 1964, he established and became director of the Institute for African American Affairs at NYU, a position in which he served until 1977. His publications include authorship of *The Black Experience*, co-editorship of *The Negro Almanac*, as well as many articles in learned journals. Brown hosted a weekly radio program, *Soul of Reason*, and three major New York television series, one of which won an Emmy Award in 1973.

Dr. Brown serves on the boards of many nonprofit organizations, including the National Board of the Boys and Girls Clubs of America, the American Council on Education, the YMCA of Greater New York, the New York Botanical Garden, and the Franklin and Eleanor Roosevelt Institute. He is a member and past president of One Hundred Black Men, an influential group of civic-minded African Americans in New York City. He was appointed by the governor of New York to the boards of the New York State Job Training and Partnership Council and the New York State Health, Fitness and Sports Council. He is chair of the Urban Issues Group, a think tank devoted to the concerns of the African American community, and he serves on the board of the Jackie Robinson Foundation.

Dr. Brown, who is divorced, has four grown children: Doris, Diane, Dennis, and Donald. He maintains his commitment to physical fitness and has completed the New York City Marathon nine times.

## Sources

"Black Ex-Fighter Pilots Recall Exploits." *New York Times* (November 15, 1976).

Brown, Dr. Roscoe C. "Are Black Officials 'Targets of Opportunity'?" *New York Amsterdam News* (February 29, 1993): 13, 37.

Dr. Roscoe Brown President InterOrg Communications. Http://www.interorg.com/BROWN.HTM. December 17, 1999.

Harney, James. "Tuskegee Pilots: Men on a Mission." *USA Today* (July 30, 1992): 6a.

The Jackie Robinson Foundation—News. "Jackie Robinson Announces New Board Members." Http://www.jackierobinson.org/Features/Comm/Docs/Press/05–1297.html. May 12, 1997.

Leuthner, Stuart, and Oliver Jensen. *High Honor.* Washington, DC: Smithsonian Institution Press, 1989: 238–247.

"Negro Flyer's Feat Doesn't Surprise Wife." *New York Herald-Tribune* (March 31, 1945).

Salzman, Jack et al., eds. *Encyclopedia of African American Culture and History.* New York: Macmillan, 1996: 454–455.

Tuskegee War Hero Fought Nazis and Racism. Http://moonjrn.columbia.edu/BronxBeat/indces/020998/tuskegee.html. December 17, 1999.

# Willa Brown

Willa Brown. Courtesy of National Air and Space Museum, Smithsonian Institution (SI Neg. No. 90-13119).

**Full Name at Birth:** Willa Beatrice Brown

**Born:** January 22, 1906, Glasgow, Kentucky

**Died:** July 18, 1992, Chicago, Illinois

**Education:** Wiley High School, Terre Haute, Indiana, 1923; A.B. in Commerce and French, State Normal School (now Indiana State University), Terre Haute, 1931; student pilot's license, 1937; private pilot's license, 1938; commercial pilot's license, ground instructor's rating, and radio license, 1939.

**Positions Held:** Teacher, department head, commercial subjects, Roosevelt Annex High School, Gary, Indiana, 1927–1932; federal coordinator, Civilian Pilot Training Program (CPTP), Chicago, 1939–1943; co-founder and director, Coffey School of Aeronautics, 1938–1945; teacher, commercial subjects and aeronautics, Chicago high schools, 1962–1971.

**Awards, Honors:** Cited in the 76th Congressional Record, 1939, for achievements in aviation; first African American woman to receive a commercial pilot's license, 1939; Dwight H. Green Trophy for distinguished contributions to aviation, 1942; first African American member of Illinois Civil Air Patrol, 1942; first African American member of Federal Aviation Administration's Women's Advisory Committee, 1971–1974; honored as a pioneer in the "Black Wings" exhibition, National Air and Space Museum, 1982.

**Summary:** Willa Beatrice Brown is often credited as the person most responsible for bringing about the training and inclusion of African American pilots into the mobilization required by World War II. She cofounded the National Airmen's Association of America and the Coffey School of Aeronautics and worked tirelessly to promote aviation among African Americans. Brown was also the first black woman to make aviation her career.

## Early Years

Born on January 22, 1906, in Glasgow, Willa Beatrice Brown was the only daughter among the four sons of Hallie Mae Carpenter Brown and Eric B. Brown. While in Kentucky, where Mr. Brown owned his own farm, the family included James, born in 1904, and Charles Guy, born in 1908. After 1910, the family, as part of the great internal migration of African Americans from the rural south to northern cities, moved to Terre Haute, Indiana. They hoped for greater opportunities in employment and education. Mr. Brown worked in a creosote factory and was a minister. He pastored the Holy Tri-

umphant Church in 1920 and the Free Church of God in 1929, according to city directories. Two more sons were born to the Browns in Terre Haute, Simeon in 1916 and David in 1921. During the 1920s, the household also included a young nephew, Wilford Howard.

While in high school, Brown was in the 100-member school chorus in 1921, one of only seven black students pictured in *The Red Pepper*, the school's yearbook. The next year the Terre Haute city directory listed her working as a maid, certainly part-time employment as she was still in high school. Brown graduated from Wiley High School in 1923, although she is listed among the members of the class of 1924.

## Higher Education

On October 1, 1923, Brown matriculated at the Indiana State Normal School, a teacher training school that is now part of Indiana University. She majored in business subjects, then called commerce, minored in French, and belonged to the Alpha Kappa Alpha sorority. In 1925, the city directory again lists Brown as a domestic. She had completed most of her coursework by 1927, and she is pictured in that year's *Sycamore*, the yearbook of Indiana State Normal School. Brown, however, did not officially receive her bachelor's degree until August 21, 1931, by which time she had been teaching in Gary for four years, some of them as head of the department of business subjects.

Brown took graduate evening courses at Northwestern University's School of Commerce in Chicago in 1937, but she didn't earn a degree. Interest in aviation had begun to occupy all of Brown's spare time from the mid-1930s. She received a master mechanic's certificate in 1935, and her private pilot's license in June 1938. Her commercial pilot's license, with ground instructor's rating, followed in 1939. Brown was the first African American woman to attain this license.

## Career Highlights

In 1927, having completed four years of teacher training, Brown was ready to begin her career. She headed for Gary, then the city in the United States most noted for the educational innovations of its school system, and with a large black population. Founded in 1906, the same year Brown was born, by U.S. Steel and named for its president, Elbert H. Gary, the city was planned to produce steel. Part of the plan included the transformation of its workers, mainly immigrants of eastern European origin, into an American workforce. When Brown arrived, the "City of the Century" was undergoing rapid population growth, a building boom (banks, theaters, hotels, an armory, a city hall, an auditorium), and receiving accolades for its schools. The system was a model for the rest of the nation as leading educators studied the well-equipped schools (swimming pools, laboratories) and the evening classes that offered both vocational and academic subjects to adults. But the schools, as well as the parks, cemeteries, theaters, and housing, were largely segregated. They became even more so as Gary's African American population swelled as the northward migration continued. A contributing factor was the entrance of the United States into World War I in 1917, and the greater need for steelworkers. The number of black schoolchildren rose from 267 in 1916 to 1,125 in 1920. By 1930, the figure had soared above 4,000.

Calls for segregation and related tensions finally erupted in the Emerson School Strike of 1927, the year Brown arrived to teach at the all-black Roosevelt Annex. On September 26, more than 600 white Emerson students walked out of their classrooms to protest the transfer of 18 black students to their school, which already had six students of color. The number of strikers grew and the strike garnered national attention, with editorial writers commenting that "the governing body of a municipality has permitted itself to be dictated to by school pupils." The strike was settled in a week, with segregation more entrenched than ever. Plans were made for a new all-black school, Roosevelt, which did open in April 1931. At a cost of one million dollars, the school had an auditorium for 1,200 people, an Olympic-sized swimming pool, two gymnasiums, a cafeteria, and 24 classrooms, all with modern silent clocks.

Brown headed the commercial department, with subjects such as typewriting and stenography. She organized a typewriting club for the best students, which met every other Saturday, and she devised creative assignments for her classes. She also taught typewriting to adults in the evening school. Her young students played a role in producing the school newspaper, *The Annex News* (vol. 1, no. 1, October 15, 1927), said to be the only student paper in the Gary school system. Brown continued to return to Terre Haute during the summers of 1928, 1929, and 1931 to complete her degree.

On November 24, 1929, she and Wilbur J. Hardaway were married at the Israel CME (Colored Methodist Episcopal) Church. Hardaway, a graduate of Tuskegee Institute, and the newly elected alderman of the 5th Ward, had been one of the first nine African American firemen in Gary, when a "colored" fire station was established in 1927. Divorced in the fall of 1931, Brown remained as a teacher until the 1932 school term ended. She then moved to Chicago.

Although these were the Depression years, Brown was never unemployed because of her secretarial skills. From 1932 until 1939, she held a host of positions—some private, some with the federal government. Her more prominent employers included Dr. Julius H. Lewis, the first Negro on the faculty of the University of Chicago's medical school, 1937–1938; Horace Cayton, co-author of *Black Metropolis*, a sociological study of Chicago, 1939; and Dr. Theodore K. Lawless, a dermatologist, 1938–1939. In February 1946, *Ebony* called him "skin wizard of the world" and marveled that "white patients forget skin color and flock to ace Negro doctor." In that time and place, segregation was the norm, and the magazine's wonder was not exaggerated. At his death in 1971, Lawless was world renowned as a philanthropist as well as a dermatologist.

Brown in 1934 was working as a cashier in a Walgreen's drug store when she met John C. Robinson, a pilot. He introduced her to Cornelius Coffey, an expert pilot and mechanic, and to the other members of the Challenger Aero Club, which Robinson had founded in 1931. Being at the Harlem Airport was exhilarating for Brown, who said she "was always an outdoor person." She began to take preparatory courses at Chicago's Aeronautical University, which had been established in 1929 by the Curtiss-Wright Flying Service. That there were classes for African Americans at all was due to the outstanding performances of Robinson and Coffey, who had threatened the school with legal action before they were admitted some years earlier. Afterward they were hired to teach other African Americans.

On May 13 of that year, Brown was seriously injured in a car accident in which her companion, John B. McClellan, was killed. McClellan, a teacher of Spanish and science at Wendell Phillips High School, and Brown were returning from a Mother's Day visit to her family. Brown was hospitalized with a broken arm, several broken ribs, and a fractured vertebra (*Chicago Defender, Gary American*, both May 19, 1934, p. 1).

She recovered and continued her enthusiasm for flying. Brown's energy, charisma, and talent for publicity were evident when she arrived at the *Chicago Defender* to request coverage for an airshow that a group of 30 flyers were going to stage. Enoch P. Waters, an editor, who knew of only two black pilots, Hubert F. Julian and John C. Robinson, reported her effect: the older reporters "polished their eyeglasses to get an undistorted view . . . [of Willa Brown who] made such a stunning appearance in white jodhpurs, white jacket, and white boots, that all the

typewriters suddenly went silent." The fliers got their publicity, and Waters became so caught up with this group of young flyers that he became part of their history.

It was he who suggested forming a national organization to serve as a clearinghouse for information about the aviation activities of African Americans, and which would be a vehicle to increase black participation in the technology of the future. On August 16, 1937, the National Airmen's Association of America (NAAA) received its charter, with the *Defender* providing a mailing address. The charter members, besides Waters and Brown, included Cornelius Coffey, Chauncey Spencer, Dale White, Harold Hurd, Marie St. Clair, Charles Johnson, Grover C. Nash, Edward Johnson, Janet Harmon Waterford, and George Williams. Brown, as secretary, took on all the public relations duties. From then on and for nearly a decade, her life became one of ceaseless and aggressive promotion for the inclusion of blacks into the aviation mainstream, and into their country's war effort. "Her presence was extremely dynamic," recalled Felix J. Kirkpatrick (interview, July 18, 1995), who became a Tuskegee Airman.

Brown and Coffey founded the Coffey School of Aeronautics in 1938, with Coffey as president and chief flight instructor and Brown as director. She ran a food service called Brown's Luncheonette, or the Clubhouse, but left the cooking to her brother Simeon, also a pilot, and to others. Chauncey Spencer (interview, June 3, 1995) remembered Simeon with "very much the personality of Willa, outgoing, exciting." Spencer continued, "Willa was persistent and dedicated. She was the foundation, framework, and the builder of people's souls. She did it not for herself, but for all of us. She had a spirit and energy you wouldn't believe." In May 1938, as part of an NAAA initiative, Spencer and Dale L. White flew to Washington, DC, to lobby for the right of blacks to become pilots in the Army Air Corps. The NAAA sponsored a "national air meet" August 25–27, 1939, in Chicago, which brought together about 40 pilots from 16 states. The group's membership grew and chapters were formed as a result of Brown's letter writing, flying visits to black colleges, and radio addresses.

When in 1939, the government initiated the Civilian Pilot Training Program (CPTP) to serve as a source of manpower with some training, in case war began, the Coffey School wanted to be certified as a training center, even though the CPTP was working through colleges only. Brown conducted for officials separate demonstration classes of college and noncollege youths. She wanted to disprove a 1925 War Department report that claimed Negroes could not assimilate technical education. She did, and came to the attention of *Time* magazine, which stated: "she has labored mightily to whip up interest in flying among Negroes, get them a share in the CAA's training program." From 1939 to 1945 they trained more than 200 pilots. She and the NAAA, with other organizations, continued the campaign for the admission of blacks into the Air Corps, which finally resulted in the segregated air field at Tuskegee and the formation of the 99th Pursuit Squadron. Many of the instructors and cadets of the 99th were graduates of the Coffey School.

In February 1940, Brown was appointed federal coordinator for the Chicago unit of the CPTP. About 30 students were enrolled at the first evening classes she taught at Wendell Phillips High School under the auspices of the Coffey School. They also had government-supplied equipment worth $100,000. Rachel Carter Ellis, the only woman in Brown's first class, said in an interview on July 22, 1995, "I admired her greatly, she was serious, and [wanted] the 'youngsters' to succeed."

In 1942, Brown was the first African American member of the Civilian Air Patrol (CAP) in Illinois, as lieutenant and adjutant of the 613–6 squadron. The segregated unit had 25 pilots, several light planes, and four army training biplanes. Brown was one of 400 pilots accepted of the 1,560 state pilots who applied. She also joined the Aircraft Owners and Pilots Association (AOPA) that year, and she was still a member in 1975.

Soon after the war ended in 1945, the Coffey School closed. Brown and Coffey were married on February 7, 1947, but the marriage didn't last. (Although most sources cite 1939 as the date of their marriage, the Cook County, Illinois (Chicago), Vital Statistics Department has no record with that date.) Several articles report that Brown ran unsuccessfully for public office in 1946, 1947, 1948, and 1950, but a search of Chicago newspapers did not uncover any details or mention. Brown married for the third time in 1955. Her husband was the Reverend J.H. Chappell, whom she met when they both worked at the Great Lakes Naval Training Base in Waukegan. Pastor of the West Side Community Church in Chicago, he retired in 1970. Brown, an active church worker, returned to teaching business subjects and aeronautics in high schools from 1962 until her retirement in 1971.

Brown achieved another first in 1971 when she became the first black woman appointed to the Federal Aviation Administration's Women's Advisory Committee on Aviation, where she served until 1974. For her leadership in promoting aviation among African Americans, Brown was invited to address the Tuskegee Airmen at their fourth annual convention in Detroit, Michigan, in August 1975. Although she was unable to attend, her speech was read at the convention. She outlined the work of the NAAA and the Coffey School in establishing flight training for African Americans. She said, "We desperately wanted blacks to fly and we desperately wanted them to be accepted into the Army Air Corps as . . . cadets." She continued, "As a matter of fact we threw the word 'I' out of our vocabulary altogether. We needed everybody's help." The groups they joined with included the YMCA, the Chicago Urban League, the Chicago Board of

Education, the NAACP, "and of course, churches of all denominations." Reclusive in her last years because of ill health, Brown died of a stroke on July 18, 1992, and was buried in Lincoln Cemetery, Chicago.

### Sources

"About People." *Essence* (April 1988): 46.

Cohen, Ronald D. *Children of the Mill: Schooling and Society in Gary, Indiana, 1906–1960.* Bloomington: Indiana University Press, 1990.

Jakeman, Robert J. *The Divided Skies: Establishing Segregated Flight Training at Tuskegee, Alabama, 1934–1942.* Tuscaloosa: University of Alabama, 1992.

Johnson, Jesse J. *Black Women in the Armed Forces 1942–1974: A Pictorial History.* Hampton, VA: Hampton Institute, 1974; 25–26.

"School for Willa." *Time* (September 25, 1939): 16.

Waters, Enoch P. *American Diary: A Personal History of the Black Press.* Chicago: Path Press, 1987. See Chapter 13, "Little Air Show Becomes National Crusade"; 195–210.

*Willa Beatrice Brown—An American Aviator.* Film. Writer/Director Severo Perez, California Department of Education, 1999.

"Willa Brown, Famed Aviatrix Returns to Chicago Teaching." *Baltimore Afro-American* (May 5, 1962): 18.

"Willa Brown Chappell, 86, Trained Black WWII Pilots." *Chicago Sun Times* (July 20, 1992): 41.

Willa Brown Chappell, Chicago, to Chauncey E. Spencer, Highland Park, Michigan, August 7, 1975, with copy of her speech.

# William E. Brown Jr.

**Full Name at Birth:** William Earl Brown, Jr.

**Born:** December 5, 1927, Bronx, New York

**Education:** B.S., Pennsylvania State University, 1949; Squadron Officer School, Maxwell Air Force Base, Alabama, 1956; Armed Forces Staff College, Norfolk, Virginia, 1966; Industrial College of the Armed Forces, Fort Lesley J. McNair, Washington, D.C., 1973; advanced management program, Harvard Business School, 1973.

William E. Brown Jr. Courtesy of U.S. Air Force.

**Positions Held:** Jet pilot in the U.S. Air Force; assigned to the Department of Defense, Manpower and Reserve Affairs Office of the Pentagon, in 1971, as special assistant for domestic actions to the assistant secretary of defense; deputy commander for operations, 64th Flying Training Wing, Reese Air Force Base, Texas; base commander, later commander, of the 82nd Flying Training Wing, Williams Air Force Base; commanded First Composite Wing, Military Airlift Command, Andrews Air Force Base, Maryland, 1975; chief of security police, Headquarters U.S. Air Force, June 1977, Tyndall Air Force Base, Florida, Headquarters U.S. Air Force; commander, Air Defense Weapons Center, Tyndall Air Force Base, Florida; commanded 17th Air Force, Germany, from July 1980 to September, 1982; commander of Allied Air Force Southern Europe and deputy commander in chief, U.S. Air Force in Europe; commander, 17th Air Force, headquartered in Germany from July 1980 to September, 1982; retired in 1985.

**Awards, Honors:** Distinguished Service Medal, Legion of Merit with two oak leaf clusters, Distinguished Flying Cross, Air Medal with four oak leaf clusters, Air Force Commendation Medal, and Purple Heart.

**Summary:** William E. Brown Jr. was among the first pilots who flew jet planes in the 1950s, completing 225 missions during the Korean War. He subsequently rose to the rank of lieutenant general, retiring in 1985.

## Early Years

William E. Brown Jr. was born on December 5, 1927, in the Bronx, New York, the oldest of three children of William E. Brown Sr. and Rose Brown. Three months after his birth, Brown's family moved to Englewood, New Jersey, a place he still considers his hometown. His father was a chauffeur for a wealthy family. Young Brown went to public elementary school and Dwight Morrow High School, both in Englewood.

It was while attending high school that he began delivering two African American newspapers, the *Baltimore Afro-American* and the *New York Amsterdam News*. One of the advantages of delivering these papers was that the Brown family received free copies. Through these newspapers, he learned of the exploits of the black flyers of World War II known as the Tuskegee Airmen. Reading about the heroism of these men inspired Brown to become a pilot himself. According to Brown, who is quoted in an article in the *Metropolitan Times* (June 7, 1995): "These papers were filled each week with news of the black fliers. . . . Their training at Tuskegee, their missions overseas, and their individual stories provided me with a whole series of role models who were doing something that I had never dreamed a black man would be allowed to do."

The youth began to look up into the sky at the airplanes that frequently passed overhead. They were numerous, as Englewood was located under the main exit airway from LaGuardia Airport in New York. "There had always been airplanes overhead while I was growing up, but I had never looked at them until the Tuskegee Airmen began their exploits." A trip with his uncle to Teterboro Airport, where Charles Lindbergh had kept his airplane, further stimulated his interest in flight. "I got my first ride in an airplane, once around the pattern for five dollars. I was really hooked then."

## Higher Education

Brown worked hard at both academics and athletics in high school. He felt that "because I'm black, people would expect me to fail. I always try to disappoint them in that regard." This hard work paid off when it came to applying to college. Brown was admitted to several colleges. He chose Pennsylvania State University. Majoring in premedical science, he originally intended to become a physician. Despite having to work to support himself in college, Brown excelled in academic work and managed to be lettered in track.

## Career Highlights

Upon graduation in 1949, Brown later remembered, "no medical school seemed to think me ready for acceptance. . . . The summer of 1950 found me working as an ambulance attendant in Harlem Hospital in New York City . . . until I could apply to medical school again. Instead, the Korean War began that summer and I applied for the Aviation Cadet Program."

He received his basic flight training at Randolph Air Force Base. Though the Air Force had been newly integrated, some instructors were reluctant to train black students. The six African American flight students were all trained by two instructors. Brown was fortunate in his flight instructor. "Captain Philip P. Plotkin . . . was the first of a long line of fair-minded, supportive people I have met, both in the Air Force and in civilian life." Of the six African Americans, only Brown and one other successfully completed the rigorous training.

Brown was then sent to Craig Air Force Base, Selma, Alabama, where he was trained on the P-51 Mustang, a propeller-driven plane. Jet planes were just being introduced to military service, and Brown was one of the first pilots to learn to fly them. At Williams Air Force Base, where he took Jet Transition Training, he met "a fighter pilot who became my role model, mentor, and lifetime friend [a] new major named Woody Crockett," who had flown in more combat missions than any other Tuskegee Airman. "He set an outstanding example of how a proud Air Force officer should act and look, and I tried to imitate his sharp appearance and military bearing. . . . [F]or 40 years, he has been a friend."

After 20 hours of jet training, Brown was transferred to Nellis Air Force Base, near Las Vegas, Nevada. Casualties were high at Nellis, where Brown and the other pilots were trained for combat in the new planes. Being an innovator had its dangers: "It was always exciting. . . . The engines were unreliable. We were very fortunate [to survive]." In a speech given in 1992, Brown wryly remarked: "[M]ore pilots were being killed at Nellis in training than in combat in Korea. The young fighter pilots would say that if you could live through Nellis, Korea would be a piece of cake." He noted: "In Tom Wolfe's *The Right Stuff* [a book about the first crew of astronauts] he has a chapter about '50s jet aviation, and it scared me to death when I read it. . . . I had no idea at the time what we were up against."

During the Korean War, on September 4, 1952, Brown was flying with then captain Frederick "Boots" Blesse when they encountered enemy fighters. According to Brown, "Blesse got some good hits on one MiG" but "As we turned to leave, we spotted another." Brown and Blesse succeeded in knocking out the engine of the other plane: "That slowed the MiG down so much I was able to pull

up right next to the cockpit and look the pilot right in the eye. He must have decided the game was up, because at that moment I watched him position his body for ejection and he bailed out." Brown earned the Distinguished Flying Cross for this mission.

Brown flew more than 5,100 hours, in South Korea, Thailand, Spain, and Germany, moving up through the ranks from second lieutenant in 1951 to colonel in 1971. He had 225 combat missions to his credit when he was assigned to the Department of Defense Manpower and Reserve Affairs Office at the Pentagon, where he served as special assistant for domestic actions to the assistant secretary of defense.

In 1973, he was assigned as deputy commander for operations, 64th Flying Training Wing, at Reese Air Force Base in Texas. He was next assigned to Williams Air Force Base, first as base commander and then as commander of the 82nd Flying Training Wing. In February 1975, Brown took command of the First Composite Wing, Military Airlift Command, Andrews Air Force Base, Maryland. On August 1, 1975, he was promoted to brigadier general.

In June 1977, General Brown was named chief of security police, Headquarters U.S. Air Force. In October, 1978, he was transferred to Tyndall Air Force Base in Florida, where he served as commander of the Air Defense Weapons Center. After a stint as commander of the 17th Air Force, he was headquartered in Germany from July 1980 to September 1982. His next move and promotion to lieutenant general found him assigned as commander of Allied Air Force Southern Europe and deputy commander in chief, U.S. Air Force in Europe for the Southern Area, stationed in Naples, Italy.

In 1985, General Brown retired from the Air Force. He was not idle upon retirement, however. He became a consultant for Burdeshaw Associates, a firm involved in the aerospace industry. One of the activities he values most is his volunteer work as a docent at the National Air and Space Museum of the Smithsonian Institution.

This avocation is very important to Brown. He had always felt drawn to the museum: "When I come in the building, I walk in like the village priest walking into the Vatican: I don't understand everything, but I know I'm in the right place." Many other retired pilots serve as docents in the museum: "[w]e tend to gravitate to where the planes are." He had always enjoyed touring the museum, and showing visiting friends around. In the course of these tours, Brown became quite knowledgeable about the museum and its collections. Despite his familiarity with the exhibits, when Brown volunteered as a docent he had to undergo 10 months of docent training. He learned a great deal, particularly about the space program. Now he shares his knowledge of aviation history and space flight with groups of visitors to the museum on a regular basis.

In retirement, Brown and his wife, the former Gloria H. Henry, live in northern Virginia, an easy commute to the museum. They are the parents of three children, Nancy, Louis, and William III. In his hours away from the museum, Brown enjoys water and snow skiing.

## Sources

Brown, William Earl. *A Fighter Pilot's Story*. Washington DC: Smithsonian Institution, 1992. National Air and Space Museum Occasional Paper Series Number 4.

Dabbs, Henry E. *Black Brass; Black Generals and Admirals in the Armed Forces of the United States*. Freehold, NJ: Afro-American Heritage House, 1984.

Outerbridge, Laura. "New Mission for Ex-Pilot." *Metropolitan Times* (June 7, 1995): C10, C11.

Smithsonian National Air & Space Museum, http://www.nasm.edu/nasm/pa/nasmnews/history/bhistory/BROWN.HTM. Accessed March 17, 1999.

U.S. Air Force. Secretary of the Air Force. *Biography: Lieutenant General William E. Brown Jr.* Washington, DC: U.S. Air Force Office of Public Affairs, 1982.

# Eugene Jacques Bullard

Eugene Jacques Bullard. Courtesy of Betty Gubert Collection.

**Full Name at Birth:** Eugene James Bullard

**Born:** October 9, 1895, Columbus, Georgia

**Died:** October 12, 1961, New York, New York

**Education:** Completed third grade, Columbus public schools, 1906; briefly attended night school, Scotland, 1912; military pilot's license #6950, French Aviation Service, May 5, 1917.

**Positions Held:** Amusement park performer and boxer, England, 1912–1914; performer, Freedman's Pickaninnies traveling vaudeville show, England and continental Europe, 1913–1914; boxer and interpreter, Paris, 1914; French Foreign Legion and French Aviation Service, 1914–1919; jazz musician, Paris, 1919–1924; boxer, Egypt, 1921–1922; manager and owner, nightclubs and Gene Bullard's Athletic Club, Paris, 1924–1940; French counterintelligence, 1939–1940;

French 51st Infantry, 1940; longshoreman, Queens, New York, 1940–1946; sales positions, New York State, late 1940s; interpreter for jazzman Louis Armstrong, 1952; elevator operator, RCA Building, New York, New York, late 1950s.

**Awards, Honors:** Received 15 medals from the French, among them the Médaille Militaire, Croix de Guerre, Médaille de Verdun, Croix du Combattant volontaire, 1914–1918, Croix du Combattant, Médaille de la France Libérée, Médaille Interalliée, Médaille Commémorative Française, 1914–1918, Médaille Commémorative Française, 1939–1945, L'Insigne de Blessés Militaires and Croix de la Légion d'Honneur; inductee, Georgia Aviation Hall of Fame, August 26, 1989; posthumous commission as second lieutenant, U.S. Air Force, September 14, 1994.

**Summary:** The first African American combat pilot, Eugene Jacques Bullard served with the French Foreign Legion and the Lafayette Escadrille during World War I, almost 25 years before African Americans were permitted to serve as combat pilots in the U.S. Army Air Corps. After World War I, Bullard remained in France, working as a boxer, musician, and nightclub owner. Early in World War II, he provided counterintelligence for the French. Fleeing France after Germany's takeover in 1940, Bullard returned to the United States, working in New York City until his death. France awarded him the Légion d'Honneur, equivalent to the American Medal of Honor, in 1959.

## Early Years

Eugene Bullard's father was born into slavery in Stewart County, Georgia, on the plantation of Wiley Bullard, and was a small child when the Civil War ended. Later in life, Eugene Bullard would write that his father's ancestors were brought from Africa to Martinique, then to Mississippi before the American Revolution. William O. Bullard's parents were born in South Carolina; Bullard family members recalled that William Bullard was "one-quarter Creek Indian."

In 1882, at the age of 19, William married Josephine Thomas (sometimes called Joyakee or Yokalee), who also had Creek ancestry. They moved to Columbus, Georgia, in the early 1890s. Josephine bore 10 children, of whom Eugene was the "lucky seventh," as his father said. Josephine died in 1902, when Eugene Bullard was seven.

In the unpublished memoir Eugene Bullard wrote late in his life, he recalled that his father told stories of their ancestors and of faraway France, where slavery did not exist and black men were treated as well as white men. This was not the case in the South in which they lived; some time after his father narrowly escaped lynching, young Eugene Bullard determined to run away to France.

The details of Bullard's departure are not clear. In his memoir, Bullard wrote that at the age of eight he left home simply "to find France." Some historians quote the recollections of neighbors, in which Eugene was somewhat older and left home following a severe beating. Lloyd cites records indicating that Bullard attended the Columbus public schools at least until June 1906. After several abortive attempts, Bullard ran away from Columbus, perhaps as early as late 1906. He wandered throughout Georgia and, briefly, into Alabama and Florida, holding jobs on farms, in a sawmill, and with a band of gypsies who taught him to work with horses.

In 1912, in Norfolk, Virginia, he stowed away on a German freighter bound for Europe. After three days at sea, he was put to work lugging bags of cinders from the boiler room to the deck. He was sent ashore in Aberdeen, Scotland, where he found himself surrounded by white faces for the first time. Bullard was 16 years old.

Supporting himself with odd jobs, Bullard made his way south toward the English Channel and France. He became a slapstick performer with Belle Davis's Freedman's

Pickaninnies, a touring vaudeville troupe, and began to train as a professional boxer. Boxing became his entrée to Paris: on November 28, 1913, Bullard and his mentor, Aaron Lester Brown, the "Dixie Kid" both fought matches there. At the age of 18, Bullard had reached Paris only eight months before the start of World War I.

## Career Highlights

Early in 1914, Bullard toured continental Europe with Freedman's Pickaninnies. "When the troupe left Paris," Bullard wrote, "you may be sure I did not leave with them. . . . None of the people in the countries which I had gone to in Europe had shown any prejudice on account of my color. It was just that for me it was France I had yearned for all my life. So I made my home in Paris." He continued to box and learned to speak French and German. His linguistic abilities enabled him also to work as an interpreter for foreign boxers.

War broke out in August and Bullard decided to volunteer to defend his adoptive country. Special "marching regiments" of the French Foreign Legion were created in which foreigners could enlist for the duration of a war not expected to last for more than a few months. Bullard enlisted on October 9, 1914, his 19th birthday. During the war and thereafter, Bullard used the Francophone rendering of his name, Eugene Jacques Bullard (pronounced Bull-AR, with no "d").

After five weeks of intensive training, the Third Marching Regiment was sent to the front at the Somme in northern France, already notorious for the high losses the French suffered there. They fought at the Somme until April 1915, when they were moved northward to join in the battle of Artois on May 9–10. In two days, France sustained 175,000 casualties. Out of the 250 members of Bullard's company, only 54 answered at roll call on the second day. The Legion continued to suffer heavy losses. In

July the Third Marching Regiment was dissolved.

On July 13 Bullard was promoted to soldier second class of the First Regiment of the French Foreign Legion. After several months in the mountains of Alsace, the Legion was sent to Champagne, where once again they sustained crippling losses. The remaining volunteers in the Legion were given the choice of transferring to regular French regiments.

Bullard transferred to the 170th Infantry, a crack regiment known to the Germans as the "Swallows of Death," which was also fighting in Champagne. In February 1916, the 170th was sent to Verdun, notorious as the "bloodiest of all battlegrounds." In early March Bullard received a severe leg wound. During the slow transferral to hospital in Lyon, he was surrounded by thousands of wounded soldiers. Later he wrote, "After being a part of all this, I was then even more convinced than before that all blood runs red." His unpublished memoir was entitled, *All Blood Runs Red: My Adventurous Life in Search of Freedom.*

While recovering in Lyon, Bullard was awarded the Croix de Guerre and the Médaille Militaire, two prestigious French military decorations for his actions at Verdun. During his convalescence, he made the acquaintance of the commander of a nearby air base. When the commander asked Bullard about his future, Bullard expressed his wish to be an air force gunner or a pilot. Military fliers were still relatively unusual, but fliers did not use their legs the same way as the infantry. The commander promised to ask for Bullard's transfer. Later Bullard wrote, "Imagine hearing that you really might have the opportunity to be the first Negro military pilot!"

On October 6, 1916, Bullard reported for training as an aviation gunner at Caz-au-lac, near Bordeaux in southwestern France. Transferring from gunnery to aviation school for pilot training, he moved to Tours, in the Loire valley, in mid-November 1916. He received his pilot's license on May 5, 1917, and was sent to Chateauroux for advanced training on bimotor planes. He next was sent to Avord, France's largest air school, for additional combat training. There he was put in charge of the sleeping quarters for the American flyers.

Bullard related that after some weeks he noticed that pilots who had arrived at Avord after him were receiving orders for the front. It became apparent that Bullard was being passed over, and that the obstacle was a highly placed American who "believed Negroes ought not be fliers," as Bullard later wrote. He asked his captain's permission to write to an acquaintance, the inspector-general of the French aviation schools, to inquire why he was held back when pilots were desperately needed.

Although he was denied permission to write, Bullard was transferred to Plessis Belleville, near Paris, in August 1917. On August 27, 1917, he was assigned to Escadrille Spad 93, one of five squadrons in the top-notch Groupe Brocard.

Bullard's first sortie was on September 8, 1917, when Spad 93 flew a reconnaissance mission near Verdun. He first saw combat during his second patrol, and continued to fly patrols regularly thereafter, flying with his mascot, a spider monkey named Jimmy, buttoned in the jacket of his uniform. On September 13 Bullard was transferred to Spad 85, which also flew in the Verdun sector in the region of Vadalaincourt and Bar-le-Duc. He remained with Spad 85 until he left "l'Aviation" in November 1917. In total he flew at least 20 missions.

On November 7, he later wrote, he forced a German Fokker triplane down behind enemy lines after an air battle that left 96 holes in his own plane and caused him to make an emergency landing immediately behind the French lines. Since the Fokker crashed behind enemy lines, his "score" was unverified. A few days later, again on patrol, his squadron crossed paths with some German Pfalzes.

Momentarily separated from his comrades by mist, Bullard maneuvered himself into a position behind the line of German planes and picked off the last Pfalz in the column before returning to find his patrol.

Despite Bullard's acceptance by his French comrades and his prowess in action, his relations to his own country remained equivocal. The United States entered the Great War on April 6, 1917, and later that year Bullard, with other Americans of the Lafayette Flying Corps, applied for a transfer to the U.S. Army Air Corps, understanding that all that was required for a pilot to receive a commission as an officer was an application and a physical examination.

The American doctors who conducted Bullard's physical in Paris in October 1917 questioned him about his flight training before his health. The physical showed that he had flat feet. "I explained that . . . I did not fly with my feet." They told him he had large tonsils. "To this I replied that I was . . . not an opera singer." Finally he was told that he had passed the examination.

The other American flyers were transferred to the American Army Air Corps, one after another, while Bullard received no word. At last he realized that all the other flyers were white. The United States did not commission an African American aviator until 1942, when Benjamin O. Davis Jr. and four other cadets completed their training at Tuskegee, Alabama.

This discrimination hurt Bullard deeply, but he derived some comfort from the knowledge that he was able to fight on the same front and in the same cause as his fellow American citizens. "And so in a roundabout way, I was managing to do my duty and to serve my country," Bullard later wrote.

Not long after this, and only days after the forays in which he engaged with the Fokker triplane and the Pfalz, Bullard was summarily removed from the flying service. Bullard's abrupt removal from the Lafayette Escadrille may have stemmed from one of several causes. In his memoir, Bullard recalls a quarrel with an officer who would not return Bullard's salute. Shortly thereafter, he writes, he was "evacuated" to recuperate from the thigh wound that had originally forced him out of the Infantry. Several sources cite versions of an incident in which Bullard apparently struck an officer, but was transferred rather than court-martialed due to his excellent combat record. Lloyd cites possible pressure on the French by American military authorities to remove Bullard from aviation duties in order not to affect the "morale" of incoming American troops, white and black, "given the American establishment's conviction of black inferiority."

In any event, Bullard's aviation career was over. According to Carisella and Ryan, the log book of Spad 85 records that, on November 16, Bullard was reassigned to the 170th Infantry, his old regiment. He returned to active duty with the 170th on January 11, 1918, and he was assigned to noncombatant service duties for the remainder of the war. Bullard's final discharge date was October 24, 1919, 11 months after the Armistice.

Bullard remained in Paris after the war. Although he would fight two "comeback" engagements in Egypt in 1921 and 1922, his wounds prohibited the serious resumption of his boxing career. Instead he became a jazz drummer and the artistic director for Zelli's nightclub in the Montmartre section of Paris.

Using his Paris connections and his growing business savvy, in the autumn of 1924 Bullard became manager of Le Grand Duc, in Montmartre. In the 1920s and early 1930s, Le Grand Duc was one of the most renowned jazz clubs in Paris. Bullard also gave private physical culture lessons and massages: these he parlayed into the founding of Gene Bullard's Athletic Club. Becoming owner of Le Grand Duc in 1929, he sold the club in the early 1930s and opened another, L'Escadrille.

On July 17, 1923, Bullard married Marcelle Straumann. He recalled that their marriage, which had the full approval of Marcelle's parents, caused a stir only because the bride was socially prominent and the groom was not. The following June their first child, Jacqueline, was born. Eugene Jr. was born in October 1926 but died the following April. Their second daughter, Lolita Josephine, was born in December 1927. Although the marriage began happily, Bullard and his wife separated in 1930, Bullard preferring the management of his businesses to his wife's socialite lifestyle. The couple were divorced in 1935 and Bullard retained custody of his daughters. Marcelle Straumann lived in Paris until her death on February 18, 1990.

As Nazi power increased in the late 1930s, it became clear that war was inevitable. Early in 1939, a Paris police detective asked the German-speaking Bullard to report any information about Nazi activity overheard either in his nightclub or in his gym. Bullard continued his espionage until he was forced to flee Paris in May 1940, shortly after the Germans launched a full invasion of France.

Failing to reconnect with the 170th Infantry, east of Paris, Bullard volunteered with the 51st Infantry at Orléans. He saw action with them June 15–18, before suffering a spinal injury.

Bullard reached New York in July 1940. He found lodging in Harlem and a series of jobs to pay for his medical treatment. His daughters joined him early in 1941. During the war he was active with the Federation of French Veterans of the Great War, and with French Forever, the international arm of the de Gaulle-led Free French movement. After the war, he worked as a salesman of French perfumes. In 1950–1951, he returned to Paris, where he unsuccessfully sought compensation for the loss of his nightclub and gym. In 1952, he toured Europe as an interpreter for jazzman Louis Armstrong.

He returned to Paris in 1954 at the invitation of the French government, to assist at the relighting of the eternal flame at the Arc de Triomphe. On October 9, 1959, he was installed as a Chevalier de la Légion d'Honneur, the French equivalent of America's Medal of Honor. When President Charles de Gaulle visited New York in 1960, Bullard was invited to the reception, where he was warmly greeted by de Gaulle.

His last job was as an elevator operator in the RCA Building at Rockefeller Center in New York City.

Bullard died of stomach cancer on October 12, 1961, at the age of 66. At his request, he was buried in the uniform of the French Foreign Legion, in the French War Veterans' plot at Flushing Cemetery, Queens, New York.

He has since been honored at Gunter AFB, Montgomery, Alabama; the Columbus, Georgia, Metropolitan Airport; and the National Air and Space Museum of the Smithsonian Institution. On August 26, 1989, he was inducted into the Georgia Aviation Hall of Fame and, on September 14, 1994, was posthumously commissioned a second lieutenant in the U.S. Air Force.

## Sources

Carisella, P.J., and James W. Ryan. *The Black Swallow of Death.* Boston, MA.: Marlborough House, 1972. Quotes extensively from Bullard's unpublished memoir.

Cockfield, Jamie H. "All Blood Runs Red." *Legacy: A Supplement to American Heritage* (February–March 1995): 7, 10, 12–15.

"Gene Bullard, French War Hero, Is Dead." *New York Amsterdam News* (October 21, 1961): 1, 13.

Lloyd, Craig. *Eugene Bullard: Black Expatriate in Jazz-Age Paris.* Athens: University of Georgia Press, 2000. Cites Bullard's unpublished memoir and other contemporary sources.

Smith, Mary H. "The Incredible Life of Monsieur Bullard." *Ebony* (December 1967): 120–122, 124–126, 128.

Stovall, Tyler. *Paris Noir: African Americans in the City of Light.* New York: Houghton Mifflin, 1996.

# Isham A. "Rusty" Burns

Isham A. "Rusty" Burns. Courtesy of Isham A. "Rusty" Burns.

**Full Name at Birth:** Isham Albert Burns Jr.

**Born:** July 24, 1925, New Orleans, Louisiana

**Education:** David Star Jordan High School, Los Angeles, 1943; Tuskegee Air Corps, 1944; Pepperdine University, Los Angeles, 1949–1951; pilots' licenses in 1945 (Commercial/instrument), 1956 (Instructor), and 1960 (Multiengine).

**Positions Held:** Post office employee, 1946–1954; owner, Rusty's Flying Service, 1954–1968; Teledyne, 1969; Woods Industries, 1970–1971; buyer and managerial positions, North American Rockwell, 1972–1988; owner, Four Winds Ultralites, 1982–1986.

**Awards, Honors:** President of Los Angeles chapter of Tuskegee Airmen, Inc., 1991; Award of Honor, County of Los Angeles, Board of Supervisors, 1995; numerous commendations for his role in making a diverse public aware of black aviation history.

**Summary:** Rusty Burns, a pilot well trained at Tuskegee Airfield, found only a post office job awaiting him at the end of World War II. Nevertheless he was able to use his skills in aviation and business to make a career in aviation, apart from the corporate world, as the owner of a private flying service, and within it, as a corporate manager at North American Rockwell, an aerospace company.

## Early Years

Isham Albert Burns Jr. was born on July 24, 1925, in New Orleans, Louisiana. He was the first of five children of Nona Bertrand and Isham Albert Burns Sr. The family was not well-to-do, often moving "when the rent came due." Burns Sr. worked for the post office and Mrs. Burns stayed at home to care for Rusty (as he later came to be known) and Beverly, Clara, Kermit, and Geraldine. Young Burns's passion was building model airplanes. His attention to detail was so great that he nipped off the heads of straight pins to use as rivet heads along the surface of the wings and fuselage of his models.

As did many other African Americans, the Burns family moved from the south to Los Angeles for the greater economic and social opportunities that were available, arriving in 1939. While at David Star Jordan High School, Burns's favorite subject was math, and he played basketball and tennis. He graduated in June 1943.

## Higher Education

With World War II raging, Burns enlisted in the U.S. Army Air Corps on his 18th birthday. "Ever since I was a little kid I wanted to fly. It was a fantasy until I was a senior in high school." At the time the Air Corps discriminated against blacks, and there were to be, in effect, separate air forces. African Americans were trained at Tuskegee, Alabama, in an "experiment," that was expected to fail. The military was doubtful that blacks could be trained to fly. But by the end of the war in 1945, nearly 1,000 African Americans had won their wings as pilots. During his course at Tuskegee, Burns took the name of "Rusty" from a now-forgotten comic-strip character, because his own name

was often mangled in the pronunciation. This nickname was perhaps more suited to the daredevil exploits favored by the young Burns. With the fearlessness of youth, Burns often engaged in forbidden activities such as flying under bridges, buzzing the town (causing windows to break), and challenging white navy pilots to mock dog fights. Any one of these activities would have been cause for him to be washed out of flight training, the term used for expulsion from the course. Tuskegee's white commanding officer, Colonel Noel F. Parrish, reprimanded Burns, but did not expel him, and Burns became a pilot on December 28, 1944. (Parrish was unusual in believing the "Tuskegee Experiment" would succeed. At the graduation of the first class in 1942, Parrish said, "Flying is an individual proposition. There is no colored way to fly.")

Burns flew P-40s, P-47s, and P-51s, but not in combat because the war ended six months after his graduation. Nearly 50 years later, he recalled that flying military aircraft "was the most outstanding pleasure in my career." About being part of the Tuskegee experience he said, "It is something you can never duplicate. I did not realize it at the time, but there is a great sense of accomplishment now for having been a part of it."

Burns continued his interest in flying and obtained the following licenses: commercial and instrument ratings in April 1945, instructor's rating in 1956, and multiengine rating in 1960. From 1949 to 1951, Burns attended Pepperdine University, then in Los Angeles, but now in Malibu. He left soon after his marriage to Treneta C. Davis on March 11, 1950. They raised four children: Keith K. (now Khephra, a writer), Vicki M., Michael A., and Cheryl A. Mrs. Burns held various management positions with Blue Cross of California, and when she retired in June 1990, she was a systems analyst/data consultant. Treneta Burns, taught by her husband, received her pilot's license in 1963. At the time she was reputed to be the only licensed African American woman pilot west of the Mississippi.

## Career Highlights

Burns worked at the post office from 1946 to 1954, and, expanding upon his early passion for model planes, he built small single-engine operable airplanes in the family garage. Leaving the post office, Burns started Rusty's Flying Service at Compton Airport at Compton, California. Here he provided flying lessons as well as aircraft maintenance, sales, and service. He bought wrecked airplanes that he rebuilt for sale, and he provided charter flights for many customers. He was a corporate pilot as well. While operating Rusty's Flying Service, which during the 1960s had 13 aircraft, Burns also flew in motion pictures. As an extra he did not receive credit, but he flew in various productions from 1961 to 1967. The highly acclaimed film *It's a Mad Mad Mad Mad World* (1963) was among the many films he had a role in.

Burns also flew in national and local air shows produced during the 1960s. As an aerobatic pilot he received star billing as he flew a Stearman P-40 and P-51 aircraft through classic aerobatic maneuvers. He also piloted planes for "wing walkers," daring young men and women who walked on the airplanes' wings, made mid-air transfers from one plane to another, and swung from rope ladders, while crowds below gasped and applauded.

Burns sold his flying service in 1970. In January 1972, Burns joined North American Rockwell, an aerospace corporation, as a buyer of airplane parts. He was steadily promoted: in 1974 to senior buyer in the Rocketdyne division; in 1975 and 1978 to managerial positions in the transportation division. From 1986 to 1988, Burns was corporate manager of travel services for the company, whose annual travel budget exceeded 50 million dollars. Burns retired from this position in 1988.

From 1982 to 1986 Burns ran a small business that he considered a weekend hobby. Called Four Winds Ultralites to describe the small lightweight aircraft used, which evolved from hang gliders, Burns rented out one two-seat trainer and two single seaters. He also gave lessons to those who wanted to fly these planes.

Rusty and Treneta Burns continue to fly their twin-engine Cessna 310 for the pleasure of it, and they also enjoy golf. Burns is an active member of the Los Angeles chapter of the Tuskegee Airmen, Inc., one of the country's largest. He served as their president in 1991. To inspire and motivate young people, Burns and his fellow Tuskegee Airmen speak to school children, community groups, and university students about the little-known role African Americans played in aviation history. They urge young people to do their best, and to follow their own dream, not someone else's. TAI provides scholarships for minority youngsters who wish to make aviation their career.

In 1995, Burns received an award for outstanding and exemplary service from the county of Los Angeles Board of Supervisors.

## Sources

Burns, Khephra, New York, to Betty K. Gubert, New York, e-mail, March 13, 1999.

Burns, Rusty, Simi Valley, California, to Betty K. Gubert, New York, e-mail and correspondence, April 1; June 1, June 3, 1999.

Millican, Anthony. "Spreading Their Wings." *Los Angeles Times* (July 12, 1992): B1, B5.

# C

## Yvonne Cagle

Yvonne Cagle. Courtesy of NASA.

**Full Name at Birth:** Yvonne Darlene Cagle

**Born:** April 24, 1959, West Point, New York

**Education:** Novato High School, Novato, California, 1977; San Francisco State University, B.A., biochemistry, 1981; University of Washington, Seattle, M.D., 1985; Transitional Highland General Hospital, Oakland, California, internship, 1985; School of Aerospace Medicine, Brooks Air Force Base, Texas, aerospace medicine certification, 1988; Ghent Family Practice Center, Eastern Virginia Medical School, Norfolk, Virginia, completed residency in family practice, 1992; Federal Aviation Administration, senior aviation medical examiner certification, 1995.

**Positions Held:** U.S. Air Force (active and reserve), 1985– ; flight surgeon, 1988–early 1990s; occupational physician and deputy project manager; NASA-Johnson Space Center, Occupational Health Clinic, 1994–1996; astronaut, National Aeronautics and Space Administration (NASA), 1996– .

**Awards, Honors:** Outstanding Young Women of America; National Defense Service Medal; Air Force Achievement Medal; U.S. Air Force (USAF) Air Staff Exceptional Physician Commendation; National Technical Association Distinguished Scientist Award; Commendation Marin County Board of Supervisors; Commendation Novato School Board; Alumna of the Year, San Francisco State University, 1999.

**Summary:** The second African American woman to be selected for the space program,

Cagle, a medical doctor, completed her astronaut training in 1998 and is qualified for assignment as a mission specialist aboard future space missions. Her medical specialties include the practice of family medicine and astromedicine.

## Early Years

Yvonne Darlene Cagle has been involved with science and the U.S. Air Force all of her life. Her parents, an X-ray technician and flight records handler, both served with the air force and were stationed at West Point, New York, when Cagle was born. During the first few years of Cagle's life, her family moved frequently, spending four years in Japan and additional time in New York State. When Cagle was in the third grade, the family moved to Novato, California, where they were stationed at Hamilton Air Force Base. Cagle remembered slipping into her father's library to look at X-ray images. "It really intrigued me," she told a reporter for the University of Washington alumni magazine. "They were the coolest pictures." The family remained in Novato and Cagle regards the Marin County area as home.

"You can prepare for your career very early in life," Cagle has said. "Young people should have the courage to dream high because once you start your journey, you'll find yourself amazed by your potential." She realized that she could become an astronaut when, at the age of nine, she watched Neil Armstrong make history as the first man to walk on the moon. She realized then, she told an ABC interviewer on *Nightline* on October 29, 1998, that "there really was a man on the moon—and a pathway to get there . . . [and he] doesn't look like the man in the moon I know. He looks more like me."

## Higher Education

Graduating from Novato High School in 1977, Cagle continued her studies at San Francisco State University, earning a bachelor's degree in biochemistry in 1981. Moving to Seattle to pursue a medical degree at the University of Washington, she became involved in an innovative program that allowed her to spend time both in downtown Seattle, working with medically underserved people, and in Alaska, working with physicians. Through those experiences she gained an abiding interest in the practice of family medicine "and in the comprehensive view of the family unit and the continuity of care—knowing a family and growing up with them." She received her doctorate in medicine in 1985.

## Career Highlights

Cagle's medical school training was financed by the U.S. Air Force's Health Professions Scholarship Program, and she was commissioned as a USAF reserve officer. She completed an internship at Transitional Highland General Hospital in Oakland, California, and her board certification in family practice. On her initial tour of active duty, Cagle was stationed at Royal Air Force Lakenheath in the United Kingdom when she was selected for the School of Aerospace Medicine at Brooks Air Force Base in Texas. After logging many hours in diverse aircraft, she became a certified flight surgeon in April 1988. She was involved in the provision of medical support and rescue in various aeromedical missions.

"Even though I could fly with pilots, I felt I wasn't flying fast enough," she later recalled. In May 1989, while serving as a flight surgeon with the 48th Tactical Hospital in the United Kingdom, Cagle volunteered to serve as the Air Force Medical Liaison Officer for the STS-30 Atlantis Shuttle Mission, which was to test the Magellan spacecraft designed for a later mission to Venus. Cagle was sent to the Trans-Atlantic Landing (TAL) Site at Banjul in West Africa, a contingency landing site, to provide emergency treatment should the shuttle crew be forced to land there. Leaving active duty, Cagle joined the residency program at the Eastern Virginia Medical School's Ghent Family Practice Center in Norfolk, Virginia, where she completed her residency in 1992.

Cagle served as occupational medicine physician at the Kelsey-Seybold Occupational Health Clinic at NASA's Johnson Space Center, serving as deputy project manager there from 1994 to 1996. She was a member of a NASA Working Group and traveled to Russia to establish international medical standards and procedures for astronauts. She also conducted health screening of the Russian Federation's support staff for the Mir cosmonauts who were aboard the STS-71 Atlantis Shuttle Mission in 1995, when Atlantis docked with the Mir Space Station and exchanged the Mir-18 and Mir-19 cosmonaut groups.

One of 35 astronaut candidates selected by NASA on May 1, 1996, including 25 mission specialist candidates and 10 pilot candidates, Cagle completed her astronaut training in 1998 and is qualified for assignment as a mission specialist aboard future space missions, possibly as a crew physician and medical researcher on the International Space Station. Assigned technical duties in the Astronaut Office Operations Planning Branch, she also takes part in public relations and educational events.

One young student who heard Cagle speak while attending a space shuttle launch in the summer of 1999 described an inspiring analogy: "[Cagle] said that women are like caterpillars crawling back and forth on a limb. It is the caterpillar that takes a risk to become a butterfly that will be able to soar to new heights, meaning women must have the will and desire to change, then have the motivation to act, and then they will be great."

Cagle has contributed ongoing data to the Longitudinal Study on Astronaut Health. She also works on the development of methods for space telemedicine, by which doctors would be able to evaluate, diagnose, and even operate on patients who are distant from the doctor. For example, an Earth-based doctor might one day be able to perform surgery on an injured astronaut who might be on a manned mission to Mars, using specialized tools and a connection to a remote surgery machine. "You can't predict all the medical contingencies that could happen while you're in space," Cagle explained. "So to be able to work in a virtual environment and have real-time impacts can make all the difference in the world." Such methods also have Earth-based application in connecting the resources of metropolitan hospitals with patients in remote areas.

Nine days before reporting for NASA training in August 1996, Cagle married Darryl Safford, an investment real estate professional. "He's in land, and I'm in space," said Cagle. She enjoys athletic activities ranging from juggling to skating and hiking, and she also pursues interests such as music, writing, and reading historical novels. She is active with the Boys and Girls Club and the Third Baptist Church and is a member of the Aerospace Medical Association and the American Academy of Family Physicians.

## Sources

"Astronaut Biographical Data: Y. Cagle." Johnson Space Center, National Aeronautics and Space Administration. January 1999. Http://www.jsc.nasa.gov/Bios/htmlbios/cagle.html. Accessed April 2, 2000.

Cagle, Yvonne. Interview with Kevin Newman. *Nightline.* ABC. October 29, 1998. *FDCH ABC Nightline.* Online. Ebsco MasterFile Premier.

Marmor, Jon. "Yvonne Cagle, UW Medical School Grad Turns Astronaut." *Columns, The University of Washington Alumni Magazine* (September 1996). Online, http://www.washington.edu/alumni/columns/sept96/cagle.html. Accessed April 2, 2000.

National Aeronautics and Space Administration. Various pages, http://www.nasa.gov. Accessed April 2, 2000. Keywords: Yvonne, Cagle.

# George R. Carruthers

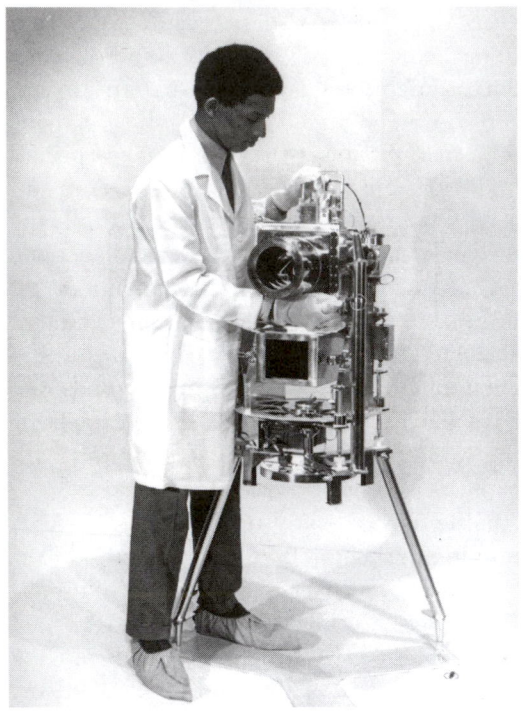

George R. Carruthers. Courtesy of NASA.

**Full Name at Birth:** George Robert Carruthers

**Born:** October 1, 1939, Cincinnati, Ohio

**Education:** Englewood High School, Chicago, Illinois, 1957; College of Engineering, University of Illinois at Champaign-Urbana, B.S., aeronautical engineering and astronomy, 1961; M.S., nuclear engineering, 1962; Ph.D., aeronautics and aeronautical engineering, 1964.

**Positions Held:** rocket astronomy research physicist, Space Science Division, Naval Research Laboratory (NRL), Washington, D.C., 1964–1982; head, Ultraviolet Measurements Branch, NRL, 1980–1982; senior astrophysicist, NRL, 1982–    .

**Awards, Honors:** National Science Foundation fellowship in rocket astronomy, 1964; U.S. patent no. 3,478,216 for the Image Converter for Detecting Electromagnetic Radiation Especially in Short Wave Lengths, November 11, 1969; Arthur S. Fleming Award, Washington Jaycees, 1971; Apollo 16 Exceptional Science Achievement Medal, NASA, 1972; Warner Prize, American Astronomical Society, 1973; honorary doctorate of engineering, Michigan Technological University, 1973; Samuel Cheevers Award, National Technical Association, 1977; Black Engineer of the Year Award, 1987.

**Summary:** An astrophysicist employed at the Naval Research Laboratory in Washington, D.C., for more than 30 years, George R. Carruthers has specialized in the study of ultraviolet emissions from massive stars. Early in his career, he was the first scientist to positively detect hydrogen molecules in interstellar space. He is best known for the invention of the Far Ultraviolet Camera. This camera uses ultraviolet light, which allows gases that are invisible in natural light to appear in colors, thereby allowing scientists to observe atmospheric compounds. Carruthers's FUV Camera/Spectrograph was sent to the moon on the *Apollo 16* mission in 1972.

## Early Years

George Carruthers, the oldest of four children, was born in Cincinnati, Ohio, where his father, also named George, was a civil engineer for the U.S. Army Air Corps. When young George was seven years old, the family moved to Milford, a suburb east of Cincinnati. There, while he was attending elementary school, George Carruthers's interest in exploring space was sparked by the adventures of Buck Rogers, a comic-book hero who traveled to Mars. His father encouraged his enthusiasm, and Carruthers read widely in astronomy and mathematics as well as science fiction. At the age of 10, Carruthers constructed his first working telescope from lenses he bought from a mail order company and cardboard tubing he found at home.

When Carruthers was 12, his father died and his mother, Sophia, moved the family to the South Side of Chicago to be closer to relatives. Sophia Carruthers found a job with the U.S. Post Office.

When George Carruthers enrolled in Englewood High School in Chicago, the faculty there recognized his scientific aptitude. With their encouragement, Carruthers explored the educational resources of the Chicago area museums, including the Chicago Planetarium, the Field Museum, and the Museum of Science and Industry, and he continued to build bigger and better telescopes. While in high school, Carruthers won three science-fair prizes, including a first prize for a telescope project.

## Higher Education

Carruthers was an experienced amateur astronomer by the time he graduated from high school in 1957 and entered the College of Engineering at the University of Illinois at Champaign-Urbana. He designed his own undergraduate major, a combination of astronomy and aeronautical engineering. The Soviet Union and the United States were beginning to launch satellites into space, and Carruthers recognized the potential for sending telescopes into space to make observations without the interference of the Earth's atmosphere.

Awarded a B.S. degree in 1961, Carruthers enrolled in the graduate program at the University of Illinois, and was awarded a masters degree in nuclear engineering in 1962 and a doctorate in aeronautics and aeronautical engineering in 1964. His graduate work led to a dissertation on atomic nitrogen recombination, an area in which he has continued to research.

## Career Highlights

Once he had received his Ph.D., Carruthers joined the Naval Research Laboratory in Washington, D.C., where he has continued to work throughout his career. From the beginning he has specialized in the study of ultraviolet emissions. Ultraviolet light, which cannot be seen by the human eye, allows gases that are invisible in natural light to appear in colors, thereby allowing scientists to identify the gases that make up Earth's atmosphere and also to observe the gases in a comet's tail or in the "empty" space between stars.

Carruthers invented the Far Ultraviolet Camera, which takes pictures using ultraviolet light. It was sent into space on a unmanned rocket flight in 1967. Carruthers continued to improve the camera; in 1969, when he was only 30 years old, he was awarded a patent for the invention, called "the Image Converter for Detecting Electromagnetic Radiation Especially in Short Wave Lengths." The specification sheet filed with the Patent Office stated, "This disclosure is directed to a system for detecting radiation in the far ultra-violet region by use of a windowless tube with a solid photocathode and an internal mirror for converting the radiation to visible light."

The following year, Carruthers sent an ultraviolet-wavelength telescope 120 miles into space aboard a sounding rocket (a rocket that does not achieve orbit). It took a spectrographic image—an image that shows the spectrum of light of one or more elements—which recorded the existence of hydrogen molecules in interstellar space. Scientists had theorized that hydrogen gas was present in the space between stars and galaxies, but no one had been able to prove it, since Earth's atmosphere distorts observations so that the interstellar hydrogen could not be detected from Earth's surface.

Carruthers gained national recognition in April 1972, when his Far-Ultraviolet Camera/Spectrograph was sent to the moon on the Apollo 16 mission. More than 175 pictures were brought back from that mission, although the device itself—a fifty-pound, gold-plated instrument mounted on a large tripod—was left on the moon. The pictures captured additional proof of the existence of interstellar and intergalactic hydrogen and other gases, evidence of developing nebulae and galaxies, images of the spectra and colors of stars and nebulae in the Milky Way, and data about the auroras near the Earth's poles, the geocorona (the far-ultraviolet light from the sun that is reflected off the cloud of neutral hydrogen surrounding the Earth), and the Earth's airglow by day and at night. The FUV Camera/Spectrograph sent to the moon was the first observatory humans ever placed on another celestial body. It demonstrated the value of sending telescopes outside of Earth's atmosphere, a role now played by the Hubble Space Telescope and other orbiting observatories.

Carruthers's far-ultraviolet cameras have been placed on high-altitude rockets to study comets. In 1974, the far ultraviolet electronographic camera flew on Skylab 4 to take pictures of the hydrogen halo of Comet Kohoutek.

In designing far-ultraviolet cameras for specific applications, Carruthers has to think about not only the data the camera is intended to collect but also the environment in which it will operate. For the *Apollo 16* mission, the camera had to operate in a near-weightless environment, collect very specific and technical data, but also be easy for the astronauts to set up and operate accurately on uneven ground. A spectrographic telescope on a sounding rocket had to be able to find and track a specific star and collect accurate data during a flight only five minutes long. Far-ultraviolet cameras have since been used on space shuttle flights and, in providing data about the Earth's ozone layer and interstellar gases such as chlorine and carbon monoxide, have been instrumental in leading to emissions regulations for industrial products such as refrigerators, air conditioning units, and motor vehicles.

In late 1997, Carruthers became a member of an Independent Science Review (ISR) group advising the Hubble Space Telescope

Project on high-level issues that would affect what steps would be taken to maintain and enhance the Hubble telescope on future servicing missions. The ISR team assessed the feasibility of mounting a cryocooler—a high-tech, mechanical cryogenic cooler to counteract an anomaly in Hubble's operating mechanism—on Hubble's Near Infrared Camera and Multi-Object Spectrometer (NICMOS) during a servicing mission scheduled for late 1999. All of the costs, the installation risks, the potential benefits of new equipment, and the conditions under which the equipment will operate are considered in detail long before a shuttle crew is sent into space to make a change or repair to the Hubble Space Telescope or other satellite.

Carruthers has also worked on ARGOS, the Advanced Research and Global Observation Satellite launched by the U.S. Air Force. This three-ton research and development satellite was launched to collect data on the global environment of Earth and for military space programs. ARGOS is testing advanced sensor technology that may be used for the International Space Station and on the Cassini mission to Saturn. In addition, ARGOS is carrying an X-ray sensor and three ultraviolet (UV) imaging experiments. The ultraviolet experiments include the High Resolution Airflow/Aurora Spectroscopy (HIRASS), the Global Imaging Monitor of the Ionosphere (GIMI), and the Extreme Ultraviolet Imaging Photometer (EUVIP). Working all at the same time, the results from these four experiments will be correlated to provide, for the first time, a three-dimensional picture of weather in the ionosphere, the Earth's outer atmosphere.

Described as a dignified, private person, Carruthers is committed to his research and to the education of young people. He recently served as chairman of the board of trustees of the Young Technocrats Mathematics and Science Public Charter School in northeast Washington, D.C. Carruthers not only makes speeches to groups of scientists but also visits high schools and grade schools in the Washington, DC, area, to encourage students' interest in science. "Not even the sky is the limit to what a person can accomplish," Carruthers has told students.

High school students working in his laboratory as research apprentices have, over the years, assisted in assembling and testing components for space shuttle astronomy experiments. "It's of value to us and it's of value to them," Carruthers commented. "I wish I had something like that when I was in high school instead of delivering newspapers." He has offered training workshop for teachers and students through Project SMART (Science, Mathematics, Aerospace Research and Technology), an organization that advocates minority involvement in science and technology.

His professional affiliations have included the National Technical Association, which provides a support network for scientists of color throughout the United States, and also the American Astronomical Society, the American Geophysical Union, the American Institute of Aeronautics and Astronautics, the American Association for the Advancement of Science, and the National Society of Black Physicists. In his free time, he is a bicycle rider and amateur photographer.

## Sources

Feinberg, Lawrence. "Area Students Launched into Science for Summer; Youths' Interest in Research Is Goal of Effort." *Washington Post* (August 20, 1988): B3.

Henderson, Susan K. *African American Inventors II.* Mankato, MN: Capstone Press, 1998; 17–21.

Jones, J. Sydney. "George R. Carruthers." *Notable Twentieth-century Scientists.* Vol. 1 Detroit: Gale Research, 1995; 319–320.

Kessler, James H. et al. "George R. Carruthers." *Distinguished African American Scientists of the 20th Century.* Phoenix, AZ: Oryx Press, 1996; 36–37.

National Aeronautics and Space Administration. Various pages, http://www.nasa.gov. Accessed April 2, 2000. Keywords: Carruthers, George.

Spady, James G. "Blackspace." *Blacks in Science: Ancient and Modern.* Ed. Ivan Van Sertima. New Brunswick, NJ: Transaction, 1983; 258–262.

*Who's Who among African Americans, 1996–1997.* Detroit: Gale Research, 1996; 248.

# Fred V. Cherry

**Full Name at Birth:** Fred Victor Cherry

**Born:** 1929, Suffolk, Virginia

**Education:** East Suffolk High School, Suffolk, Virginia, 1947; B.S., Virginia Union University, Virginia. 1951, Air Force pilot training, 1951.

**Positions Held:** Fighter pilot, Korea, Thailand, and Vietnam, 1951–1965; prisoner of war, 1965–1973; Colonel, United States Air Force, retired 1981.

**Awards, Honors:** Distinguished Flying Cross, Silver Star, 1953; Air Force Cross, Legion of Merit, two Bronze Stars, two Purple Hearts, 1973; installed in Hall of Heroes, Pentagon, 1981; Ira Eaker Fellowship, 1983.

**Summary:** Fred V. Cherry, a fighter pilot in the U.S. Air Force, was the first black officer and the highest ranking black man to be captured in the Vietnam War. After his release in 1973, he set a legal precedent in successfully suing the air force for allowing his unfaithful wife to spend his military pay and his savings while he was imprisoned.

## Early Years

Fred Cherry was born in Suffolk, Virginia, in 1929. His parents, John and Leola Cherry, had eight children in all, four boys and four girls. John Cherry, a farmer, supplemented his farming income with employment as a laborer. Neither parent had gone beyond elementary school. Church attendance was an important part of their lives.

The neighborhood where the Cherry family lived was an integrated one, and they were on good terms with their white neighbors. When it came to schooling, however, there was strict segregation. According to Cherry, "The whites had buses. We had no buses. So, on the rainy days, the snowy days, the half-full buses would drive past us." Though the neighbors were friendly, he noticed that his family had to call white people Mr. and Mrs., while the whites called blacks by their first names. "It was sort of understood you had your place."

Cherry was in elementary school during World War II. There was a U.S. Navy auxiliary base near the town where he lived where naval pilots were trained and he was fascinated by the airplanes that came and went. He described the impression this made on him in the book *Bloods*: "All day long these aircraft would be flying by at very low altitudes. Very slow. You could see the pilot and we would wave to him. . . . I could see them do combat maneuvering, and I said 'that's adventure.' I was still in elementary school, but I knew I wanted to fly." In the *Afro-American* and the *Norfolk Journal & Guide*, which were African American newspapers of the day, Cherry followed the exploits of the Tuskegee Airmen in the 99th Squadron, an all-black squadron that was acquitting itself creditably over the skies of Italy. Their heroism fed the youngster's desire to be a pilot. "[W]hen I read that Lucky Lester shot down those three Nazi planes . . . I said to myself, I'm going to be a fighter pilot just as soon as I get old enough."

John Cherry died when Cherry was 11 years old and the child was sent to live with his elder sister Beulah and her husband, Melvin Watts. His sister was a stickler for school attendance. She set very high standards for her brother, pushing him to excel in his studies. She was ambitious for him to be a doctor when he grew up.

Cherry attended East Suffolk High School, which, though segregated, he remembers as a fine high school. The teachers "really cared." Discipline was strict but fair.

## Higher Education

Cherry attended Virginia Union University in Richmond, Virginia. He majored in biology, intending to go to medical school. But, while in college, he realized that what he really wanted to do was fly.

Having heard of a program in which students who had completed two years of college would be eligible for aviation cadet training, Cherry went to a naval recruiter in Portsmouth. When Cherry told the recruiter that he wanted to be a pilot, the recruiter put him off with endless delays and excuses. Leaving his flying ambitions aside temporarily, Cherry returned to college and completed his last two years. But he still was determined to fly. Just before graduation, in May 1951, Cherry took the test for flight school at Langley Air Force Base in Richmond, Virginia. Cherry was the only African American to take the test that day. Of the 20 men taking the test, he had the highest score. He started flight school in October 1951.

## Career Highlights

On June 25, 1950, in the early hours of the morning, the North Koreans had launched an attack on South Korea. The United States led a United Nations force in repelling the invasion. After successfully completing flight school, Cherry was immediately sent to Korea, where he was in the thick of the battle. He flew 53 missions in the F-89G fighter-bomber, bombing bridges, dams, and railroads behind enemy lines. His plane carried 1,000 pound bombs, napalm, five-inch rockets, and .50 caliber machine guns. With these incendiary items aboard, there was great danger of being hit by ground fire, which could cause the plane to catch fire or explode. "I never encountered enemy aircraft, but I had to worry about ground fire. I was hit in the tailpipe once while carrying napalm, but I made it home."

Early in the 1950s Cherry got married. The couple had four children: Donald, born in 1953, Fred in 1955, Debbie in 1957, and Cynthia in 1959. Cherry remained in the service when the Korean War ended. Meanwhile, U.S. involvement in the war in Vietnam was increasing. At first, only a few military "advisers" were involved, but as the war escalated, more and more American troops were sent into the fray. In the early 1960s Cherry was sent to Vietnam. He was flying a F-105, a tactical bomber. His targets were primarily roads, bridges, and military installations.

On October 25, 1965, Cherry was leading a squadron in an attack on a radar installation. The squadron flew at low altitude in order to place their bombs more accurately. Cherry's plane was hit by rifle fire from the ground. The plane caught fire and exploded almost immediately. Cherry parachuted out of the burning aircraft. "I could feel the bullets zinging [while] I was coming down," he recalled.

On the ground, he found himself surrounded by a dozen militiamen with guns. His left shoulder was shattered and his left wrist and ankle broken. Despite his injuries, Cherry was made to walk three miles to the nearest village, where he received superficial medical treatment. His broken bones were not attended to. From this village, he was escorted another five miles on foot to a military vehicle, in which he was taken to Hoa Lo Prison, known to prisoners as the Hanoi Hilton. Cherry was the 43rd prisoner to be taken by the Viet Cong, and the first African American. Many of his captors had never seen a black man.

Upon arrival at Hoa Lo, Cherry was interrogated all night. The interrogation techniques included torture:

> They would kick the chair out from under me and bang my head on the table. I thought . . . that really hurts. Then, I'd just relax and think of something pleasant. . . . Anything far away from this.

> Just before daybreak they took me to this cell. It had the biggest rats you ever saw in your life. . . . And I was sleeping on a concrete floor. No blanket. Just my flight suit. . . . Every morning they would take me to a place we called Heartbreak. These cells were their torture chambers.

At this prison, he was able to talk briefly with his fellow inmates, exchanging information with them and receiving encouragement from them. On November 16, he was removed from Hoa Lo and taken to Cu Loc prison, known to the men as "the Zoo." In this prison, he was kept from contact with other prisoners. He did manage to communicate with the prisoner in the cell next to his, a naval officer named Rodney Knutson, by means of tapping on the wall. On the 27th, another prisoner, Porter Halyburton, a lieutenant junior grade, was brought to share his cell. Halyburton was a white man who had grown up in the South. At first, the two did not trust each other; each thought the other must be a spy. Halyburton could not believe that a black man could be a pilot, and a major to boot.

Gradually, the two overcame their mutual mistrust. Halyburton, who had been imprisoned longer, taught Cherry the code of knocks that the men had devised so that they could communicate with those in adjoining cells. This means of communication made the men feel less isolated and kept their morale up in a dangerous and difficult situation.

In December of that year, Cherry's broken ankle had swollen tremendously, and his captors put a cast on it.

The following year, in February 1966, President Lyndon B. Johnson called a halt to bombing North Vietnam and offered a peace plan. For a while, the prisoners received better treatment. Cherry's torso was put in a cast after an operation on his shoulder. Then hopes for peace faded, and his captors abruptly withdrew medical treatment. Cherry, still in a cast, was seriously ill. His incisions had become infected. He was delirious, had a raging fever, and was close to dying.

His white roommate provided the only care he got. Halyburton shared his food with Cherry and cared for him in other ways as well. "I couldn't stand up. Hally would take me to the wash area, hold me up against the wall, . . . and wash my whole body."

At last, he was taken to a hospital where the cast was removed. He had lost weight, dropping from his normal weight of 135 pounds to 80 pounds. He was washed down with gasoline, given a blood transfusion, and fed intravenously. Still, his wounds did not heal. In April, he was taken to a hospital for surgery. The operation to remove the infected areas lasted for three hours and was performed without anesthetic.

Having recovered from this ordeal, Cherry was again subjected to torture every day, for periods lasting as long as five hours and he was kept in manacles and leg irons most of the rest of the time. He again became ill and was hospitalized to remove a rib that had pierced his lung, probably as a result of the torture sessions.

Upon his return from the hospital, Cherry was placed in solitary confinement where he would remain for 53 weeks. The daily interrogation sessions continued. His captors wanted Cherry to denounce the war and the U.S. government. There would have been great propaganda value in having Major Cherry, an African American officer, urge other African Americans not to fight. "They never got to home plate . . . [W]hen they would beat me, I always kept in mind I was representing 24 million black Americans. . . . I'm just not going to denounce my government or shame my people."

At last, in February 1973, the war wound down and the prisoners were repatriated. Cherry had spent 700 days in solitary confinement, had gone through bouts of infection caused by his untended wounds and the harsh treatment he received, and had suffered permanent damage to his shoulder and

arm. Released at last after seven years in captivity, he returned home to find himself in a very distressing personal situation. His wife Shirley, who received the first letter from Cherry in 1969, had never written to him and had told the children he was dead. Shortly after Cherry's capture, she had begun a relationship with another man and had given birth to his child. Meanwhile, the air force had given his monthly allotments and his savings to his wife, even though his sister, Beulah Watts, had informed them of the situation.

Upon his return to the United States, Cherry obtained a divorce. He then sued the Air Force for negligence. Air Force records showed that Shirley Cherry's continual requests for "emergency" money for such reasons as unverified losses of cash, bad investments, and medical treatment should have alerted Air Force officials. In addition to receiving and spending Cherry's monthly allotments, she had plundered his savings account of $17,000. Although the Air Force attempted to settle the case for a lesser amount, Cherry was successful in the Court of Claims. This was a lengthy process, and the case was not settled until 1982, nearly 10 years after his return from Vietnam. Cherry felt vindicated and hoped that his case would set a precedent.

In September 1981, after 30 years of service, he retired on 70 percent disability with the rank of colonel. He suffered from deafness in one ear, vision problems, and the after-effects of the fractures that had been neglected and could not now be remedied. He has kept in touch with his comrade Halyburton, and they remain good friends. His hometown of Suffolk, Virginia, honored him by establishing a scholarship fund, called the Colonel Fred Victor Cherry Scholarship Fund, to help deserving low-income students attend college. He now lives in Maryland and is a member of the Tuskegee Airmen, Inc. As a representative of the association, Cherry speaks to young black people, encouraging them to study engineering, science and technology, and to aspire to aviation careers.

## Sources

"Black Pilot's Portrait to Hang in Pentagon's Hall of Heroes." *Jet* (March 12, 1981): 5.

Cherry, Fred V., as told to Wallace Terry. "One Brave Man's Ordeal." *Parade* magazine (July 29, 1984): 15–17.

"Col. Cherry Gets Partial Claim in USAF Pay Case, Vows to Continue Fight." *Jet* (March 7, 1983): 32.

Franklin, Ben A. "Ex-P.O.W. Seeks Money Paid to Wife." *New York Times* (June 30, 1981).

———. "Former P.O.W., Money Taken by Wife, to Reject Court Award." *New York Times* (April 25, 1982).

Terry, Wallace. *Bloods: An Oral History of the Vietnam War by Black Veterans.* New York: Random House, 1984.

# Cornelius Coffey

Cornelius Coffey. Courtesy of National Air and Space Museum, Smithsonian Institution (SI Neg. No. 91-6605).

**Full Name at Birth:** Cornelius Robinson Coffey

**Born:** September 6, 1903, Newport, Arkansas

**Died:** March 2, 1994, Chicago, Illinois

**Education:** Chicago School of Automotive Engineering; Master Mechanic, Curtiss-Wright Aeronautical University, 1932.

**Positions Held:** Automobile mechanic and garage owner, Detroit, mid-1920s; founder and director of the Coffey School of Aeronautics, Chicago, 1938–1945; instructor, Lewis School of Aeronautics, Lockport, Illinois; aviation mechanics instructor, Dunbar Vocational High School, Chicago, 1957–1969; aircraft and engine examiner designated by the Federal Aviation Authority (FAA) until 1993.

**Awards, Honors:** Dwight H. Green Trophy, 1941; Cofey Fix, July 10, 1980 (a five-letter navigational aid in aeronautics); Cornelius R. Coffey Day in Chicago, July 22, 1980; honored as a pioneer at the "Black Wings" exhibition, National Air and Space Museum, 1982; inducted into Illinois Aviation Hall of Fame, 1984; Elder Statesman of Aviation, National Aeronautic Association, 1991; Cornelius R. Coffey Aviation Education Foundation, founded by a group of admirers, 1992.

**Summary:** Cornelius R. Coffey's focus on opportunities in aviation for African Americans, as he pursued his own dream in the field, successfully challenged American racist ideas of black inferiority. Coffey founded and directed the Coffey School of Aeronautics in Chicago in 1938, where until 1945 he trained hundreds of pilots, many of whom became instructors of, or pilots later known as, Tuskegee Airmen during World War II. A pilot himself since 1928, Coffey was instrumental in making Chicago the center of African American aviation activities. In 1932, he became one of the country's first black airplane mechanics. Coffey was a charter member and first president of the National Airmen's Association of America (NAAA), founded in 1937.

## Early Years

Cornelius Robinson Coffey was born to Henry Coffey and Ada Wright Coffey on September 6, 1903, in Newport, Arkansas. His sister, Vina, was born about 1897 and his brother, Vernon, was born about 1907. Their father was "a railroad man in the days when an Afro-American could hook a train together and drive a locomotive from the roundhouse to the station. But he could never become a full-fledged engineer." According to the 1910 census, Henry Coffey, by then a widower, lived with his widowed mother-in-law, Cyntha Wright. The household included, besides the three Coffey children, two other granddaughters, Arline and Annie Wright, who were 15 and 20 years old. Annie Wright worked as a seamstress for a white family.

Always fascinated by the workings of machines and used to seeing steam locomotives in Newport, Coffey became interested in the latest form of energy, the internal combustion engines that were used to power automobiles, known earlier as "horseless carriages." While still in grade school, he rode a motorcycle to deliver mail for the local postmaster, who paid him eight cents for each special delivery letter. By the age of 12, Coffey could drive a Model-T Ford, the car that solidified America's automobile craze. Coffey recalled, "The car dealer in town hired me to show customers how to drive. Folks were so excited by their first car, they'd take lessons from a black child."

A few years later a barnstorming pilot, a veteran of World War I, arrived in Newport to take people for airplane rides. A barnstormer was one who engaged in daredevil feats or offered rides, both popular entertainments at the time. Coffey jumped at the chance to experience flight. He certainly did, as the pilot put the plane through rolls and spins, upside-down flying, and nose diving, only to pull up at tree-top level. The pilot was surprised by the teenager's lack of fear, and upon landing, told Coffey to think about flying, as he had a feel for it. Coffey was happy to do so, believing that the new technology would be less bound by the prejudices of the past. As Coffey said (Grossman 1993), "My spirit was kindled to go into a line of work where I wouldn't be bound by the limitations my father had to put up with."

## Career Highlights

After graduating from high school in the early 1920s, Coffey decided to become an automobile mechanic. School after school turned him down because of his color. At last the Chicago School of Automotive Engineering accepted him. Coffey graduated in the mid-1920s and moved to Detroit where his sister and brother-in-law had settled. He owned a repair shop for cars and motorcycles in Detroit's Black Bottom section, which was not only a ghetto but also a center of illegal activities, gambling, and drinking.

Here he met John C. Robinson (1903–1954), a motorcycle stunt rider and auto mechanic from Chicago, who had an avid interest in flying. They became good friends, often talking about the difficulties, both financial and societal, of learning to fly. The memory of Bessie Coleman (1892–1926), who had to go to France to be licensed as an aviator, fueled their determination to fly. Robinson convinced Coffey to return to Chicago with him, where opportunities would be greater. They pooled their money and bought a kit from the Heath Parasol Airplane Company. They displayed the airplane they built, a one-seater, at a Christmas party at the Dreamland Dance Hall to raise money for their study group, the South Town Aviation Club. They wanted to interest other African Americans in aviation, first, to honor Bessie Coleman, and second, to give the lie to ideas of black inferiority. They also knew there was strength in numbers, because lessons and planes were expensive. Not many white instructors could be found to teach blacks, and at that time a black often had to own a plane if he wanted to fly it.

In 1928, Coffey earned his private pilot's license. To obtain a transport pilot's license, then the highest license one could obtain, and which would permit him to fly commercially, he needed 200 more hours of flying time. With airplanes renting for $10 an hour, almost a week's salary, Coffey convinced Robinson they should become aircraft mechanics and gain master mechanic certificates. They then could barter their skills for flying time. Accepted at the Curtiss-Wright School of Aeronautics, they made their tuition payments by mail. When they appeared in person the school offered to refund their money, as it did not accept blacks. Coffey and Robinson refused. They were encouraged by Emil Mack, the owner of the auto dealership where both men were employed. He threatened court action; Curtiss-Wright accepted the two young African Americans. Their performance convinced the school to hold classes for 35 other African Americans, albeit at night. Coffey and Robinson were hired as instructors.

Coffey's master mechanic's license, dated July 26, 1932, is perhaps the first awarded to a black in the United States.

Through the early and mid-1930s the two friends continued to work at Mack's Elmwood Park Motor Sales. But what really occupied them was turning their dream of flight into reality. In 1936 Coffey developed a carburetor heat control so light planes could fly in winter weather. Although he didn't patent his ideas, many are still in use today. They formed numerous clubs, called at various times, the Brown Eagle Aero Club, Challenger Aero Club, and Challenger Air Pilots Association. The club members were based at Robbins Airport near the all-black town of Robbins, Illinois. With the support of the mayor, grass was cleared to build runways, and the group constructed a hangar themselves. The three planes owned by Coffey, Robinson, and Janet Waterford, later Bragg, were for group use. The plane owned by Earl Renfroe, a dentist, was for his own use.

In 1933, a winter storm destroyed the hangar and the planes inside. The Challengers then moved to Harlem Airport on the south side of Chicago, where they occupied an area away from the white clientele. By 1935 Willa Brown (1906–1992) had joined the group. She had been a teacher in Gary, Indiana, and learned to fly after she met Robinson. Brown, Coffey, Chauncey Spencer, Harold Hurd, Dale White, Enoch Waters, Janet Waterford, Marie St. Clair, Charles Johnson, Grover C. Nash, Edward Johnson, and George Williams were the charter members of the National Airmen's Association of America (NAAA). It was founded in August 1937 "to further stimulate interest in aviation and to bring about a better understanding in the entire field of aeronautics." Studying the statistics reveals that of 62,200 licensed pilots in the United States, 130 were black (*Time*, September 25, 1939.) The *Chicago Defender*, an important black newspaper, provided office space, a mailing address, and feature stories about aviation activities in Chicago and nationally.

In 1938, Coffey and Brown also established the Coffey School of Aeronautics; Coffey was president and chief flight instructor and Brown was the director. The school became so busy that Coffey lived in a trailer at the airport to save commuting time. Their differing personalities—he the quiet instructor and master mechanic and she the dynamic publicist and organizer—centered the group. They turned the school into a major arena for training black pilots, who eventually were permitted to join the Army Air Corps. These young pilots became known as the Tuskegee Airmen and their skill and bravery were factors in the desegregation of the armed forces in 1948. Their organization, NAAA, sponsored a national air meet in Chicago, August 25–27, 1939. Forty to 50 African American pilots, some flying their own planes, came to Chicago to meet each other and to exchange information. Coffey was president at the time.

In September 1939, in order to prepare for the coming war, a Civilian Pilot Training Program (CPTP) was instituted to create a reserve of pilots. The Civil Aeronautics Authority (CAA) certified 220 colleges and universities for participation. Willa Brown, secretary of the NAAA, flew to colleges to stir interest in flying. Chauncey Spencer and Dale White, NAAA members, flew to Washington, D.C. to meet lobbyists and congressmen; and the black press and civil rights groups worked tirelessly to demand the inclusion of African Americans in the CPTP.

Their efforts resulted in six historically black colleges and universities being chosen by the government as training sites: West Virginia State College, North Carolina Agricultural and Technical State University, Tuskegee Institute, Hampton Institute, Howard University, and Delaware State College. The Coffey School was also chosen for the program, one of only two noncollegiate units. The role the NAAA played in African American aviation history was to open doors for African Americans to participate in mainstream American life. Several graduates of the Coffey School became the first instructors to train cadets for the 99th Pursuit Squadron, the first group of the Tuskegee Airmen. The Coffey School began secondary training in December 1940, the only secondary course equipped with two army primary training aircraft. The school closed in 1945, when World War II ended, and with it, its training contracts. Coffey took a course in instrument flying at the Lewis School of Aeronautics in Lockport, Illinois, and remained there as an instructor for six years. He continued to work as a mechanic. Although most sources cite 1939 as the date of Coffey's and Willa Brown's marriage, the actual date was February 7, 1947, according to records kept at the Cook County (Chicago) Vital Statistics Department. From 1957 until his retirement in 1969, Coffey was an aviation

and mechanics teacher at Dunbar Vocational High School in Chicago. He continued to advance his knowledge, and he was appointed a designated Federal Aviation Administration (FAA) Aircraft Examiner in the 1970s and continued until 1993, the year before his death. Coffey flew his own plane in his 80s.

In recognition of Coffey's more than 50 years as a pioneer African American aviator, the Great Lakes Region of the FAA named an aerial navigation fix for him on July 10, 1980. A "fix" is a specific geographical position determined by visual or electronic means. Pilots use it to report their position to ground controllers. The Cofey Fix (only five letters are permitted) is 12 miles southeast of Midway Airport. At the ceremony, Coffey himself flew his Cessna 150 over the Fix named in his honor. He later said, "It's nice to enjoy your flowers while you're still living." In 1982, Coffey was again honored in ceremonies at the National Air and Space Museum's seminal exhibition, "Black Wings: The American Black in Aviation." It has since become a permanent exhibition at the museum in Washington, D.C. Two years later, Coffey was inducted into the Illinois Aviation Hall of Fame. A group of admirers established the Cornelius R. Coffey Aviation Education Foundation in 1992 to assist students at the American Airlines Maintenance Academy. When he died in March 1994, his second wife, Ann, or Anna Mae, survived him.

## Sources

Allen, Henry. "To Fly, to Brave the Wind." *Washington Post* (September 26, 1979): B1, 6.

Golab, Art. "Black Aviator Still Flies High." *Chicago Sun-Times* (July 14, 1993):24.

Grossman, Ron. "A Flight against the Wind." *Chicago Tribune* (July 25, 1993): 1,3.

Helse, Kenan. "Cornelius Coffey, Early Black Aviator." *Chicago Tribune* (March 4, 1994).

Hunt, Rufus A. *The Cofey Intersection.* Chicago: JRDB Productions, 1982.

Simmons, Thomas E. *The Brown Condor: The True*

*Adventures of John C. Robinson*. Silver Spring, MD: Bartleby Press, 1988.

Waters, Enoch P. *American Diary: A Personal History of the Black Press*. Chicago: Path Press, 1987.

# Bessie Coleman

Bessie Coleman. Courtesy of National Air and Space Museum, Smithsonian Institution (SI Neg. No. 80-12873).

**Full Name at Birth:** Bessie (or Elizabeth) Coleman

**Born:** January 26, 1892, Atlanta, Texas

**Died:** April 30, 1926, in Jacksonville, Florida. Buried Lincoln Cemetery, Chicago, Illinois.

**Education:** Completed eighth grade, Waxahatchie, Texas. Attended preparatory division, Colored Agricultural and Normal University (now Langston University) in Langston, Oklahoma, for one semester. Studied manicuring at Burnham's School of Beauty Culture, 1915. Trained as a pilot in France, 1920–1922, at Ecole d'Aviation des Frères Caudron at le Crotoy.

**Awards, Honors:** Represented in a monument recognizing Black American aviators and astronauts from 1917 to 1990 unveiled in 1990 at Lambert-Saint Louis International Airport. A stamp in her honor was issued in 1995 by the United States Postal Service.

**Summary:** Bessie Coleman became the first black woman to earn a pilot's license. As a stunt flier, she barnstormed all over the United States before dying in an airplane accident at age 34. Her exploits were widely celebrated in the African American press, making Coleman a hero and a role model to countless others who came after her.

## Early Years

Bessie Coleman was born in Atlanta, Texas, on January 26, 1892, the 12th of 13 children born to Susan and George Coleman. Her father was three-quarters Choctaw Indian and one-quarter African American. Shortly after her birth, the family moved to Waxahatchie, Texas, where they earned their living picking cotton.

When Coleman was seven, her father returned to Choctaw country in Oklahoma Territory, leaving her mother and the younger children, four girls, to survive as best they could. Several of the older children had grown up and left, some for Chicago. Coleman was the oldest of those left at home, and she looked after her three younger sisters. All the children worked from an early age, picking cotton and doing domestic work. Coleman strenuously objected to picking cotton— a first instance, perhaps, of the strong-mindedness that would govern her life. As she was clever and showed mathematical aptitude, she was exempted from this onerous job and became the family bookkeeper.

The family's main source of entertainment was to have Coleman read aloud from the Bible every evening. She also read stories borrowed from a traveling library, about the achievements of famous African Americans such as Paul Lawrence Dunbar, Harriet Tubman, and Booker T. Washington. These may have inspired Coleman's ambition to do something for her people.

## Higher Education

Coleman showed so much ability in school that her mother allowed her to keep her earnings from taking in laundry to finance her college education. She graduated from eighth grade, which was quite unusual in a time when southern black children often got only two or three years of education. She attended college at Colored Agricultural and Normal University (now Langston University), in Langston, Oklahoma, for one semester, until her savings ran out.

A small incident that took place at this time illustrates Coleman's spirit. Upon learning that a church in her hometown was planning a party to welcome her back, Coleman brought along her school's brass band to brighten the occasion.

## Career Highlights

Opportunities for African Americans in the South at the time were limited or non-existent, particularly for women. Around 1915, Coleman emigrated to Chicago, where two of her older brothers lived. There she attended manicuring school and upon completion of the course, became a manicurist at the White Sox Barber Shop. The shop was situated on the Stroll, an eight-block stretch of State Street where black-owned businesses flourished. This was a strategic location for Coleman, enabling her to meet such influential African Americans as Robert S. Abbott, founder and publisher of the *Chicago Defender*, and Jesse Binga, a real estate promoter.

World War I was raging in Europe at the time, and the newspapers were full of the ex-

ploits of the flying aces. It had been but a few years since the Wright Brothers had made the first successful flight, in 1903, and the idea of human flight was still a thrilling novelty. Working in the barber shop, listening to the talk of men who had returned from the war, and reading newspaper accounts of their exploits, she became interested in learning to fly. She was so confident that she could be a successful flier, she quit her job to pursue her dream.

At the time, it was unthinkable that an African American—and a woman—could fly. At the time, women suffered many legal disabilities; they were not even permitted to vote until 1921. Coleman was denied admission to all the aviation schools to which she applied. According to her niece, she could have been admitted if she would agree to pass for white, but she refused. At last, Robert S. Abbott encouraged her to go to France to study. He offered financial support as well. He saw in this attractive, flamboyant woman a great potential for publicity, which would lead to increased circulation for his paper. Jesse Binga, founder and president of the Binga State Bank and another prominent Chicago African American, also provided financial support.

She learned French and went to France, where she attended the prestigious Ecole d'Aviation des Frères Caudron, receiving her pilot's license in 1921—the first black woman to do so. Upon her return from France, she found herself an overnight sensation, due at least partly to Abbott's publicity. She was met at the ship's dock by reporters, both black and white. Coleman had a great sense of drama and enjoyed the attention. She was good copy. In an interview with the *Chicago Defender*, she boasted, "I thought it my duty to risk my life to learn aviating and to encourage men and women of the Race. . . . I tried and was successful." She went on to say, "Did you know you have never lived until you have flown?"

In 1922, returning to France for further study, she became the first woman ever to win an international pilot's license. Coleman was now ready to plan for the future.

Coleman had formulated three goals when she first became interested in flight. The first, to earn a pilot's license, had been reached. Now she set out in pursuit of her other goals: to become a stunt flier, and to start an aviation school for black Americans—"to turn Uncle Tom's cabin into an airplane hangar." Coleman envisioned a vital role for aviation in the future, and she wanted her people prepared to be a part of it. The two goals were interrelated. The publicity and acclaim she was to receive for her barnstorming performances would raise her visibility and enable her to raise money for her flight school.

In these early years of aviation, barnstorming, or stunt flying, was a popular form of entertainment. Crowds would turn out to watch loop the loops, midair stalls, and other such dangerous and daring stunts. Coleman now set her sights on becoming a successful barnstormer. Almost immediately, she was engaged to appear in an air show on the outskirts of New York City, sponsored by Abbott and the *Chicago Defender*. Six weeks later she appeared in another show, this time in Chicago. Onlookers were dazzled by her youth, beauty, and daring. According to the *Defender*, spectators "witnessed some of the most marvelous flying feats that have ever been performed by the most daring aviators."

In 1922, she signed a contract to star in a full-length feature film, but walked off the set when asked to perform in what she considered a demeaning manner. Her parting shot was, "No Uncle Tom stuff for me!"

This show of determination proved to be a setback for Coleman: she became known in the press as headstrong and temperamental. The contretemps left her without a sponsor or a plane. But she was not to be diverted from her goals. She found sponsorship from one of her students who was an executive with a California tire company and was able to purchase a plane. She could then arrange an exhibition flight in Los Angeles, on February 4, 1922.

The flight was a disaster. Her plane stalled at 300 feet, and smashed into the ground. Coleman suffered a broken leg, three broken ribs, and serious lacerations. She begged the doctor who had rushed to the scene to patch her up so that she could resume her flight. Instead, she was hospitalized. She was in the hospital for three months, and when released, her leg was in a cast. This setback slowed the momentum of her career but did not deter Coleman. She returned to Chicago for a time, but then relocated to Texas, where she gave lectures and resumed stunt flying.

Having made her mark with mostly white audiences in the North, she drew largely African American audiences in the South. Wherever she went, local black people opened their homes and their hearts to her. Coleman's beauty, courage, and skill captured the public imagination. Not just a skilled pilot, she was also adept at presenting herself and courting publicity, and was widely known as "Brave Bessie" and "Queen Bess."

At last, with help from a wealthy Florida businessman, Coleman was able to complete the purchase of a plane. Unfortunately, its engine was worn and poorly maintained. Friends expressed their doubt about the safety of the plane. According to her niece Marion Coleman, "The airplanes she was flying, they were just old things, thrown away. . . . They weren't worth a darn." The family also expressed doubts about William Wills, Coleman's collaborator. They were mistrustful of his piloting skills, as he was basically a mechanic. Coleman shrugged off these doubts.

Coleman was planning to do a parachute jump, so she asked her mechanic to take her up in the plane ahead of time to scout likely landing places. As this was an exploratory flight, and Coleman wanted to be able to lean out of the plane to assess the territory, she did not wear her seat belt. Wills, the mechanic, lost control of the plane, and Coleman, with neither seat belt nor parachute, was hurled to her death. She was 34 years old.

Bessie Coleman never realized her dream of starting a flying school for black people, but her influence lasted, and still lives on. Within a few years of her death, William Powell founded the Bessie Coleman Aero Club, honoring her and striving to pursue her goals. Many young black people were inspired to fly by her example. Every Memorial Day, black men and women aviators fly in formation and drop bouquets of flowers over her grave in Lincoln Cemetery, in honor of her brave and undaunted spirit.

## Sources

"Air Woman's Stamp Tribute." *Voice* (April 4, 1995).

"Aviator to Get Stamp." *Air Force Times* (February 13, 1995).

"Aviatrix Must Sign Life Away to Learn Trade," *Chicago Defender* (October 8, 1921).

Barr, Agnes. "Bessie Coleman," *The Ninety-nines.* Http://www.ninety-nines.org. Accessed October 14, 1998.

"Bessie Coleman and White Pilot in 2,000 Ft. Crash," *New York Amsterdam News* (May 6, 1926).

Bois, Danuta, "Bessie Coleman (1893–1926)." Http://www.netsrq.com/dbois/coleman.html. Accessed October 7, 1998.

Brown, Ross D. *Afro-American World Almanac.* Chicago: the author, 1948.

Hodgman, Ann, and Ruby Djabbaroff. *Skystars: The History of Women in Aviation.* New York: Atheneum, 1981.

Molotsky, Irwin. "Pioneers: Women Who Led the Way in Aviation." *New York Times* (November 25, 1985): C12.

Moolman, Valerie. *Women Aloft.* Alexandria VA: Time-Life Books, 1981.

Rich, Doris L. "My Quest for Queen Bess." *Air and Space* (September 1994).

———. *Queen Bess: Daredevil Aviator.* Washington, DC: Smithsonian Institution Press, 1993.

Turnage, Sheila. "Claiming the Sky." *American Legacy* (spring 2000).

"U.S. Postal Service Honors Aviator Bessie Coleman with Stamp." *Jet* (December 5, 1994).

Whitman, Sylvia. "Barnstorming Bessie Coleman." *Cobblestone* (February 1997).

# Patricia S. Cowings

Patricia S. Cowings. Courtesy of National Air and Space Museum, Smithsonian Institution (SI Neg. No. 97–15073).

**Full Name at Birth:** Patricia Suzanne Cowings

**Born:** December 15, 1948, Bronx, New York

**Education:** State University of New York at Stony Brook, B.A. (cum laude) in psychology, 1970; University of California at Davis, M.A., Ph.D. in psychology, 1973.

**Positions Held:** Research assistant in psychology, SUNY at Stony Brook, 1968–1970; teaching assistant, Department of Psychology, University of California at Davis, 1970–1971; guest investigator, Rockefeller University of New York, 1971–1972; research assistant/research psychologist, Summer Student Program, NASA, 1971 and 1972; post-doctoral associateship, National Research Council, NASA-Ames Research Center, Mountain View, California, 1973–1975; research specialist, San Jose (CA) State University Foundation, 1975–1977; research psychologist, principal investigator, Psychophysiological Research Laboratory, NASA Ames Research Center, 1977–   .

**Awards, Honors:** Distinguished Scholarship Award, University of California at Davis, 1971; Best Aerospace Medicine Research Paper by a Young Investigator Award, Space Medicine Branch of the Aerospace Medical Association, 1976; NASA Group Achievement Award, Spacelab Mission Development-III, Project Support Team, Principal Investigator, 1977; NASA Individual Achievement Award, Spacelab Mission Development-III, Scientist Astronaut, 1977; NASA Group Achievement Award, Spacelab-3 Payload, Principal Investigator Team, 1985; Ames Honors Award for Excellence in the Category of Scientist, 1985; Candace Award for Science and Technology, National Coalition of 100 Black Women, 1989; Innovative Research Award, Biofeedback Society of California, 1990; Black United Fund of Texas Award, 1991; NASA Group Achievement Award, Spacelab-J, 1993; NASA Individual Achievement Award, Principal Investigator of flight experiment, Spacelab-J, 1993; NASA Incentive Award for Contributions to the development of biomedical flight hardware, 1993; Black Engineer of the Year Award, for contributions to aerospace technology and science, Maryland Space Grant Consortium, 1994; NASA African American Advisory Group, Public Services Award, 1994.

**Summary:** The first African American woman to receive scientist astronaut training, in 1976–1977, Cowings has been a psychophysiologist at NASA's Ames Research Center since 1977. Her research in "zero-gravity sickness syndrome" has been instrumental in helping astronauts combat the effects of motion sickness and therefore allows them to spend longer time periods in space.

## Early Years

The only daughter of Sadie B. and Albert S. Cowings, Patricia Cowings grew up in New York City. "Both my parents were seriously into academics as a way of getting out of the Bronx," Cowings recalled. "When going to my father's grocery store I would have to do my homework in the telephone booth so he could see me working on it." Albert Cowings was a grocery store owner-operator for 30 years in the Bronx, and later worked as a guard at the Metropolitan Museum of Art. Sadie Cowings earned an associate degree in psychology when she was 55 and became an assistant preschool teacher in the New York City school system. Her parents' insistence on the importance of education paid off: in addition to Patricia Cowings's own success as a scientist, her three brothers are a two-star army general, a jazz musician, and a freelance journalist.

Cowings says that she was about nine years old when "I looked around and noticed that all the good jobs were for men, and mainly for white men." Her father, however, told her, "You're not just a short round brown girl from the Bronx. What you are is a human being, and a human being is the best animal on the whole planet." Human beings "can achieve anything through learning," Cowings insists, and her interest in science, and especially space, developed early. "Ever since I could read, I was interested in science fiction . . . I was not so good at math (I admit) as a kid. I learned to use it as a tool. But science was always a game! . . . Scientists are eternal students. We ask questions for a living . . . I was encouraged by my parents to do what I *wanted* to do, not what someone else thought I *should* do."

## Higher Education

After graduating from Music and Art High School in New York City, Cowings attended a New York junior college for her freshman year. She then transferred to the State University of New York at Stony Brook, renowned for its psychology department.

Graduating with honors in psychology from Stony Brook in 1970, Cowings continued her psychology studies at the University of California at Davis. She began her long association with NASA while still a graduate student, working in NASA's Summer Student Program in 1971 and 1972. During this period she also served as a guest investigator at Rockefeller University under Neal E. Miller, a pioneer in "visceral learning" research—known today as biofeedback. Biofeedback would become a key element in Cowings's contributions to helping astronauts avoid motion sickness.

Later Cowings would say,

> I took a course in graduate school . . . [that] was to design features for the space shuttle, from the point of view of a person using the equipment . . . the class was full of men and they were all engineers. . . . So I told the professor, "You have no women in this class. Everybody's designing zero gravity tables. . . . Nobody is looking at what impact that environment could have on animals, such as human beings. You need a life science woman in this class." . . . That particular course truly launched my career. . . . I wrote a paper for the course about 12 possible applications of mind work that could be used for solving biomedical problems [of manned spaceflight]. The first one was a treatment for space motion sickness. I got an A in the course, but more importantly, I discovered Ames Research Center and have been here ever since.

## Career Highlights

Cowings was awarded both her masters and doctoral degrees in 1973, then took up a post-doctoral associateship at Ames for the next two years. In 1976 she was selected as a payload specialist for Spacelab Mission Development SMD-3, thereby becoming the first African American woman to be trained as a scientist astronaut.

> I was the alternate and never got a chance to fly but that experience is something I will never forget. . . . It was a joint effort between Johnson Space Center and Ames . . . and was the first simulation of a life science dedicated space shuttle mission. . . . There were two years of fairly intense science development and crew training—half the time [at Ames] and the other at JSC. . . . "much ado" was made about my selection (some good, some bad).

Also in 1976, Cowings was awarded the Space Medicine Branch of the Aerospace Medical Association's award for Best Paper by a Young Investigator, for a paper that Cowings and her colleagues J. Billingham and W.B. Toscano published the following year, "Learned control of multiple autonomic responses to compensate for the debilitating effects of motion sickness." William B. Toscano, one of Cowings's co-investigators at Ames, with whom she has since published or presented more than 30 papers, is also her husband. They have one son, Christopher Michael Cowings Toscano.

In 1977 Cowings became a research psychologist and principal investigator in the Psychophysiological Research Laboratory at Ames. Her research there has focused on "zero-gravity sickness syndrome," which is similar to gravity-based "motion sickness." As astronauts spent longer periods of time in space on the shuttles, Cowings was asked to develop a drug-free way for the astronauts to combat motion sickness symptoms. With her colleagues, Cowings has devised a training system, Autogenic Feedback Training Exercise, which she has described as "a way in which people learn how to control up to 20 of their bodily responses so that they can keep themselves from getting sick due to motion sickness." As Cowings explained,

Autogenic is Latin for "self-generated." My treatment . . . combines Autogenic therapy (a psychotherapy that involves self-hypnosis), with Biofeedback (showing a person his own physiological responses, like heart rate, in real-time), Training (because the more you do it, the better you get . . . ) and Exercise, because what you're really learning . . . is to exercise or control "smooth" muscle—the muscles of your heart, blood vessels, and gut. Plus, you learn to regulate glandular responses as well. In my lab when we say "don't sweat" we mean just that. We can teach you how to increase or decrease sweat—on command!

Cowings's experiments were flown on Space Shuttle Missions STS 51-C and 51-B in 1985, and STS-47 Spacelab J in 1992. In addition to AFTE's applicability in increasing the efficiency of the space shuttle crews, Cowings's projects now include helping medical patients learn to control fainting and nausea and working with helicopter pilots to improve their performance and safety.

## Sources

Bruno, Leonard C. "Patricia S. Cowings." *Notable Twentieth-century Scientists*. Ed. Emily J. McMurray. Detroit: Gale Research, 1995. Vol. 1, 417–418.

Cowings, Patricia Suzanne. Curriculum Vitae. NASA ARC Psychophysiology Research Laboratory. February 9, 1997. Http://lifesci.arc.nasa.gov/psychophysio/patvita.html. Accessed February 5, 2000.

Goodson, Martia Graham. "Patricia S. Cowings." *Notable Black American Women, Book II*. Ed. Jessie Carney Smith. Detroit: Gale Research, 1996; 150–151.

Graves, Curtis, and Ivan Van Sertima. "Patricia Cowings." *Blacks in Science: Ancient and Modern*. New Brunswick, NJ: Transaction Books, 1983; 252–254.

"Meet: Patricia Cowings, Ph.D." Shuttle/Mir Online Research Experience (S/MORE) Team. Fall 1996. Http://quest.arc.nasa.gov/smore/team/pcowings. html. Accessed February 20, 2000.

Murray, James B. *Black Visions '90: African Americans in Space Science*. New York: Mayor's Office of Minority Affairs, 1990; 15.

"Patricia S. Cowings, Ph.D." Women of NASA. Biography and QuestChat Archives. April 22, 1999; February 9, 2000; March 7, 2000. Http://quest.arc.nasa.gov/women/bios/pc.html, http://quest.arc.nasa.gov/women/archive/. Accessed February 20, April 15, 2000.

# Woodrow W. Crockett

**Full Name at Birth:** Woodrow Wilson Crockett

**Born:** August 31, 1918, Texarkana, Arkansas

**Education:** Dunbar High School, 1939; Dunbar Junior College, 1939–1940.

**Positions Held:** Tuskegee Airman, 1942–1945; pilot, flight instructor, 1945–1972.

**Awards, Honors:** Distinguished Flying Cross, Presidential Unit Citation, two Soldiers Medals for Bravery, the Air Medal with four oak leaf clusters, Meritorious Service Medal; inducted into Arkansas Aviation Hall of Fame, 1992; inducted into Arkansas African American Hall of Fame, 1995.

**Summary:** Woodrow W. Crockett was a member of the Tuskegee Airmen, the first group of black pilots who served in the U.S. Army Air Corps (later the Air Force) during World War II. He made the Air Force his career, serving as a flight instructor and pilot, and retired after 30 years of service.

## Early Years

Woodrow W. Crockett was born on August 31, 1918, the fifth of six children. Both his parents were schoolteachers in Homan, Arkansas, when he was of school age, and the boy, nicknamed "Woody" by his classmates, attended the school where they were teaching. It was a two-room school; his mother taught grades one through four, his father, five through eight. There was no instruction for African American children beyond the eighth grade and Crockett remembers that he realized before the age of 10 that an eighth-grade education "would not hack it in the world even in 1930." The family was strongly in favor of education; his mother had received her college degree at the age of 60.

To go further in his education, the youth had to leave Homan for Little Rock, where he lived with his sister. The move was necessary in order to attend Paul Laurence Dunbar High School, a black secondary school that had recently opened. According to Crockett: "Black kids from all over the state descended on it."

Crockett has remembered that he "just didn't know what to think of . . . this huge school, three or four stories high, taking up almost a full block, with marble-like floors." To his surprise, the teachers were specialists in their subjects and each had his or her own classroom. More important, in Dunbar High School the young man was able to pursue his interest in mathematics, with the encouragement of his math teacher, Lillian M. Weaver.

## Higher Education

After receiving his high school diploma in 1939, Crockett attended junior college, also at Dunbar. He was so proficient in mathematics that he taught Mrs. Weaver's high school and junior college classes when she took a two-week vacation one semester.

## Career Highlights

Financial hardship forced him to leave Dunbar in 1940 to enlist in the U.S. Army. The Great Depression that had gripped the nation during the 1930s still prevailed, and Crockett was unable to afford the six-dollar-a-month tuition charge.

The young man's talent was recognized by his superiors: "My first sergeant thought I should go to West Point, but they said I was too old. Then they said I should go to Officers Candidate School (OCS), but only the infantry was open to black officers. I would have been the first black to attend Artillery OCS, except that this announcement showed up on the orderly room wall." The poster advertised that a flying officer could earn $245 a month. At the time, he was earning only $21 a month. He had an additional reason: "I was tired of sleeping in the mud and in the back of trucks. . . . I thought I'd take my chances getting blasted out of the sky during the day, so I could sleep well at night."

Shortly after his enlistment, war began to appear inevitable. The Axis powers, Germany, Japan and Italy, began their wars of conquest in Europe and Asia, compelling President Franklin D. Roosevelt and his advisers to prepare the United States military for the coming conflict. On December 7, 1941, the surprise bombing attack on Pearl Harbor caused the United States to enter World War II.

After passing rigorous tests, Crockett was sent to Tuskegee Institute in Tuskegee, Alabama, for preflight orientation in 1942. The instructors were civilian pilots, most of them black. C. Alfred "Chief" Anderson, one of the first African Americans to get a pilot's license, was in charge of instructors. The whole operation at Tuskegee was led by Colonel Noel Parrish. Though a southern white man, he was not a racist and treated everyone decently.

Some of the base leaders clearly expected the men to fail; "They said we didn't have the intelligence, the demeanor, the courage to be combat pilots. . . . They learned differently. It was never about color; it was always about education and opportunity. All we needed was a chance and training. And we seized it when it came."

"We were the first class to expand from the normal 20 per class. There were 35 in our class, including 15 who had previous Army experience. After nine weeks we were left with only 15. . . . They washed out 75 percent of the cadets they took in . . . this was white boys. The 'washing machine' was going. . . . I was properly motivated to be in the upper 25 percent." Crockett had another reason for working hard: He had recently married a classmate at Dunbar, Daisy Juanita McMurry of Little Rock. Because cadets were not permitted to marry, Crockett kept the marriage a secret until the conclusion of his training. They later had four children: Marcia J., Rosemary F., Woodrow W., and Kathleen Y.

Crockett successfully completed his training, and in April 1943 was sent to North Africa as a member of the 99th Pursuit Squadron. They were then folded into the 332nd Fighter Group, based in Italy. The group relieved a white unit near Salerno, Italy.

The group were used as long-range bomber escorts with the 12th Tactical Air Force: "We escorted over 200 missions from the south of France clockwise to Romania, but our greatest claim to fame is we never lost one bomber to an enemy fighter." The work was dangerous: 66 of the Tuskegee Airmen lost their lives in combat, and an additional 32 were shot down and became prisoners of war.

Crockett told an interviewer: "I flew 107 missions in four months. There were no replacement black pilots—Tuskegee had to furnish to the 99th Pursuit squadron. We knew this was an experiment, and we continued to fly." On one of his final missions the group had to provide cover for bombers flying over Berlin. Crockett and the other escorts shot down three of the German ME-262 jet aircraft and damaged five others.

In May 1945, after the war in Europe had ended, Crockett returned home to Fort Patrick Henry, Virginia, where, despite his service in the war, which included saving a man from a burning plane, he was denied access to the officers' club, while German prisoners on the post were permitted to enter.

Crockett decided to make the military his career. He became a pilot instructor at Tuskegee and flew in the Korean War and in the Marshall Islands during A-bomb testing on Eniwetok, an island in the Pacific. He also served with the Strategic Air Command. After 30 years, he retired with the rank of lieutenant colonel.

Crockett is active in retirement. He and his wife settled in Annandale, Virginia. Having taken up tennis at the age of 60, he held the senior doubles championship twice in Virginia and three times in Northern Virginia. In 1996, when he was 78, he was still an avid skier and tennis player. Mrs. Crockett died on June 24, 2000.

Crockett also enjoys speaking at area schools and civic groups, and has spoken about the Tuskegee Airmen at the Smithsonian Air and Space Museum. Men whose bombers he accompanied are appreciative of his service during the war: "About once a year we have a bomber pilot come up and say, 'If it weren't for you, I probably would not be speaking today,' and that's a good feeling."

In 1994, President Bill Clinton selected Crockett to accompany him to Europe for the celebration of the 50th anniversary of the invasion of Normandy. In Cambridge, England, Crockett led the president down the wall of Missing Airmen, an event that was captured in a front page photograph in *The New York Times.*

Asked whether he still enjoyed flying, Crockett responded: "I haven't flown since [retirement from the military]. I guess I got it out of my system with 20 years' jet time." In summing up his career, particularly the obstacles he encountered because of race, Crockett says: "I . . . could've spent the rest of my life feeling resentment and would've ended up doing nothing. If we'd have waited until the playing field was level, we would've never gotten into the game."

## Sources

Funeral program of Daisy Juanita Mc Murray Crockett, August 30, 1921–June 24, 2000.

Holway, John B. *Red Tails, Black Wings: The Men of America's Black Air Force*. Las Cruces, NM: Yucca Tree Press, 1997.

"Lonely Eagles." Http://www.af.mil/news/airman/0299/tusk2.htm. Accessed March 7, 2000.

Senna, Bethany. "Tuskegee Airman Celebrates 30th Year in Retirement." *The Connection* (Fairfax, Virginia) (February 17–23, 2000).

"Woodrow L. Crockett, Class of 1939." Http://www.uair.edu/-lrsd/crockett.htm. Accessed March 7, 2000.

# Robert L. Curbeam Jr.

Robert L. Curbeam Jr. Courtesy of NASA.

**Born:** March 5, 1962, Baltimore, Maryland

**Education:** Woodlawn High School, Baltimore County, Maryland, 1980; B.S. in aerospace engineering, United States Naval Academy, Annapolis, Maryland, 1984; M.S. in aeronautical engineering, 1990; Degree in aeronautical and astronautical engineering, 1991; Naval Postgraduate School, 1991, Monterey, California.

**Positions Held:** As member of Fighter Squadron 11 (VF-11), made overseas deployments to the Mediterranean and Caribbean Seas, 1986; deployed to the Arctic and Indian Oceans on board the USS *Forrestal* (CV-59); project officer for the F-14A/B Air-to-Ground Weapons Separation Program, Strike Aircraft Test Directorate. Instructor, U.S. Naval Academy, Weapons and Systems Engineering Department, 1994; astronaut, Johnson Space Center, assigned to the Computer Support Branch of the Astronaut Office; mission specialist on STS-85, 1997; currently, spacecraft communicator (CAPCOM)STS-85 (August 7–19, 1997) a 12-day mission during which the crew deployed and retrieved the CRISTA–SPAS payload, operated the Japanese Manipulator Flight Demonstration (MFD) robotic arm, studied changes in the Earth's atmosphere, and tested technology destined for use on the future International Space Station.

**Awards, Honors:** Fighter Wing One Radar Intercept Officer of the Year for 1989, U.S. Naval Test Pilot School Best Developmental Thesis (DT-II) Award, two Navy Commendation Medals, the Navy Meritorious Unit Commendation, the Armed Forces Expeditionary Medal, the National Defense Service Medal, the Navy Battle Efficiency Award, and the Sea Service Deployment Ribbon.

**Summary:** Robert L. Curbeam, a 1984 graduate of the Naval Academy, became a test pilot in 1991 and was chosen for the astronaut program in 1995. Now a spacecraft communicator responsible for relaying voice communication between Mission Control and Space Shuttle crew, he made three space walks during the on-orbit construction of the International Space Station, in February 2001.

## Early Years

Robert L. Curbeam was born in Baltimore on March 5, 1962. He attended local public schools. Even as a small boy, he was interested in airplanes. According to his grandmother, Beatrice Curbeam, he was always "in love with airplanes and cars and things. He just always stuck with it . . . a real smart kid. And he had ideas of his own." His favorite playthings were toy planes; he dreamed of being a flyer. Curbeam attended Woodlawn High School in Baltimore, graduating in 1980.

## Higher Education

In the fall of 1980, Curbeam matriculated at the U.S. Naval Academy, in Annapolis, Maryland. He also attended Navy Fighter Weapons School (Topgun). Upon graduation in 1984, Curbeam commenced Naval Flight Officer training. He attended Test Pilot School and was qualified as a test pilot in December 1991.

## Career Highlights

In 1986, Curbeam reported to Fighter Squadron 11 (VF-11) and made overseas deployments to the Mediterranean and Caribbean Seas and the Arctic and Indian Oceans on board the USS *Forrestal* (CV-59). During his tour in VF-11, upon completion of Test Pilot School in December 1991, he reported to the Strike Aircraft Test Directorate where he was the project officer for the F-14A/B Air-to-Ground Weapons Separation Program. In August 1994, he returned to the U.S. Naval Academy as an instructor in the Weapons and Systems Engineering Department. He applied for the astronaut program and was selected by NASA in December 1994, one of 19 chosen out of 2,962 candidates.

Curbeam reported to the Johnson Space Center in March 1995. He completed a year of training and evaluation and was assigned to the Computer Support Branch of the Astronaut Office. In 1997 he flew as a mission specialist on STS-85. In completing his first flight, Curbeam logged 284 hours and 27 minutes in space.

STS-85 (August 7–19, 1997) was a 12-day mission during which the crew deployed and retrieved the CRISTA–SPAS payload, operated the Japanese Manipulator Flight Demonstration (MFD) robotic arm, studied changes in the Earth's atmosphere and tested technology destined for use on the future International Space Station. The mission was accomplished in 189 Earth orbits, traveling 4.7 million miles in 284 hours and 27 minutes.

Curbeam served as a spacecraft communicator (CAPCOM) responsible for relaying all voice communication between Mission Control and crews aboard the Space Shuttle.

On February 7, 2001 Commander Curbeam was part of the six-person crew on an 11-day mission to install the "Destiny" space laboratory as part of the International Space Station. "Destiny" is the scientific heart of the station and a crucial element to control the entire outpost. The laboratory's size, 28 feet long by 14 feet wide, increases the habitable part of the station by 41 percent. It is intended to handle "cutting edge science experiments over the next 10 to 15 years." Curbeam and Thomas D. Jones made three space walks during the trip to install "Destiny," and to perform the emergency drill known as "the dead guy test." The two took turns at "rescuing" each other, in preparation for the eventuality that an astronaut may become incapacitated.

Curbeam is married to Julie Dawn Lein. The couple and their two children live in Houston, Texas. Curbeam enjoys weightlifting and biking. He is a member of the U.S. Naval Academy Alumni Association and the Association of Old Crows.

## Sources

"Astronauts Bolt Laboratory to Space Station." *New York Times* (February 11, 2001): p 34.

"Astronauts Play Dead Men Space Walking." *New York Times* (February 15, 2001):p 29.

"Black Astronaut Aboard *Discovery* Space Shuttle Slated to Help Build Space Station." *Jet* (August 25, 1997).

"Crew Tears the Wrapping Off Space Lab." *New York Times* (February 12, 2001): p 1, 16.

Lyndon B. Johnson Space Center. "Biographical Data." Http://www.jsc.nasa.gov/Bios/htmlbios/curbeam/html.

"NASA Set to Deliver Station's Scientific Core." *New York Times* (February 6, 2001): p F3.

"STS-85 Crew: Robert L. Curbeam Jr." Http://www.spaceflight.nasa.gov. Accessed July 24, 2000.

# Lemuel R. Custis

Lemuel R. Custis. Courtesy of U.S. Air Force.

**Full Name at Birth:** Lemuel Rodney Custis

**Born:** June 4, 1915, Hartford, Connecticut

**Education:** B.S., Mathematics, Howard University, Washington, D.C., 1938; attended the University of Connecticut School of Law, 1950 or 1951.

**Positions Held:** Policeman, Hartford Police Force, 1939–1940; Squadron Operations Officer, 99th Fighter Squadron, World War II; Tax Department of the State of Connecticut, 1952–1982; chief of sales tax, 1975–1982.

**Awards, Honors:** Distinguished Flying Cross, Air Medal with oak leaf clusters, several campaign medals, African and Italian campaigns, World War II, honored as a pioneer at the "Black Wings" exhibition at the National Air and Space Museum, 1982.

**Summary:** Lemuel R. Custis was one of Tuskegee's first class of five graduates on March 7, 1942. The others were Benjamin O. Davis Jr., Charles H. DeBow Jr., George S. Roberts, and Mac Ross.

## Early Years

Lemuel Rodney Custis was the only child of Mary C. Goodwin Custis and Charles W. Custis, an employee of the Aetna Life Insurance Company in Hartford. He was born on June 4, 1915, and attended public elementary school and high school. As many youngsters do to earn some pocket money, Lemuel Custis had a paper route and he cut the neighbors' lawns.

## Higher Education

Custis earned a degree in mathematics from Howard University in Washington, D.C., in 1938. When Custis completed his time in military service, retiring at the rank of captain in 1947, he returned to the academic world by enrolling at the University of Connecticut's School of Law, which he attended for one year, 1951 or 1952.

## Career Highlights

When Custis graduated from Howard, the country was still in the midst of the Great Depression. He returned to Hartford, then known as "the Insurance Capital of the World," hoping to find employment with one of the city's insurance companies. He began sending out resumés, "knocking on doors for a job," but no jobs were forthcoming. Raised by his parents to be productive and hard working, Custis took a job with the police department, "walking a beat." He thereupon became Hartford's first African American police officer. He preferred that to "standing on a corner, with no money in your pocket." When the U.S. Air Corps began admitting black cadets, Custis "jumped at the chance and never regretted it."

As cadets, Custis and Benjamin O. Davis Jr., both started from ground zero—neither man knew how to fly. The other cadets had learned to fly at Civilian Pilot Training Programs at the colleges they had attended or graduated from. Davis, the son of the army's first black general and a West Point graduate himself, became the leader of the group. Custis called himself, "a real greenie who had to start from scratch. We [himself and Davis] had to climb a little higher mountain than the others did." Custis successfully climbed that mountain and became one of the first five black men, out of the first class of 13 cadets, to become a pilot in the U.S. Army Air Corps. Besides mastering the necessary piloting skills, the men had to pass ground school and be judged for their overall conduct and attitude. Custis told author John Holway, "I was consumed with making it, not washing out. Next to my wife [Ione Williams], flying has been the greatest love of my life."

Appointed squadron operations officer of the 99th Fighter Squadron, Custis served in the European/Mediterranean Theater during World War II. As a pilot, he was in the battle at Anzio, Italy, which established a beachhead there in early 1944. In order to liberate Rome from fascist rule, it was necessary to go through Anzio. That proved to be a critical turning point for the black pilots, as it demonstrated their ability in combat. During that battle, on January 27, 1944, Custis shot down an enemy aircraft, an FW-190.

Normally, pilots flew 50 missions before receiving "R and R," rest and recreation. But the men of the 332nd Fighter Group (the 99th, the 100th, the 301st, and the 302nd squadrons) routinely flew many more. They did not have the luxury of replacements that white pilots had, because so few black pilots had been trained. Custis himself flew 92 missions and he recalls that Howard Baugh flew 135 missions before he was relieved. One of the traditions associated with the 50-mission mark was the "crushed cap." When the pilots had flown that number, they removed the grommets from their caps, which had kept the top stretched flat. Now the caps had a jauntier, devil-may-care look that mirrored the men's achievement. Custis remained in the air force until 1947, when he retired with the rank of captain. His assignments were varied when the war ended, and Custis remarked that the brass "didn't know what to do with us [combat pilots]." The armed forces were not desegregated until 1948, when President Truman issued Executive Order 9981, which was meant to eliminate discrimination in all branches of military service. This was a landmark event in the long battle for the civil rights of African Americans, and the performance of the Tuskegee Airmen played an important part in President Truman's decision.

After the war was over, Custis returned to Tuskegee Army Air Field, where he served as a flight instructor from 1945 to 1946.

Returning to Hartford in 1947, Custis enrolled at the University of Connecticut's School of Law. He remained for about a year, 1950 to 1951. He left the university to take employment with the Tax Department of the state of Connecticut, where he worked for 30 years. In 1975, he became the first African American chief of sales tax, and remained until his retirement in 1982.

In his retirement, Custis kept up his interest in, and love of, aviation. He attended the 25th Annual National Convention of the Tuskegee Airmen in Seattle, Washington, from August 26 to September 1, 1996. He talked to the young pilots who attended and was surprised, but gratified, by their avid interest in the events of 50 years ago in which he had participated. Custis told them, "We were aware of the burden we were carrying, but we were oh-so determined to succeed. It was tough at times, but we had to prove to people we could do anything. All we wanted was an opportunity. When we finally got it, we took it."

Custis is active as an adviser to the Connecticut Aeronautical Historical Association. He was a member of the Board of Directors of the New England Air Museum, near Bradley International Airport, until just recently. He still retains his association with the museum's programs and activities.

## Sources

Cooper, Charlie, and Ann Cooper. *Tuskegee's Heroes: Featuring the Aviation Art of Roy LaGrone.* Osceola, WI: Motorbooks International, 1996.

Custis, Lemuel R., Wethersfield, Connecticut, to Betty K. Gubert, New York, telephone interview and correspondence, April–May 2000.

Harris, Jacqueline. *The Tuskegee Airmen: Black Heroes of World War II.* Parsippany, NJ: Dillon Press, 1996.

Holway, John. *Red Tails Black Wings: The Men of America's Black Air Force.* Las Cruces, NM: Yucca Tree Press, 1997.

McKay, Bud. "Volunteers Inspired by Working with Tuskegee Airmen." Http://www.af.mil/news/Sep 1996/n19960910_960909.html. Accessed April 9, 2000.

# D

## Dorothy Darby

**Born:** Around 1909, Cleveland, Ohio

**Summary:** Dorothy Darby was primarily known as a parachute jumper at air shows. Darby was born around 1909 in Cleveland, Ohio. She was inspired toward a career in aviation by Bessie Coleman, the first black woman pilot in the world. Coleman earned her license in France in 1921 and died in a plane accident in Florida in 1926.

Darby took lessons at the Curtiss-Wright Aeronautical University in Chicago and during the summer of 1932, she made her first parachute jump. After making several successful jumps at exhibitions, Darby met with a serious accident on October 8. Jumping from a plane at the St. Louis, Missouri, airport, she landed badly and broke both her ankles. She suffered internal injuries as well. She recovered, and thereafter she was in demand at air shows, a popular entertainment of the times. She was a parachute jumper with a repertoire of daring stunts. Darby also parachuted for publicity purposes, such as in 1935 at the Joe Louis training camp, for a forthcoming prize fight.

During 1937–1938 she continued flying lessons at the Pontiac Municipal Airport in Michigan. She was granted a pilot's license in 1938. One of the first flights Darby made was on Memorial Day, when she flew over the grave of Bessie Coleman, in honor of the pioneer aviator. This memorial tribute, which included dropping a wreath of flowers over the gravesite, was organized by African American aviators in the Chicago area.

Three weeks later, on June 21, Darby took off from Paterson, New Jersey, on the Joe Louis Victory Flight, to his camp at Pompton Lakes. She delivered 50,000 signatures that had been gathered in Detroit and other cities of Michigan to wish "the Brown Bomber" success with his fight with Max Schmeling in New York.

### Sources

"Girl Flyer Is Injured As She Leaps from Plane." *Chicago Defender* (October 15, 1932): 1.

"Granted Pilot's License." *Chicago Defender* (May 21, 1938): 1.

## Christine Mann Darden

**Full Name at Birth:** Christine Voncile Mann

**Born:** September 10, 1942, Monroe, North Carolina

Christine Mann Darden. Courtesy of National Air and Space Museum, Smithsonian Institution (SI Neg. No. 97-15071).

**Education:** B.S., Hampton Institute, Hampton, Virginia, 1962; M.S., Virginia State College, Petersburg, Virginia, 1967; Doctoral degree in Science, George Washington University, Washington, D.C., 1983.

**Positions Held:** Director, Aero Performing Center Programs, National Aeronautics and Space Center (NASA), Langley Research Center, Hampton, Virginia.

**Summary:** Christine Mann Darden became one of the first black women to pursue a scientific career as an aeronautical engineer, and achieved distinction at the National Aeronautics and Space Administration (NASA). Darden specializes in studying the effects of sonic boom on aircraft design.

## Early Years

Christine Mann was born on September 10, 1942, in Monroe, North Carolina, the youngest of five children of Noah Horace Mann Sr. and Desma Chaney Mann, both schoolteachers. Monroe was a small country town of 7,000, surrounded by cotton fields. Her father left teaching for a job in a publishing firm and then took a position with the North Carolina Mutual Insurance Company and her mother taught at a school in Union County, just outside of Monroe.

When Darden was about three, her mother began to bring her along to the schoolroom where she was teaching. At first, the child was content to play quietly in the back of the classroom, but she soon wanted to join the class in their work. At the age of four, she began second grade work at Winchester Avenue school in Monroe.

She did very well in school and showed unusual mechanical aptitude. Like many children who go on to engineering careers, Darden loved to take things apart to see how they worked, and she learned not only to fix her bicycle but to perform maintenance on the family car. Her hobbies were roller skating, baseball, and playing the piano.

In the 11th grade, Darden transferred to Allen High School, in Asheville, North Carolina. Allen had been founded by the Methodist Church to educate talented minority students. She had always been interested in literature and had been a great reader, but at Allen she discovered an aptitude for mathematics.

## Higher Education

Graduating from high school at 15, Darden entered Hampton Institute, in Hampton, Virginia. Although her primary interest was in mathematics, she majored in education, as opportunities for African American women were few in the mathematics field. She received her bachelor's degree in 1962, graduating with high honors. While at Hampton, she was active in the civil rights movement, participating in sit-ins and working on voter registration drives.

After graduation, she taught junior high

school for a year, at the same time taking evening courses in mathematics at Virginia State College. In 1963, she married Walter L. Darden Jr. After teaching for another year, she decided to pursue her studies full-time at Virginia State, and was able to receive a research assistantship in the physics department. Her research involved the use of light beams to study the proportion of gases and particulate matter in the atmosphere. By observing how light was refracted or absorbed by different elements, the quality of air could be determined. Her research on this topic formed the basis for her master's thesis. In 1967, she received her masters degree.

## Career Highlights

Upon receiving her degree, Darden received several job offers in the field of mathematics. She accepted a position at NASA as a data analyst in 1967. Her job involved solving mathematical problems with the aid of mechanical calculators. However, more modern and complex computers were being developed, and Darden soon began to develop software for these. As she wanted to develop as a scientist and engineer, she soon realized that programing computers was becoming a routine task which could be done by those with much less education than she had, and did not employ her talents to the full.

To gain the educational skills necessary for advancement, she enrolled at George Washington University, which had a branch campus in Hampton, seeking a doctorate in engineering. Hitherto, Darden had attended primarily black colleges, but at George Washington, the students were predominantly white. In her particular field of engineering, there were at that time few African Americans and few women of any race. However, Darden was able to cope with her studies successfully while continuing to work full-time at NASA and caring for her children, two daughters and a stepdaughter.

Her work on her doctorate dovetailed nicely with her current assignment at NASA, which was to study the environmental impact of supersonic transport aircraft (SST). This new design of aircraft, which moved faster than the speed of sound, had many potential problems. The most important of these was sonic boom—a boom caused by a wave of pressure created by the aircraft. This boom was potentially powerful enough to break windows and even damage structures. Darden created a computer program that was able to simulate the effects of various factors in the design of aircraft on sonic boom. This simulation provided an effective and cost-saving method of assessing aircraft design and other factors on sonic boom.

In 1991, the breakup of the Soviet Union ushered in a new era of cooperation between American and Russian space scientists, and Darden was part of that cooperative effort. Darden was an aerospace engineer in the High-Speed Research Program Office, which directed work on technologies to build a new generation supersonic transport.

In September 1998, Darden was named director of aero performing center programs at Langley Research Center. This office's areas of concern include information technology (uses of computers in airplane research, systems, and operations); airspace capacity (research in increasing the air traffic system capacity), and rotorcraft (reducing noise and improving safety of rotorcraft).

## Sources

"Aerodynamics Research Engineer." *Ebony* (January 1985): 7.

"Careers behind the Launchpad." *Black Enterprise* (February 1983): 59–60, 64.

Christine Darden. Http://www.nsf.gov/od/lpa/nstw/kids/cards/world/christin.htm. Accessed January 9, 1999.

Graves, Curtis M., and Ivan Van Sertima. *Blacks in Science.* New Brunswick, NJ: Transaction, 1983.

Kessler, James H. et al. *Distinguished African Ameri-*

*can Scientists of the Twentieth Century.* Phoenix, AZ: Oryx Press, 1996.

Robinson, Rosetta. "Space Is the Place." *Essence* (November 1984): 38.

*Who's Who among Black Americans.* 7th ed. Detroit: Gale Research, 1992.

# A. Porter Davis

A. Porter Davis. Courtesy of A. Portia Davis King and Edward W. King III.

**Full Name at Birth:** Albert Porter Davis

**Born:** November 13, 1890, Palestine, Texas

**Died:** September 1, 1976, Kansas City, Kansas

**Education:** Lincoln High School, Palestine; Meharry Medical College, Nashville, Tennessee, 1913; postgraduate courses at Sumner Junior College and University of Kansas; private pilot's license, 1928.

**Positions Held:** Physician and surgeon for 50 years, Kansas City.

**Awards, Honors:** Dwight H. Green Trophy, 1939; Keynote speaker at NAACP conventions in Junction City, Kansas, 1944 and 1945; President of National Medical Association, 1953.

**Summary:** A. Porter Davis was a pioneer African American aviator, earning a pilot's license in 1928. Financially secure as a doctor, Porter was able to participate in and publicize aviation activities among African Americans.

## Early Years

Albert Porter Davis was born in Palestine, Texas, to Louisa Craven and William W. Davis, a white physician, on November 13, 1890. At Lincoln High School he played football until a knee injury prevented continued participation in the sport.

## Higher Education

After graduating from high school, Davis entered Meharry Medical College in Nashville, Tennessee, and graduated in 1913. Meharry (est. 1876), one of the historically black educational institutions established after the Civil War, answered the need for black physicians. White medical schools only rarely accepted African Americans, certainly not in the numbers required for a population underserved in every way, and routinely denied treatment by white doctors and hospitals. After obtaining his medical degree, Davis moved to Kansas City, where he practiced family medicine and surgery. At that time, it was the practice for students to go to medical school from high school. So Davis continued his studies at Sumner Junior College and the University of Kansas. He kept his medical knowledge up-to-date and pursued other courses as well. He served as lieutenant in the U.S. Army Medical Corps Reserve during World War I. The many interests he followed reveal an enthusiastic and gregarious man: he was a fan of jazz, he wrote music, and in 1921, he starred in *The Lure of a Woman.* The five-reel silent film, shot in black and white, was the first black film produced in Kansas City. The George P. Johnson Collection at UCLA holds three of the five reels.

On September 1, 1926, Davis and Hazel White, a schoolteacher, were married. Their daughter, A. Portia, was born on February 18, 1940. Soon after the marriage, Davis began his quest to fly in earnest. His first instructor was a French flyer, as it was difficult to find white Americans who would teach blacks. Later Davis took flying lessons at the Porterfield Flying School at the Old Richards Air Field in Kansas City, Missouri. On May 16, 1928, Davis received his license, No. 3902. The same day he bought his first plane, an American Eagle, which he kept until 1935. Ed Porterfield, an early aviation enthusiast, built the plane. The U.S. Department of Commerce began licensing pilots only in 1926, making A. Porter Davis one of the earliest licensed pilots of any race. African American licensed pilots were rarer still, as certified by the department itself. Eleven years later in January 1939 it issued a list of 81 licensed black pilots, of whom 46 were students. There were about 50 others who had let their licenses expire.

## Career Highlights

A. Porter Davis was an active pilot involved in aviation activities for much of his life. His career, however, was that of a physician. He engaged in numerous entrepreneurial undertakings and in civil rights activities as well. At the outset of his career, Davis, who spoke Spanish, was able to treat the many Mexican immigrants who had come to build the railroad. He had offices in both Missouri and Kansas, but finally established his office in Kansas, at 422 Minnesota.

Dr. Davis founded the Davis Maternity Sanitarium for Unwed Mothers in 1920, and it operated into the early 1940s. There was a dearth of such facilities for Negro women, and the Davis Sanitarium provided a range

of services that included prenatal care, education, and adoption assistance if requested.

In 1926, Davis became the first Negro to be appointed assistant health director in Kansas City, a post he held until 1932. He served on the staffs of Wheatley-Provident Hospital, General Hospital no. 2 in Kansas City, Missouri, and Douglass Hospital in Kansas City, Kansas. In 1927, Davis founded both the Red Top taxicab company and the Service Finance Corporation, a savings and loan association. Both were the first such black-owned institutions in Kansas. Davis was deputy coroner of Wyandotte County from 1950 to 1952. In 1953, he was elected president of the National Medical Association, the group established by African American physicians in 1895. This parallel institution was founded because black doctors were denied membership in the American Medical Association, which was incorporated in 1847. Also in 1953 Davis built, at a cost of $47,000, the Kansas Trailer Village along Highway 40. It held 50 spaces for permanent and transient tenants, who were all white, and provided amenities such as sidewalks, patios, public showers, a laundromat, streetlights, a playground, and buses to the town school. Davis headed the all-white Wyandotte County Mobile Homes Association in 1956, and he served as the vice president of the local branch of the National Association for the Advancement of Colored People (NAACP.)

A. Porter Davis was a pioneer aviator who learned to fly when aviation was in its infancy, and Americans were just at the dawn of what was called "airmindedness." He earned his license just three years after the U.S. Army's infamous 1925 report declared that Negroes could not fly because they are not smart or strong enough. Probably Davis hadn't read the report, for in 1929 he flew his plane to Yackey Checkerboard Airfield, just outside of Chicago. The Universal Aviation Association sponsored the first national aviation meet of Negro flyers. Davis, however, was the only pilot among seven who was not from Chicago. Returning home, the plane crashed into a tree leaving Davis unhurt, but without a way to get his plane home. He bought a pickup truck, loaded the damaged plane onto it, and drove back to Kansas City.

Davis continued to fly for pleasure, to attend political rallies and speaking engagements, and he often had to land in wheatfields and cow pastures because there were no landing strips. In 1935, he bought his second plane, a Porterfield Cabin Monoplane, and in 1938 he set himself the goal of flying daily for consecutive days. By mid-April, he had flown for 75 days, but the final count is unknown.

Ten years after Davis's 1929 flight to Chicago to meet other black aviators, another such meeting was scheduled, this time more successfully. After months of planning, on August 16, 1937, the National Airmen's Association of America (NAAA) was incorporated in Chicago by Cornelius R. Coffey, Willa B. Brown, Chauncey E. Spencer, Dale L. White, and Harold Hurd, among others. They held an air conference on August 25–27, 1939, to which all licensed "Race" flyers were invited. Some 40 to 50 pilots attended, six of whom flew to Chicago in their own planes. The NAAA's aim was not to conduct a spectacular air show, which was a popular entertainment at the time. Rather, they wanted the conference to provide a chance "for Negro pilots to know each other better socially," and to "discuss problems common to all air pilots, and especially to our particular group. Negro pilots have never met in a national body in this manner . . . it would be a great experience for us."

It was at this conference that A. Porter Davis was awarded the Dwight H. Green Trophy for having contributed the most to the advancement of aviation during 1938. The trophy was named for a Republican Party politician and former army aviator who had fought in World War I. Green later became governor of Illinois from 1941 to 1949.

Davis was also elected one of the seven vice presidents (the NAAA planned to set up local chapters), and he invited them to hold the 1940 conference in Kansas City.

As part of the festivities for the renovation of the Kansas City Municipal Airport in January 1940, Davis flew in his open cockpit Porterfield monoplane. His passenger was his wife, eight months pregnant with their daughter. The following year Davis bought his third plane, also built by Porterfield, a Columbia 75c. By 1950, Davis had logged 2,200 flying hours in the nearly 23 years since he earned his license. His fourth plane was a Navion, which he flew eight to 10 times a month, sometimes making professional calls. Davis reported that it has been 10 years since he "encountered airport Jim Crow."

His health in decline since 1969, A. Porter Davis died on September 1, 1976. In March 1999, Dr. Davis's home at 852 Washington Boulevard was given Historic Landmark status in Wyandotte County, Kansas City, Kansas. Built in 1938, Castle Rock, as the home is known, was cited for its "high integrity of design, workmanship, setting, and association." Continued occupancy by the family has contributed to its preservation. Adding to the home's architectural interest is its history: it had to be built in the downtown area where African Americans were segregated, and not in the location where people of Davis's socioeconomic status lived. When the Davises moved into their new home in 1938, they held an open house for 400 guests. A newspaper article of the time pointed out the unusual modern features: fireproof construction, phone jacks throughout the house, air conditioning, and central heating.

The Kansas City Jazz Museum holds some items relating to Davis's life as an aviator, such as his log book and a restored propeller from one of his planes, as well as other memorabilia.

## Sources

Carras, John. " 'Castle Rock' . . . Is Declared a Landmark." *Kansas City Kansan* (March 28, 1999): 1, 3.

"Doctor Wins Aviation Award." *Chicago Defender* (September 2, 1939): 1, 2.

King, A. Portia Davis, and Edward W. King III, Kansas City, Kansas, to Betty K. Gubert, New York, telephone interviews, e-mail, correspondence, clippings, March–May 1999.

"Private Plane Owners." *Ebony* (December 1950): 76, 78, 80–81.

Ruse, Jim. "KC Doctor a Pioneer in Aviation." *The K.C. Flyer* (July–August 1998): 1, 6.

"Trailer Park Landlord." *Ebony* (August 1956): 107–110.

*Who's Who in Aviation, 1942–43: A Directory of Living Men and Women Who Have Contributed to the Growth of Aviation in the U.S.* Chicago: Ziff-Davis, 1943; 104.

# Benjamin O. Davis Jr.

Benjamin O. Davis Jr. Courtesy of National Air and Space Museum, Smithsonian Institution (SI Neg. No. 94-3550).

**Full Name at Birth:** Benjamin Oliver Davis Jr.

**Born:** December 18, 1912, Washington, D.C.

**Education:** Central High School, Cleveland, Ohio, 1929; Western Reserve University, Cleveland, 1929–1930; University of Chicago, 1930–1931; U.S. Military Academy, West Point, New York, B.S., 1936; Infantry School, Fort Benning, Georgia, 1938; Advanced Flying School, U.S. Army Air Corps, Tuskegee, Alabama, March 6, 1942; Air War College, Maxwell AFB, Alabama, 1949; advanced fighter gunnery school, Nellis AFB, Nevada, 1953.

**Positions Held:** Army of the United States, 1936–1941, including instructor of military science, Tuskegee Institute, 1938–1941; aide to General Benjamin O. Davis Sr., 1941; U.S. Army Air Corps, 1942–1948, commands included 99th Fighter Squadron, 1942–1943; 332nd Fighter Group, 1943–1945; 477th Composite Group, 1945–1946; Lockbourne AFB, Ohio, 1946–1947; U.S. Air Force, 1949–1970, commands included 51st Fighter Interceptor Wing, South Korea, 1953–1954; vice commander, Air Task Force 13 (Provisional), Taipei, Formosa, 1955–1957; deputy chief of staff for operations, Headquarters, USAFE, Wiesbaden, Germany, 1957–1961; chief of staff, United Nations Command and U.S. Forces in Korea, 1965–1967; commander, 13th Air Force, Clark AFB, Phillippines, 1967–1968; deputy commander in chief, U.S. Strike Command, MacDill AFB, Florida, 1968–1970; director of public safety, city of Cleveland, Ohio, 1970; director, Office of Civil Aviation; director, United States Department of Transportation, 1970–1971; assistant secretary for Environment, Safety and Consumer Affairs, U.S. Dept. of Transportation, 1971–1975; Member, Presidential Commission on Military Compensation, 1977; American Battle Monuments Commission, 1978; Board of Visitors, U.S. Military Academy (USMA) at West Point, 1994–1998?; president, Board of Visitors, USMA, 1995–    .

**Awards, Honors:** Distinguished Service Medal with two oak leaf clusters; Silver Star; Distinguished Flying Cross, Legion of Merit with two oak leaf clusters; Air Medal with five oak leaf clusters; Croix de Guerre with Palm; Star of Africa; honorary degrees include DMilSc, Wilberforce University, 1948; LLD, Tuskegee Institute, 1963; honored as a pioneer at the "Black Wings" exhibition, National Air and Space Museum, 1982; Alabama Aviation Hall of Fame, 1986; Virginia Aviation Hall of Fame; National Aviation Hall of Fame, 1994.

**Summary:** Davis, a West Point graduate, became commander of the 332nd Fighter Group, the "Tuskegee Airmen," in World War II and, by proving through the men he commanded that African Americans could excel as combat pilots, was instrumental in the eventual integration of U.S. military services. Davis remained on active military duty until his 1970 retirement from the U.S. Air Force at the rank of lieutenant general; he was awarded the fourth star of a full general in 1998.

## Early Years

Born in 1912, Benjamin O. Davis Jr., was the second child and only son of Elnora Dickerson Davis and Benjamin O. Davis Sr., a career Army officer who retired in 1948 with the rank of brigadier general. Elnora Dickerson Davis traveled from Wyoming, where B.O. Davis Sr., was stationed at Fort D.A. Russell as a second lieutenant of cavalry, to the family home in Washington, D.C., for the baby's birth. She then returned to Wyoming with Benjamin Jr., and his older sister Olive. "This kind of extra effort was typical of the Davises," Davis remarked in his autobiography.

Davis's mother died in 1916, a few days after the birth of his sister Elnora. Shortly thereafter, his father, now a lieutenant colonel, received orders for transfer to service in the Phillippines. Davis and his sisters were sent to live with their paternal grandparents in Washington. In 1919, Davis's father married a family friend, Sadie Overton, and the following year was assigned to Tuskegee Institute in Alabama, in a strictly segregationist area.

In the early 1920s, an event occurred that Davis remembered as "the night of the Klan." Protesting the construction of a hospital for African American veterans near Tuskegee Institute, the Ku Klux Klan announced a march in support of all-white staffing of the hospital. The institute officially instructed its employees to remain indoors, without lights, in order not to provoke the Klansmen. But Lieutenant Colonel Davis refused to hide and, on the night of the demonstration, the entire Davis family sat quietly on their front porch, the colonel "resplendent in his white dress uniform." The only lights visible in the area were the Davis's porch light and the flaming torches of the Klansmen passing just feet away in their masked and hooded white robes.

When Colonel Davis's tour at Tuskegee was completed in 1924, the family moved to his next assignment in Cleveland, Ohio, where Davis entered Central High School.

In the summer of 1926, while the Davises were visiting family in Washington, Davis's uncle took him to Bolling Field to watch an air show. Davis convinced his father to take him to the airfield again, and to spend five dollars for an airplane ride. "[My father] was not a frivolous spender, and $5 was a considerable sum. . . . I can only guess that he was looking far into the future and . . . realized in some mysterious way that I would benefit from the experience." Davis remembered little of that first flight other than the takeoff, the exhilaration of looking down at the city of Washington, and "a sudden surge of determination to become an aviator."

Davis worked at a variety of jobs during

high school, including a newspaper route that, Davis recalled, "certainly developed my voice." With a close friend, Davis bought his first car for $25; but the two forgot to add sufficient oil and the engine froze. Davis graduated from Cleveland High School in 1929 at the age of 16, president of the student council and first in his class.

## Higher Education

Davis enrolled at Western Reserve University in the fall of 1929, but he had little interest in his intended major, mathematics. He still wanted to be an aviator, but there was little hope that, as an African American, he could become a professional pilot. He considered becoming an engineer and pursuing a career in South America, as other African Americans had done. In the spring of 1931, however, his intentions clarified, and he determined to apply to the U.S. Military Academy at West Point.

As a first step, he moved to Chicago, to establish residency in the home state of Congressman Oscar De Priest, the only African American congressman at the time. He thus became eligible for De Priest to appoint him to West Point. In the fall of 1930, Davis enrolled at the University of Chicago, and took the entrance examinations for West Point in February 1931. Notification that he had failed his exams only crystallized Davis's determination. "I fully resolved to go to West Point, graduate, and seek a career in the Army Air Corps; I never had further doubts of any kind about my future, which I was completely convinced lay in the military service." Studying intensively for the next year, Davis repeated the examinations, passed with high grades, and reported to West Point on July 1, 1932.

Shortly after his arrival, however, Davis realized that his experience would not be the same as other cadets':

> Apparently certain upperclass cadets had determined that . . . they were going to enforce an old West Point tradition—"silencing"—with the object of making my life so unhappy that I would resign. Silencing had been applied in the past to certain cadets who were considered to have violated the honor code. . . . In my case there was no question of such a violation. . . . I was to be silenced solely because cadets did not want blacks at West Point. Their only purpose was to freeze me out. What they did not realize was that I was stubborn enough to put up with their treatment to reach the goal I had come to attain.

For four years, Davis roomed alone and was spoken to by no one except in the line of duty.

Davis applied for the U.S. Army Air Corps in late 1935 and was rejected. There were no African American units in the Air Corps. He graduated from West Point on June 12, 1936, ranked 35th in a class of 276, and was commissioned as a second lieutenant in the infantry, with orders to report to the 24th Infantry Regiment at Fort Benning, Georgia, on September 12.

## Career Highlights

On June 20, 1936, Davis married Agatha Scott of New Haven, Connecticut, whom he had first met in Chicago during Christmas leave, 1933. The last two years of his silencing had been in some part alleviated by her frequent visits to West Point.

Reporting to Fort Benning in September 1936, the newly wed Davises found that the silencing of West Point was continued in the regular Army, and that they were excluded from social activities on the base. To a greater or lesser extent, the silencing would continue until the integration of the military services was decreed in 1948.

In 1937, Davis was detailed to Infantry School at Fort Benning, a year earlier than was customary. Following his graduation in

1938, he was assigned to Tuskegee Institute as an instructor of military science.

In early 1941, Davis was reassigned to Fort Riley, Kansas, as aide to his father, now a brigadier general in command of the 4th Cavalry Regiment. Shortly after Davis's arrival at Fort Riley, however, the chief of the Army Air Corps requested Davis's release for pilot training. The Roosevelt administration had directed the War Department to form an African American flying unit, later known as the 99th Pursuit Squadron. Davis was to command the squadron.

Davis returned to Tuskegee in the late spring, and the first class started ground training in July 1941 and flight training the following month. Five members of that first class graduated on March 7, 1942, and continued training at Tuskegee Army Air Field through the spring. In May Davis received three sets of orders. The first promoted him to the rank of major; the second, to the rank of lieutenant colonel. Both of these were retroactive to March 1, 1942, the date on which the rest of the West Point class of 1936 were promoted to lieutenant colonel. The third order designated Davis as commander of the 99th Pursuit Squadron.

As additional pilot classes graduated, the 99th reached its full strength in July 1942. Training rigorously under Davis's command, the 99th was deployed to North Africa in spring 1943. They flew their first combat missions in early June and were part of the repeated attacks against the island of Pantelleria, which surrendered on June 11, the first defended position ever defeated solely by air power.

Davis led a 12-plane escort over Sicily on July 2; on that mission, Lieutenant Charles Hall shot down an enemy fighter, the first time that an African American pilot had done so. The 99th's base of operations was moved to Sicily in July, after that island's invasion.

Davis was unexpectedly recalled to the United States in September 1943, to assume command of the 332nd Fighter Group, then stationed at Selfridge AFB, Michigan. On his arrival in the United States, however, he learned that Army Air Force officials were still skeptical of African American pilots' combat abilities and were preparing to remove the 99th and other African American flight forces from any combat position. Davis vigorously defended the combat record and capabilities of the 99th before a Pentagon committee; the African American flight forces remained in place.

Assuming command of the 332nd on October 7, 1943, Davis trained the group to combat readiness; they were deployed to the Mediterranean theater in December 1943. Arriving in Italy early in 1944, the 332nd was transferred to the 15th Fighter Command in May, charged with offensive fighter missions. On May 29, 1944, Davis was promoted to colonel. In late June, the 99th was transferred from the 12th Air Force to the 15th, joining the 100th, 301st and 302nd squadrons as part of the 332nd Fighter Group.

Davis stressed repeatedly that the 332nd was not to chase the enemy for personal glory, but to stay with the bombers they escorted. "I never considered wandering off, and I'm a pretty independent person," Lee A. Archer Jr. would recall. "Some of the people I knew, who were *extremely* independent, would not take on Colonel Davis." Another of Davis's men recalled, "He stressed the awful price of failure. He brooked none, and he got none." Captain George "Spanky" Roberts, Davis's second in command, described Davis as "very bright, ambitious, and self-controlled, which in my opinion was a result of his Academy days. His intensity to achieve made many people think of him as a martinet. That made him [seem] cold, and he's not; he's a very warm person. . . . Davis led every major raid when he was in Europe. Usually we alternated, but if there were two biggies in a row, he'd take both of them. He considered the place of a leader to be out in front."

Under Davis's rigorous leadership, the

332nd held a record unequalled by any other fighter group in World War II: they never lost a single bomber under their escort. The 332nd remained in action until the end of the war in Europe in May 1945.

Davis returned to the United States in June 1945 to command the 477th Composite Group at Goodman Field, Kentucky, and later assumed command of Goodman Field. In March 1946, he assumed command of Lockbourne AFB, near Columbus, Ohio. In July 1947, he retained command of the 332nd Fighter Wing, stationed at Lockbourne.

In early May 1949, the Air Force issued its historic Letter 35–3, that "there shall be equality of treatment and opportunity for all persons in the Air Force." Immediately thereafter, Davis was detailed to attend the prestigious Air War College at Maxwell AFB, Alabama. After graduation, he served as a planning officer within the Air Force Directorate of Operations at its headquarters in Washington.

Davis went on to command the 51st Fighter Interceptor Wing in South Korea in 1953. In 1954, he was promoted to the rank of brigadier general, and became commander of Air Task Force 13 (Provisional) in Taiwan from 1955 to 1957, where he had to create and develop a force to defend against a Chinese Communist attack. Moving on to assignments in Germany, Davis was advanced to major general in December 1957 and assigned as deputy chief of staff for operations at the USAF headquarters in Wiesbaden, where he remained until 1961.

Returning to Washington for a four-year assignment at USAF headquarters, Davis received his third star, that of major general, in 1965, and was assigned as chief of staff of the United Nations Command and U.S. Forces in Korea. Two years later he assumed command of the 13th Air Force at Clark AFB in the Philippines, 1967. His last assignment was as deputy commander in chief, U.S. Strike Command, and concurrently, deputy commander in chief for the Middle East, Southern Asia and Africa south of the Sahara, based at McDill AFB in Florida.

Retiring from active military service on February 1, 1970, Davis served briefly as director of public safety for the city of Cleveland, Ohio, before joining the U.S. Department of Transportation, where he served first as director of civil aviation security and later as assistant secretary for environment, safety and consumer affairs. He was instrumental in instituting airport procedures to counteract the series of aircraft hijackings taking place at the time, and active in the early encouragement of the national 55-mile-per-hour speed limit. He retired from the civil service in 1975.

Davis refused a request in the early 1970s that his portrait be painted for prominent display at West Point. In his refusal, Davis wrote, "I . . . belong to the school that would treat all servicemen alike in every respect and in no way take official notice of their race. . . . [I]t would be inconsistent for me to have my portrait displayed as 'a source of both satisfaction and inspiration' for black cadets, the reason simply being that there is a strong implication of the existence of a separate group in the Corps of Cadets."

In his autobiography, Davis agreed with President Theodore Roosevelt's remark that "divisive nomenclature," which identifies people by ethnic group, diminishes Americanism. "We are all simply Americans," wrote Davis. "I do not find it complimentary to me or to the nation to be called 'the first black West Point graduate in [the twentieth] century.' "

In his retirement, Davis continued to be active in matters of aviation and education, serving as a member of the Presidential Commission on Military Compensation and of the American Battle Monuments Commission, among others, and playing an advisory role during the formation of the Smithsonian Institution's seminal "Black Wings" exhibition in 1982. Appointed to the U.S. Military Academy's Board of Visitors by President

Clinton in 1994, he became the board's president in 1995.

On December 9, 1998, President Clinton awarded Davis his fourth star, elevating him to the rank of full general.

The December 6, 1999, issue of *Jet* magazine reported that both General and Mrs. Davis had been admitted to Walter Reed Hospital with Alzheimer's disease.

### Sources

*Benjamin O. Davis Jr., American: The Video.* Videocassette. Smithsonian Institution Press, Video Division, 1991.

Booker, Simeon. "Ticker Tape." *Jet* (December 6, 1999): 10.

Davis, Benjamin O. Jr. *Benjamin O. Davis Jr., American: An Autobiography.* Washington, DC: Smithsonian Institution Press, 1991.

"Davis, Benjamin O(liver) Jr." *Current Biography.* New York: H.W. Wilson, 1955; 150–152.

"Davis, Benjamin Oliver Jr.—1994." National Aviation Hall of Fame. 1997. Http://www.national aviation.org/enshrinee/davis.html. Accessed June 13, 2000.

Goldsworthy, Joan. "Benjamin O. Davis Jr." *Contemporary Black Biography.* Detroit: Gale Research, 1994. Vol 2: 51–53.

Holway, John B. *Red Tails, Black Wings: The Men of America's Black Air Force.* Las Cruces, NM: Yucca Tree Press, 1997.

*Who's Who among African Americans.* 12th ed. Detroit: Gale Research, 1999; 320.

# Charles H. DeBow Jr.

**Full Name at Birth:** Charles Henry DeBow Jr.

**Born:** February 13, 1918, Indianapolis, Indiana

**Died:** April 4, 1986, Indianapolis

**Education:** Crispus Attucks High School [1936]; Indiana University, premedical studies [1936–1938]; Hampton Institute, Virginia, business subjects and private pilot's license [1938–1940]; master's degrees, Butler University, Indianapolis; Indiana University, Bloomington.

**Positions Held:** Commander (Captain), 301st Fighter Squadron, Italy, 1943–1944; teacher of English, high schools in Indianapolis; associate lecturer in English, Indiana University-Purdue University [early 1980s]; equal employment opportunity specialist, U.S. Department of Labor.

**Awards, Honors:** Invited by President Reagan to attend the launch of the space shuttle *Challenger*, August 1983.

**Summary:** Charles H. DeBow Jr. was one of Tuskegee's first class of five graduates on March 7, 1942. The others were Benjamin O. Davis Jr., Lemuel R. Custis, George S. Roberts Sr., and Mac Ross. DeBow commanded the 301st Fighter Squadron in Italy in 1943–1944.

### Early Years

Charles Henry DeBow Jr. was born on February 13, 1918, in Indianapolis. It could not be determined if there were siblings other than Mary Elizabeth Winston, who survived him at the time of his death. His father was a porter in a white barbershop, and his mother worked as a maid in a department store. Education was valued in the DeBow home, and his parents "gave up comforts and vacations to see [him] through school." Young DeBow worked, too; at the age of seven, he started delivering newspapers. In high school, he delivered orders for a drug store, between the hours of four and midnight. Later, he did stints as a janitor and general utility man at a shoe store. DeBow wrote in *The American Magazine*, "Studies came fairly easy, and I spent an abnormal amount of time, in class and out, daydreaming. Mostly about flying." Flying became a symbol of liberation, emancipation from crowded streets and rooms. He built model airplanes and dreamed of "smashing speed records." While still in high school, DeBow tried to enlist in the U.S. Army. He was turned down at least six times because, "There just wasn't room for Negroes."

## Higher Education

After his graduation from Crispus Attucks High School, DeBow entered Indiana University to major in premedical studies, as his parents wished. Although they sent him a monthly allowance, he still needed part-time jobs to meet college expenses. Office work and washing dishes for a white fraternity saw him through. After two years, DeBow decided that medicine was not for him, and that he "wanted to go to a colored school where no doors would be closed to me." He transferred to Hampton Institute, now University, in Virginia, and changed his major to business subjects. During the fall of his second year, 1939, Hampton was selected as a Civilian Pilot Training Program (CPTP) site. The federal government established the CPTP at more than 200 colleges and universities to have a ready supply of trained pilots for the war that was on the horizon. DeBow passed all the exams, got his parents' consent, and became one of the 20 students who were chosen from among the 300 applicants. During one of his first flights, DeBow experienced a shiver of exhilaration shooting through his spine when he realized, *That ship was tilting because I was making it tilt.* Man alive, I was flying."

Once DeBow had soloed 35 hours to obtain his private pilot's license in 1940, he knew he couldn't meet the expenses of both college life and flying lessons. Flying lessons won out, and on January 2, 1941, DeBow moved to Chicago where there were "plenty of colored fields where I could rent a plane." He worked as an oven operator in a steel manufacturing factory to pay for the hours of air time he needed to keep his license current.

Before DeBow moved to Chicago, he sent an application to the War Department, even though they were not accepting African Americans as pilots. But soon after, the policy was reversed, and DeBow wrote again. This time he was appointed to the first class of Negro cadets who were to be trained at Tuskegee, Alabama.

When DeBow arrived at Tuskegee Army Air Field in 1941, he was in a class of 13 students. The preflight course lasted five weeks, from five in the morning until ten at night. Then came Basic Training, and after that, Advanced Training. On Graduation Day, March 7, 1942, there were only five men left to receive those "bright silver wings that had never been awarded to any colored men before." Later, on a street in nearby Montgomery, a white passerby asked him, "What do you boys want to fly for anyhow?" DeBow mulled the question over and he decided he was fighting for a democratic future instead of a fascist future, for his mother and father who made many sacrifices for him, and "for every one of the 12,000,000 Negroes in the United States." He continued, "all of us at Tuskegee feel that way. We've got a double duty—to our country and to our race." DeBow included Tuskegee's support staff as well as the ground crews, doctors, executive officers, radio specialists, and supply men.

## Career Highlights

When the black pilots were sent to Italy in 1943, DeBow was named Commander of the 301st Fighter Squadron. He was promoted to captain, and he flew 52 combat missions over Germany. He also flew support missions for the Italian and D-Day (June 6, 1944) invasions.

After the war ended, DeBow returned to Indianapolis and earned master's degrees from Butler University in Indianapolis, and from Indiana University at Bloomington. He joined the Air Force Reserve, but teaching English in high school became his postwar career. He taught at his alma mater, Crispus Attucks High School, as well as at School

No. 26 and Thomas Carr Howe High School. He also held the position of associate lecturer in English at Indiana University-Purdue University for several years before his death. In 1981, DeBow worked for the U.S. Department of Labor, as an equal employment opportunity specialist.

He and his wife Aurelia Jane Stewart DeBow had seven children: Charles H. DeBow III, William, Johnathon, Kay DeBow-Alford, Emily, LeCheryl Smith, and Myra Mason. A stepdaughter, Natalie Jane Brown, completed the family.

### Sources

"Charles DeBow Mourned; One of 1st Black Airmen." *Indianapolis Star* (April 13, 1986).

"Charles DeBow, 68, Dies; Was Original Tuskegee Airman." *Indianapolis Recorder* (April 26, 1986): 10.

"Charles H. DeBow Jr." *New York Times* (April 15, 1986).

Cooper, Charlie, and Ann Cooper. *Tuskegee's Heroes: Featuring the Aviation Art of Roy LeGrone.* Osceola, WI: Motorbooks International, 1996.

DeBow, Charles [as told to William A.H. Birnie]. "I Got Wings." *The American Magazine* (August 1942): 28–29, 104–105.

Wills, Edward. "Blacks Fought Prejudice As well As Axis to Become Pilots in World War II." *Indianapolis Star* (February 15, 1981): Section 2, 1, 10.

# Robert W. Deiz

**Full Name at Birth:** Robert William Deiz

**Born:** June 17, 1919, Portland, Oregon

**Died:** April 6, 1992, Columbus, Ohio

**Education:** Franklin High School, Portland, 1937; University of Oregon, attended [1937–1938]; University of Omaha, graduated in 1959; Army Command and General Staff School, Fort Leavenworth, Kansas.

**Positions Held:** U.S. Army Air Corps/Air Force, 1941–1961, retired as major; Cambridge Research Center, Massachusetts, mid-

Robert W. Deiz. Courtesy of U.S. Air Force.

1950s; researcher, Weapons Analysis Group, North American Aviation, Columbus, 1961–1964; parole officer, 1964–1967, parole supervisor, 1967–198?, Ohio Adult Parole Authority.

**Awards, Honors:** Air Medal; Portrait on wartime poster, "Keep Us Flying!"

**Summary:** Robert W. Deiz was one of the first Tuskegee Airmen, graduating in September 1942. Responsible for the downing of two enemy planes in 1944, Deiz was also among the first Air Force pilots to test jet aircraft. His portrait is featured on one of the popular wartime posters, "Keep Us Flying! Buy War Bonds."

### Early Years

Robert William Deiz was born on June 17, 1919, to Elnora Foster Deiz and William Carlos Deiz, in Portland. Their second son, Carl Henry, completed the family when he was born in December 1920. Their father had emigrated from Jamaica, West Indies, and worked as a waiter on the Union Pacific Railroad. When Deiz was six, his mother taught him to play the piano, but because he wouldn't practice, they tried the violin next. Deiz had a good ear for music and he couldn't stand the wrong notes he played on the violin.

When he reached Franklin High School, he played football. He also set track records in both the 100-yard dash and the 220-yard race, as well as in relay races. He now turned to a new musical instrument, the trombone. Since there were too many trombonists, Deiz chose the bass horn.

## Higher Education

Deiz, the recipient of a track scholarship, enrolled at the University of Oregon after his high school graduation. He played a number of instruments—tuba, bass viol, double bass, and sousaphone—proficiently enough to be included as a member of both the Portland Junior Symphony and of the University's orchestra. About 1939–1940, Deiz learned to fly through the Civilian Pilot Training Program (CPTP), a plan instituted by the federal government to ensure a ready supply of trained pilots for the war that was beginning to seem inevitable. He already had about 300 hours of flying time when he was accepted into the Air Cadets training course at Tuskegee, Alabama. He earned his silver wings, the designation of pilot with the rank of second lieutenant, on September 6, 1942. His younger brother, Carl, was a supply officer at Tuskegee, and he earned a private pilot's license near the end of the war.

Deiz left the University of Oregon in his junior year to enlist in the service. After the war he earned a degree from the University of Omaha in 1959. While at Tuskegee Army Air Field, Deiz was chosen as the model for a poster the U.S. Treasury Department produced to aid the war effort. It portrays Deiz in uniform, with cap, goggles, and his para-chute strapped on. He is looking upward, against a background of vivid blue sky. The text on the poster reads "Keep Us Flying! Buy War Bonds."

## Career Highlights

Deiz's unit, the 99th Pursuit Squadron, was assigned to combat in Italy in 1943 and 1944, under the command of Benjamin O. Davis Jr. and, later, George S. Roberts. Before going overseas Deiz and Ruby Butler were married. They had one son, Robert Everett.

While in Italy Deiz flew 93 missions with the 332nd Fighter Group, which was made up of the 99th, 100th, 301st, and 302nd pursuit squadrons. In 1944 he shot down two German fighter planes, one each on January 27th and January 28th. Other actions he saw were the bombing and strafing missions during the battle of Anzio, fought in January and February. A war correspondent for the newspaper *PM*, reporting from the front, described Deiz as "this Spanish-looking youth," who "has as varied talents as any man I have met in the U.S. Army." He then noted Deiz's prewar accomplishments in music, and his teaching of painting and sculpture in classes of an adult education project in Portland. Deiz told the correspondent, "It irks us when people refer to us as an experiment. We are not conceited, but we feel we can fly as well as anybody else."

In an interview nearly 50 years later (Mahar 1992) Deiz still felt that way about the "Tuskegee Experiment," so called because the military establishment, as well as civilian society, did not really believe blacks could succeed as pilots. "Among those in control, some wanted to see us succeed, and others wanted to see us fail. For a while, the ones who wanted to see us fail had the upper hand. We couldn't get near combat. [The black pilots were not sent into combat until 1943; they just kept on training.] But combat came to us. . . . At Anzio, we got the job of protecting the beachhead. After that, they couldn't ignore us." Deiz added that "Prejudice made it a lot tougher for a black fellow to get his wings. It made us the best of the best, and helped to create a strong fighting force." Carl Deiz judged his brother, "a very careful pilot" and although he could perform daring stunts, he was "the soul of propriety" when he flew.

After the war ended in 1945, Deiz was sent to Tuskegee as an instructor. He decided to remain in the Air Force, as it became known in 1949. As a test pilot he was among the first to fly jet aircraft. In the mid-1950s, he was with the Cambridge Research Center in Massachusetts, working on more efficient landing procedures for planes when air traffic was heavy. Deiz had risen to the rank of major by the time he retired in 1961. He settled in Columbus, Ohio, and went into aeronautical research. He told author John B. Holway, who called him "a reluctant warrior," in his book, *Red Tails Black Wings*, "I was more proud of what I did after I got out of fighters and into flying experimental planes and into electronic research. I was at Cambridge Research Center, and then at North American Aviation, in their weapons analysis group." Deiz worked at North American Aviation, in Columbus, from 1961 until 1964. In his after-work hours he played in the company's orchestra, just as he did in community orchestras as he moved from one air force assignment to another.

From then until 1967, Deiz was a parole officer for the Ohio Adult Parole Authority. He then became a supervisor for the agency for the next 17 years, until his last retirement in 1984. Among his activities in retirement, until his death of a heart attack in 1992, were work as a volunteer for the local chapter of the American Cancer Society, and playing with the Columbus Orchestral Society. He also served on a suicide hotline, but gave that up after a year and a half because, "It gets you down after a while. When you look at the average Negro pilot, you're looking at a guy who has his sanity. But he fought

for it. If we let the things we went through bother us, we would be a bunch of nuts walking around."

## Sources

Deiz, Carl H., Portland, Oregon, telephone interviews with Betty K. Gubert, New York, March–April 2000.

Deiz, Ruby, Columbus, Ohio, telephone interview with Betty K. Gubert, New York, April 21, 2000.

Holway, John B. *Red Tails Black Wings: The Men of America's Black Air Force*. Las Cruces, NM: Yucca Tree Press, 1997; 94–97, 303–304, and passim.

Knickerbocker, H.R. "Few Air Squadrons Work Harder than Modest 99th." *PM* (New York) (February 17, 1944).

———. "Negro Flyers Bat Down 16 Planes at Beachhead." *PM* (New York) (February 16, 1944).

Mahar, Ted. "Robert W. Deiz, Ex-Track Star, WWII Fighter Pilot, Dies at 72." *The Oregonian* (April 8, 1992): D7.

"Service Planned for One of Original Tuskegee Airmen." *Columbus Dispatch* (April 8, 1992): 6B.

# Elwood T. Driver

**Full Name at Birth:** Elwood Thomas Driver

**Born:** August 20, 1921, Trenton, New Jersey

**Died:** March 26, 1992, Reston, Virginia; buried in Arlington National Cemetery.

**Education:** B.S., Trenton State Teacher's College (now The College of New Jersey), 1942; Masters in Safety Engineering, New York University.

**Positions Held:** Joined the Army Air Corps in 1942 as one of the Tuskegee airmen; served in the 99th Fighter Squadron; transferred to the Air Force in 1947; stationed in the United States and Japan; retired in 1962 with the rank of major; worked for North American Aviation in Anaheim, California, until 1967; director of crash worthiness and crash avoidance, National Traffic Safety Administration; Department of Transportation; appointed to the National Transportation

Safety Board; served as vice chairman until 1981; senior consultant, Institute of Safety Analysis 1981–1986; director of the aircraft management office of the National Aeronautics and Space Administration (NASA), 1986–1991, president, Elwood T. Driver and Associates, 1982–1992.

**Awards, Honors:** Air Medal with clusters, 1943; Distinguished Flying Cross, 1943; Commendation Medal, 1962; Certificate of Achievement in North American Aviation, 1965; Special Achievement Award, U.S. government, 1970.

## Early Years

Elwood Thomas Driver was born on August 20, 1921, in Trenton, New Jersey, one of four children of Robert Thomas Driver and Mary Susan Morris Driver. As a youngster, "Woody," as he was known, worked as a newspaper delivery boy and a grocery delivery boy. He was a member of the Boy Scouts Mounted Troop, affiliated with the 112th Field Artillery in Eggert Crossing, New Jersey, and an expert horseman. He excelled at scouting, becoming an Eagle Scout and a Life Scout, and attended a Boy Scout Jamboree in Holland, one of the first boys from New Jersey to attend an international jamboree.

## Higher Education

Driver graduated from Trenton Central High School and won a scholarship to Rutgers University, but he was unable to attend, as the scholarship did not cover room and board. By working three jobs, he was able to finance his education at Trenton State Teachers College (now The College of New Jersey). He received his bachelor's degree in 1942. He later received a master's degree in safety engineering from New York University. Driver was the first black person to learn to fly at Mercer County airport, where he washed planes in exchange for flying lessons.

A gift of $50 from one of his college professors allowed him to train on a Piper Cub.

## Career Highlights

In 1939, the federal government came to the realization that the United States would inevitably be involved in the war that was beginning in Europe. The military would need pilots to fight the war successfully, and there was a shortage of trained men. Furthermore, it was a time-consuming process to train a pilot properly, a process that took months. Pilot training was expensive as well, and many of those who might be interested could not afford the cost. To get around these difficulties, the Civilian Pilot Training Program (CPTP) was established. At first, participation was limited to white men, but under intense political pressure, the government relented and set up separate programs for African Americans. The United States had entered World War II in December 1941 after the attack on Pearl Harbor, and upon graduating from college in 1942, Driver applied to the Naval Academy. Though he ranked first on the exam, he was denied admission on the grounds of his race. He immediately joined the Army Air Corps. He was sent to the Tuskegee Institute, Tuskegee, Alabama, for basic training and flight instruction. Because the Tuskegee Institute already had in place a civilian pilot training program, Tuskegee had been given a contract to train black pilots for the armed forces. Driver was graduated in October 1942 in the class of 42-I, and was assigned to the 332nd Fighter Group.

In August 1943, Driver was sent to Lacarta, Sicily, as a replacement pilot with the 99th Fighter Squadron. Spann Watson, who conducted his combat flight orientation, described him as "an alert and outstanding pilot who had the guts to fight with an airplane."

The 99th was assigned to patrol the Anzio-Nettuno beachhead during the Allied attack on Anzio, a task which involved vicious dogfights with the German air force. The squadron acquitted itself with honor and distinction, downing a total of 16 German planes. Driver shot down a German FW-190 over Anzio Beach on February 14, 1944. A *Chicago Defender*, February 19, 1944, interview about this incident quotes Driver: "It was over the beach. There were seven of us and 17 Focke-Wulfs, and when I saw them they were pulling out at 300 feet. I made a diving left turn and got on the tail of one at about 100 yards distance, but he was faster than my plane . . . but I kept shooting long bursts. . . . My ammunition began to run out and all my machine guns quit on me, except one. At that very moment when I had given up hope of getting him, he began to burn." Driver had flown 43 missions at the time. In all, he flew 123 combat missions during the course of the war. For his heroism, he received the Air Medal with clusters and the Distinguished Flying Cross. At the end of the war, Driver elected to remain in the service. In 1947, he transferred from the Army to the U.S. Air Force, which had just been organized as a separate branch of service.

In 1947, both his parents died, two months apart, and he became responsible for his young sister, Barbara. He also influenced both his brothers toward military careers; Russell became a cadet at Tuskegee Air Base and Earl joined the U.S. Marines. There were great changes in the transportation field in the early postwar period. Air travel was rapidly replacing other means of transportation, particularly over long distances. A trip from New York to California, for instance, which would have taken days by rail, car, or bus, took only a few hours by plane. In 1941, a total of 134,405,836 passenger miles were flown; in 1946, the first year after the war, there were 309,888,684. And the number was rapidly rising. With so many passengers involved, and with the increase in all modes of travel resulting from the end of the war and the expanding economy, issues of safety became of paramount importance. Safety of aircraft was also of vital importance to the

military, which began to expand its capabilities with the advent of the Cold War between the United States and the Soviet Union.

This increased emphasis on safety dovetailed neatly with Driver's experience. He had long been educating himself and developing expertise in safety issues. This specialization would influence his career for the rest of his life. His next Air Force assignment was as assistant director of safety training and safety engineering, 1949–1953. From 1954 to 1956, he was director of safety, Far East Logistic Forces, Japan. He then served as commander, Shows Air Station, from 1956–1958. In addition, he flew aircraft missions in Korea from 1954 to 1956.

In 1960, he married Shirley Martin, a professional social worker. It was the second marriage for both of them. There were no children from this marriage, although Driver had a son, Timothy, by an earlier marriage, which had ended in divorce. He retired from the military in 1962, and the couple moved to Riverside, California, where Driver became chief of safety for Minuteman missiles at North American Aviation.

Driver returned to government service in 1967, as director of crash worthiness and crash avoidance of the National Highway Traffic Safety Administration, U.S. Department of Transportation.

In 1978, he was chosen by President Jimmy Carter and confirmed by the U.S. Senate as a board member and vice chairman of the National Transportation Safety Board. In this capacity, he directed the 1979 investigation of the American Airlines jetliner crash in Chicago, which killed all 271 people on the aircraft and two on the ground.

With the change in administrations in 1981, Driver left the board and became a private consultant on safety issues, heading up his own firm, Elwood T. Driver and Associates. He returned to government service in 1986, as director of aircraft management for the National Aeronautics and Space Administration. He retired from this position in the fall of 1991, when he became ill with liver cancer. He died of this disease on March 26, 1992, in Reston, Virginia.

## Sources

"All-Negro Squadron Ready for Action." *Click* (September 1943).
Booker, Simeon. "Ticker Tape U.S.A." *Jet* (December 15, 1977).
"Elwood Driver, Safety Official, Tuskegee Airman, Dies at 70." *Washington Post* (April 1, 1992): D4.
Erstein, Hap. "The Eagles Who Touched the Sky." *Insight* (March 4, 1991): 53–55.
Knickerbocker, H.R. "Few Squadrons Fight Harder than the 99th." *PM* (New York) (February 17, 1944): 13.
Lambert, Bruce. "Elwood Driver, 70, Wartime Pilot and Transportation Safety Expert." *New York Times* (April 4, 1992): 31.
"Tuskegee Airman Heads Chicago Air Crash Probe." *Jet* (June 14, 1979): 5.
"A Victory Celebration Commemorating the Life, Labor and Successes of Elwood Thomas 'Woody' Driver." Memorial Booklet, March 1992.
Walker, Kenneth. "Black Pilots Recall War's Woes, Glory." *Washington Star-News* (August 12, 1973): B2.
*Who's Who among Black Americans 1992/1993.* Detroit: Gale Research, 1993.

# Charles W. Dryden

**Full Name at Birth:** Charles Walter Dryden

**Born:** September 16, 1920, New York, New York

**Education:** Stuyvesant High School, New York, 1937; City College of New York, 1937–1940; Civilian Pilot Training Program, 1940–1941; Advanced Flying School, U.S. Army Air Corps, Tuskegee, Alabama, April 29, 1942; Hofstra College, Hempstead, New York, B.A. in political science, 1955; Columbia University, New York, M.A. in public law and government, 1957.

**Positions Held:** U.S. Army Air Corps, 1941–1949; U.S. Air Force, 1949–1962; manager, special markets department, Pepsi-Cola Company, 1964–1968; executive director, Presbyterian Economic Development Corporation, 1968–1970; executive assistant to the president, Martins-Jamaica, 1972–1973; professional personnel administrator, Lockheed-Georgia Company, 1975–1983; training services officer, Lockheed-Georgia, 1983–1988.

**Awards, Honors:** Air Medal with six oak leaf clusters; Air Force Commendation Medal; Man of the Year, Ben Hill United Methodist Church, Atlanta, Georgia, 1987; honorary Doctor of Humane Letters, Hofstra University, 1996; Order of Gentlemen of the Palmetto, South Carolina, 1997; Outstanding Georgia Citizen, 1997; inductee, Georgia Aviation Hall of Fame, 1998.

**Summary:** A graduate of the second class at Tuskegee Army Air Field in 1942, Charles W. Dryden Sr. saw action in North Africa and the Mediterranean with the 99th Pursuit Squadron. On June 9, 1943, Dryden was in command of a flight of the 99th which was the first African American flight squadron to engage in enemy combat. He flew 30 combat missions in World War II and 50 during the Korean War, retiring at the rank of lieutenant colonel in 1962.

## Early Years

Charles Walter Dryden was born in New York City in 1920, the eldest child of Charles "Robin" Levy Tucker Dryden and Violet "Vie" Adina Buckley Dryden, who were both from Jamaica. Dryden's parents had met while teaching at neighboring schools in Kingston, Jamaica, but postponed marriage plans until Dryden's father returned from duty in Belgium during World War I, as a sergeant in the Jamaican Expeditionary Force.

Born into a "tranquil home and supportive family," surrounded by many relatives, Dryden recounts that, at the age of two, he threw scraps of paper into the air, pretending they were airplanes. Four years later Dryden's brother Denis Alvin was born, followed in five years by his sister Pauline.

Dryden's parents emphasized the importance of good education, good manners, and good grammar. Outside of school hours, Dryden recalled, "summer vacations included reading at least one book of our choice and attending some craft activity. . . . And year round there was time for a hobby." Dryden built model airplanes: solid, rubber-band powered planes. Everyone on their block in the Bronx "knew about the crazy black kid who wanted to fly." He read everything he could find about flying, especially a pulp magazine about a fictional World War I pilot, *G-8 and His Battle Aces*. In his final year at Stitt Junior High School, J.H.S. 164, Dryden was elected class president, "my first leadership opportunity," he recalled.

Needing the background of a rigorous science curriculum, Dryden went on to study at Stuyvesant High School on the lower east side of Manhattan.

## Higher Education

Upon graduation from high school, Dryden enrolled at the School of Mechanical Engineering of the City College of New York (CCNY). Dryden wanted to be a pilot, although neither military nor commercial airlines were open to African Americans in the late 1930s. His family could not afford to send him to New York University to study aeronautical engineering. At tuition-free CCNY, Dryden discovered that engineering was not, after all, his forte. In his third year there, he enrolled in CCNY's new Civilian Pilot Training (CPT) program, through which he could earn his private pilot's license.

Flight training was held at Roosevelt Field on Long Island, from which Lindbergh had taken off on his historic transatlantic flight in 1927. Dryden completed flight training handily, earned his private pilot's license and was accepted into the advanced CPT course. In 1941 the U.S. Army Air Corps at last accepted African American cadets; Dryden, with his pilot's license and CPT training under his belt, passed the necessary examinations and, in August 1941, was ordered to report to Tuskegee, Alabama.

Dryden was part of the second class of aviation cadets to attend the Army Air Corps's Advanced Flying School at Tuskegee. Of the 11 members of Dryden's class who started the course in August, only three would graduate. Given a 10-days' leave in early December, Dryden traveled to New York to visit his family. On December 7, however, leave was cut short and everyone ordered to return to base at once: the Japanese had attacked the U.S. naval fleet in Pearl Harbor, Hawaii.

Dryden's class, now numbering only four, began its next phase of training at once, moving from Moten Field, where preliminary training took place, to Tuskegee Army Air Field (TAAF) itself. Graduation took place on April 29, 1942, and the newly commissioned officers continued training at TAAF through the spring as the 99th Pursuit Squadron gained in strength with the addition of succeeding pilot-class graduates.

## Career Highlights

Reaching its full strength in July 1942, the 99th trained rigorously under the command of Lieutenant Colonel Benjamin O. Davis Jr. until their deployment to North Africa in spring 1943.

Once in North Africa, the 99th familiarized themselves with their new shipment of P-40L fighters. Dryden and his ground crew, all New Yorkers, named theirs *A-Train*, for the current Duke Ellington jazz hit, "Take the A-Train," and for the famous New York subway express that inspired it.

On June 9, 1943, Lieutenant Dryden was leading a flight on patrol just west of the island of Pantelleria when they were alerted that bombers were approaching:

> Six P-40's wheeled around . . . in a gut-wrenching 180-degree tight turn . . . as they prepared for this first air battle with the enemy by any of the 99th pilots. Suddenly facing the thirty-six .50-caliber machine guns of our flight, the attacking planes scattered.
>
> We all took after them like quail. . . . When I saw the swastikas on those ME-109s [I] felt the urge to "go get 'em" and a surge of adrenaline at the prospect of being the first Negro to shoot down an enemy airplane in aerial combat. . . . As it turned out none of us scored a victory on that mission. . . . Twenty minutes later we landed, ending a historic flight. Pantelleria surrendered on June 11, the first defended position ever defeated solely by air power.

On July 2, Colonel Davis led a 12-plane escort flight over Sicily; on that mission, Lieutenant Charles Hall shot down an enemy fighter, the first time that an African American pilot had done so. On the same mission, Dryden and his wingman, Lieutenant James B. Knighten, fought fiercely against four German fighters, dodging and striking repeatedly until the Germans reached the end of their range and broke off the attack. When Dryden returned to base, he found a grapefruit-sized hole in his wing; the wing was so precariously attached that a victory roll would have destroyed it.

The base of the 99th's operations was moved to Sicily on July 19 after the island's invasion.

When Colonel Davis was recalled to the United States in September 1943 to assume command of the 332nd Fighter Group, Dryden and four others were also recalled to serve as combat instructors in the 332nd at Selfridge Field, Michigan. In mid-September, Dryden flew his 30th and final combat mission of World War II, over the Salerno beachhead.

Arriving at Selfridge in late November, Dryden was offered the chance eventually to return overseas as a squadron commander and major. Dryden declined, since he had been married at Tuskegee just weeks before, on November 16, to Irma "Pete" Cameron, an Army nurse from New Jersey whom he had met in the spring, hours before the 99th shipped out to North Africa.

The Drydens remained married for 32 years and had three children, Charles Jr., Keith, and Eric. Following their divorce, Dryden married Marymal Morgan in the late 1970s, gaining four stepchildren, George, Anthony, Kenneth, and Cornelia.

Remaining at Selfridge Field after the 332nd shipped out to Europe at Christmas 1943, Dryden was transferred to Walterboro, South Carolina, early in 1944, with others who had attempted to integrate the Selfridge officers' club. At Walterboro, the African American officers were denied privileges granted to German prisoners of war. Furious, Dryden took a flight over the town water tower, to demonstrate an attack on a machine gun tower:

> I was going to show . . . I could fly. . . . You can imagine a quiet sleepy Sunday morning with four P-39s at full power roaring across town. . . .
>
> I was given a general court martial and dismissed from the Service. But I was granted a second trial because . . . one member of the court was heard to say they were going to throw the book at me, which is a prejudicial statement.

Dryden was suspended from promotion eligibility for a year, but he was not dismissed. "After the court martial, Major [Bill] Campbell, [commander of the 99th], was seeking volunteers to join the 477th to be sent to the Pacific. I was so fed up with the South and Jim Crow, I said, "Take me! Please!"

He was transferred at once to Godman Field, near Louisville, Kentucky, where the

477th Composite Group, including two bomber squadrons and the reconstituted 99th fighter squadron, was in training. However, when the Japanese surrendered on August 14, 1945, the 477th was not sent to the Pacific. As bases were demobilized after the end of the war, Tuskegee fliers were transferred to Godman and, in early 1946, the 477th was transferred to Lockbourne Army Air Base near Columbus, Ohio. On July 1, 1947, the 477th was deactivated and the 332nd Fighter Group reactivated. A year later, the desegregation of the armed forces was mandated, and the segregated forces at Lockbourne were phased out. In 1949, Dryden was promoted to captain and assigned to communication officer school at Scott AFB, Illinois.

Dryden was transferred to Japan in 1950, then to a K-2 airstrip near Taegu, Korea. He flew a tour of 50 combat missions, then spent an additional tour as a communications officer with the 934th Signal Battalion and the Fifth Communications Group. Assigned to Mitchel Air Base, Long Island, in 1952, Dryden volunteered for the Associate Intelligence Course at the Air University at Maxwell AFB, Alabama. He returned to Mitchel at the rank of major, assigned to intelligence for the headquarters of the Continental Air Command. While stationed at Mitchel, Dryden earned a bachelor's degree in political science at nearby Hofstra College in 1955 and a master's in public law and government from Columbia University in 1957. He was then transferred to Ramstein Air Base, Germany, to the Combat Intelligence Section. In 1959 he was assigned to Howard University in Washington, D.C., where he served as assistant professor of air science until 1961.

Retiring from the Air Force on August 31, 1962, at the rank of lieutenant colonel, Dryden became manager of Pepsi-Cola's special markets department in 1964. He served as a municipal councilman in Matawan, New Jersey, in 1965 and 1966. Leaving Pepsi-Cola in 1968, he became the executive director of the Presbyterian Economic Development Corporation, a post he held until 1970. In 1972–1973 he served as executive assistant to the president of Martins-Jamaica. He joined the Lockheed-Georgia Company in 1975, working as a professional personnel administrator until 1983, then as a training services officer until his retirement in 1988.

Dryden was president of the Atlanta Chapter of Tuskegee Airmen in 1983–1986, and a member of the Military Academies Selection Committee, 5th Congressional District, during the same years. A member of the NAACP and the Urban League, he became a member of the Honorable Order of Kentucky Colonels in 1987 and also served on the board of directors of the Georgia Aviation Hall of Fame beginning in 1989. In 1995 he chaired the Tuskegee Airmen convention in Atlanta.

His autobiography, *A-Train: Memoirs of a Tuskegee Airman*, was published in 1997. He is a frequent speaker to educational groups. Also in 1997, he became a member of the Metro Atlanta Lions Club's order of Dacdalians. He was inducted into the Georgia Aviation Hall of Fame in 1998.

## Sources

Dryden, Charles W. *A-Train: Memoirs of a Tuskegee Airman*. Tuscaloosa: University of Alabama Press, 1997.

Francis, Charles E. *The Tuskegee Airmen: The Men Who Changed a Nation*. 4th ed., revised and updated by Adolph Caso. Boston: Branden Publishing Co., 1997.

Holway, John B. *Red Tails, Black Wings: The Men of America's Black Air Force*. Las Cruces, NM: Yucca Tree Press, 1997.

*Who's Who among African Americans*. 12th ed. Detroit: Gale Research, 1999; 368.

# Edward J. Dwight Jr.

**Full Name at Birth:** Edward Joseph Dwight Jr.

**Born:** September 9, 1933, Kansas City, Kansas

Edward J. Dwight Jr. Courtesy of National Air and Space Museum, Smithsonian Institution (SI Neg. No. 99-40505).

**Education:** Ward Catholic High School, Kansas City, Kansas, 1951; Kansas City Junior College, 1953; Arizona State University, Tempe, Arizona, B.S. in aeronautical engineering, cum laude, 1957; Aerospace Research Pilot School, Edwards Air Force Base, 1963; University of Denver, Colorado, M.F.A. in sculpture, 1977.

**Positions Held:** U.S. Air Force, 1953–1966; jet instructor, Williams AFB, Arizona 1955–1957; B-57 bomber pilot, Japan, 1957–1958; chief of collateral training, Strategic Air Command, Travis AFB, California, 1958–1961; test pilot training program and candidate for astronaut training, Aerospace Research Pilot School, Edwards AFB, 1961–1963; assigned to Bomber Operations, deputy for flight test, Aeronautical Systems Division, Wright-Patterson AFB, Ohio, 1964–1966; co-founder, Jet Training School, Denver, Colorado, 1967-early 1970s; realtor, late 1960s-mid 1970s; sculptor and owner, Ed Dwight Studios, Denver, Colorado, 1980– .

**Awards, Honors:** National Preparedness Award, Los Angeles Urban League, 1963; "dozens of other awards and citations," 1963; Arizona State University, honorary L.H.D., 1987.

**Summary:** The first African American to be appointed to the fledgling astronaut training school in 1962, Edward J. Dwight Jr. faced significant resentment from his fellow students and instructors for what was viewed as a political, racially motivated assignment. Shortly after President Kennedy's assassination, Dwight was reassigned out of the Aerospace Research Pilot School. He resigned from the U.S. Air Force in 1966 and today is a sculptor of international renown, whose works include bronze statues of African American historical figures in public spaces throughout the United States.

## Early Years

Born on September 9, 1933, in Kansas City, Edward Joseph Dwight Jr. grew up near Fairfax Airport, a municipal airport that was turned into an Army Air Force base during World War II. Dwight's grandfather, Lobe, had moved his family from Dawson, Georgia, to Kansas City, where he went to work in a meatpacking plant.

Edward J. Dwight Sr., Lobe's son, quit school at 15 to play professional baseball in the Negro Leagues. While on a road trip, he met Georgia Baker in Sioux City, Iowa. After a long-distance courtship, they married and settled in Kansas City, where their five children were born. Eventually Edward Dwight Sr. became chief chemist with the Kansas Grain Department.

Young "Eddie" Dwight attended Our Lady of Perpetual Help grade school; his parents were devout Catholics, and Dwight and his four sisters were taught by example the importance of hard work and diligent use of time. Thrift was also important in those Depression years. The Dwights planted a large vegetable garden, which helped to keep food on the table and gave young Dwight a lasting love for the land. With his cousins and friends, he fished for crawdads and hung around the fence surrounding the airfield, watching the planes in action.

When Dwight was 10, he and some friends saw a P-39 fighter spin out of control and crash in a nearby field. As live ammunition exploded and the plane's cockpit flamed, burning the motionless body inside, Dwight thought that the pilot must have made some kind of mistake. He thought "and if *I'm* ever a pilot, I won't let that happen to me!"

After the war, Fairfax Airfield returned to its civilian status and the boys did odd jobs around the hangars, hoping to be taken flying in exchange. Eventually a pilot offered Dwight a ride in a Piper Cub two-seater, which Dwight found both exciting and scary. "Landing was the best part!" he would recall.

At the age of 12, Dwight saved enough money from two newspaper routes to purchase a 1929 Model A Ford, although his Kansas driving permit only allowed daytime driving. When he was 14, Dwight's father "loaned him out" as a summer farmhand, an experience that stayed with him always.

Throughout junior high and high school, Dwight was "possessed with this airplane stuff" and he studied the sample pilot's tests in books at the library. "I [was] unwittingly working toward taking the real test, playing this imaginary pilot guy. . . ."

In 1951, Dwight was the first African American male to graduate from Ward Catholic High School, where he was a member of the National Honor Society. He excelled at track and football, although, at 104 pounds, he was said to look more "like the team mascot . . . than the school's star halfback." Later he was a Golden Gloves boxer, winning the state 118-pound championship.

## Higher Education

Enrolling at Kansas City Junior College, Dwight became even more interested in avi-

ation. He began visiting the local Air Force recruiting office, asking for an application to train as a pilot. Despite President Truman's 1948 order to desegregate the armed forces, Dwight was repeatedly told that the Air Force was not for "his kind." Nevertheless, an aviation cadet evaluation team visited his college campus, and Dwight and some fellow students were sent to Lowry Air Base in Denver to take the pilot's exam. Dwight was the only one who passed. "Well, everybody got really upset about this. . . . But nobody thought about the fact that I had practiced. I just zoomed right through the test because it was the same test I'd got . . . out of the books in the library!"

After graduating from junior college, Dwight joined the Air Force on August 7, 1953. He took airman basic and cadet preflight training at Lackland Air Force Base in Texas, followed by primary flight training at Malden Air Base in Missouri. He earned his wings and was commissioned second lieutenant in 1955. Soon after that, he married Sue Lillian James, whom he had first met in high school in Kansas City.

The Air Force assigned Dwight to Williams Air Force Base, Arizona, where he began training as a jet aircraft pilot. He was the first in his class to solo in the T-33 jet trainer. He became a jet instructor and remained at Williams AFB for two and a half years. He continued his education at the same time, attending night classes at Arizona State University in nearby Tempe. He graduated in 1957 with a B.S. cum laude in aeronautical engineering.

## Career Highlights

After his assignment at Williams AFB, Dwight was stationed in Japan for about a year as a B-57 jet bomber pilot. He returned to the United States to become chief of collateral training—the ground education program of the Strategic Air Command—at Travis Air Force Base in California.

The early 1960s were a time of rising civil rights awareness, as segregation laws were challenged and the Kennedy administration emphasized the integration of government programs. At the same time, the space race was underway, and the first-generation astronauts of the Mercury program were among America's new heroes. A Kennedy spokesman questioned the Department of Defense: Did the Air Force "have any Negroes in the new aerospace research pilots' course being set up at Edwards Air Force Base?" The answer was no.

The Air Force began to search for an African American pilot with the right credentials. They found Captain Edward Dwight, with a degree in aeronautical engineering and more than 2,000 hours of jet flight time to his credit. Dwight recalled receiving a letter from President Kennedy, offering him an opportunity to "be one of the greatest Negroes who ever lived."

> So I got duly excited about it. . . . [A]gainst everybody's advice and wishes, I sent my information in. In the fourteen years I was in the service, I never saw the Air Force react so swiftly. Within a couple of days I was sent to Edwards AFB for an evaluation. And I knew full well . . . that if, in fact, I did succeed, . . . I would be on one of the lunar missions. Kennedy had this dream of having a black and an Asian on the first moon mission.
>
> Because I kind of knew, it allowed me to take all that gaff that I was getting down there [at Edwards AFB]. Because they did not want me. . . . I heard . . . how a certain high-ranking officer called in several of the staff of the test pilot school and made a comment . . . that "Washington is trying to cram a nigger down our throats, and . . . it'll hurt this program and will destroy everything you people have been putting together."
>
> . . . I represented an incredible fear that Kennedy was going to be like Branch Rickey and turn the space program into what Branch Rickey did to

baseball. And I was kind of like Jackie Robinson, and I was going to be the experiment. The bigger fear with the integration of any area of our society has always been not so much the first black person who moves into the neighborhood or sport or what have you, but the numbers of black people who follow.

Competition was keen among the 25 officers chosen for the rigorous seven-month test pilots' training course at the Aerospace Research Test Pilots' School at Edwards AFB. Although initially Dwight felt a camaraderie with the other students, as the course progressed "it became a game of survival." Every one knew that even successful completion of the training did not guarantee selection by NASA for an astronaut assignment. Dwight began to see himself as a target, the one candidate who, due to President Kennedy's interest, was assured selection by NASA.

Dwight's experience at Edwards AFB has been likened to the experience Benjamin O. Davis Jr. underwent as a cadet at West Point. Other students would not talk to him. He recalled that he "caught hell" from the faculty: "I remember car pooling with four other guys. We'd arrive simultaneously, and I was the only one chewed out for being four minutes late. Most of the guys would spend up to an hour and a half in debriefing (after test flights), and I only got five minutes."

Dwight complained about the change in attitude toward him—all the way to the White House. The attorney general's office sent investigators to Edwards. Most notable were Dwight's confrontations with the school commandant, renowned test pilot Colonel Charles Yeager, which Dwight later described in a 15-page report and in interviews. "Who got you into this school?" Yeager is reported to have said. "[D]id President Kennedy send the word down that you're supposed to go into space? . . . As far as I'm concerned, there'll never be [a 'colored guy'] to do it. And if it was left to me, you guys wouldn't even get a chance to wear an air force uniform!"

Despite the extensive intimidation, Dwight graduated eighth in his class, and, as one of the higher ranked students, was eligible for phase II training at the Aerospace Research Pilots' Training School, the next step before selection by NASA. Apparently in light of his experience during test pilot training, Dwight wrote to Kansas senator Frank Carlson rather than submitting his application for phase II training through the Air Force. Senator Carlson forwarded Dwight's letter to the White House, and shortly thereafter the Air Force announced Dwight's inclusion among the 14 officers in the next aerospace research pilot class, scheduled to begin on June 17, 1963.

As a member of the phase II training class, Dwight, like his colleagues, was encouraged by NASA to take part in public relations events: Dwight made 176 speeches that year, was awarded "dozens" of citations by organizations all over the nation, and was featured in a filmstrip used by the NASA Spacemobile Education Program. An associate of that program commented, "I saw . . . the reaction of black youngsters who looked at Captain Dwight and how they reacted to his message—it did a lot of good. He was the closest person to an astronaut our group could identify with." Dwight himself emphasized his belief in the equality of opportunity: "There are no racial barriers for anyone who wants to be a man in space. All that counts is whether you can do the job."

But the public relations glitter had a darker side. Dwight recalled "an incredible amount of social discrimination"—meals not served to Dwight when the astronaut candidates spoke at certain country clubs and restaurants, rooms reserved for everyone but Dwight at hotels, and orders "not to dance with any more white women" at officers' club parties: "Trouble was, it was the white women [who] asked me to dance!"

In the fall of 1963, the astronaut selection board "recommended without qualification" to NASA eight of the members of Dwight's class, including Dwight himself. But NASA selected only two of the eight—Captain Theodore C. Freeman, who was killed shortly thereafter in a T-33 jet crash, and Captain David R. Scott, who later flew on the *Gemini 8* and *Apollo 9* missions and commanded the *Apollo 15* lunar mission.

Dwight's ARPS class graduated in December 1963. Less than a month before, President Kennedy had been assassinated in Dallas. Dwight was given orders to be a liaison officer to Germany's test pilot school and (nonexistent) space program. Dwight refused to go, and instead was assigned to bomber operations in the aeronautical systems division at Wright-Patterson AFB, Ohio. An Air Force press release in February 1964 stated that Dwight was "considered a candidate for future selection on aerospace projects by either" NASA or the Air Force.

But Dwight and his wife, Sue, were faced with harassment both on and off base in Ohio, ranging from property damage to personal attacks. They divorced, and Dwight retained custody of their two young children, Tina and Dwight III.

President Johnson signed the Civil Rights Act into law in June 1964. Riots broke out in many cities that summer. In 1965, an article appeared in *Ebony* magazine, chronicling Dwight's "troubles" in the Air Force space pilot training program. Newspapers across the country picked up the story. NASA issued a general statement: "If [Dwight] was not selected as an astronaut, it does not mean he was not qualified. It means that someone more qualified was selected ahead of him." Commentary from African Americans who were former members of the armed services agreed with Dwight's allegations: "Captain Edward Dwight's experiences were very similar to incidents that are everyday occurrences," wrote one.

Between the NASA pass-over and the ongoing media turmoil, it became clear to Dwight that his military career was over. "What would they do with me? How could I accept a regular air force job? . . . I [was] constantly going to be on somebody's list." Dwight resigned his commission in the Air Force in 1966.

In June 1967, Robert H. Lawrence Jr. became the first designated African American astronaut. He was killed on December 8, 1967, in a simulated space ship landing at Edwards AFB. After Lawrence's death, there were no other African American astronauts until 1978, when Guion S. Bluford Jr., Frederick D. Gregory, and Ronald E. McNair were appointed.

After a second marriage which lasted 30 days, Dwight married another childhood friend from Kansas City, Barbara, "who brought me back to earth, because I was about to go crazy," Dwight would later say. Moving to Denver, Dwight became a realtor and co-founded the Jet Training School in 1967. However, one day the other six flight instructors took off in a plane without Dwight, who had stayed on the ground to complete a real estate deal. Fifteen minutes later the plane crashed, killing everyone aboard. Dwight never flew again.

In the mid-1970s, Dwight returned to a long-standing avocation, sculpture. He earned a master of fine arts degree in sculpture at the University of Denver and taught there for a time. Dwight now heads the Ed Dwight Studios in Denver and has produced bronze sculptures for both public installations and for private collectors all over the world. Among his most noted works are statues of Hank Aaron and Dr. Martin Luther King Jr., in Atlanta; the Frederick Douglass Memorial in Washington, D.C., and also six jazz figures

at the Smithsonian Institution's National Museum of American History. He has been commissioned to design a 90-foot installation to commemorate African American patriots in the Revolutionary War, intended for the Mall in Washington near the Lincoln Memorial and the Washington Monument.

## Sources

Burns, Kephra, and William Miles. *Black Stars in Orbit: NASA's African American Astronauts.* New York: Gulliver Books/Harcourt Brace and Co., 1995; 16–23.

Cohen, Jean Lawlor. "Ed Dwight: The Realistic Dreamer." *American Visions* (April–May 1992): 26–31.

McNeill, Lydia. "Dwight, Edward Joseph Jr." *Encyclopedia of African American Culture and History.* Vol. 2. New York: Macmillan, 1996.

Perez-Giese, Tony. "Little Big Man." *Denver Westword.* May 29, 1997. Online, http://westword.com/1996/052997/feature2–1.html. Accessed October 29, 1999.

Phelps, J. Alfred. *They Had a Dream: The Story of African American Astronauts.* Novato, CA: Presidio Press, 1994; 1–46.

Robinson, Louie. "First Negro Astronaut Candidate." *Ebony* (July 1963): 71–85.

Sanders, Charles L. "The Troubles of 'Astronaut' Edward Dwight: Official Excuses Cloud Routine Assignment of Nation's Only Negro Trained for Role in Space." *Ebony* (June 1965): 29–32, 34–36.

Seymour, Gene. "The Black Pilot Who Almost Made It into Space." *San Francisco Sunday Examiner & Chronicle* (August 28, 1983): A17.

White, Frank. "The Sculptor Who Would Have Gone into Space." *Ebony* (February 1984): 54, 56, 58.

Yeager, Chuck, and Leo Janos. *Yeager: An Autobiography.* Toronto: Bantam Books, 1985; 269–272.

# E

## Aprille Ericsson-Jackson

Aprille Ericsson-Jackson. Provided by NASA Goddard Space Flight Center.

**Full Name at Birth:** Aprille Joy Ericsson

**Born:** April 1, 1963, Brooklyn, New York

**Education:** Massachusetts Institute of Technology (MIT), Cambridge, Massachusetts, B.S. in aeronautical and astronomical engineering, 1986; Howard University, Washington, D.C., M.E. in engineering, 1991; Ph.D. in mechanical engineering, aerospace option, 1993.

**Positions:** Aerospace engineer, National Aeronautics and Space Administration (NASA), Goddard Space Flight Center, 1992–present; adjunct professor of mathematics, Bowie State University, Bowie, Maryland; adjunct professor of mechanical engineering, Howard University, Washington, D.C.

**Awards, Honors:** Top 50 Minority Women in Science and Engineering, National Technical Association, 1996, 1997; Women in Science and Engineering Award, Best Female Engineer in the Federal Government, 1997; Special Recognition Award, Black Engineers Award Conference, 1998; NASA Goddard Honor Award for Excellence in Outreach (Individual), 1999; Center of Excellence Award for the TRMM Project (Group) 1999, and numerous other awards.

**Summary:** Aprille Ericsson-Jackson was the first woman to receive a Ph.D. in mechanical engineering from Howard University and she became an aerospace engineer at the NASA Goddard Space Center.

## Early Years

Aprille Ericsson-Jackson was born on April 1, 1963, the oldest of four daughters of Corrinne Elaine Breedy and Henry Anthony Ericsson. She grew up in Bedford-Stuyvesant, a minority neighborhood in Brooklyn. The family lived in the Roosevelt projects, a public housing development. When she was eight, her parents separated.

Ericsson-Jackson attended New York City public schools, where she was an outstanding student and athlete. She was a Girl Scout and attended camp or went camping every summer. In junior high, she developed what was to be a lifelong interest in science and math. The only black student to be enrolled in the Special Progress Program, she came in second in the school's science fair.

Ericsson-Jackson remembers herself as a "tomboy." She loved participating in sports, particularly basketball. She was also a member of the school band. She believes that her mother's support and encouragement gave her the confidence to excel in all these areas: "She was always behind me whatever I wanted to do."

Upon graduating from junior high school, she was accepted at several prestigious selective public schools in New York City. When she won a full scholarship to the Cambridge School, a private school in Weston, Massachusetts, she decided to attend high school there. She moved to Cambridge, Massachusetts, where she lived with her maternal grandparents while attending the school as a day student.

During her high school years, Ericsson-Jackson was an honor student, excelling in all her academic subjects. She also found time to participate in athletics. She was on the school basketball and softball teams, and volunteered as a physical education teacher in Cambridge elementary schools.

Of her high school ambitions, Ericsson-Jackson says, "I did not know that I would choose to be an engineer. I became interested in the first grade when I got a chance to see the U.S. go to the moon. But through the years I thought I might be an artist, a track star, a karate expert, a lawyer." She credits a summer program at The Massachusetts Institute of Technology (MIT) with making her realize "how the pieces fit together."

## Higher Education

The summer program which she had attended at MIT took place in her junior year of high school. She realized that she "loved to figure out how things work and . . . I loved putting things together." The brief exposure to MIT opened her eyes to her own potential and motivated her to apply to the institution. She was accepted, and after graduation from the Cambridge School, matriculated at MIT, one of the foremost teaching and research universities in the fields of science and technology in the United States, if not the world.

Ericsson maintained her excellent academic record at MIT. As an undergraduate, she was involved in several projects that were geared toward manned space flight. Her ambition at the time was to participate in manned space missions. After receiving her degree in aeronautical/astronautical engineering, she applied to be an astronaut. However, a catastrophic event intervened, in 1986, the year Ericsson-Jackson graduated. The *Challenger*, a manned spacecraft, exploded upon launching, killing all those aboard. In the aftermath of this event, the future of the space program looked doubtful. Career opportunities in manned space flight dried up; no applications were being accepted. The following year, she applied to be an astronaut. Her application was rejected on medical grounds, on the basis of an old knee injury and a chronic condition of asthma.

With this option closed to her, at least for a time, Ericsson-Jackson decided to pursue advanced degrees in her field. A good friend recommended that she continue her studies at Howard University, a historically black institution in Washington, D.C. Ericsson-Jackson matriculated there in 1987. She received her master's degree from Howard in 1991.

Ericsson-Jackson continued her studies at Howard in pursuit of a Ph.D. degree, and, in the summer of 1992, she was hired at the National Aeronautics and Space Administration as an intern. At the end of the summer, she converted to a cooperative program, combining her studies at Howard with employment at NASA.

On October 11, 1992, she married Mark Jackson, a licensed mechanical engineer, but the marriage ended after eight years. She continued to work at NASA and to pursue her Ph.D. in mechanical engineering. She received many grants and fellowships to enable her to continue her studies. In 1995, Aprille Ericsson-Jackson made history by becoming the first woman to receive a Ph.D. in mechanical engineering. This made her the only African American at Goddard Space Flight Center with this advanced degree.

Ericsson-Jackson continues to work at NASA as an engineer. At present, her work involves conducting computer simulations of spacecraft designs. She also teaches mathematics at Bowie State College, Bowie, Maryland, and has taught vibration analysis at Howard.

Ericsson-Jackson has a mission to "help spur the interest of minorities and women in . . . math, science, and engineering." In pursuit of that mission, she is an active participant in the NASA Goddard Space Flight Center Speakers Bureau, and she has served as career adviser and mentor to a number of young people. She still enjoys playing football, basketball, softball, cycling, and tennis. She is a member of a top-ranked, world-class coed softball team, the Hardrock Senators. She enjoys reading and particularly likes the works of Stephen King.

In an e-mail discussion group, Ericsson-Jackson was asked if she felt discriminated against as a woman. She felt this was not a problem, but perceived a bias against her as an African American: "People still believe that blacks are lazy and . . . stupid. I try to prove them wrong every day!"

Recently, Ericsson-Jackson reapplied to the astronaut program and is eagerly awaiting NASA's selections, which are scheduled for 2002.

## Sources

"Aprille Ericsson-Jackson, Ph.D." Http://quest.arc. nasa.gov/women/bios/ae.html. Accessed February 2, 1999.

"Dr. Aprille Joy Ericsson-Jackson, NASA, Code 572, Guidance, Navigation and Control Center." Publicity release, National Aeronautics and Space Administration.

Ericsson-Jackson, Aprille. "Re: Bio and Resume [e-mail to Miriam Sawyer]," (May 4, 1999).

———. "Re: a Few Last Details [e-mail to Miriam Sawyer]," (October 4, 1999).

———. "Re: No Subject [e-mail to Miriam Sawyer]," (November 8, 1999 and May 4, 2001).

"Female Frontiers Questchat Archive; Featuring Aprille Ericsson-Jackson, Aerospace Engineer, Goddard Space Flight Center, Greenbelt, MD." Http://quest.arc.nasa.gov/space/frontiers/chat-archives/ericsson02–02-09.html. Accessed February 2, 1999.

# Jean R. Esquerre

**Full Name at Birth:** Jean Roland Esquerre

**Born:** December 28, 1923, Yonkers, New York

**Education:** Morris High School, Bronx, New York, 1942; Tuskegee Air Field, 1942–1945; evening classes in mechanical engineering at City College of New York, 1947–1948; industrial management courses at New York University, 1951–1952; B.S. in engineering technology, Empire State College, 1977.

**Positions Held:** Various draftsman positions in mechanical engineering, 1949–1953; prin-

Jean R. Esquerre. Courtesy of Jean R. Esquerre.

cipal design engineer, Republic Aviation Corporation, 1953–1963; fluid system engineer, 1963; test director of Lunar Module No. 4 (LM 4), 1966; engineering supervisor of rocket engine systems on LM 4, 1968; assistant to the president and director of the Opportunity Development Department, 1969, Grumman Aerospace Corporation, until retirement in 1987.

**Awards, Honors:** Elected first African American member of board of directors, Grumman Aerospace Corporation, August 16, 1973; Grumman Achievement Award; National president of Tuskegee Airmen, Inc., 1981 and 1986; Town of Huntington (NY) proclamation honoring exemplary service and for providing opportunities for minorities in aviation, February 26, 1989.

**Summary:** Jean R. Esquerre, a Tuskegee Airman with 3,500 hours of flying time, has been able to provide opportunities in his career in the aerospace industry for minorities in the field of aviation. As president of the Tuskegee Airmen, Inc., and as the first African American elected to the board of directors of a major corporation, Esquerre has recorded outstanding achievements and has inspired many young people to achieve success.

## Early Years

Jean Roland Esquerre was born on December 28, 1923, in Yonkers, New York, to Jean Bertram Esquerre and Marie Bates Esquerre. In World War I, his father served with the all-black 369th Infantry in North Africa and in France. Because he spoke French, he was assigned to the intelligence division to teach the language. When the war ended, the elder Esquerre returned to the United States and could only find work as a waiter in a railroad dining car. Esquerre's grandfather, Howard Gale, served in the 24th Infantry (Colored) before World War I. He spoke five languages and gave young Jean his first encyclopedia and Morse Code kit. He also told him about the first African American man and woman to become pilots. They were Eugene J. Bullard, who flew for the French in World War I, and Bessie Coleman, who became a pilot in France in 1921. As a child, Jean Esquerre built model airplanes and flew them off the roof of his apartment house. He was thrilled one day when his grandfather introduced him to Bullard, who had returned to Harlem from Paris, where he had lived until 1940.

Esquerre, in his teens, earned money by shining shoes. Although African Americans weren't permitted to work in the lucrative Times Square area, an exception was made for him. The policeman on this beat was the brother of Gene Tunney, the undefeated heavyweight boxing champion of the world. The elder Esquerre boxed, for sport, at the same gym as the champion, and consideration was shown for his son.

After graduating from high school in 1942,

Esquerre volunteered to join the Army Air Corps. He was refused because of his race and was told "the Air Corps wasn't ready for us." This was a politer rejection than the one received by a volunteer in California, "Get the hell out of here boy, the Army ain't training night fighters."

boxed on the pro circuit, which disqualified them as amateurs, a requirement for the Olympics." Esquerre also studied industrial management at New York University in the early 1950s. In 1977, Esquerre graduated from Empire State College with a degree in engineering technology.

## Higher Education

Esquerre entered military service at the newly established all-black air training field at Tuskegee, Alabama. Unable to become a pilot because he was color blind, Esquerre was trained as a radio gunner on a B-25 bomber, attaining the rank of sergeant. He also trained on B-17s. The men assigned to the 477th Medium Bomber Group were in training for a possible invasion of Japan, which did not happen because the atomic bomb attacks on Japan in 1945 effectively ended the war.

During the Tuskegee years (1940–1946), about 1,000 African American men were trained as pilots, of whom about 450 flew combat missions abroad, and another 10,000 served as essential ground support. While at Tuskegee Air Field, the men were given wooden rifles in basic training and were denied access to churches of their choice. They buoyed up their spirits as best they could. The soldiers worked at calisthenics to maintain their physical well-being. They sang "Fly Me to the Moon," and developed a spirit of camaraderie that endures more than 50 years later. Finally, in 1943, they were permitted to fly in combat.

The war over, Esquerre left the armed services and entered City College of New York. He attended evening classes in mechanical engineering, and he became the first colored (the term then in use) member of the college's boxing team. The team lost their chance of participating in the 1948 Olympic Games, Esquerre recalled, "because the assistant coach took the boys up to a summer resort area to work as bellhops. They also

## Career Highlights

Esquerre began his professional life in Brooklyn as a draftsman designing electro-mechanical and electronic devices for military use, from 1949 to 1952. For the next two years he worked for the New York Transit Authority as a mechanical engineering draftsman in the New Construction and Maintenance Department. In late 1953 he moved to Republic Aviation Corporation, where he remained for nearly 10 years. Esquerre's title was principal design engineer. In this capacity he was involved with the design of missiles, space and rocket engines, fluid systems, and other aeronautical components.

In August 1963, Esquerre left Republic for Grumman Aerospace Corporation on Long Island, New York. He remained with Grumman until his retirement in December 1987. Esquerre started as a fluid systems engineer, and in 1966 he became test director of LM-4 (Lunar Module.) Two years later he was named an engineering supervisor of rocket engines on the lunar module. A later assignment was that of price analyst in subcontract negotiating.

Ten years after joining Grumman, in August 1973, Esquerre was elected to the board of directors, becoming the first African American to join that body. Grumman's announcement noted that Esquerre was "one of only a few score blacks among several hundred thousands of whites in the country who are instrumental in directing the affairs of tens of thousands of corporations." Esquerre was the director of the Opportunity Development Department, responsible for all equal employment and affirmative action programs throughout the entire corporation. At his retirement in 1987, he was the assistant to the corporate president.

Over the years, Esquerre has belonged to many organizations. The one dearest to him, and in which he is most active, is the Tuskegee Airmen, Inc. (TAI). He was elected national president twice, in 1981 and in 1986. He belongs to local chapters in New York and Florida. He was the founding president and chief instructor of the Grumman Martial Arts Club, and he is affiliated with other karate associations here and in Japan. He belongs to the Society of Automotive Engineering, Alpha Phi Alpha fraternity, and the City College of New York Boxing Alumni Club. The civil rights organizations of which he is a member include One Hundred Black Men, Urban League of Long Island, which he founded, Edges Organization, Transafrica, Inc., and the Huntington, New York, branch of the NAACP. He has served on numerous boards of directors, including Huntington Hospital, Springfield College, Massachusetts, and United Way of Long Island.

Moving to Tampa, Florida, in 1994, with his wife Maria Edman, hasn't slowed down Esquerre's activities. He is an elder in the Village Presbyterian Church, a volunteer driver for the Veterans Relief Fund, a member of the local chapter of the Urban League, and he continues to study karate. As a Tuskegee Airman, he speaks before groups about the role African Americans have had in the history of aviation and in the defense of the United States. Esquerre's wife was born in Solna, Sweden, and became a school teacher. Her father was Sweden's first private, as distinguished from military, pilot. They have two daughters, Malin Elisabet Esquerre Langfitt and Johanna Maria, a licensed pilot who is pursuing a doctorate in psychology.

## Sources

Bosch, Steven John. "Black History Month—Esquerre Pays Back." *Westbury* (New York) *Pennysaver* (February 4, 1989).

Delatiner, Barbara. "A Black Eagle Recalls His War." *New York Times* (February 12, 1989): Long Island section, 19.

Esquerre, Jean R., Tampa, Florida, to Betty K. Gubert, New York, telephone interviews, correspondence, clippings, January–May 1999.

"Flight Testing: New Opportunities in the Air." *Encore* (March 17, 1975): 41–42, 45.

Francis, Charles E. *The Tuskegee Airmen: The Men Who Changed a Nation.* Boston: Branden Publishing Co., 1988.

Reddick, Tracie. "Tuskegee Airmen." *Tampa Tribune* (February 9, 1997).

# F

## Albert E. Forsythe

Albert E. Forsythe. Courtesy of National Air and Space Museum, Smithsonian Institution (SI Neg. No. 2001-1895).

**Born:** February 25, 1897, Nassau, Bahamas

**Died:** May 4, 1986, Atlantic City, New Jersey

**Education:** Tuskegee Institute, Tuskegee, Alabama, 1913; MD., Ph.D. McGill University Medical School, Montreal, Canada

**Positions Held:** physician until retirement in 1977; aviation pioneer, licensed in early 1930s.

**Awards, Honors:** Award as "Pioneer in the Field of Aviation" at the "Black Wings" exhibition, National Air and Space Museum, Smithsonian Institution, 1982; "Albert E. Forsythe Day" acclaimed by the City of Newark, New Jersey; Inducted into Aviation Hall of Fame, Teterboro, New Jersey, 1985.

**Summary:** Albert E. Forsythe was a New Jersey physician and a pioneer in black aviation in the 1930s. With his friend and partner, C. Alfred Anderson, he undertook three historic flights, most notably the first cross-country round trip by African Americans in 1933, to demonstrate that African Americans were capable of being pilots, thus paving the way for other African Americans to achieve successful careers in aviation.

### Early Years

Albert E. Forsythe was born on February 25, 1897, to Maude Bynloss and Horatio A.

Forsythe, a civil engineer. Little is known of his childhood. Forsythe had a brother, Roger, and four sisters, Mary, Carmen, Erma, and Kathleen. The family lived for a time in Jamaica, West Indies, where he received his early education.

## Higher Education

In 1912, Forsythe came to Tuskegee Institute in Tuskegee, Alabama, an institution for higher education for black Americans founded by Booker T. Washington. His original intention was to study architecture. While there, he was a student of Dr. George Washington Carver, the renowned African American scientist. At some point during his time at Tuskegee, he abandoned his plans to be an architect and decided on a career in medicine.

After graduating from Tuskegee, he next attended McGill University Medical School in Montreal, Canada, from which he received his medical degree as well as his Ph.D. degree.

## Career Highlights

Forsythe established a medical practice in Atlantic City, New Jersey. It was while he was living in Atlantic City that he became interested in aviation. At about this time, he became acquainted with C. Alfred Anderson, who had already trained extensively and was a skilled pilot. Accounts differ as to whether Anderson taught Forsythe to fly, or whether his tutor was Ernest Buehl, the former German World War I pilot who had tutored Anderson. At any rate, Forsythe did learn to fly and the two became fast friends. Forsythe and Anderson were looking for a way to use their aviation skills to promote careers for young African Americans, to "open doors" for them. The field of aviation was new and promising and not weighted down by a tradition of racism. Forsythe also believed that if he could encourage young

African Americans to enter this field, it would eventually lead to advancement in many other areas.

The two men determined to show the world that black pilots could do anything white pilots could do. To prove their point, they planned three daring long-distance flights—to be known as "good will" flights—one from Atlantic City to Los Angeles and back, a second from Atlantic City to Montreal, and a third from Miami, Florida, to the West Indies and South America. The purpose of these trips was to show the world that African Americans could fly airplanes—the generally accepted wisdom being that African Americans were inferior and incapable of flying. Forsythe and Anderson planned their trips for maximum publicity, to let the world know that black people could indeed pilot aircraft.

Their first trip was to be a cross-country flight from coast to coast and back. According to Forsythe, "The trip was purposely made to be hazardous and rough, because if it had been an ordinary flight, we wouldn't have attracted attention." In July 1933, the "good will" pilots started for California to the roar of cheering crowds. Their Fairchild monoplane, *The Pride of Atlantic City*, was equipped only with a compass and an altimeter. They had no radio, lights, or parachutes. They used a Rand McNally road map to chart their course—until it blew out of Forsythe's hands on their return flight. Nevertheless, despite heavy rain and strong winds, they made it to Los Angeles and back, making history as the first round-trip transcontinental flight made by African American pilots.

This trip was a success in generating publicity. Upon their return to the East Coast in September 1933, the two pilots were given a rally and parade in Newark, New Jersey. The parade, which went down Newark's main thoroughfare, was attended by 15,000 persons, according to contemporary newspaper reports. Their second trip, from Atlantic City to Montreal, Canada, took place in late

1933, was just as successful, and set another record, making them the first black pilots to fly over an international border.

Their third and last good will trip took them to the Caribbean and Latin America, where they were to land in 25 different countries, bearing a scroll to be signed by government officials in each of the countries. For this journey, they purchased a Lambert Monocoupe plane in St. Louis, Missouri. In the course of negotiating the purchase, they met Charles Lindbergh. Lindbergh attempted to discourage their plans; it was his belief that only white men could fly. But the two refused to be discouraged. They went ahead with their plans and purchased a plane, which was christened the *Spirit of Booker T. Washington*, in a ceremony at the Tuskegee Institute. Nettie H. Washington, Booker T. Washington's granddaughter, was among those at the ceremony, which was attended by hundreds of enthusiastic students and faculty, as well as members of the public. The two embarked on their journey on November 8, 1934.

The Caribbean flight was the most difficult of all; in many places there were no runways or landing fields, and the men were often forced to land on a city street or a playing field. In Nassau, where they arrived at night after an unexpected delay, cars surrounded the runway, their headlights on to illuminate the plane's landing.

Contemporary newspaper accounts show the pair being enthusiastically greeted at every port of call. The first leg of their trip was to Nassau, Bahamas. "There wasn't any landing strip or airport in those days," Forsythe is quoted as saying, "but our friends in my home town . . . had cut down brush and . . . moved all the telephone poles in the area and shifted their wires." They created history by landing in Nassau; only seaplanes had landed there before.

The governor of the Bahamas greeted them ceremoniously in the presence of a large crowd numbering 5,000 persons, including the U.S. consul and other government officials. This was a great triumph for Forsythe, who was a native of the Bahamas. Forsythe presented the governor with a scroll conveying a greeting from the people of the United States. His parents were among the honored guests who welcomed the two men.

Their next stop was in Kingston, and on the way there, they circled Port Antonio, Forsythe's home town, where a waiting crowd gave them a big ovation. On the way to Cuba, their next stop, the tropical rain was so hard, it "peeled the paint off the struts," as Anderson recalled in a 1988 interview with *People* magazine.

Upon reaching Havana, Cuba, their next stop, they were received by the officials of that island; they then proceeded to Santiago, Cuba, where several receptions in their honor were held. However, they never reached South America; as they left Trinidad, strong tailwinds forced them off course, and they crash-landed, seriously damaging the plane. The remainder of the trip was canceled. Despite this forced shortening of their trip, the two were feted when they returned to New Jersey, in September 1935.

In late 1935, having proved his point, Forsythe returned to the practice of medicine in Atlantic City. "[M]y main business was medicine, surgery. I was not interested in becoming involved much in aviation. We just made a series of flights for the sole purpose of opening the road for blacks who wanted to fly."

For the next 17 years, Forsythe continued to practice medicine in Atlantic City. In 1945, he married Frances Turner, a nurse. The couple moved to Newark in 1952, where Frances Turner Forsythe became a nurse in the public school system, while Forsythe continued to practice medicine until his retirement in 1977. After retirement from medicine, Dr. Forsythe took up art as a hobby; many of his art works decorated his apartment and the homes of friends. In 1985, he was inducted into the Aviation Hall of Fame at Teterboro, New Jersey. In his later years Forsythe was made the subject of a television broadcast, and a 1982 Smithsonian exhibition, "Black Wings," on the early years of black aviation honored his contribution to African American aviation.

On May 4, 1986, Dr. Forsythe died. In a tribute to Forsythe's pioneer role, representatives of Negro Airmen International, the Tuskegee Airmen, and the Black Pilots Association were honorary pallbearers. His old comrade, C. Alfred Anderson, speaking at the funeral service, was moved to tears and almost lost his composure. A tribute by the mayor of Atlantic City was read, recognizing his death as a loss to Atlantic City, to New Jersey, and to "the people in the forefront of making history for black people throughout the world."

## Sources

Brock, Pope. "Chief Anderson." *People* (November 28, 1988): 149+.

"Dr. Albert Forsythe, 88, Dies; Among First Black Aviators." *New York Times.* (May 6, 1986).

"Four Added to Aviation Hall of Fame." *New Jersey Historical Commission Newsletter* (April 1985): 2.

Hardesty, Von, and Dominick Pisano. *Black Wings; The American Black in Aviation.* Washington, DC: National Air and Space Museum, Smithsonian Institution Press, 1983.

Jakeman, Robert J. *Divided Skies.* Tuscaloosa: University of Alabama Press, 1992.

"Negro Fliers in Havana." *New York Times* (November 10, 1934).

"Negro Fliers Land In Dominican Hills." *New York Times* (November 18, 1934).

Scott, Lawrence P., and William A. Womack Sr. *Double V; the Civil Rights Struggle of the Tuskegee Airmen.* East Lansing: Michigan State University Press, 1994.

Terrell, Stanley E. "Dr. Albert Forsythe, Pioneer Black Aviator." *Newark Star-Ledger* (May 7, 1986).

U.S. Postage Stamp to Honor "Chief Anderson and Dr. Forsythe." *Negro Airmen International News* (December 1988): 1.

Webber, Harry E. "Dr. Albert Forsythe, Pioneer Black Airman Leaves Great Legacy." *New Jersey Afro-American* (May 7, 1986): 1, 7.

# Louis L. Freeman

Louis L. Freeman. Courtesy of Louis Freeman and Southwest Airlines.

**Full Name at Birth:** Louis Lawrence Freeman

**Born:** June 12, 1952, Austin, Texas

**Education:** Woodrow Wilson High School, Dallas, Texas, 1970; B.S. in sociology and psychology, East Texas State University, Commerce, Texas, 1974; U.S. Air Force Pilot Training, Reese Air Force Base, Texas, August 1974 to August 1975.

**Positions Held:** Co-Pilot, pilot, instructor pilot, 454th Flight Training Squadron, Mather Air Force Base, California, August 1975–August 1980; first officer, captain, assistant chief pilot (Phoenix, Arizona), chief pilot (Chicago, Illinois), Southwest Airlines, November 1980–   .

**Awards, Honors:** Squadron Pilot of the Year, 454th Flight Training Squadron, U.S. Air Force; Winning Spirit Award; President's Award, Southwest Airlines; Corporate Trailblazer Award, *Dollars & Sense Magazine*, September 1993; Keynote speaker, Black History Month Celebration, Miami International Airport, 1996.

**Summary:** In 1980, Louis L. Freeman became the first black pilot to be hired by Southwest Airlines. His professional skills enabled him to become Southwest's first African American captain as well, and later, chief pilot for the Chicago pilot base of the airline.

## Early Years

Louis Freeman was born on June 12, 1952, the second of four children of Alphine and Rodis Freeman, in Austin. His father was a master sergeant in the U.S. Army, and his mother was a nursery school teacher. His older brother, Alphine III, trained as an architect, but he now owns and directs a medical consulting firm. His younger brother John also works there. Their sister Cynthia, the youngest of the children, is a nurse. Louis Freeman and his older brother were among the first 10 black students to integrate Woodrow Wilson High School in Austin in 1967. The school's population was nearly 2,000 at the time. The black high school the Freemans had transferred from, Madison, did not have as good equipment as the white Wilson high school, but Freeman and his brother credit their teacher at Madison, William Marx. The director of the band, Marx instructed and inspired them. Louis played the tuba and Alphine played the trombone, and both were members of the band. They were the first African American band members, as well as the first African American assistant drum majors at Wilson. From this experience, Freeman learned a valuable lesson: that he could compete successfully against those with special advantages, in this case, white

students who had had the benefit of private music lessons, as well as a school with superior facilities.

Freeman was also the first African American cadet corps commander in the school's ROTC (Reserve Officers Training Corps). He graduated in 1970.

## Higher Education

Freeman continued to add to his string of firsts in college. He enrolled at East Texas State University in Commerce, and he once again became the ROTC's cadet corps commander, the first African American to hold that position. During his freshman year, he took the Air Force Officers' Qualifying Test, but he failed the pilot aptitude section. He did well on the navigator's part, however, thanks to family vacations where it was his job to read the map and give directions. But Freeman was not used to failing and the following year he passed the test. His philosophy that "if you stumble and fall, get up and run harder," was strengthened by this experience.

He was a member of the student senate, and he was resident assistant for one of the many dorms at the university. He graduated in 1974 with a B.S. in sociology and psychology. From August of that year until graduation in August 1975, Freeman attended the Air Force's Undergraduate Pilot Training at Reese Air Force Base (AFB) in Texas. Although the class started out with 60 students, only 38 remained at graduation. The rest were unable to meet the instructor's requirement of "110 percent of effort."

## Career Highlights

His training over, Freeman was assigned to the 454th Flight Training Squadron at Mather AFB in California. He flew T-43 planes, and he was the first second lieutenant to become a squadron scheduler. He was also one of the first lieutenants to become an instructor pilot as well as a supervisor of flying. Freeman remained with the Air Force until August 1980, when he decided to seek employment in civilian aviation.

In November 1980, Freeman was hired by Southwest Airlines, headquartered in Dallas. He was the airline's first black pilot, and in June 1983, Freeman became its first black captain. Freeman recalled that in 1987, there were three black pilots employed by Southwest. In 1995, the number had risen to 26, out of a total of 2,100 pilots. Still with the company in 2000, Freeman has held the positions of first officer, captain, and check pilot. He was assistant chief pilot at Southwest's Phoenix pilot base from 1989 until 1992. Freeman then became Southwest's chief pilot at Chicago's Midway Airport. As the immediate supervisor of more than 500 pilots, Freeman's responsibilities include their oversight and evaluation. He also assists in the development of policy for Flight Operation. Freeman has described Southwest Airlines as "the perfect place for me . . . the company's personality fits me like a glove."

Freeman and the former Stephanie Wood-fork are the parents of a daughter, Nikki, born in 1987, and a son, Stephen, born in 1990. Stephanie Freeman is a radiologist, and the two met at Mather AFB, where she was assigned to complete her medical school clerkship for the Air Force. Freeman enjoys playing chess with his children, and he accompanies them to soccer tournaments in other states, traveling by car or airplane. He also speaks to school classes on subjects as far ranging as the role geography plays in aviation or the military history of African Americans, going as far back as the French and Indian War, which was fought from 1754 to 1763.

## Sources

*Blacks in Aviation 1996, A Commemorative Brochure.* Miami, FL: Metro-Dade Aviation Department, 1996; 63–64.

"Chief Pilot." *Ebony* (April 1993): 6.

Freeman, Lou, Chicago, Illinois, telephone interview with Betty K. Gubert, New York, March 26, 2000.

Jones, Del. "Workforce Moves Steadily toward Diversity." *USA Today* (May 15, 1995): 3B.

Undated resumé of Louis Freeman.

# G

## Edward A. Gibbs

**Full Name at Birth:** Edward Albertis Gibbs

**Born:** December 12, 1919, New York City

**Died:** 1969

**Education:** Hampton University, Virginia, 1940; B.S. in business administration, New York University; J.D., New York Law School (dates unknown).

**Positions Held:** Flight instructor, Schumacher Flying Service and Coffey School of Aeronautics, Chicago, early 1940s; civilian flight instructor, Tuskegee Army Air Field, Alabama, 1942–1945; instructor, Lyon's Flying School, Long Island, New York, 1946; owner, Atlantic School of Aviation, Wilmington, North Carolina, 1947–1951; assistant commissioner of federal code enforcement, New York City Housing and Development Administration, until 1969.

**Summary:** In his short life, Edward A. Gibbs played an important role in increasing opportunities for African Americans in aviation. In the 1940s, he taught those who became Tuskegee Airmen. In 1967 he founded, and served as the first president of, the Negro Airmen International (NAI). From a handful of black flyers, the organization has now grown to include 31 chapters and hundreds of members.

### Early Years

Edward A. Gibbs was born in New York City on December 12, 1919, to a family with roots in the West Indies. He grew up in New York and attended the city's public schools.

### Higher Education

Gibbs enrolled at Hampton Institute, now University, in Virginia, where he planned to study accounting. While he was a student there in 1940, a Civilian Pilot Training Program (CPTP) was instituted at the college. This program was launched by the federal government to ensure a supply of trained pilots in case war should break out. Hampton was one of the first six black colleges chosen for this endeavor. The number was later increased to 10 institutions, chosen from a total of 200. He received his private pilot's license in Newport News, near Hampton, in 1940. It was so exhilarating that Gibbs said he felt like Charles A. Lindbergh, the pilot who made a nonstop 33-and-a-half hour flight across the Atlantic Ocean in May 1927.

Gibbs was married in 1940 to Dicey V. Thomas and they had one daughter, Beryl.

After Gibbs took another CPTP course, in aerobatics, in 1941, he was hooked on the idea of aviation as a career. It was also a livelihood that was better paying than many others. Gibbs realized that even if he could obtain work at a "Negro college or a Negro newspaper," he would earn only $200 a month. From Virginia he went to Chicago, where he "was lucky . . . to get into another CPTP group . . . an instructor's course at Harlem Airport." Sometimes the airport's name was spelled "Haarlem," because it was named after the city in The Netherlands and not the neighborhood in New York. It was operated by Fred Schumacher (Shoes), a man of Dutch origin. Gibbs met Cornelius Coffey and Willa Brown, who ran the Coffey School of Aeronautics at the northern end of Harlem Airport. Because of their efforts, Chicago became the center for blacks who were interested in aviation.

Despite the gibes of a prejudiced flight instructor, Gibbs earned both his flight instructor's and ground instructor's ratings, and he began teaching at Schumacher's school. Later, Gibbs earned a B.S. in business administration from New York University and a law degree from New York Law School.

## Career Highlights

After a government official who was visiting Schumacher's school pressured him to fire Gibbs because he didn't like the idea that Gibbs was teaching white women, he left for Tuskegee. "Where else?" he commented. He taught there as a civilian flight instructor for about three years, until the war ended in 1945.

He then returned to New York and became an instructor for Lyon's Flying Service at Zahn's Airport on Long Island. Even though business grew through Gibbs's efforts, he was passed over for the position of chief pilot. Gibbs left, feeling that he could not stay under those circumstances. Hearing of an opening for a black instructor at the Atlantic School of Aviation on Bluethenthal Field, in Wilmington, North Carolina, Gibbs applied for and was given the job. The owners wanted a black instructor because under the G.I. Bill (a government-sponsored benefit for veterans), many black veterans were enrolling at schools and colleges since their tuition would be fully or partially paid. By 1948, Gibbs was the owner of the business because the two partners couldn't agree, and each sold his half to him.

The school qualified its students as private commercial pilots or flight instructors. The curriculum included flight training and ground courses on aircraft and theory, and on mechanics, such as engine inspection. There were four airplanes. Gibbs planned for growth, and he hoped his school would be a major source of new black pilots. Soon after becoming the owner of the school, he said, "For Negroes, the ceiling is unlimited." Gibbs ran the school for three-and-a-half accident-free years. But the business finally failed due to "overt and covert discrimination and financial sabotage."

Because the G.I. Bill only partially funded aviation training, causing students to go on to other fields, Gibbs drew up plans to increase government assistance. He elaborated in an interview in *Flying* (July 1969) that after he submitted a curriculum plan that both the state board of education and the CAA (Civilian Aeronautics Administration) approved, he approached the Veterans' Administration (VA) for a contract. "They realized for the first time that the complexion of the school had changed. Right after that, their voucher payments began getting slower and slower. I was getting squeezed out."

Even though another school, the Pennington Flying Service, offered to supply his school with gas, and the County Commission complained that the VA was discriminating, Gibbs had to give up his school and his dream. He grew bitter enough to take a detour if he saw an airport sign along the road he was driving on.

Gibbs entered the field of public housing as an administrator while still living in North Carolina. He remained in this field, and he eventually became the assistant commissioner of federal code enforcement for the New York City Housing and Development Administration.

His love of flying superseded his bitterness, and he founded the Stick and Rudder Club of New York. His lasting contribution to the promotion of African Americans in aviation, however, came in 1967. On February 17th of that year, Negro Airmen International (NAI) was incorporated in New York. Gibbs was the founder and first president. The group's first convention was held in July 1969, in Pine Bluff, Arkansas. Starting with about 20 members, the NAI in 2000 counted 31 chapters throughout the United States and the Caribbean. Since July 1973, NAI has run a summer flight academy for 24 students from the age of 12 to 19. The preamble to their constitution clearly states their purpose, "Recognizing the imperfections of our society, and in order to secure those noble principles of equality and freedom so cherished by men of whatever state or persuasion, we hereby create this organization dedicated to promote aviation and to enable its members to more fully participate in."

Before Gibbs died in 1969, he also established an air taxi and maintenance service at the Harry S Truman Airport on St. Thomas, in the Virgin Islands. It was called West Indies Airline and Air Service. His legacy may be described as a life of entrepreneurial energy, far-ranging visions, and, most important of all, an ideal of collegiality.

## Sources

"Ceiling Unlimited." *Our World* (August 1948): 48–49.

Connes, Keith. "Can a Black Man Fly?" *Flying* (July 1969): 53–57.

"What Is Negro Airmen International?" Accessed March 27, 2000, http://seflin.org/nai/nai.2html.

"Negro Airmen International Inc. A Short History." Http://www.blackwings.com/history.htm. Accessed December 29, 1998.

# Isaac T. Gillam IV

**Full Name at Birth:** Isaac Thomas Gillam IV

**Born:** February 23, 1932, Little Rock, Arkansas

**Education:** Dunbar High School, Little Rock, Arkansas, 1948; B.S., mathematics, Howard University, Washington, D.C., 1953; pilot's wings, U.S. Air Force, 1953; graduate studies in mathematics and physics, Tennessee A & I State University, 1957–1961.

**Positions Held:** U.S. Air Force, 1952–1963; assistant professor of air science, Air Force ROTC, Tennessee State University, 1957–1961; missile crew commander, Strategic Air Command, 1961–1963; resource management specialist, NASA, 1963–1966; assistant program manager, Delta Launch Vehicle, NASA, 1966–1968; Delta program manager, NASA, 1968–1973; program manager, Small Launch Vehicles and International Projects, NASA, 1973–1976; director of Space Shuttle Operations, NASA's Dryden Flight Research Center, 1976–1977; deputy director, Dryden, 1977; acting director, Dryden, 1977–1978; director, Dryden, 1978–1981; special assistant, NASA, 1981–1982; assistant associate administrator, NASA, 1982–1984; assistant administrator in charge of commercial programs, NASA, 1984–1987; Orbiting Astronomical Observatory Corporation (OAO), Greenbelt, Maryland, 1987–1998; vice president for mission and computer support, OAO, 1988–1989, senior vice president, aerospace systems group, OAO, 1989–1998; communications network program manager, Allied Signal Technical Services, Pasadena, California, 1998–   .

**Awards, Honors:** Distinguished Service Medal, NASA, 1976; Exceptional Service Medal, NASA, 1981, 1982; Distinguished Alumnus, for successful pursuits in Space Engineering, Howard University, 1981; AIAA Space Commerce Award, 1985; NASA Equal Opportunity Medal, 1985; Presidential Meritorious Excellence Award, 1986.

**Summary:** Isaac T. Gillam IV has had a lengthy career in aerospace engineering and administration. He was manager of NASA's Delta program, which was responsible for launching weather and communications satellites into orbit. Gillam also was director of space shuttle operations during the early flight tests of the shuttle program. He later became director of NASA's Dryden Flight Research Center where shuttle testing took place, and thus was the first African American to lead a NASA research center. His later career included achievements in NASA's Washington headquarters, where he began development of a space station. From there, he moved into private industry.

## Early Years

Born in Little Rock, Arkansas, to Isaac Thomas and Ethel McNeal Reynolds Gillam, Isaac "Ike" Gillam IV grew up in his grandparents' home, attending school in Little Rock where his grandfather was a high school principal. He spent summers with his parents in Washington, D.C., where his mother worked for the State Department and his father for the U.S. Post Office.

## Higher Education

After graduating from high school in Little Rock, Gillam enrolled at Howard University in Washington, D.C., where both his father and grandfather had studied. A newsreel about the Tuskegee airmen sparked his interest in flying, and he joined the Air Force ROTC at Howard.

## Career Highlights

Upon graduating from Howard with a degree in mathematics, Gillam was commissioned as a second lieutenant in the U.S. Air Force and served as a pilot during the Korean War. In 1956, he married Norma Jean Hughes, a former teacher; they have four children. The following year, Gillam was assigned to Tennessee State University as an assistant professor of air science in the ROTC program. While at Tennessee State, he also pursued graduate studies in mathematics and physics. From 1961–1963, Gillam was a launch crew commander in underground missile silos for the Strategic Air Command, which required 24-hour shifts.

Gillam left the Air Force in 1963 with the rank of captain to join NASA, working at NASA's Washington headquarters as a resource management specialist. Three years later, he was appointed assistant manager for the Delta program, which was responsible for "launch vehicles" (i.e., missiles), which launched weather and communications satellites into orbit. In 1968, he became the manager of the Delta program.

In 1973, he was appointed program manager for small launch vehicles and international projects, which included both the Delta and Scout launch vehicles. During this time, NASA launched satellites not only for U.S. agencies but also for companies in other countries, including the European Space Agency, France, Germany, Italy, Indonesia, Canada, and Japan. He was awarded NASA's highest award, the Distinguished Service Medal, in 1976 for his work in the international satellite launch program.

In 1976, Gillam left NASA headquarters to become director of space shuttle operations at NASA's Dryden Flight Research Center in Edwards, California. The first phase of the space shuttle program took place during Gillam's tenure, and he was responsible for coordinating the efforts of scientists from both government agencies and private companies. Critical tests of space shuttle operations at this time included takeoff and landing processes.

In August 1977, Gillam was named deputy director of Dryden, and three months later, acting director. On June 18, 1978, he was named director of Dryden, the first African American to lead a NASA research center. He held that post for three years. In 1981, Gillam returned to NASA's Washington headquarters as a special assistant, working on the development of a national space policy, under assignment to the Office of Science and Technology Policy at the White House. The following year he was named an assistant associate administrator for NASA's Office of Space Flight, responsible for assisting with the management of the shuttle program and the early development of the space station program. From 1984 to 1987, Gillam headed NASA's newly created Office of Commercial Programs, leading efforts to expand U.S. private sector investment and involvement in civil space-related activities.

In 1987, Gillam moved into the private sector, joining the Orbiting Astronomical Observatory Corporation, an aerospace firm in Greenbelt, Maryland, which provides technological and information support to government agencies, including NASA, as well as private companies. He was named vice president for mission and computing support at OAO in 1988, and, in 1989, senior vice president of OAO's aerospace systems group, with responsibility for all engineering and science support activities that OAO provides to military and civil space programs. While at OAO, Gillam served on several committees of the NASA Advisory Council, such as the Scientific Research, Mission to Planet Earth, and Space Technology Committee of NASA's Federal Laboratory Review Task Force, which conducted an interagency review of federal research and development in these areas, and on the Technology and Commercialization Advisory Committee, which focused on assessments of the viability of commercializing space exploration.

In 1998, Gillam moved from OAO to Allied Signal Technical Services (now Honeywell) in Pasadena, California, where he is program manager for a NASA-commissioned communications network that makes it possible for control centers to communicate with spacecraft at great distances.

## Sources

Graves, Curtis M., and Ivan Van Sertima. "Space Science: The African American Contribution." *Blacks in Science: Ancient and Modern.* New Brunswick, NJ: Transaction, 1983; 246–247.

Moite, Sally M. "Isaac Thomas Gillam, IV." *Notable Black American Scientists.* Detroit: Gale Research, 1999; 128–129.

National Aeronautics and Space Administration. Various pages, http://www.nasa.gov. Accessed on April 2, 2000. Keywords: Gillam, Isaac.

*Who's Who among Black Americans, 1990–1991.* Detroit: Gale Research, 1990; 469.

# Joseph P. Gomer

**Full Name at Birth:** Joseph Philip Gomer

**Born:** June 20, 1920, Iowa Falls, Iowa

**Education:** Ellsworth College, Iowa Falls, Iowa

**Summary:** Joseph P. Gomer was a member of the Tuskegee Airmen, the first group of black pilots who served in the U.S. Army Air Corps during World War II. He later pursued a career in the Air Force as pilot and maintenance officer. Retiring from the military in 1964, Gomer then served in the U.S. Forest Service for a number of years.

## Career Highlights

Joseph P. Gomer was born in Iowa Falls, Iowa, on June 20, 1920. The Gomer family was one of only two African American families in the town of 5,000 residents. In a newspaper article, Gomer stated that he encountered no prejudice in his early years, and he remembers being fully accepted in the community. It "was a nice way of growing up." It was an unusual upbringing for an African American child of the period. In a speech given in 1997, Gomer wryly stated that "I have known assimilation, segregation, and integration." As a child, he was fascinated with airplanes, and enjoyed building model planes.

It was while Gomer was attending college that war began to loom. The Axis Powers, Germany, Japan, and Italy, were starting to overrun Europe and Asia, causing President Franklin D. Roosevelt and his advisers to prepare the United States military for the coming conflict. The United States entered the war on December 7, 1941, after the surprise bombing attack on Pearl Harbor.

Gomer enlisted in the army in July 1942. Ellsworth College in Iowa Falls, Iowa, which he had been attending, offered pilot training, so he had learned to fly before his enlistment. Soon after, Gomer applied and was accepted for Aviation Cadet Training. After passing rigorous tests, the men were sent to Tuskegee Institute in Tuskegee, Alabama, for preflight orientation. The instructors were civilian pilots, most of them black. C. Alfred "Chief" Anderson, one of the first African Americans to get a pilot's license, was in charge of instructors. The whole operation at Tuskegee was led by Colonel Noel Parrish. Though a southern white man, he was not a racist and treated everyone with respect.

Gomer earned his wings on May 28, 1943. The Airmen were next shipped to Italy, where the group were assigned to escorting bombers on their missions, under the command of Lieutenant Colonel Benjamin O. Davis Jr. Their superb teamwork and discipline caused them to excel in this function, and the group could boast that they never lost a bomber to enemy fire. Known as the "Red Tails" because of the distinctive markings on their planes, the unit flew 1,500 sorties in Italy, and downed 111 enemy aircraft

as well as sinking one German navy destroyer. Sixty-six members of the group were killed in action.

This creditable showing did not prevent the men of the 332nd Fighter Group from being treated as second-class citizens. They had to eat in segregated dining halls, and they had to suffer the humiliation of observing German prisoners of war being fed in white dining halls. Gomer later observed, "We shared the sky with white pilots, but that's all we shared. We never had contact with each other. German prisoners lived better than black serviceman."

Although white pilots had to complete a maximum of 50 sorties before being shipped home, Gomer flew 68 sorties before completing his tour of duty. Despite the prejudice he encountered, Gomer was convinced of the rightness of his cause: "We were fighting two battles. I flew for my parents, for my race, for our battle for first-class citizenship. We were fighting for the 14 million black Americans back home. . . . But we're all Americans. That's why we chose to fight. I'm as American as anybody. My black ancestors were brought over here, perhaps against their will, to help build America. My German ancestors came over to build a new life. And my Cherokee ancestors were here to greet all the boats."

At the war's end, civilian piloting jobs were still not open to African American men. Gomer decided that the military offered better opportunities than civilian life, and became a career officer. Black and white units were still segregated. Gomer became a flight test maintenance officer with the 332nd, which was stationed at Lockbourne Air Force Base in Ohio. In 1948, the armed forces were integrated by an executive order issued by President Harry S Truman. In 1949, the Air Force, at the time a branch of the Army, became a separate command, and Gomer married Elizabeth Evelyn Caperton on March 12, 1949.

After Lockbourne, Gomer was transferred to Langley Air Force Base in Virginia, where he became chief maintenance officer for reconnaissance and helicopter aircraft. On this tour of duty, he qualified as a helicopter pilot.

During the Korean War, Gomer served in Japan and Korea, flying troop transports. When the war ended, he was assigned to Andrews Air Force Base in Maryland, where he set up the first helicopter flights used to carry President Dwight D. Eisenhower and other high government officials. His final assignment took him to the French River, just north of Duluth, Minnesota.

After 22 years of service, Gomer retired as a major in 1964. He and his wife elected to remain in Duluth, where they had raised their two daughters, Tanya and Phyllis G. Douglass. Gomer embarked on a second career as an employment officer for the Superior National Forest, part of the National Forest Service. He retired from this position in 1985.

Fifty years after the end of World War II, Gomer was invited to a reunion of the 359th Bombardment Group, one of the groups which the 332nd Fighter Group had escorted. When he was introduced, he was greeted with a standing ovation. It was the first time that white bomber crewmen and one of their black fighter escorts had met. One of the bomber crewmen told Gomer, "I've waited 50 years to thank you for saving my butt."

## Sources

Fortner, Larry. "We Shared the Sky with White Pilots, but That's All We Shared." *Northlife & the Senior Reporter* (February 2000): 8–11.

"The Tuskegee Airmen: A Tribute to my Father." Http://www.geocities.com/Pentagon/Quarters/1350. Accessed June 5, 1998.

# Robert O. Goodman Jr.

**Full Name at Birth:** Robert Oliver Goodman Jr.

**Born:** November 30, 1956, San Juan, Puerto Rico

**Education:** B.S. in operations analysis, United States Naval Academy, Annapolis, Maryland, 1978; M.S. in systems technology (Space), Naval Postgraduate School, Monterey, California, 1987.

**Positions Held:** A6 Intruder bombardier-navigator, United States Navy.

**Summary:** Robert O. Goodman Jr. became the first American military person to be taken prisoner of war since the conclusion of the Vietnam War when he was captured by Syria in 1983. His release from captivity was secured by the efforts of the Reverend Jesse L. Jackson. Jackson, at the time a presidential candidate, traveled to Syria as a private citizen and persuaded Syrian president Hafez al-Assad to release Goodman.

## Early Years

Robert O. Goodman Jr. was born in 1956 in San Juan, Puerto Rico, where his father, Robert O. Goodman Sr., an Air Force pilot, was then stationed. Marylyn Joan Dykers Goodman, his mother, is a fashion show coordinator and professional model. Goodman has two brothers, Tyron, who is in the Coast Guard, and Marvin, who is in the Navy.

Because of his father's military assignments, the Goodman family moved frequently during Robert's youth. Lieutenant Harry Woods, a close friend, recalls Goodman's reminiscences of his school years: "I remember Bob talking about all the places he had lived . . . [H]e said he was the only black kid in the school he went to in Puerto Rico. He had a varied background." Among the places where he resided was Portsmouth, New Hampshire, where he spent many of his school years.

## Higher Education

Upon graduation from high school, Goodman enrolled in the Naval Academy, at Annapolis, Maryland. Woods, who was a classmate of Goodman's at the Academy, recalled that Goodman had always wanted to be a navy pilot. His role models were his father and General Daniel "Chappie" James, the first black flag officer to receive a fourth star.

## Career Highlights

After completing his studies at Annapolis, Goodman was commissioned as an officer in the navy and became a navigator-bombardier.

In August 1982, the American military became involved in efforts to stabilize Lebanon, where Syria, Israel, and contending Lebanese factions were engaged in conflict. On December 3, 1983, Syrian antiaircraft batteries attacked two unarmed U.S. reconnaissance planes. In retaliation, on December 4, 28 carrier-based U.S. warplanes struck at Syrian antiaircraft batteries at Hammana, in the mountains east of Beirut, Lebanon. Two of these planes were shot down by the Syrians.

Goodman, who was serving as navigator-bombardier on one of the planes, was captured by the Syrians. The other crewman on Goodman's plane, Navy Lieutenant Mark A. Lange, was killed.

Upon learning of Goodman's capture, U.S. Defense Secretary Caspar Weinberger attempted to open negotiations with Syria to secure his release. The Syrians refused to free him, declaring their intentions to detain Goodman "until the end of the Lebanese war and the departure of the Americans from Lebanon."

The situation appeared to be at a stalemate when the Reverend Jesse Jackson, a prominent civil rights leader and at the time a candidate for the Democratic Party nomination for president, sent a telegram to Syrian president al-Assad asking for Goodman's release as a "humanitarian gesture." The telegram led to an invitation from al-Assad for Jackson and a group of American clergy to

visit Damascus to "discuss Middle East issues and the specific question of your concern—the release of Goodman." Jackson called the invitation "a good sign," adding, "I had not intended to go when I sent the telegram. . . . But their response appealed to me to go, and so if I can help within the law to set the climate in which Goodman would be released I will contribute that service."

On December 27, Jackson said he would reconsider making the trip if President Reagan, who had expressed misgivings about the idea, asked him not to go. Goodman's father, Robert O. Goodman Sr., shared the White House's doubts: "I don't see what good would come about if Jackson went . . . I am assured this government will see to it that Robert is returned home." Nevertheless, Reagan did not try to prevent the trip, and Jackson departed for Syria on December 29, 1983.

Jackson met with Goodman on December 31; the captured airman described himself as "relatively comfortable," and had but one request: "Send me home."

Before leaving the United States, Jackson received no guarantees that he would be allowed to meet with President al-Assad. After several days' delay, Jackson was granted the interview with Syria's president. Further discussions followed, and on January 3, Jackson announced at a news conference that "our prayers have been answered." Goodman was to be allowed to leave. The Syrian government stated that the release was a response both to Jackson's "human appeal" and to the demands of the U.S. government.

Later on January 3, Jackson, Goodman, and the 14 other members of the group left Syria, arriving at Andrews Air Force Base early on January 4. On the last leg of his trip home, Goodman made clear to reporters that he would steer clear of politics and let "politicians deal with political issues." "I am a naval officer," Goodman reportedly declared. "I am not a hero. It's just a matter of fate that it happens to be me sitting here, instead of Mark."

Upon arrival at Andrews, Goodman embraced his family and made a brief speech: "I want to quote a gentleman, a POW from Vietnam, when he returned home: God bless America." He said that he had been especially heartened by 60,000 Christmas cards and letters that he had received from Americans while in captivity. After being examined by Air Force doctors at Bethesda Naval Hospital and pronounced in good condition, Goodman and Jackson were honored at a reception at the White House. Reagan professed himself delighted with Jackson's effort: "You don't quarrel with success."

In interviews with reporters, Goodman said his treatment by the Syrians was "generally good." He explained the injuries he had sustained as the result of ejection from the aircraft: "Any time you eject from an aircraft going in excess of 450 knots, you're going to get injured, even in the best circumstances." He said jokingly that "plebe summer (at the naval academy) was worse."

For Goodman, the worst part of his imprisonment was the uncertainty he had to live with. When interrogated, Goodman gave his questioner vague answers, as he had been taught at a survival, evasion, resistance, and escape school. Though frightened and uncertain of his fate, Goodman maintained that he "did the things that are right to do."

Goodman, in a May 1987 interview with *Ebony*, refused to rule out the possibility of participating in another air strike: "I'm not a warmonger or anything like that, but if the situation presented itself and I was called upon, I wouldn't hesitate to do the same thing again."

After his return from Syria, Goodman was assigned to Attack Squadron 85, based in Oceana, Virginia. In April 1985, he was sent to the Naval Postgraduate School, Monterey, California, to prepare for a postgraduate degree in space systems. He graduated from the program in 1987.

Goodman and his wife, Terry Lynn Bryant Goodman, reside in Virginia Beach, Virginia. They have two daughters, Tina, born in 1976, and Morgan, born in 1982.

## Sources

"Black Pilot to Be Captive until U.S. Leaves Lebanon." *Jet* (December 26, 1983): 31.

Burgess, Tom. "Friends Describe Flier As Level-Headed, Optimistic." *Navy Times*, n. d.

———. "Goodman: Believe in Self, Country." *Navy Times* (January 16, 1984): 1, 10.

"Ebony Update; Lt. Robert O. Goodman." *Ebony* (May 1987): 124, 126.

"Syria Releases Captive U.S. Flyer to Rev. Jackson." Http://www.2facts.com/stories/index/198400000 10.asp. Accessed May 30, 2000.

# Marlon D. Green

**Born:** 1930, Lansing, Michigan

**Summary:** When Marlon D. Green, who had been a captain in the U.S. Air Force, was refused a position in commercial aviation, he turned to the Colorado Anti-Discrimination Commission and then to the courts. His case, which began in 1957, resulted in the landmark decision by the U.S. Supreme Court in 1963 that it was unconstitutional for the airlines to discriminate on the basis of race. Green's six-year fight not only gave him employment as a pilot but also opened the door to fair employment to those who came after him.

## Career Highlights

Marlon D. Green was born in 1930. A native of Lansing, Michigan, Green served as a captain in the U.S. Air Force and as a pilot in several installations in the United States. He was sent to Tokyo, Japan, in 1955, and served with the 36th Air Rescue Squadron until leaving the military in 1957. Green attempted to put his air force training to use in civilian life as a pilot for a commercial airline, but he was rejected by 600 commercial and private airlines all over the world. Green, who was married and had six children, could only find work flying for the Michigan Highway Patrol. This job ended in

1960, after three years. Green then worked at a dairy for a time. The family was supported by the earnings of his wife, a schoolteacher.

At last, he applied to Continental Airlines and omitted mentioning his race on the application form. Though qualified for the job and having passed all the tests, Green was rejected because of his race. Four other men, all white, who applied at the same time as Green, were hired.

In June 1957, Green took his case to the Colorado Anti-Discrimination Commission, which had jurisdiction over Continental, at that time based in Denver. The commission ruled in his favor. Continental was ordered to enroll Green in its next pilots' training class. The company appealed the order, first to the Denver District Court, and then in the Colorado Supreme Court. According to Continental's attorneys, being forced to obey the executive order would result in an "undue burden upon commerce." The Colorado Supreme Court concurred, ruling that the Colorado commission had no jurisdiction over the airline, as it was an interstate carrier, operating out of nine states. Green and his attorneys then appealed to the U.S. Supreme Court.

In 1963, the Court ruled in Green's favor. The decision made history. Justice Hugo Black delivered the Supreme Court's opinion, which was unanimous. He stated that "the Colorado statute as applied here to prevent discrimination in hiring on account of race does not impose a constitutionally prohibited burden upon interstate commerce. . . . We are not convinced that commerce will be unduly burdened if Continental is required by Colorado to refrain from racial discrimination in its hiring of pilots in that state."

Justice Black went on to state: "[U]nder our more recent decisions any state or federal law requiring applicants for any job to be turned away because of their color would be invalid under the due process clause of the fifth amendment and the due process and equal protection clauses of the fourteenth amendment."

In support of this decision, Justice Black referred to the railway labor act, the civil aeronautics act, and several federal executive orders.

Ben King, then vice president in charge of public relations for the airline, claimed that "discrimination was not a factor." In defense of the airline's position, King claimed that Green was not hired after the company learned that he had filed complaints against six other airlines. According to King, "We wanted cockpit harmony. . . . We didn't want anybody with a cause in the cockpit."

After the decision was handed down, Green was elated. "I am very impressed with the prompt decision, and most impressed with the fact that the decision was a unanimous one. . . . I am now awaiting notification from Continental that they want me to come to work."

The consequences of Green's successful lawsuit were enormous. The Supreme Court decision opened doors for other African Americans to participate in the prestigious and lucrative piloting jobs that had formerly been reserved for whites. Within two years, Green and three other black men were employed as pilots by major carriers. While much remained to be done in terms of recruitment, by 1986, 175 African Americans were employed as pilots, among them Marlon Green.

## Sources

"Again: Caught Between." *Interracial Review* (March 1963): 5.

"Breakthrough on the Airlines." *Ebony* (November 1965): 112–114, 116, 118–119.

Hearst, Joseph. "Kansas Debt Law Upheld by High Court." *Chicago Tribune* (April 23, 1963).

"Lansing Pilot Awaits Job Call After High Court's Bias Ruling." *Detroit News* (April 23, 1963): 8a.

Leary, William M., ed. *Encyclopedia of American Business History and Biography; The Airline Industry.* New York: Facts on File, 1992: 10.

"Michigan Highway Pilot." *Ebony* (February 1958): 4.

White, Frank III. "Spreading Their Wings." *Ebony* (February 1986): 775–776, 778, 782.

# John W. Greene Jr.

John W. Greene Jr. Courtesy of National Air and Space Museum, Smithsonian Institution (SI Neg. No. 2001-1897).

**Full Name at Birth:** John William Greene Jr.

**Born:** December 25, 1900, Atlanta, Georgia, or December 25, 1901, Chattanooga, Tennessee

**Died:** March 23, 1989, Washington, D.C.

**Education:** Elberton High School, Elberton, Georgia; mechanical engineering degree, Hampton Institute, Virginia, 1922; airplane mechanics degree, Boston Trade School, Boston, Massachusetts.

**Positions Held:** Engine mechanic and transport pilot, Wiggins Flying Service, Boston; instructor, Phelps Vocational School, Washington, D.C., 1940–?; instructor, Armstrong High School, 1940s?; co-owner/operator, Columbia Air Center, 1941–1956; aircraft mechanic, Camp Springs Army Air Field (now Andrews Air Force Base), during World War II; instructor, University of Colorado National Aviation Education workshop; retired from teaching, 1975.

**Awards, Honors:** Received private pilot's license in June 1929. In August 1930, Greene was one of only three African Americans to hold a transport pilot's license. By 1932, he held U.S. Department of Commerce, limited commercial license no. 15,897 and mechanics license no. 10,658. Member, Caterpillar Club. The Maryland chapter of Negro Airmen International is named for him.

**Summary:** Greene was the second African American to receive a commercial pilot's license in the United States, and the first to receive an aircraft engine mechanic's license. The founder and co-owner of the Columbia Air Center in Croome, Maryland, Greene was a lifelong advocate of aviation education for young people.

## Early Years

John William Greene Jr. was the son of John W. Greene Sr. and Rosa Reasley Greene. In Charles E. Francis's book (1997 ed.), Greene's birth date and place are listed as December 25, 1900, in Atlanta, Georgia. In John M. Walton Jr.'s book (1996), Walton claims that Greene was born on December 25, 1901, in Chattanooga, Tennessee. Several sources claim that Greene completed grade school in Chattanooga; he may also have attended public school in Atlanta, and he graduated from high school in Elberton, Georgia, east of Atlanta.

## Higher Education

Greene first became interested in flying while visiting Langley Field, Virginia, while he was a student at Hampton Institute (now Hampton University) in southeastern Virginia. Following his graduation from Hampton in 1922 with a degree in mechanical engineering, he enrolled at the Boston Trade School for instruction in airplane mechanics. After flight training at Denison Airport in Quincy, Massachusetts, he received his private pilot's license in 1929, the first African American to do so in that state.

## Career Highlights

Following completion of his training at Boston Trade School, he worked as an engine mechanic for Wiggins Flying Service, based in Boston. Over the next several years, he earned licensing as a limited commercial pilot, able to pilot all types of licensed airplanes but not to instruct students commercially, and as a transport pilot, allowed to instruct students commercially and to carry passengers for hire within areas specified on the particular pilot's license. In a contemporary news article, Dutton Ferguson wrote, "True to all aviators, Pilot Greene has his pet peculiarities. He always flies bare-headed and wears his parachute. . . . He is nothing short of being among one of America's top rank pilots in the science of air navigation."

In August 1939, Cornelius Coffey, president of the newly founded National Airmen's Association, invited Greene to take part in a proposed national conference of African American air pilots, to be held in Chicago later that month. Greene subsequently became one of the vice presidents of the National Airmen's Association. The National Airmen's Association worked with the nonmilitary federal Civil Aeronautics Authority to establish a flight training center in Chicago for African Americans. In March 1940, Willa Brown, then director of Flight Training for the National Airmen's Association, invited Greene to come to Chicago as one of the instructors.

It is not evident why Greene did not join this effort; however, when Greene left Boston in 1940, he relocated not to Chicago but to Washington, D.C. There he established an aviation mechanics course at Phelps Vocational School, which began instruction on September 20, 1940. "No longer is the airplane to be viewed as an unsafe method of transportation and a plaything for a few," Greene wrote several years later:

> No longer are military leaders skeptical of its value as an offensive weapon. Aviation as an industry is definitely here to stay. The continuous growth of aviation, however, could not have been possible without the mechanic, who is coming to the fore at this time. . . . The increased importance given to the mechanic is of great interest to the Negro, for at present the mechanical field offers the best possibilities of employment for the Negro.

By the time Greene's article appeared, nearly 100 students had received instruction in the course at Phelps, of whom 60 percent had achieved "occupational levels." It continued,

> To serve more fully the community's aviation activities, the school authorities allowed the instructor at Phelps [Greene] to work with an aviation club in the District [of Columbia]. He taught the members flying, ground school, and airplane mechanics. Under the guidance of the instructor, the club selected and developed an airport which compared favorably with the privately owned airports in the community, and today it is operating commercially with two new airplanes.
>
> The work with the Aviation Club is the greatest contibution the course at Phelps has offered. . . . Future plans are to develop at Phelps within the next five years such aviation courses as Airplane Mechanics, Engine Mechanics, Propeller Mechanics, Instrument Mechanics, and Radio Mechanics, and such flying activities as elementary, advanced and instrument flying.

Greene later taught also at Armstrong High School.

The District of Columbia's "Cloud Club"

initially was based at Beacon Field near Alexandria, Virginia. Following some "unpleasantness" there, however, several members of the club began a search for their own field, with Greene's enthusiastic assistance. Finding the District itself too congested, they searched further afield, and eventually established the Columbia Air Center in Croome, Maryland, approximately 35 miles east of Washington. The group signed a lease on the land, laid out the runways, were donated an office, and built a hangar. Their first program, sponsored by the Civil Aeronautics Authority, took place as scheduled, but in December 1941 Pearl Harbor was bombed and the United States entered World War II. The Navy took over the Columbia flying field, and many of the Air Center's operators and students went off to war. Greene himself worked as an aircraft mechanic at Camp Springs Army Air Field (now Andrews Air Force Base).

Back in business after the war, by 1946 Columbia Air Center was the largest air field in the country owned and operated by African Americans. Its flying school was integrated, however, and approximately half of its 60 students were white. The airport could handle as many as 150 arrivals and departures each hour on its eight runways. A contemporary newspaper article describing the facilities concluded, "With men like John Greene breaking the trail, more and more Negroes are likely to find that flying is good business and, what's more, it's fun."

John Greene operated the Columbia Air Center until 1956. At some time he was also employed as an instructor at the University of Colorado's National Aviation Education workshop; he retired from teaching in 1975. He remained in the District of Columbia area for much of his life, "sharing his love and knowledge of aviation with all who would listen." He was honored as part of the Smithsonian Institution's "Black Wings" exhibition in 1982. A Maryland chapter of the Negro Airmen International is named in his honor. On March 23, 1989, Greene died in Washington, D.C.

## Sources

Ferguson, Dutton. "Colored America on the Wing." n.d., n.p.

Francis, Charles E. *The Tuskegee Airmen: The Men Who Changed a Nation.* 4th ed., revised and updated by Adolph Caso. Boston: Branden Publishing Co., 1997; 32–33.

"Fun on the Wing." *The Easterner* (April 1, 1946): 5–6.

Greene, John W. "National Defense Program in Action: Aviation Mechanics at Phelps Vocational School." n.p., n.d.

Hardesty, Von, and Dominick Pisano. *Black Wings: The American Black in Aviation.* Washington, DC: National Air and Space Museum, Smithsonian Institution Press, 1983; 70.

"Negro and White Study Together: High School Students Take Active Part." *The Easterner* (April 1, 1946): 7.

Powell, William J. *Black Aviator.* Washington, DC: Smithsonian Institution Press, 1994; 148–149.

Walton, John M. Jr. "This Week in County History." *Prince George's Journal.* December 1996. Http://www.jrnl.com/news/96/Dec/jrn189271296.htm. Accessed March 26, 2000.

# Frederick Drew Gregory Sr.

Frederick Drew Gregory Sr. Courtesy of NASA.

**Full Name at Birth:** Frederick Drew Gregory

**Born:** January 7, 1941, Washington, D.C.

**Education:** B.S., United States Air Force Academy, Colorado Springs, Colorado, 1964; M.S. in information systems, George Washington University, Washington, D.C., 1977.

**Positions Held:** Helicopter rescue pilot, Vance Air Force Base, Oklahoma, combat rescue pilot, Vietnam; Space Shuttle Crew, 1978; piloted the *Challenger*, Spacelab 3 mission, April 1985; spacecraft commander, orbiter *Discovery*, 1989; mission control lead spacecraft communicator for subsequent flights of the space shuttle; pilot, orbiter *Atlantis*, 1992; associate administrator, Office of Safety and Mission Assurance, National Aeronautics and Space Administration (NASA), Washington, D.C., 1992–  .

**Awards, Honors:** Defense Superior Service Medal; the Legion of Merit; two Distinguished Flying Crosses; Defense Meritorious Service Medal; 16 Air Medals; the Air Force Commendation Medal; the Air Force Meritorious Service Medal, the NASA Distinguished Service Medal; 1967; three NASA Space Flight Medals; a NASA Outstanding Leadership Award; National Intelligence Medal of Achievement; National Society of Black Engineers Distinguished National Scientist Award and George Washington University Distinguished Alumni Award.

**Summary:** Frederick Drew Gregory Sr. was one of the first three African Americans chosen to participate in the astronaut program and the first African American to pilot an American spacecraft. After logging 455 hours in space, Gregory retired from the U.S. Air Force in 1993, becoming associate administrator, Office of Safety and Mission Assurance, National Aeronautics and Space Administration (NASA).

## Early Years

Frederick Drew Gregory was born on January 7, 1941, in Washington, D.C., the only child of Francis Anderson Gregory and Nora Drew Gregory, both teachers. He came from an illustrious family; his maternal uncle was Dr. Charles Richard Drew, a surgeon and a pioneer in blood plasma production and preservation during World War II, and his paternal grandfather was a Congregational minister. His great-grandfather, James Monroe Gregory, had been a member of Howard University's first graduating class in 1872.

Gregory grew up in an integrated neighborhood, but was bussed across town to an all-black school until he was in eighth grade, when local schools were integrated. His family tried to shield him from racism although his father had suffered from its effects. An electrical engineer, the elder Gregory was unable to find work in his profession and had become a teacher. He had a distinguished career in education, eventually becoming assistant superintendent of schools in Washington, D.C.

The family was solidly middle class. His parents, college graduates, owned the house they lived in and were active in civic and community associations. According to Barbara Archer Gregory (Gregory's wife), who grew up in the same environment: "We had everything white society had, but no one knew it but us."

Gregory was "adventuresome," according to his mother. He enjoyed racing small boats off Columbia Beach, Maryland, and was active in his Boy Scout troop. But education was of primary importance to the Gregory family. At the time local schools were integrated, in 1954, whites staged a boycott and threatened any African American who attended with bodily harm. Most stayed home. Gregory attended and was the only student in his class to show up.

Despite occasional harassment in the form of taunts and jeers from whites, Gregory did well in high school. He became a member of the Junior Reserve Officers Training Corps (ROTC), and he developed an interest in flying during visits to Andrews Air Force Base. This interest was further stimulated when he met a member of the Thunderbirds, an Air Force acrobatic flying team, and learned that the new U.S. Air Force Academy was to open shortly in Colorado.

## Higher Education

As his graduation from Anacostia High School, Washington, D.C., drew nearer, Gregory still wanted to train as a military pilot, but he enrolled in Amherst College, at Amherst, Massachusetts, which his father and grandfather had attended, instead. Francis Gregory, observing that his son truly desired a military career, persuaded Representative Adam Clayton Powell of Harlem, a celebrated civil rights leader and influential politician, to nominate him for the Air Force Academy. He left Amherst College when he was admitted to the Academy—the only African American in his class. Despite encountering some hostility and studied indifference from whites, Gregory excelled in scholarly, military, and athletics subjects, graduating in 1964. Shortly after graduation, he married Barbara Ann Archer, his high school sweetheart.

## Career Highlights

After graduation, Gregory underwent helicopter flight training at Stead Air Force Base in Nevada. He received his wings in 1965, and after a short stint as a helicopter rescue pilot at Vance Air Force Base in Oklahoma, was sent to Vietnam as a combat rescue pilot, flying 550 combat missions during a single year. In 1967, he was awarded a Distinguished Flying Cross for rescuing four Marines from a downed helicopter during intense enemy fire.

Gregory then underwent training on fixed wing aircraft and was assigned to the F-4 Phantom Combat Crew Training Wing, an unusual move, as most pilots specialized in only one type of aircraft. In 1970, he attended the U.S. Naval Test Pilot School at Patuxent River Naval Air Station, Maryland.

Upon completion of this training, he joined the 4950th Test Wing where he tested both helicopters and fixed-wing aircraft. In 1974, he was sent to Langley Air Force Base in Virginia as a research test pilot.

Gregory had wanted to be an astronaut since his youth, and in 1977 he asked the Air Force to forward his application to NASA. The Air Force was at first reluctant to do so, as most of his experience was in piloting helicopters while most astronauts had been high performance jet pilots. Gregory, a man who "does everything to the max" according to Curtis M. Graves, director of civil affairs at NASA, persisted. He submitted two applications, one as a civilian and one as an Air Force officer. If chosen as a civilian, he was willing to resign his commission in order to be accepted. This proved unnecessary.

In 1978, he was one of 35 candidates chosen, along with two other African American candidates, Ronald E. McNair and Guion S. Bluford Jr. After training and evaluation, Gregory qualified as a pilot on space shuttle crews. He worked for NASA in a variety of assignments for four years, and in 1985 he was chosen to pilot the *Challenger* on the Spacelab 3 mission, which was launched in April 1985.

As leader of the seven-man crew, he was the first African American to pilot an American spacecraft and was responsible for the scientific operations performed on the flight, which included medical and materials processing experiments and satellite deployments.

Gregory was deeply moved by this first voyage. The experience fortified his belief in God. In an article in *Ebony*, he is quoted as saying: "[W]hen you're in space . . . looking down on earth and you see this perfect globe . . . and the organization and non-chaos, you have to feel, as I did, that there was one great Being—one great force that made this happen."

Gregory next served as mission control lead spacecraft communicator for subsequent flights of the space shuttle. On January 28,

1986, it was he who was communicating with the *Challenger* shuttle when the craft exploded, killing all on board.

In 1989, he was appointed spacecraft commander of the orbiter *Discovery*, both piloting the plane and landing it after its successful five-day flight. On this mission, Gregory orbited the earth 79 times, deploying classified Department of Defense cargo.

His next mission was at the helm of the orbiter *Atlantis* in 1991. This shuttle deployed the Defense Support Program missile-warning satellite and conducted other military-related operations. After the completion of this mission, Gregory had logged over 455 hours of time in outer space.

During his career as an astronaut, Gregory gave high priority to encouraging young African Americans to pursue careers in astronautics and in aviation generally. He spoke at numerous high schools, always stressing the message that any young man or woman could be an astronaut with hard work and perseverance. African American pilots, according to Gregory, "are what we need a whole lot of."

He retired from the Air Force with the rank of colonel in 1993. Since then, he has been in his present position, associate administrator, Office of Safety and Mission Assurance, at NASA's Washington, D.C. headquarters. In this capacity, he is responsible for the safety, reliability, and quality of all NASA programs. His 7,000 hours of flight experience in 50 types of aircraft make him ideally suited to this assignment.

He and his wife are the parents of a son, Frederick Drew Gregory Jr., who is in the Air Force, and a daughter, Heather Lynn Gregory Skeens, a social worker.

Gregory is an active participant in several professional organizations, including the Society of Experimental Test Pilots, American Helicopter Society, Air Force Academy Association of Graduates, the Air Force Association, Sigma Pi Phi Fraternity, the National Technical Association, and the Tuskegee Airmen, Inc. He is on the board of directors of the Young Astronaut Council, the Challenger Center for Space Science Education, Kaiser-Permanente, Fisk University, and the Maryland Science Center. He is also on the executive committee of the Association of Space Explorers.

## Sources

"Black Leads Spaceship." *New York Amsterdam News* (December 10, 1988): 13.

Broad, William J. "Shuttle Atlantis Is Launched with Military Satellite." *New York Times* (November 25, 1991): A7.

Gregory, Frederick. "D.C. Astronaut Locks onto a View of Unity from Space." *Washington Times* (January 12, 1980).

Hunt, Rufus A. "Profile of an Astronaut Candidate." *Chicago Defender* (March 2, 1982): 6.

"Marchbanks, Gregory Are Lauded by Air Force Assn." *Jet* (October 21, 1985): 6.

Marriot, Michel. "Astronaut's Dream Comes True." *Washington Post* (April 28, 1985): A1, 18.

Milloy, Courtland. "An Inspiring Alumnus." *Washington Post* (June 4, 1985).

Narine, Dalton. "First Black Space Commander." *Ebony* (May 1990): 78, 80, 82.

Phelps, J. Alfred. *They Had a Dream: The Story of African American Astronauts.* Novato, CA: Presidio Press, 1994.

# H

## Charles B. Hall

Charles B. Hall. Courtesy of National Air and Space Museum, Smithsonian Institution (SI Neg. No. 99-15449).

**Full Name at Birth:** Charles Blakely Hall

**Born:** August 25, 1920, Brazil, Indiana

**Died:** November 22, 1971, Oklahoma City, Oklahoma

**Education:** Eastern Illinois State Teachers College, Charleston, Illinois, 1938 to 1941; Tuskegee Army Air Field, Pilot's wings, July 3, 1942.

**Positions Held:** Second Lieutenant, Captain, U.S. Army Air Corps. 1942–1946; manager, DuSable Hotel Lounge, Chicago [1946–1947]; production control specialist and scheduler, Tinker Air Force Base, Oklahoma, 1949–1967; equipment maintenance specialist, Federal Aviation Administration, Oklahoma City, 1967–1971.

**Awards, Honors:** Distinguished Flying Cross; Air Medal with three oak leaf clusters; Charles B. Hall Chapter of the Tuskegee Airmen, Inc., at Tinker AFB; portrait in the Military Hall of Fame, Washington, D.C.; plaque and portrait in the Ralph Ellison Library, Oklahoma City, 1978.

**Summary:** Charles B. Hall was the first African American pilot to shoot down a German plane in World War II. It gave an enormous boost to the 99th Pursuit Squadron's morale, whose combat prowess was continually in question by white military brass. Hall downed the plane on July 2, 1943, and he was credited with two more hits on January 28, 1944, for which he received the Distinguished Flying Cross.

## Early Years

Charles B. Hall was born to Anna and Frank Hall in Brazil, Indiana, on August 25, 1920. He had an older sister, Victoria (Phillips). According to the *Pittsburgh Courier*, in 1943 the black population of Brazil stood at 698, about half of the total inhabitants. Hall was known as a good student and an outstanding athlete.

## Higher Education

While a student at Eastern Illinois State Teachers College, now Eastern Illinois University, Hall played varsity football as an offensive halfback, ran track, and worked in a campus restaurant to meet his expenses. A yearbook description called him "a fast and flashy freshman." He left the college in November 1941, just weeks before the Japanese bombed Pearl Harbor on December 7, and the United States entered the war. He joined the U.S. Army Air Corps, considering it "a fine future for Negroes and a chance to show that we could do the same things that white men were doing in the war." When he joined the army, his mother moved from Brazil to Fort Wayne, Indiana, to live with her sister. Hall was sent to Tuskegee Army Air Field in Alabama, where he earned his silver wings and second lieutenant's commission on July 3, 1942. He also acquired his nickname, Buster, or, Little Buster, at Tuskegee.

## Career Highlights

The 99th Pursuit Squadron, the first group of African American pilots in the U.S. military, set sail for Africa and Italy on April 15, 1943, traveling on a converted luxury liner, the SS *Mariposa*. Arriving in Casablanca, French Morocco, nine days later, they embarked again on April 29, for Tunisia. Their assignment was to provide support for Operation Husky, as the Allied invasion of Sicily was dubbed. Their planes were 27

new P-40 Warhawks, and their instructor turned out to be the much-decorated Colonel Philip P. Cochran. Besides his fame as a fighter pilot, Cochran was the model for the Flip Corkin character in the popular comic strip, *Terry and the Pirates*.

"Spanky" Roberts, second in command of the 99th, called him, "one of the finest things that happened to us. . . . Flip moved in with us, slept with us, ate with us, flew with us, talked with us, spent 24 hours a day with us for a week, and poured out information, lore, understanding, like a coffee pot that you turn up to pour out coffee." He demonstrated particulars of desert flight, combat formation, dogfight tactics, and aerial teamwork.

Hall first went into combat on June 2, along with William Campbell, Clarence Jamison, and James Wiley. They had been assigned by Commander Davis to escort bombers over Pantelleria, an Italian island. On June 11, when Pantelleria surrendered, it marked the first time in military history that a battle had been won by air power alone.

The following month, on July 2, Hall made history and brought wide recognition to the 99th Pursuit Squadron. He became the first African American airman to down a German plane, and have "the honor to paint a swastika on his ship." He was rewarded by his fellow pilots with the one bottle of Coca-Cola that had been kept in the safe for this special occasion. Lou Purnell brought back a block of ice from a town 15 miles away, and the celebration was on. Further, more official, recognition came with the personal visit and congratulations of General Dwight D. Eisenhower, commander of all U.S. forces in Europe. Three other generals arrived with him: Carl Spaatz, head of a joint American-British unit; James H. Doolittle, 8th Air Force commander, and leader of the first raid over Tokyo; and John K. Cannon, commander of the North African Training Command. Some sources give the fourth general as Air Marshall Cunningham (or Coningham) of the British Royal Air

Force. The ceremony was broadcast over Allied radio to all American troops.

Hall's next two "kills" came on January 28, 1944. The German planes he downed, Focke-Wulfs (FW-190), were technically advanced aircraft, superior to the American P-40 Warhawks and P-51 Mustangs in speed and firing power. From January 22 to 28, the 99th downed 16 German planes, eight of them on January 27. The war correspondent, H.R. Knickerbocker, wrote that, "Nobody regards the Negro squadron as a curiosity any more . . . they have gone from a position of comparative obscurity to one of leadership in pursuit and combat." Hall told him he had flown 75 missions, but he did not want to go home just yet, saying, "Home isn't any place for a man in this war," but added, "Of course I would like to visit my home, but I don't want to quit the war until we have won it everywhere."

Hall eventually flew 108 missions before returning home. Usually, pilots in a squadron share an aircraft, but Hall had his own plane, which he named *Knobby II*. (Knobby was the nickname of his crew chief, Staff Sergeant William Cyrus Hall, who was no relation.) Some accounts say the name "Maxine" was painted on one side of the plane. The plane replaced the first *Knobby*, worn out in April after fierce combat. Flying over North Africa, Sicily, and Italy, the plane had seven holes caused by flak and had had to have its shot-up tail replaced. Hall, by now a captain, received the Distinguished Flying Cross. His citation read, in part: "Attacking so aggressively that he completely disorganized the enemy formation, Captain Hall shot down two enemy aircraft and his comrades destroyed two FW-190s and dispersed the remainder without loss or damage to the P-40s . . . his steadfast devotion to duty and outstanding proficiency as a combat pilot has reflected great credit upon himself and the armed forces of the United States."

Hall returned a hero to the African American public, and he went on a 105-day war

bond tour, to urge support for the men overseas. He remained in the U.S. Army Air Corps until 1946, as an instructor of fighter pilots at Tuskegee, and then he moved to Chicago. *Ebony* reported in January 1947, "Today his wings are stuffed away in a dresser drawer and he spends all his time on the ground as the manager of the DuSable Hotel's lounge." Hall expressed his disappointment by saying he would like to fly for the airlines but, "There isn't a single Negro pilot employed by a major airline in the country. Many who are qualified are being denied jobs because of color discrimination." Hall went on, "More white people have more respect for Negroes than they used to have. But it isn't quite enough . . . little additional freedom has been won."

Hall worked for an insurance company in Nashville, Tennessee, where he met Jeanne (or Emma Jeanne) Ackiss, an employee of Fisk University. They married, and by June 1948 they had moved to Oklahoma City, where Hall managed a drugstore owned by Dr. R.P. Perry, his wife's stepfather. In 1949, likely weary of being "in the store most of the 24 hours each day," Hall took a job at Tinker Air Force Base in Oklahoma City. He worked as a production control specialist and he scheduled the workload of the electrical and pump units. The Halls' marriage ended in the early 1950s, and Hall and Ida Mucker (1929–1987) had a daughter in 1957, Peggy Ann. On January 13, 1961, Delois Miles became his second wife. The couple had two daughters, Sherri Lynn and Kelli Ann. When the Federal Aviation Administration (FAA) established its Maintenance Analysis Center at the Will Rogers Airport in 1967, Hall was the only one selected from outside the FAA ranks for employment there. He was an equipment maintenance specialist, working on identifying reliability factors in air carrier equipment. He remained there until 1971, the year of his death. Hall was a member of the 9835th Reserve Squadron, where he achieved the rank of major. On

October 26, 1978, a plaque and an oil portrait of Hall were installed in the Ralph Ellison Library as a memorial to Hall's wartime achievement. An Air Force honor guard participated in the ceremony.

Hall's beliefs were perhaps best summarized by a letter he wrote to the residents of Charleston, Illinois, on December 21, 1943, when he was in Italy. Some excerpts are: "Up in the blue it doesn't make any difference where you come from, what color you are, etc. I can appreciate the land, sea, engineers, cooks, nurses, the Red Cross, tanks, defense workers, people buying bonds, and a thousand and one other things. I look at them and say, 'This is worth fighting for.' "

## Sources

Allin, Lawrence. "Charles B. Hall: Pilot Left His Mark on Air Force History." *Tinker Take Off* (June 19, 1992): 14.

Francis, Charles E. *The Tuskegee Airmen*. Boston: Branden Publishing Co., 1988.

Funeral program of Charles B. Hall, November 24, 1971.

Holway, John B. *Red Tails Black Wings: The Men of America's Black Air Force*. Las Cruces, NM: Yucca Tree Press, 1997.

"Indiana Youth Bests Deadly Focke-Wulf in Air Battle Above Clouds over Sicily." *Pittsburgh Courier* (July 10, 1943): 1, 7.

Knickerbocker, H.R. "99th Record Tops All Squadrons in Italy." *Chicago Defender* (February 19, 1944). (Reprinted from the *Chicago Sun*).

Mitchell, Mitch. "First Blood: The Saga of the 99th Fighter Squadron." *Air Classics* (February 1987): 14–20, 84, 86–87.

Read, Harry. "Black EIU Student Made History in the Air." *Times-Courier* (Charleston, Illinois) (September 17, 1985): B 12.

"Where are the Heroes?" *Ebony* (January 1947): 5–10.

Wilkinson, Edmund L., Oklahoma City, to Betty K. Gubert, New York, e-mail messages, interview transcript, and clippings, June 14, 22, 23, 28, 30, July 6 and 14, 2000.

Wilkinson, Edmund L., Oklahoma City, interview with Peggy Ann Hall, July 2, 2000.

# Bernard A. Harris Jr.

Bernard A. Harris Jr. Courtesy of NASA.

**Full Name at Birth:** Bernard Anthony Harris Jr.

**Born:** June 26, 1956, Temple, Texas

**Education:** Sam Houston High School, San Antonio, Texas, 1974; B.S. in biology, University of Houston, 1978; M.D., Texas Tech University School of Medicine, Lubbock, 1982; M.S. in biomedical science, University of Texas Medical Branch at Galveston, 1996.

**Positions Held:** Clinical scientist and flight surgeon, NASA Johnson Space Center, Texas, 1987; several faculty appointments at Baylor College of Medicine and at other schools of the University of Texas; NASA astronaut 1990–1996, as mission specialist conducting research in physical and life sciences, and also as payload commander; chief scientist and vice president of Spacehab Inc., Houston, Texas.

**Awards, Honors:** NASA Sustained Superior Performance Award, 1988, 1989; American

Astronautical Society's Boynton Award for Outstanding Contribution to Space Medicine, 1993; NASA Space Flight Medals, 1993, 1995; National Technical Association, Physician of the Year, 1993; election of Fellowship in the American College of Physicians, 1994; Morehouse School of Medicine, Atlanta, Georgia, Honorary Doctorate 1996; NASA Outstanding Leadership Medal, Ronald E. McNair Foundation's Challenger Award, Association of Black Cardiologists Award of Achievement; Texas Tech University created the Dr. Bernard A. Harris Jr. Premedical Society (DHPS) in 1998 to assist students preparing for medical careers.

**Summary:** Bernard A. Harris Jr. was the first African American astronaut to walk in space. On February 9, 1995, Harris stepped outside the STS-63, the first flight of the joint Russian-American space program. He remained in space for four hours and 25 minutes. An astronaut since 1991, Harris had also flown in space in 1993.

## Early Years

Bernard Anthony Harris Jr. was born on June 26, 1956, in Temple, Texas, to Gussie Emanual and Bernard Anthony Harris Sr., the first of their three children. When he and his sister, Gillette, and his brother, Dennis, were young, their parents divorced. Mrs. Harris moved with her children to San Antonio, a larger city, but one plagued with urban problems. When Harris was about seven, his mother found work as a teacher with the Bureau of Indian Affairs. The family moved again, first to Arizona and then to a Navaho reservation in New Mexico. Living in a housing complex for employees, the Harrises were one of two black families on the reservation. At first, the different groups of Indian, white, Mexican, and black children tossed verbal insults at each other. After three weeks, Harris recalled, "[W]e all ended up playing together." As they grew older there were hiking excursions in the moun-

tains. These early experiences with people of different ethnicity had a dramatic effect on Harris's perceptions of them, and of his relation to them.

Back in Texas to attend high school, Harris was caught up in the excitement of NASA's space flights, especially the one in which Neil Armstrong walked on the moon on July 20, 1969. He drew rocket ships in his notebooks, and he was an early and faithful "Trekkie," the nickname for fans of the television program, *Star Trek*. Harris graduated from Sam Houston High School in 1974, not yet sure of his career path.

## Higher Education

At the University of Houston, Harris majored in biology, with the idea of becoming a doctor so he could heal ill or injured people. He played the saxophone in a group called *Purple Haze*, as his summer job. During the school year, he also played with the band at football games. After his graduation in 1978, Harris was accepted by the Texas Tech University of Medicine. In 1982, having earned his medical degree, Harris went to the Mayo Clinic in Rochester, Minnesota, to perform his three-year residency in internal medicine. Dr. Joseph Combs, a rheumatologist who participated in NASA's Gemini launches, rekindled Harris's interest in space. "When he talked about the obstacles . . . in sending the first man up in space . . . I knew the combination of medicine and space was for me."

## Career Highlights

With his residency completed in 1985, Harris went to NASA Ames Research Center, Moffett Field, California, on a National Research Council fellowship. His research there was in the field of musculoskeletal physiology and disuse osteoporosis. In 1987, he moved to NASA Johnson Space Center, Houston, as a clinical scientist and flight surgeon with the Medical Science Division. Harris was the project manager for the clinical investigations of space adaptation and the development for countermeasures for extended duration flight. These studies examined ways to offset the deconditioning of body tissues that may occur in space: smaller heart, muscle atrophy, and bone resorption.

Following an old but persistent dream, Harris now decided to try for the astronaut training program one more time. His first application in 1987 had been unsuccessful. In September 1989 Harris was selected as one of the 106 astronaut candidates, culled from a pool of 2,500 applicants. The training program, from January 1990 to July 1991, included rigorous physical activities as well as intellectual matter. Harris thought it was like medical school, and described it as, "A whole bunch of smart guys sitting out there absorbing material." With official astronaut status conferred in July 1991, Harris was ready for assignment as a mission specialist on future space shuttle crews. While waiting, Harris helped design exercise equipment and routines for astronauts who remain in space for extended periods, and therefore, are at risk for musculoskeletal weakness.

Harris's first assignment was aboard the *Columbia* (STS-55) as a mission specialist. The trip lasted from April 26 to May 6, 1993. It was a joint space trip with German astronauts and numerous medical experiments were conducted. The scientists also studied the growth of tiny cells in the absence of gravity. Harris and Hans W. Schlegel of Germany used a wall-mounted laboratory with more than 600 containers, measuring devices, process chambers, incubators, and centrifuges. They grew human disease-fighting lymphocyte cells, bone-forming collagen cells, fungi, and tobacco. Busy as they were, Harris had time to note the beauty of the colors of the atmosphere. The speed of their ship was, "just incredible—you're over Australia—you turn your head to do something and 10 minutes later, you're off the coast of California!"

The next mission in space catapulted Harris into history. He became the first African American to walk in space. It was while aboard the *Discovery* (STS-63), and the date was February 9, 1995, well into the trip's duration, from February 2 to 11. Harris, the payload commander, and Dr. C. Michael Foale, an astrophysicist, stepped out arm-in-arm to check how their spacesuits would handle temperatures of 90 to 125 degrees F. below zero. It was pitch black as well as icy cold because the spaceship faced away from the sun. Harris practiced moving around a 2,500-pound astronomy satellite, called *Spartan*, to help NASA learn how future space walkers can handle massive objects while constructing a space station. NASA had to cut the planned five-hour walk by 25 minutes because the gloves were not insulated well enough and both astronauts had begun to exceed the frostbite safety limits set by NASA. A highlight of the mission was the rendezvous with Mir, the Russian space station. There were lighter moments aboard *Discovery*. The Coca-Cola company financed an experiment to mix two of its liquids together in space, and when the astronauts drank it, Harris reported it tasted like Coke. Harris recalled his early experience by bringing a Navaho Indian nation flag to accompany him and to pay tribute to the multicultural composition of America.

In his career with NASA, which ended with his retirement in April 1996, Harris logged 438 hours and flew over six million miles in space. When he retired, Harris joined Spacehab Inc. at their Houston office, as vice president and chief scientist. Spacehab is a private corporation that facilitates the commercial use of space by providing access to crew-tended microgravity research environments. Among their contributions is the development and operation of habitable modules that fly aboard U.S. space shuttles.

On July 22, 1989, Harris and Sandra Fay Lewis, a systems analyst, were married. They are the parents of Brooke Alexandria, who was born on August 3, 1992. For recreation,

Harris enjoys flying, sailing, skiing, scuba diving, running, art, and music. Some of the organizations Harris belongs to include the American College of Physicians, American Society for Bone and Mineral Research, Aerospace Medical Association, National Medical Association, American Medical Association, Aircraft Owners and Pilots Association, Association of Space Explorers, and numerous local medical societies and alumni associations. He is a member of the board of directors of both the Boys and Girls Club of Houston and the Manned Space Flight Education Foundation Inc.

## Sources

"Astronauts Conduct Life Science Studies on 2d Day of Flight." *New York Times* (April 27, 1993).

"Astronauts Say Warmer Gloves Are Necessary." *New York Times* (February 11, 1995): 10.

"Bernard Harris First Black to Walk in Space." *The Syl Watkins Drum* (Orlando, Florida) (March 1995): 1–2.

Blount, Cheryl E. "Habitats for Extended Space Flight." *about . . . time* (April 1997): 6.

Broad, William J. "2 Astronauts in Deep Chill during a Test of Spacesuits." *New York Times* (February 10, 1995): A1, 10.

Harris, Bernard A., Houston, Texas, to Betty K. Gubert, New York, e-mail, correspondence, October–December 1999.

NASA Biographical Data. "Astronaut Bio: Bernard Harris 1/99." Accessed September 30, 1999. Search either NASA or "Bernard Harris"

Phelps, J. Alfred. *They Had a Dream: The Story of African American Astronauts.* Novato, CA: Presidio Press, 1994: 227–240.

# David E. Harris

**Full Name at Birth:** David Ellsworth Harris

**Born:** December 22, 1934, Columbus, Ohio

**Education:** B.S. in education, Ohio State University, 1957.

**Positions Held:** Second lieutenant, captain, U.S. Air Force, 1958–December 1, 1964; second officer, captain, American Airlines, December 3, 1964–December 1994.

**Awards, Honors:** Black Achievement in Industry Award, YMCA, 1971.

**Summary:** When David E. Harris was hired by American Airlines in December 1964, he became the first African American pilot hired by that airline. He is a pioneer among blacks who made their career in commercial aviation.

## Early Years

The son of Wilbur R. Harris and Ruth A. Estis Harris, David Ellsworth Harris was born December 22, 1934, in Columbus, Ohio. He attended public elementary and high schools in Ohio, but more information about his early years could not be located.

## Higher Education

Harris graduated from Ohio State University in 1957, with a bachelor's degree in education. After two years at the university, he joined the advanced Air Force ROTC (Reserve Officers Training Corps) after "knocking on the door three times." He feels the refusals were because of his color. Harris wanted the advance service because he "became aware that there was an opportunity to get a second lieutenant's commission and learn to fly. This would have been cost prohibitive for me otherwise, and flying airplanes at government expense seemed a great idea." Harris was finally admitted and he achieved the rank of cadet colonel, though he thought the higher position of wing commander of the outfit was denied him, again because of color prejudice.

Harris continued musing about the influence that led him to choose piloting as a career: "my interest in flying came as a matter of chance and circumstance. I cannot remember having a burning desire to be a pilot as a boy. . . . There were no minority role models out there as airline pilots. World War II and the Tuskegee Airmen had come and gone. They were not accepted and, therefore, not in the commercial arena."

## Career Highlights

Harris joined the U.S. Air Force in June 1958, and remained until December 1, 1964. During these years Harris was assigned to air bases in Bartow, Florida; Big Spring, Texas; Plattsburgh, New York; and Springfield, Massachusetts. He and his family (he married the former Lynne Purdy, and they had two children, Camian and Leslie) often had difficulty finding housing, in the North as well as in the South. With the Strategic Air Command (SAC), he was assigned to fly such jet bombers as the B-47 and the B-52.

His military service coincided with Marlon Green's struggle to become a pilot for Continental Airlines, 1957–1963. Green took his case all the way to the U.S. Supreme Court, which declared discrimination in the airline industry unconstitutional. The airlines began hiring black pilots in the mid-1960s as a direct result of the decision. At about this time, Harris, finding his career hard on his family, wrote letters to two carriers, who had placed advertisements in the *Air Force Times*. He told them he was a Negro to "save myself a trip."

On December 3, 1964, Harris was hired by American Airlines, becoming that company's first African American pilot. He stayed with American, based in Boston, until his retirement in December 1994. For Harris, who by July 1969 had been promoted to captain, "it's been a beautiful relationship. They [American Airlines] may have been as bigoted as any airline in the past, but when they came around, they went all the way." He was told he could be red, yellow, or chartreuse as long as he could meet the prerequisites and fly the plane. He knew the airline was sincere when he was approached by recruiters "to pass the word around to qualified black pilots" that they were hiring. When Harris flew with First Officer Herman Samuels, another African American, they were good-naturedly known as Sam and Dave, the Soul Patrol. As for the passengers, Harris said in 1969 none have gotten off the airplane yet. "People buy a ticket to get from Point A to Point B, and they figure if you're up there, you know what you're doing."

During his long career, Harris has flown a variety of aircraft: the DC-6, 7, Lockheed Electra, BAC 111, Boeing 747, 727, 767, and the Airbus 300. He has been a member of Negro Airmen International (NAI) and of the Organization of Black Airline Pilots (OBAP), as well as a former president of OBAP.

## Sources

*Blacks in Aviation 1996: A Commemorative Brochure.* Miami, FL: Metro-Dade Aviation Department, 1996; 42–44.

Connes, Keith. "Can a Black Man Fly?" *Flying* (July 1969): 53–57.

*Who's Who among African Americans.* Farmington Hills, MI: Gale Group, 1999.

# Marcelite J. Harris

Marcelite J. Harris. Courtesy of U.S. Air Force.

**Full Name at Birth:** Marcelite Jordan

**Date of Birth:** January 16, 1943, Houston, Texas

**Education:** Kashmere Gardens Junior-Senior High School, Houston, 1960; Spelman College, Atlanta, Georgia, B.A. in speech and drama, 1964; Officer Training School, Lackland AFB, Texas, 1965; Squadron Officer School, 1975, and Air War College, 1983, both at Air University, Maxwell Air Force Base, Alabama; University of Maryland, B.S. in business management, 1986; Senior Officers in security course, 1989, and international security management course, 1994, both at Harvard University, Cambridge, Massachusetts; CAPSTONE general and flag officer course, Washington, D.C., 1990.

**Awards, Honors:** Bronze Star Medal, Meritorious Service Medal with three oak leaf clusters; Air Force Commendation Medal with one oak leaf cluster; Presidential Unit Citation; Air Force outstanding Unit Award with "V" device and eight oak leaf clusters; National Defense Service Medal with three oak leaf clusters; Republic of Vietnam Gallantry Cross with Palm; Woman of the Year (1990); Tuskegee Airmen; Living Legacy Patriot Award (1998); Women's International Center.

**Summary:** Marcelite J. Harris became the first African American woman general in the U.S. Air Force in 1990 when she became a brigadier general. In 1994, she was promoted to major general, another first. These appointments capped a career of firsts, for African Americans, women, and the Air Force. Harris was the first woman aircraft maintenance officer, the first woman deputy commander for maintenance, and one of the first two woman commanding officers at the U.S. Air Force Academy.

## Early Years

Marcelite Jordan was born on January 16, 1943, in Houston, Texas, to Marcelite Elizabeth Terrell Jordan and Cecil O'Neal Jordan Sr. Her mother was a high school librarian and her father was a supervisor in the post office. Harris's sister Elizabeth is now an attorney, and her brother Cecil is a minister. Mrs. Jordan's ancestors were prominent in education and politics. I.M. Terrell, Harris's great-grandfather, founded the first school for blacks in Fort Worth, Texas. Her great-great-grandfather, Pierre Landry, who was born a slave, served in the house of representatives and the state senate of Louisiana from 1870 to 1884. He then practiced law.

The Jordans made sure their children kept the goal of excellence before them. They emphasized the meaning of the phrase, "potential over barrier," instilling in them the idea that ability and determination can conquer obstacles.

## Higher Education

Harris attended Spelman College in Atlanta, Georgia. At the prestigious women's college, she majored in speech and drama, planning for a career in the theater. Before her graduation in 1964, Harris traveled with a USO tour to military bases in France and Germany, hoping to return one day as an actor.

That did not happen, and Harris turned to the U.S. Air Force for her career. She entered Officers Training School at Lackland Air Force Base (AFB) in Texas in September 1965. Commissioned as a second lieutenant at the end of the year, Harris continued her education, honing the skills and acquiring the knowledge that would lead to promotions within the Air Force. She enrolled at Air University's (Maxwell AFB, Alabama) Squadron Officer School by correspondence in 1975, and at its Air War College by seminar in 1983. Harris earned another bachelor's degree, this one in business management, from the University of Maryland in 1986. In 1989, Harris took the senior officers in national security course at Harvard University. A year later, she completed the CAPSTONE general and flag officer course at Fort McNair in Washington, D.C. (A flag officer is a naval term for ranks above captain.) Harris returned to Harvard University in 1994 for a course in national and international security management.

## Career Highlights

Harris's assignments have taken her all over the world. From December 1965 to January 1967 she was assistant director for administration, 60th Military Airlift Wing, Travis AFB, California. She was then assigned to Bitburg Air Base in West Germany, where she was the administrative officer with the 71st Tactical Missile Squadron until May 1969. She then became the maintenance analysis officer with the 36th Tactical Fighter Wing, also located at Bitburg. Promoted to captain on December 21, 1969, Harris remained at the base until September 1970.

Upon her return to the United States, Harris took the aircraft maintenance officer course at Chanute AFB, Illinois. Her successful completion of the course in May 1971 made her the first woman in the Air Force, black or white, to become an aircraft maintenance officer. From that August until May 1972, she was the maintenance supervisor for the 49th Tactical Fighter Squadron at the Korat Royal Thai AFB in Thailand.

Rotated back home in June 1972, Harris was once more assigned to Travis AFB in California. Her title there was job control officer with the 916th Air Refueling Squadron, a position she held until September 1973, when she became the unit's field maintenance supervisor. Captain Harris was promoted to major on April 1, 1975. Five months later, Major Harris joined USAF Headquarters in Washington, D.C. There, she was personnel staff officer and White House social aide to President Jimmy Carter. In May 1978, Harris achieved another first as an African American woman in the armed services. She became commander of Cadet Squadron 39 at the U.S. Air Force Academy in Colorado Springs, Colorado. She was one of the first two women to be designated as "air force commanding."

In July 1980, Harris was assigned to McConnell AFB, Kansas, where she remained until November 1982. She held such positions as maintenance control officer and commander of maintenance squadrons. While stationed here, she and Maurice Anthony Harris, a pilot in the air force, were married on March 29, 1980. They have two children, Steven Eric and Tenecia Marcelite. On October 1, 1981, Harris received a promotion to lieutenant colonel.

From Kansas, Colonel Harris went to Japan in November 1982, remaining at the Kadena AFB until March 1986. Her post there was director of maintenance for the Pacific Air Forces Logistic Support Center. When her tour of duty in Japan ended, she was assigned to Keesler AFB in Mississippi. Here, she was the first woman to be deputy commander for maintenance. Promoted to full colonel on September 1, 1986, Harris continued in this position until December 1988. She then received the assignment of commander of the 3300th Technical Training Wing, also at Keesler. With this assignment, Harris became the first woman wing commander in Air Training Command. She remained until September 1990. On September 8, 1990, Harris made U.S. Air Force history—she was promoted to brigadier general. She thus became the first African American woman to become a general in the air force.

From then until July 1993, Harris was vice commander at the Oklahoma City Air Logistics center, at Tinker AFB, where she was responsible for depot maintenance of various weaponry, including B-1B, B-52B, and TF-33 aircraft. Harris's command consisted of 22,000 military and civilian personnel who needed to be trained and ready to supply superior equipment, especially in wartime. Her superior officer noted her effective leadership, wealth of experience, energy, and enthusiasm, while her subordinates appreciated her approachability (*Ebony* 1992). When

Harris achieved the rank of general, there were 13,323 women officers in the U.S. Air Force, but only 15 of them were general officers, that is, officers ranking above colonel.

From July 1993 to August 1994, Harris served as director of technical training at Headquarters Air Education and Training Command, Randolph AFB, Texas. In September, she became director of maintenance at Headquarters U.S. Air Force, Washington, D.C. In this position, Harris oversaw the training and organization of a workforce of more than 100,000 technicians and managers. She developed maintenance policy and operated a $260 billion Global Reach Global Power aerospace weapons systems inventory.

Harris achieved one more promotion before her retirement in 1996. She was named a major general on May 25, 1995, another first for an African American woman. She "is sure there will be other women who come behind me." And she pays tribute to her "female predecessors . . . who have done a tremendous job of opening doors and proving capabilities." In early June, Harris represented the Department of Defense as the head of the U.S. delegation to the Committee on Women in the NATO Forces Conference in Brussels, Belgium. She stated, "As a nation which continues to benefit from the capabilities of women in our military, we are happy to share our experiences with others."

After retirement, Harris was asked to serve on the Department of Defense's Task Force on gender-integrated training, which was formed in June 1997. Their mission was to focus on current and future training programs, as well as morale and discipline issues. As more women enter the military, Harris's personal and professional knowledge puts her in demand as a speaker and consultant. Among the organizations Harris belongs to are the Air Force Association, Tuskegee Airmen, Inc., and Delta Sigma Theta.

### Sources

"The Air Force's First Black Female General." *Ebony* (December 1992): 62, 64, 66.

Lane, Linda Rochelle. "Harris, Marcelite Jordon [*sic*]" in *Black Women in America: An Historical Encyclopedia*. Brooklyn, NY: Carlson Publishing, 1993; 538–539.

"Major General Marcelite J. Harris." Women's International Center, http://wic.org. Accessed September 30, 1999.

Smith, Jessie Carney. "Marcelite J. Harris" in *Notable Black American Women*. Detroit: Gale Research, 1992; 467–468.

United States Air Force Biography (press release). Secretary of the Air Force, Office of Public Affairs, Washington, D.C. 20330. *Brigadier General Marcelite J. Harris* (December 1990), *Major General Marcelite J. Harris* (June 1995).

*Who's Who among African Americans*. New York: Gale Research, 1999.

# Wesley L. Harris

Wesley L. Harris. Courtesy of Wesley L. Harris.

**Full Name at Birth:** Wesley Leroy Harris

**Born:** October 29, 1941, Richmond, Virginia

**Education:** Armstrong High School, Richmond; B.S. with honors, aerospace engineering, University of Virginia, Charlottesville, 1964; M.A. and Ph.D., aerospace and mechanical sciences, Princeton University, New Jersey, 1966, 1968.

**Positions Held:** Assistant professor (1968–1970), associate professor (1971–1972), University of Virginia; professor, aeronautics and astronautics, director of Rotor Acoustics Group, director of Office of Minority Education, Massachusetts Institute of Technology (MIT), 1972–1985; program manager, National Aeronautics and Space Administration (NASA), 1979–1980 (on leave from MIT); dean, School of Engineering, University of Connecticut, 1985–1990; vice president and chief administrative officer, University of Tennessee Space Institute, 1990–1992; associate administrator for aeronautics, NASA, 1993–1995; professor of aeronautics and astronautics, director of the Lean Sustainment Initiative, co-director of the Lean Aerospace Initiative, MIT, 1995– .

**Awards, Honors:** Student award, American Institute of Aeronautics and Astronautics, 1964, elected Fellow, 1994; Irwin Sizer Award, MIT, 1979; Eminent Scholar, Norfolk University, 1981–1982; Herbert S. and Jane Gregory Distinguished Lecturer, College of Engineering, University of Florida, 1992; Confrérie des Chevaliers du Tastevin, 1993; Engineering Achievement Award, University of Virginia, 1994; Outstanding Leadership Medal, 1994; honorary degrees from Lane College, 1994, Milwaukee School of Engineering, 1994, Old Dominion University, 1995; elected Fellow, American Helicopter Society, 1994; holder of the Barry Goldwater Chair of American Institutions, Arizona State University, 2000–2001.

**Summary:** Wesley L. Harris, with a string of firsts in the fields of aerospace research and education at NASA and at several universities, has been a catalyst for change in these areas. While engaging in award-winning scientific research himself, he has been instrumental in bringing cultural diversity to the institutions where he has taught, mentoring minority students in physics and aeronautics.

He has been an advocate for the advancement of space sciences in American industry, research, and education.

## Early Years

Wesley Leroy Harris, one of three children of William and Rosa Minor Harris, was born on October 29, 1941, in Richmond, Virginia. Both of his parents worked in a tobacco factory, and his mother encouraged the children to get as much education as they could. Young Harris was interested in aviation, and he pursued this interest by reading all he could find on the subject and by building model planes of all types and sizes. At Armstrong High School, Harris played football and his favorite subjects were math and physics. His football coach emphasized the values of hard work and persistence as the means to success, not just on the football field, but in life itself. His teachers of math and physics, both women, were, like the coach, strong disciplinarians who insisted on hard work.

The 1957 Russian launching of *Sputnik I*, the first artificial satellite, electrified Harris, then 16 years old. His interest, already avid about the possibilities of space studies and travel, was greatly stimulated.

## Higher Education

After his high school graduation in 1960, Harris married and entered the University of Virginia at Charlottesville, hoping to study physics. But that major was not available to black students then, and Harris chose aerospace engineering. Despite the strain of being a married student, and the loneliness of being one of a handful of black students on campus, Harris graduated with honors in 1964. In his senior year he received a number of honors. His research into the flow of air over wing surfaces netted him an award from the American Institute of Aeronautics and Astronautics (AIAA). He was selected to introduce Dr. Martin Luther King Jr. when he spoke at the university. Harris became the first African American to join the Jefferson Society, the university's prestigious debating club.

Encouraged by two of his professors, both alumni of Princeton University, to enroll there, Harris earned both his M.A., in 1966, and his Ph.D., in 1968, in aerospace and mechanical sciences.

## Career Highlights

Wanting to guide more African American students into science studies, Harris returned to the University of Virginia as an assistant professor of aerospace engineering, the university's first black professor of engineering. He later became the first black professor to become tenured. Despite his teaching load, Harris was able to do research on aerodynamic noise, hypersonic airflow, and short-takeoff and landing airplane technology.

During a leave of absence from the University of Virginia, 1970–1971, Harris taught physics at Southern University, in Baton Rouge, Louisiana, a predominantly black institution. He returned to Virginia as an associate professor, and remained until 1972. That year he left for the Massachusetts Institute of Technology (MIT), Cambridge, Massachusetts, for one year. But when he was offered a position as associate professor of Aeronautics and Astronautics, he accepted and remained until 1979, serving also in the dual appointment of associate professor of Ocean Engineering. Harris was the first director of MIT's Office of Minority Affairs in 1975, having established it. An extensive database was developed on the academic performance of minority undergraduate students. Harris saw the need to encourage minority students to improve their performance and decrease their dropout rate. In 1979, he received the Irwin Sizer Award for the most significant improvement to education at MIT.

Taking a leave from MIT, Harris worked for NASA in 1979. He had two positions: manager of computational methods in the Office of Aeronautics and Space Technology and program manager in the Fluid and Thermal Physics Office. He was able to deepen his research into airflow, or computational fluid dynamics. He also planned NASA's later acquisition of supercomputers.

Harris returned to MIT in 1980 for five years, where he held both faculty and administrative positions. In 1985, he became dean of the School of Engineering at the University of Connecticut, at Storrs, and remained until 1990. He also married again in that year, and the Harrises are the parents of four children. During his five years as dean, Harris increased minority recruitment figures from about five or six students when he arrived, to 40 when he left. He initiated partnerships between the university and such companies as Pratt and Whitney, makers of aircraft engines, and United Technologies, an aerospace corporation. Harris led in the establishment of the Environmental Research Institute.

Returning south in 1990, Harris took the position of vice president and chief administrative officer of the University of Tennessee Space Institute (UTSI), at Tullahoma. He reorganized UTSI's research efforts to focus on five selected areas, which preserved resources and concentrated its activities. Harris was able to continue his research into the effects of air flow and of noise that creates shock waves at high speeds (sonic booms). Harris's research has resulted in over 100 presentations and publications in scientific journals. Further professional recognition came to Harris when the AIAA, which gave him an award in his senior year at college, named him a fellow of the prestigious institute in 1994. The American Helicopter Society (AHS) named him a fellow as well in the same year. He was honored for his research on helicopter rotor noise and air flows above and below the speed of sound, and for the advancement of engineering education.

In 1992 NASA's new administrator, Daniel S. Goldin, decided it was time to revive interest in the first "A" of the agency's name,

Aeronautics. Goldin thought that if American companies want to share in the global competition for aerospace business, which he estimated would be worth $500 billion by the end of 2005, then more research must be done. In early 1993, Harris accepted Goldin's offer to become associate administrator in NASA's Office of Aeronautics. Harris was responsible for strategy, planning, advocacy, and direction of NASA's research programs and for the institutional management of the four aeronautics centers: Ames, Langley, Lewis, and the Dryden Flight Research Center. This translated into a budget in excess of $2 billion, over 7,400 employees, and 2,000 contracts and grants.

Among his priorities were the development of a supersonic plane—High Speed Civil Transport—which could fly at 1,500 mph, but not destroy the ozone layer and remain within noise regulations; improved technologies for commercial aviation; upgrading of national resources (superstructure) such as high-performance computers and wind tunnels; and continued joint research with the Department of Defense for a hypersonic national aerospace plane. This craft is seen as a possible successor to the space shuttle, and would be able to take off and land like an airplane, but fly up to 25 times the speed of sound.

Harris returned to MIT in 1995 as professor of aeronautics and astronautics, director of the Lean Sustainment Initiative, and co-director of the Lean Aerospace Initiative. The Lean projects are housed at MIT Center for Transportation Studies. Harris was selected to fill the Barry Goldwater Chair of American Institutions at Arizona State University for the 2000–2001 academic year. He is the first engineer to hold this post, the largest endowed at Arizona State University.

Throughout the 1980s and 1990s Harris was a member of numerous advisory committees and boards of directors, many of which he continues to hold. They include the U.S. Army Science Board, the National Science Foundation Engineering Advisory Committee, several scientific committees of the National Research Council, American Helicopter Society, Federal Aviation Administration, and universities such as Hampton, MIT, Alabama A&M, Princeton, and the University of California at San Diego. Harris has also received honorary degrees from Lane College, Eugene, Oregon, 1994; Milwaukee School of Engineering, 1994; and Old Dominion University, Norfolk, Virginia, 1995. When out of the classroom or laboratory, Harris enjoys running, weightlifting, and playing squash.

### Sources

Bille, Matthew A. "Wesley L. Harris" in Kristine Krapp, ed. *Notable Black American Scientists*. Detroit: Gale Research, 1999; 149–150.

Harris, Wesley L., Cambridge, Massachusetts, e-mail to Betty K. Gubert, New York, February 8, 2000.

Harris, Wesley L. Résumé.

Kessler, James H. et al. *Distinguished African American Scientists of the 20th Century*. Phoenix: Oryx Press, 1996; 144–148.

Sawyer, Kathy. "Reviving Aeronautics." *Washington Post* (May 27, 1993); A23.

# Joseph H. Haynes

Joseph H. Haynes. Courtesy of Frances Haynes.

**Full Name at Birth:** Joseph Harold Haynes

**Born:** February 18, 1931, Brooklyn, New York

**Died:** March 2, 1997, Brooklyn; buried in Evergreen Cemetery, Brooklyn

**Education:** Haaren High School, New York, 1946; Associate degree in mechanical technology, New York City Community College, 1953; Missouri School of Mines, B.S. in mechanical engineering, University of Missouri, 1961.

**Positions Held:** Mechanical engineer in both the New Subway Car Designs Department and the Car Equipment and Shop Maintenance Department, New York City Transit Authority; accident investigator, National Transportation Safety Board, Parsippany, New Jersey, 1979 to 1993.

**Awards, Honors:** National Black Coalition of Federal Aviation Employees, September 1983; President of Negro Airmen International (NAI).

**Summary:** Joseph Haynes, a historian of aviation in general and of the role of African Americans in the field, freely shared his knowledge with generations of students. He instructed others to achieve their pilot's licenses and was a founding member of the Weeksville Society, a group dedicated to uncovering Brooklyn's African American past.

## Early Years

Joseph Harold Haynes was the third child and first son of six children born to the Reverend Joseph T. and Frances Haynes. His siblings were Charles, Frances, Alma Warner, Ivy Ballard, and Evelyn Polhill. The family lived in Brooklyn, where Joseph Haynes Sr. was minister of St. Stephen's Holiness Church of the Church of God in Christ denomination. When "Sonny," as his family called him, was eight or nine, he acquired the first volume of an encyclopedia through a promotion of the local Bohack supermarket. With articles on aerodynamics, air-

planes, and aviation, that "A" volume set Haynes on his lifelong passion for flying and for teaching others to fly. In the process he became a historian of aviation in general, and of blacks in aviation in particular. A dramatic sight that further sparked his interest was the varied aircraft as they flew overhead on their path to LaGuardia Airport in Queens, which had opened in December 1939. To Haynes it was as if a catalogue of airplanes had come alive. As a teenager, he built model airplanes and attended contests and flying shows sponsored by the city's daily newspapers.

When Haynes was about 16, he saw an article in the *New York Daily Mirror* offering free airplane rides at Floyd Bennett Field. Buddy Rogers, the star of *Wings* (1927), the first film to win an Academy Award, and a pilot, was flying his own plane to advertise his latest movie. It was a frigid day in February when Haynes reached the gate. He was ushered right in—the only person in New York who had braved the weather to show up. At Haaren High School where he took both academic and aviation mechanics courses, he befriended two other students who introduced him to the Warhawk Aviation Club. The club, located on 125th Street where the Harlem State Office Building now stands, was led by Archie Smith. Smith had been a flight instructor at Tuskegee Airfield before and during World War II. He charged $3.00 an hour for dual instruction on a wooden spar J-2 Piper Cub, flying out of Deer Park and Zahn's airports on Long Island. Haynes's parents first learned he was flying when they opened the *Sunday News* in 1947 to see a picture of their son receiving his junior pilot's license. Their surprise was even greater when he subsequently built an airplane that flew. His first solo flight came on November 11, 1948.

## Higher Education

In 1961, Haynes graduated from the Missouri School of Mines (now part of the University of Missouri) with a degree in mechanical engineering. Returning to New York, he continued flying with Archie Smith, who in 1965 began using the Westchester Airport. The pilots' licenses Haynes earned were private pilots certificate (November 11, 1966), commercial pilots certificate (July 3, 1971), and flight instructors certificate (November 20, 1971).

## Career Highlights

As Haynes wrote in 1992 for the souvenir journal of the 25th anniversary of Black Pilots of New York, a chapter of Negro Airmen International, "While flying high, I was working underground with the New York City Transit Authority." As a mechanical engineer, he designed, supervised, and inspected the construction of new subway car prototypes for nearly 20 years. He also worked for the car equipment and shop maintenance section. In 1979, he began employment with the National Transportation Safety Board, which investigates aerial and rail accidents. Haynes was a primary railroad accident investigator for the NTSB and he chaired numerous investigative boards. In October 1993, he retired from the board's regional office in Parsippany, New Jersey.

Haynes's intellect and curiosity led him to other careers besides that of mechanical engineer. He was a pilot; a teacher; a historian of aviation, black history, local history, and transportation; a genealogist; and a photographer. He was an avid collector of books and ephemera on these and other subjects, and he was exceptionally generous with his time, knowledge, money, and books, as he participated with others in these fields.

Haynes was especially active in educating young African Americans about the career possibilities available in the field of aviation. This was important because the prestigious position of commercial pilot had always been an elusive goal. In fact, it played a part in Haynes's choice of engineering as a career.

In 1969, the *Christian Science Monitor* polled major airlines and found that there were only 51 blacks out of the 35,000 employees at the cockpit level. As late as 1992, the numbers were still small. As reported by the Organization of Black Airline Pilots (OBAP) at their annual conference in Boston, there were fewer than 500 blacks out of 52,000 pilots employed by the airlines.

In 1968, soon after obtaining his private pilot's license, Haynes was walking through Brooklyn's newest museum, the New Muse, at 1530 Bedford Avenue, when he noticed that there were no aviation workshops among the many others offered to the community. He immediately volunteered to develop one, and he was welcomed. He covered such subjects as aerodynamics, navigation, meteorology, Federal Aviation Authority regulations, and the instrument board. Twice a month, Haynes rented an airplane at Teterboro Airport in New Jersey to give students hands-on practice. Other trips included visits to aviation weather stations and to a mechanics school to examine engines, aircraft frames, and other components of planes.

In 1970, Haynes taught a 33-week aviation course offered by SUNY's Manhattan Urban Center at 125th Street and 7th Avenue in Harlem. A few years earlier, Haynes had joined the Negro Airmen's Association (NAI) founded in 1967 by Edward A. Gibbs, whom he had met at Westchester Airport. He remained an active and lifelong member, and he served as the fifth president of the New York chapter.

Another long association was with the Society for the Preservation of Weeksville and Bedford-Stuyvesant History. The society grew out of Project Weeksville, a Pratt College workshop to research and find the thriving early nineteenth-century African American community named for James Weeks, a black landowner. Haynes was a founding member of the Society in 1970 and served on its board of trustees and as treasurer. Once called the "guardian angel of

Weeksville," he did more than hold various offices. In remarks made at Haynes's wake, James Hurley, former director of both the Long Island Historical Society and Project Weeksville and first president of the Weeksville Society, recalled his "somewhat unusual approach to black history." "One of the first things we did in those early days was to go up in Joe's plane and take pictures . . . to see or confirm odd or unusual property lines. . . . Although I'd been an aerial photographer in the Navy, some of my pictures didn't come out too well so Joe went up one Saturday and, flying the plane with one hand (this at a fairly low altitude,) took the pictures with the other!"

Other organizations in which Haynes was active were the Afro-American Historical and Genealogical Society, New York Society of Professional Engineers, Aircraft Owners and Pilots Association, Math Counts, and the Rog-Mark Block Association.

### Sources

Drew-Holland, Carol. "People & Places." *New York Voice* (October 1, 1983); 11.

"Gives Pupils Lofty Hopes." *New York Sunday News* (November 22, 1970).

"Joseph H. Haynes, P.E./C.F.I.I." *Black Pilots of New York—25th Anniversary Souvenir Journal*, 1992.

Maynard, Joan, and Gwen Cottman. *Weeksville Then & Now.* Brooklyn, NY: Society for the Preservation of Weeksville and Bedford-Stuyvesant History, 1983.

"Remembering Joe Haynes." *Beating Our Drum* (July 1997), newsletter of the Weeksville Society; 2.

Saxon, Wolfgang. "Joseph Haynes, 66, Found Old Black Settlement." *New York Times* (March 16, 1997): 46.

# Michael R. Hollis

**Born:** 1954, Atlanta, Georgia

**Education:** Booker T. Washington High School, Atlanta, Georgia; B.A., Dartmouth College, law degree, University of Virginia.

**Positions Held:** Attorney; vice president, Oppenheimer and Company, 1981–1983; founder and president, Air Atlanta, 1983–1987.

**Summary:** Michael R. Hollis, an Atlanta attorney, founded the first major black-owned airline, Air Atlanta, in 1984. Though the airline subsequently failed, he managed to raise more capital than any African American had ever raised before to start up the business.

### Early Years

Michael Hollis was born in 1954, the youngest of five children His father was a Pullman porter, and his mother was an official for the Atlanta Housing Authority. Both parents pushed their children to excel in school. Hollis, in an interview in *Ebony*, commented that he was raised according to the "13 commandments." These commandments comprise the original 10 commandments known to everyone, with the addition of three that were special to the middle-class African American community; "thou shalt own thy own home, thou shalt send thy sons and daughters to college, and thou shalt own thy own business." All of the Hollis children successfully completed college.

Hollis was an ambitious youth, who decided at the age of 12 that he wanted to be an attorney. He early exhibited a knack for getting ahead. At the age of 15, he was president of the Atlanta Youth Congress. According to Maynard Jackson, former mayor of Atlanta, quoted in *The New York Times*: "He remembers names and he follows up contacts like no one I've seen in my life." Among the influential men in the African American community whom he met while still in high school were Andrew Young, Julian Bond, Jackson, and the late educator, Benjamin E. Mays, the president of Morehouse College. Mays was a mentor to the youth. His motto, "If you set out to do it, you will," had a deep influence on the young man. Most important, perhaps, Mays encouraged Hollis to attend Dartmouth College and the University of Virginia Law School, both highly prestigious institutions. He graduated cum laude from Dartmouth, and at the University of Virginia, he became the first black president of the 30,000-member student law section of the American Bar Association.

## Career Highlights

Upon graduation from law school, Hollis was appointed by President Jimmy Carter, a fellow Georgian, to the commission that investigated the disaster at Three Mile Island, a nuclear power plant in Pennsylvania. After the assignment ended, he joined an Atlanta law firm, and from there he moved to New York, where he became a vice president in the public finance department of Oppenheimer and Company at the age of 26.

Two years later, Hollis returned to Atlanta, where he joined the law firm of Hansell and Post. But it was his intention to start his own airline. He had some experience in public transportation, having served briefly with the Urban Mass Transit Administration and the Bay Area Rapid Transit (BART) in San Francisco. Hollis was convinced that the time was right: "On the surface it may have appeared risky. . . . But given my appreciation for mass transportation and the fact that Atlanta is the premier transportation hub in the country, these two things together added up to an appropriate decision to build an airline."

With a well-researched business plan in hand, Hollis began calling on the black leaders he had met in his youth. Maynard Jackson arranged an introduction to Robert L. White, president of the National Alliance of Federal and Postal Employees, a largely black union whose pension fund provided the first $500,000 of seed money for the airline. An introduction to William J. Kennedy III, chairman of the African American–owned

North Carolina Mutual Life Insurance Company, followed. This firm ultimately invested almost $2.5 million in the company.

Other backers followed, among them the Equitable Life Assurance Society, the General Electric Credit Corporation, Aetna Life Insurance Company, and UNC Ventures, the nation's largest African American venture capital company. Hollis succeeded in raising more start-up capital than any other black entrepreneur had up to that time. There were signs, however, that the company was undercapitalized. Hollis had raised only half of the $50 million that he had sought to start the company. He went ahead with his plans, however. With the backing he had already received, Hollis was able to lease five vintage 727–100 Boeing jets and to hire 60 pilots, as well as maintenance personnel and flight attendants.

It was a time of great turmoil in the airline industry. Deregulation had created a cutthroat business environment. According to Dan Kolber, one-time vice president of Air Atlanta, quoted in *Black Enterprise*: "Before 1978 running an airline in the United States was like running a utility . . . the fares were structured by the government and you passed costs on. There was no real competition. It became a whole new industry in 1978." New airlines proliferated, but they were often put out of business or taken over by the major carriers.

Hollis had thoroughly thought out his strategy. He saw a gap in service at Atlanta's busy Hartsfield Airport. Atlanta's business travelers were forced to plan their schedules around the departures of connecting flights arriving at the airport—a serious inconvenience. Air Atlanta was to be "the Airline Born for Business." Flights were to depart at the convenience of business passengers and to meet their wants and needs.

Air Atlanta began offering airline service on February 4, 1984. Hollis had made the decision not to try to compete by cutting fares; the major airlines could undercut his prices were he to employ this strategy. The qualities that would distinguish Air Atlanta would be convenience, courtesy, and luxury service. The airline's fleet was outfitted with wider, roomier seats, and there were fewer seats; 88 in all, compared to an industry average of 125. The airline provided gourmet meals, complete with wine, china dishes, and silver cutlery, on every flight. Business travelers appreciated these amenities, and Air Atlanta built up a loyal group of passengers.

Staff, who were not unionized, made far less than the industry's averages. Pilots earned about a third less than comparable pilots, and the rest of the staff earned about half the standard wage. Promises of incentives to come, such as stock options, motivated the employees. A former flight attendant with the firm is quoted in *Ebony*: "Even though we worked real hard and could have made more money elsewhere, there was this feeling that if we really got it going, we were all going to be on the ground floor of something big." Hollis was a dynamic figure, by all accounts, who could arouse enthusiasm among employees. Said another employee, also quoted in *Ebony*: "He was like this charismatic preacher. . . . He would have these employee meetings and talk about how wonderful things were going to be . . . and we'd just want to go out and conquer the world."

Not all employees, including top management, were satisfied. Four presidents, all with experience in airline operations, found their way through the revolving doors of the company in three years. Three of the four highest-ranking officers resigned within a two-week period. Hollis attributed the rapid changes of management to "growing pains." Some of the managers felt differently. In the opinion of these experienced executives, Hollis insisted in being involved in every aspect of the company's operation. Some outsiders close to the situation disagreed, attributing the conflict to racial prejudice or to personal incompatibility.

Employees did not fail to notice that Hollis had provided himself with an excellent salary, and such perks as two luxuriously appointed apartments. Hollis's law firm was awarded a $13,000-a month consulting fee by the Air Atlanta board. In addition, Hollis traveled first class whenever he flew, but insisted all other company employees travel coach.

Still, the airline was off to a promising start. Due to its lower labor costs, Air Atlanta had lower overhead than other airlines. The company projected that a load of 50 percent of capacity would allow it to break even. At the end of its first year, the airline had flown 175,000 passengers, with an average load factor of 37 percent. Agreements with Eastern and Delta Air Lines permitted all three airlines to handle each other's baggage and to book flights on each other's planes.

However, the airline was undercapitalized. Twelve to 15 planes were needed to reach what the company called "critical mass," a system large enough to spread the costs. Cash flow was erratic. A major setback came when an initial public offering for Air Atlanta stock found no takers. The offering had to be withdrawn. Hollis had to spend most of his time jetting around the country seeking more investment capital.

In January 1986, the Equitable Life Assurance Company, one of Air Atlanta's largest investors, forced Hollis to hire Harry Kimbriel as chief operating officer. Kimbriel negotiated a lucrative deal for himself, insisting on being paid a consulting fee along with his salary. He and Hollis clashed immediately. By the end of the year, Kimbriel had organized a campaign to oust Hollis. He was aided by 150 members of Air Atlanta's staff, who signed a petition asking for Hollis's removal. Hollis fired Kimbriel, causing Equitable to withdraw further financial support.

Hollis made desperate efforts to salvage the company, but his other investors were also withdrawing support. The company's assets were heavily mortgaged, and without a new infusion of capital, mortgage holders were threatening to foreclose. Hollis had no choice but to suspend operations.

On April 3, 1987, Air Atlanta declared

bankruptcy, leaving 3,900 creditors, including some employees who were unable to cash their final paychecks. A disgruntled former employee is quoted in *Ebony* as saying, "Air Atlanta failed because of ego." Some observers, however, believed that Air Atlanta's history was not one of total failure. Robert L. White, a former board member and president of the National Alliance of Postal and Federal Employees, which had invested heavily in the airline, stated his belief in the same article: "Air Atlanta was a wonderful idea that gave many black professionals a chance to run a major airline. That was a rare and very valuable opportunity."

## Sources

Alexander, James Jr. "Air Atlanta's in a Holding Pattern." *Black Enterprise* 15, 11 (June 1985): 228–230.

Salpukis, Agis. "Air Atlanta's Buoyant Founder." *New York Times* (June 9, 1985): 7.

Schwartz, Jerry. "After Three Years of High Hopes, Air Atlanta Is Out of Cash." *New York Times* (April 12, 1987): 8.

Simon, Francesca. "Air Atlanta Takes Off." *Essence* 15 (September 1984): 66.

Whitaker, Charles. "The $90 Million Dream: The Rise and Fall of Michael Hollis." *Ebony* (November 1987): 188–190, 192, 194.

Witherspoon, Roger. "The Crash of Air Atlanta." *Black Enterprise* 17, 11 (June 1987): 59–60.

# Fred Hutcherson Jr.

**Full Name at Birth:** Fred Hutcherson Jr.

**Born:** July 6, 1912, Evanston, Illinois

**Died:** July 7, 1962, Evanston

**Education:** Evanston Township High School, 1930; Haines Normal and Industrial Institute, Augusta, Georgia, one year.

**Positions Held:** Captain, Royal Canadian Air Force Ferry Command, 1940–1942; pilot, British West Indian Airways, 1942–1944; flight instructor, Tuskegee Air Field, Tuske-

Fred Hutcherson Jr. Courtesy of Fred Hutcherson III.

gee, Alabama, February 1945–January 1946; co-owner, Port-au-Prince Flying School, Haiti, 1946–1948; chief pilot, Sociedad Aereonautica Medellín (SAM Airways), Colombia, 1949–early 1950s; manager, owner, Lake Airways charter service, Chicago, 1956.

**Awards, Honors:** Evanston City Council citation for wartime achievement, 1946.

**Summary:** The first African American to fly across the Atlantic Ocean was Fred Hutcherson Jr., when he was a captain in the Royal Canadian Air Force Ferry Command in 1942. He was also the only pilot of color in the unit. Hutcherson had a career in aviation—despite the barriers raised by color prejudice in the United States—by flying in Canada, Haiti, and Colombia.

## Early Years

Fred Hutcherson Jr., born on July 6, 1912, to Orain Babcock and Fred Hutcherson Sr., was their first child. His parents were originally from Georgia, and they had two more children, Joseph and Marianna. Hutcherson Sr. was a mechanic, but he later owned and managed a restaurant and bowling alley.

While at Evanston Township High School, young Hutcherson played basketball and football and he enjoyed swimming. He was interested in watching the airplanes at a nearby airport and tinkering with the engines of defunct aircraft. He graduated from high school in 1930 and spent one year at the Haines Normal and Industrial Institute, a well-regarded school founded by Lucy Laney, in Augusta, Georgia. At about this time, he married Regina Elaine Laurent of New Orleans. Because the bride was under 18 years old, they had to go to Wisconsin to marry. (The only one of their children to survive infancy was Fred Hutcherson III, who was born in 1935. He served eight years in the U.S. Air Force as a weather observer and a missile guidance mechanic. From 1962 his career has been in photography.)

Hutcherson learned to fly while still in his teens by reading books and studying cardboard depictions of instrument panels. He received his early flight training at Sky Harbor Airport, Northbrook, Illinois where his mentors were a black man, Mr. Matthews, and Roy Guthier, a German ace of World War I and an instructor at Sky Harbor. To pay for his flying lessons, Hutcherson worked as a doorman at an elegant china shop, where his duties included parking the cars of the patrons and carrying their purchases. He received his license sometime in the 1930s. Called "a natural flyer" by his fellow pilots, Hutcherson was asked to run the ground school at the airport.

## Career Highlights

After Germany declared war on Britain in 1939 it was apparent that a larger war was on the horizon. Hutcherson tried to enlist in the U.S. Army Air Corps, but because of his color he was denied the opportunity to serve his country. He was accepted by the Royal Canadian Air Force (RCAF) as a flight instructor. The RCAF soon established a Ferry Command to transport American-made bombers to Britain under an assistance program called "lend-lease." When the call came for volunteers to fly the unarmed bombers, Hutcherson immediately responded. He was accepted and commissioned as a captain. With the completion of his first delivery in 1940, Hutcherson became the first African American to fly across the Atlantic Ocean. The flight lasted eight hours and 50 minutes.

Hutcherson remained with the RCAF through 1942. On his furloughs (leaves) home, he was in demand as an example of African American achievement. Hutcherson spoke on radio programs and before civic groups in Evanston, Chicago, and St. Augustine, Florida. His dramatic tales of motors stalling low over ocean waves and of near collisions enthralled audiences. In one of these experiences, he related that a crew member's black hair had turned to pale gray in minutes. Harrowing events such as these, as well as temperatures that fell well below freezing, soon winnowed the 33-member corps to 16. Hutcherson next accepted an offer from British West Indian Airways, where he was employed as a commercial pilot from 1942 to 1944. He now had 5,000 hours of flying time, and he flew government personnel and international dignitaries along the northern coast of South America and to bases in the Caribbean.

He was finally able to serve his own country when he was appointed a flight instructor at Tuskegee Army Air Field, Alabama, on February 1, 1945. Until January 17, 1946, he instructed cadets in both single- and twin-engine aircraft. His official separation record from the Army notes his proficiency in "pilotage, dead reckoning, and radio navigation." It further states he holds an AAF Green instrument card, CAS Commercial License, and CAA Instructor's rating, as well as British Transport and British Navigator's licenses.

Mustered out of military service, and with no commercial aviation jobs available to black pilots, Hutcherson pondered the next best step to support his family. With his fellow instructors, Perry H. Young and James O. Plinton, he decided to go to Haiti in 1946 to try to start an airline. Private financial backing fell through when the government changed hands and demanded a larger share of the profits. The three stayed on in Haiti, with Hutcherson and Young opening the Port-au-Prince Flying School.

The venture failed in two years, and in 1949, Hutcherson became the chief pilot for the Colombian airline, SAM, which was the acronym for Sociedad Aereonautica Medellín. He returned to Illinois in the early 1950s where he was the manager of Sky Harbor Airport. In 1956 he founded his own company, Lake Airways, a charter service operating out of Meigs Field, Chicago. He also continued his interest in the family restaurant, and he was a member of the Illinois wing of OX-5, a club of pioneer airmen.

Hutcherson died of leukemia on July 7, 1962, in Evanston, and he is buried in Montrose Cemetery.

## Sources

"Canadian Aviation Captain First Negro to Fly Atlantic." *Pittsburgh Courier* (May 16, 1942): 1.

"Commercial Airline Pilot." *Ebony* (September 1951): 4.

"Fred Hutcherson was 1st Negro to Fly Atlantic." *Journal & Guide* (Norfolk, VA) (July 21, 1962): second section, 9.

Hutcherson III, Fred, Rockford, Illinois, to Betty K. Gubert, New York, telephone and personal interviews, correspondence, clippings, July–August 1999.

Lacy, Sam. "Tells Colorful Tale of Life in Ferry Command." *Chicago Defender* (June 26, 1943): second section.

# J

## Melva Jackman

**Full Name at Birth:** Melva Letitia Hill

**Born:** November 4, 1945, Harlem, New York

**Education:** B.S. in elementary education, City College of New York, 1966; M.S. in educational administration, C.W. Post College of Long Island University, Greenvale, New York, 1975; Doctor of Education, Hofstra University, Hempstead, New York, 1994; State University of New York, FAA-issued private pilot's license, commercial pilot's license, and instrument rating, 1975–1983.

**Positions Held:** Elementary school teacher, P.S. 194 (Manhattan), 1966–1968, 1970–1973; U.S. Department of Defense dependents school, Landstuhl, West Germany, 1968–1970; P.S. 132 (Queens), 1973–1991; adjunct professor, Hofstra University, 1991–1993.

**Awards, Honors:** Kingsborough Community College (Brooklyn), Women's History Month, 1985; TECH (Teachers Extending Computer Horizons) Grants, 1986, 1987; President, Negro Airmen International (NAI) Black Pilots of New York, 1988–1992; Black Women in Aviation, 1994.

**Summary:** Melva Jackman and her friend, Ruby L. Bostic, became the first two African American women to fly from New York to Trinidad in a single-engine plane. This feat, accomplished in February 1985, gained them entrance into the *Guinness Book of World Records*. Jackman, with a doctorate in education, has devoted her career in teaching to expanding students' interest in aeronautics and other sciences. The first woman to become president of NAI Black Pilots of New York, Jackman held the position from 1988 to 1992.

### Early Years

Melva Letitia Hill was born in Harlem on November 4, 1945, to Estelle Irish Hill and Elmore Wellington Hill. The family was completed when another daughter, Cynthia, arrived. Both parents were Harlem-born, but Mrs. Hill's parents came from St. Kitts and Nevis, West Indies. When Melva was born her father, trained as a pilot at Tuskegee Air Field in Alabama, was serving in the U.S. Army Air Corps on Guam, an island in the Pacific Ocean.

The elder Hill held a lifelong interest in aviation although he was unable to forge a career in the field. His interest attracted his first daughter's imagination. Jackman's earliest memories are of Sunday afternoons spent watching planes as they landed and took off from Little Ferry Seaplane Base in New Jersey, and from Zahn's Airport on Long Island. Her first ride in an airplane, her father's Taylorcraft, occurred when she was about four years old. Several pillows had to be piled on the seat so that the little girl would be high enough to see outside.

Hill worked for the New York City Transit Authority from 1946 until 1976, retiring as chief supervisor of road car inspectors. During this time, he also owned and piloted small land and sea planes, and he conducted sightseeing flights. These flights, along with home-cooked meals and boating, were part of the draw of the lakeside vacation lodge that the Hills purchased and ran during the summer. Their lodge was in Narrowsburg in Sullivan County, New York. As a teenager, Jackman knew that someday she would follow in her father's footsteps, and that she too would learn to fly an airplane. But she put thoughts of flying on hold as she completed high school.

## Higher Education

Entering the City College of New York (CCNY) in 1962, and working part time, Jackman decided to start flying lessons. Her father accompanied her to Zahn's Airport in Amityville on Long Island. Her enthusiasm was dampened by the discomfort of the plane itself and the cost of lessons. Fourteen dollars an hour was high for a college student. Jackman's interest in aviation was again submerged as she completed her degree in elementary education, which she obtained in 1966.

Jackman has earned degrees that include a master's in educational administration from C.W. Post College (Long Island University) in 1975, and a doctorate in education from Hofstra University in 1994. From 1975 until

1983, Jackman revived her interest in flying and she achieved licenses as a private pilot, commercial pilot, and instrument-rated pilot. Her primary instructors were John Denham and Joseph H. Haynes. Of her several flight instructors, Haynes stood out for his ability, knowledge, and kindness. They remained friends until Haynes died in 1997.

An introduction to George Gay Daniel, a co-worker of her father's and a fellow Tuskegee Airman, helped Jackman find her niche in the world of African American aviation. Daniel, who received his pilot's license in 1939, was on the membership committee of Negro Airmen International (NAI), founded in 1967 by Edward A. Gibbs and a dozen other aviators. They aimed to promote opportunities for blacks in commercial aviation and to create an association for networking and lobbying. They now provide flight training and inspiration for youth to pursue careers in aviation. The New York chapter of NAI is known as Black Pilots of New York, located in Queens.

Jackman, the first woman in the New York chapter to be a serious flight student, was put through rigorous lessons. In a Cessna 150, she was taught to handle unusual altitudes, steep banks, severe stalls, and rapid dives.

## Career Highlights

Upon graduation in 1966, Jackman began teaching at P.S. 194 in Harlem, remaining until 1968. She then went to Landstuhl, West Germany, to teach in the school for military dependents run by the U.S. Department of Defense. She joined Norman Jackman, whom she had met while they were students at CCNY, and who was now attending medical school in Germany. They were married in Basel, Switzerland, on February 13, 1968. The Jackmans lived in Hamburg for three years. Their son Terrence was born after they returned to the United States, on October 2, 1971. A graduate of Long Island University, he is studying court reporting.

Jackman continued teaching at P.S. 194 until 1973, when the Jackmans bought a home in Queens. She then transferred to P.S. 132, the Ralph J. Bunche school, in that borough. She remained at the school until 1991, with ever-increasing responsibilities above classroom duties. She specialized in developing courses and programs in all the sciences, with an emphasis on aerospace science.

While attending Hofstra University to attain her doctorate in education, Jackman was a research assistant and adjunct professor in the university's school of education, from 1991 to 1993.

Jackman continued flying for pleasure, and in February 1985, she and her friend Ruby L. Bostic, made a flight that earned them a place in the *Guinness Book of World Records*. On February 10, 1985, the women took off from Republic Airport in Farmingdale, New York, bound for Trinidad and Tobago, a trip of 5,600 miles, mostly over water. Jackman's single-engine plane, a Piper Cherokee Arrow, held only enough fuel for five hours. Among the stops they made for refueling were Myrtle Beach, South Carolina; Ft. Lauderdale, Florida; Grand Exuma Island, Bahamas; Dominican Republic; Puerto Rico; Antigua; St. Lucia; and Grenada. They reached Trinidad on February 14, just in time for Carnival celebrations. They thus became the first black women to pilot a single-engine plane from New York to Trinidad. They did not know they had set a record, nor was that their intention. They wanted to commemorate the 1934 "goodwill" flight of C.A. "Chief" Anderson and Albert E. Forsythe, pioneers in aviation, which covered some of the same route. At the completion of the flight, Jackman said, "It was a great experience, and gave me a great sense of accomplishment." They returned home on February 23, after 50 hours of flying time. Their refueling stops on the return trip were Guadeloupe; Puerto Rico; Grand Turks and Caicos Islands; Nassau, Bahamas; and Palm Beach, Florida.

Before Jackman became the president of NAI in 1988, the first woman to hold that position, she served the organization in other capacities. She was chair of the public education committee, and later, she was deputy director. She also spearheaded NAI's successful drive to purchase a building for the planned academy, as well as its ATC 610 Flight Simulator.

Besides flying as a recreational activity, Jackman has also been a pilot for prominent leaders in the African American community such as Jesse Jackson and Percy Sutton. Jackman's future plans include the development and operation of a nonprofit institution that will provide pilot training and promote aerospace career training opportunities for young African Americans in the New York City area.

### Sources

Drew, Carol. "People and Places." *New York Voice* (March 1985).

Flowers, Sandra H. *Women in Aviation and Space.* Washington, DC: U.S. Department of Transportation and Federal Aviation Administration, 1995.

Funeral program of Elmore Wellington Hill, May 1999.

Jackman, Melva, Hollis, New York, to Betty K. Gubert, New York, e-mail, August 22, December 8, 1999, March 12, 2000.

NAI Black Pilots of New York. *25th Anniversary Celebration.* Queens, NY: Negro Airmen International, 1992.

# Lewis A. Jackson

**Full Name at Birth:** Lewis Albert Jackson

**Born:** December 29, 1912, Angola, Indiana

**Died:** January 8, 1994, Ohio

**Education:** Transport Pilot Certificate, 1937; B.S. in education, Indiana Wesleyan University, 1939; commercial license with instructor rating, 1939; M.S. in education, Miami University, Oxford, Ohio; Ph.D. in higher education, Ohio State University, Columbus, Ohio, 1948.

**Positions Held:** Flight instructor, Coffey School of Aeronautics, 1939–1940; director of training, Army Air Force 66th Flight Training Detachment, Tuskegee Institute, 1940–1945; associate professor of aviation, Ohio State University; examiner, Federal Aviation Administration, (FAA) 1947–1960; successively dean of students, vice president for academic affairs, and president, Central State University, Wilberforce, Ohio.

**Awards, Honors:** OX-5 Aviation Pioneers; honored in exhibitions at the National Air and Space Museum, Washington, D.C., and the United States Air Force Museum, Wright-Patterson Air Force Base, Ohio.

**Summary:** Lewis A. Jackson was director of training, Army Air Force 66th Flight Training Detachment, Tuskegee Institute, 1940–1945, training African Americans as military pilots, a historic role, as African Americans had never been permitted to serve as pilots before. At the end of World War II, Jackson became an examiner for the Federal Aviation Administration, examining 411 pilots between the years of 1947 to 1960. Becoming a college administrator, Jackson had a long and successful career as an educator at Central State University, culminating in his appointment as the fourth president of the institution.

## Early Years

Lewis A. Jackson was born in Angola, Indiana, on December 29, 1912. His interest in flight manifested itself early: At the age of three, Jackson built his first model plane. In 1927, when he was 15 years old, he had his first plane ride, in an OX-5 Swallow. When Jackson was 16, he designed, built, and successfully flew two gliders. At the age of 17, he installed a motorcycle engine in a partially completed Alco sport Monoplane. According to Jackson, he and a friend "taxied a

great deal, but never took off." The plane was destroyed by a windstorm before they could get it off the ground.

In 1930, Jackson purchased a four-year-old Waco-10 and began formal flight training. The training involved was minimal: "On November 13, 1932, I soloed this Waco for the first time, having had a total of seven hours in four different airplanes with five different instructors over a period of three years."

## Higher Education

Jackson acquired his transport license in 1937 and a commercial license with an instructor rating in 1939. He also managed to put himself through college by flying passengers around central Indiana and Ohio, and in 1939 he received a B.S. in education from Indiana Wesleyan University. In later years, Jackson earned a master's degree from Miami University and a doctorate from Ohio State University, both in education.

## Career Highlights

After completing college, Jackson was teaching public school in 1939 when he learned that a flight instructor was needed to train African American pilots in Chicago. In Jackson's words: "I joined partnership with the Willa Brown-Cornelius Coffey School of Aeronautics which was located at Harlem Airport. I taught a private pilots' course with 15 students, nearly all of whom completed the course."

Meanwhile, events in Europe were worsening. The rise of Hitler and Mussolini and their aggression toward other countries convinced President Roosevelt and his advisers that war was likely. Pilots would be needed when war broke out, and there was a shortage of pilots. Pilot training was costly in both time and money. In the height of the Great Depression, with many people out of work, even those who might be interested could not afford pilot training. To meet the need for pilots, a plan called the Civilian Pilot Training Program (CPTP) was formed to train young American men to fly.

The program was intended only for white men, but after much lobbying and pressure from prominent African Americans, the Roosevelt administration agreed that young African American men could participate in the program. It was in conjunction with this program that Jackson was brought to Chicago.

In October 1940, Tuskegee Institute recruited Jackson to teach in the flight and ground school, which was located at Moton Field. Tuskegee, a black institution in Tuskegee, Alabama, was chosen by the U.S. Army as a segregated training site for African American pilots after the outbreak of World War II. Jackson was appointed as an instructor in the program, eventually becoming director of training for the Army Air Force 66th Flight Training Detachment, preparing pilots who eventually joined the 99th Pursuit Squadron.

The men under Jackson's tutelage did well. "Few people know it, but during one period Tuskegee topped the 23 schools in the Southeast Air Corps Training Command on the final written examinations. Our students always passed everything with flying colors!" The African Americans trained in the program went on to distinguish themselves for their courage and flying skill and became known collectively as the Tuskegee Airmen.

When the war ended in 1945, Jackson moved to Ohio, where he became a Federal Aviation Administration (FAA) examiner, testing over 400 pilots for flight certification between 1947 and 1960. In this capacity, he developed an aircraft computer (called a NAV-kit) which pilots used to obtain their licenses. He also designed several "roadable" airplanes—planes that could either be flown or driven like an automobile. During the summers, from 1953 to 1956, Jackson was employed as a crop duster by Aerial Crop Aids, Indiana.

Meanwhile, Jackson had resumed his education, obtaining a master's degree from Miami University in Oxford, Ohio, and a Ph.D. in higher education in 1948 from Ohio State University. The title of his dissertation was "A Study of Aviation Courses and Facilities in Higher Education in the United States with Predictions and Future Trends." He spent a year as associate professor of Aviation at Ohio State.

Jackson served for a time as vice president for administration at Sinclair Community College. However, most of Jackson's academic career was spent at Central State University, a historically black college in Wilberforce, Ohio. He served successively as professor, dean of students, vice president for academic affairs, and president. During these years, he had not lost interest in designing aircraft. One of Jackson's "roadable" airplanes was featured in the 1967 edition of *Janes' All-World Aircraft*. Another of his inventions was a computer-plotter-log, a device which was used for many years to teach students how to fly.

After retirement, Jackson remained active in aviation, educational, and civic organizations. He was a member of the Citizens Advisory Committee, FAA; a founder and member of the Greene County Regional Airport Authority; the Experimental Aircraft Association; and he belonged to numerous other groups.

Jackson died on January 8, 1994. He was survived by his wife of 55 years, Dr. Violet Burden Jackson, a daughter, Joyce J. Dixon, and a son, Robert L. Jackson, a dermatologist. He made one further contribution to education at his death, leaving his body to the medical school at Ohio University, Athens, Ohio.

## Sources

Campbell, Clifford J. "They're Learning to Fly in Chicago." *Opportunity* (May 1941): 132, 134.

Cooper, Charlie, and Ann Cooper. *Tuskegee's Heroes; Featuring the Aviation Art of Roy La Grone*. Osceola, WI: Motorbooks International, 1996.

"Doctor Lewis A. Jackson." Memorial Program, Wilberforce, OH: Central State University, 1994.

# Daniel "Chappie" James Jr.

Daniel "Chappie" James Jr. Courtesy of National Air and Space Museum, Smithsonian Institution (SI Neg. No. 87-3316).

**Full Name at Birth:** Daniel James Jr.

**Born:** February 11, 1920, Pensacola, Florida

**Died:** February 25, 1978, Colorado Springs, Colorado

**Education:** Washington High School, Pensacola, 1937; B.S. in physical education, Tuskegee Institute, Tuskegee, Alabama, 1942; Civilian Pilot Training Program, Tuskegee Institute, 1941–1943; Air Command and Staff College, Maxwell AFB, Alabama, 1957.

**Positions Held:** Flight leader, 12th Fighter-Bomber Squadron, Phillipines, 1949; jet fighter pilot, 58th Fighter-Inceptor Squadron, Otis AFB, Massachusetts, early 1950s; deputy assistant secretary for Public Affairs, U.S. Department of Defense, 1970–1974; commander in chief (CINC), North American Air Defense Command (NORAD) and CINC U.S. Air Force Aerospace Defense Command (ADCOM), Peterson AFB, Colorado, 1975–1977.

**Awards, Honors:** Distinguished Service Medal with one oak leaf cluster; Distinguished Flying Cross with two oak leaf clusters; Meritorious Service Medal; Air Medal with 13 oak leaf clusters; Presidential Unit Citation Emblem with one oak leaf cluster; and numerous other medals and awards for service in Korea and Vietnam. A school in Brooklyn, P.S. 183, was named the General Daniel "Chappie" James Jr. School in 1979. Tuskegee Institute named its Center for Aerospace Science and Health Education after James in 1987; five honorary doctorates, 1971–1976.

**Summary:** In 1975, Daniel James Jr. became the first African American four-star general in the history of the United States. As commander in chief of the North American Air Defense Command, he wielded enormous power. His abilities and outsize personality made him an inspiration to armed forces personnel and to civilians who heard him speak.

## Early Years

The 17th and last of the children of Lillie Anna Brown and Daniel James Sr., Daniel James Jr. was born on February 11, 1920, in Pensacola, Florida. When he was born, there were only seven surviving siblings and three of them were no longer living at home. Mrs. James, a high school graduate, strongly believed that education was the key to success, and she did not want her children to attend the inferior schools available to blacks in Pensacola. "Excellence is a standard throughout the world and no one questions its color," was one of her precepts. She set up her own school, the Lillie Anna James Private School, in their home at 1606 Alcaniz Street. As more and more neighbors took advantage of the rigorous curriculum taught by the no-nonsense Mrs. James, the school needed to expand. Mr. James first built a little red schoolhouse in the back yard and later they purchased the house next door, which they remodeled as a school. Mr. James, of Alabama, had little formal schooling. He worked as a lamplighter (there were no electric street lights in the black section) and supervised coal-dolly men in a gas plant. He taught his son to follow his goals and not to be deterred by racism. Mrs. James stressed to her son that for him there was an 11th commandment, "Thou shalt not quit."

Dan Baby, as James was called, attended his mother's school until he entered Washington High School in 1933. He was thoroughly imbued with the family's work ethic and goal of success in whatever field the children chose. In high school, he dropped his own nickname and took his brother Charles's nickname of Chappie. (Charles James was an outstanding athlete, and the first of the family to graduate from college, Florida A&M.) Daniel James played football and basketball, sang in the glee club, and performed in dramatic productions. He delivered papers and watched the planes filling the sky as they flew over Pensacola's naval air base. James wanted to fly, and he traded chores for airplane rides.

## Higher Education

In 1937, the year his father died, James graduated from high school and entered Tuskegee Institute, now Tuskegee University. Participating in sports and in campus musical and dramatic productions, James was a popular student. His exuberant personality, full of humor and confidence, as well as his height of six feet five inches, made him seem destined for greatness. An extravagant action, fighting another student, caused his expulsion from Tuskegee two months before graduation in 1941. Fortunately for James, the Civilian Aeronautic Administration

(CAA) had begun the Civilian Pilot Training Program (CPTP) in 1938 in order to have a supply of pilots in case of war. Training was segregated, as was every other activity in the United States. Tuskegee had been selected as one of the black colleges where training was to take place. James had learned to fly in his senior year and his instructor, C. Alfred (Chief) Anderson, noted he was quick to learn and "had more guts than anyone I had ever seen." Chief Anderson later became the highest-ranking instructor at the Tuskegee Army Air Field. In November 1942, James married his college sweetheart, Dorothy Watkins, on the Tuskegee campus. They had three children: Danice, born 1945; Daniel III, born 1947, who also made the Air Force his career; and Claude, born 1955. By 1943, James had completed primary, basic, and advanced training at the Tuskegee Flying School, which had now become the exclusive training site for black military personnel. He received his commission as a second lieutenant in 1943 and completed his pilot training at Selfridge Field in Michigan.

## Career Highlights

Until the end of World War II, James trained pilots for the all-Negro 99th Pursuit Squadron, later known as the Tuskegee Airmen, and flew C-37 supply planes to fields in the United States. While on supply duty at Freeman Field, Indiana, on April 5, 1945, James and 100 other pilots, all officers, tried to enter the white officers club. The airmen were arrested and threatened with court martial. A young NAACP lawyer, Thurgood Marshall, who in 1967 became the first African American on the U.S. Supreme Court, defended them. He was assisted by one of the airmen who had studied law at Harvard University, William T. Coleman, who in 1975 became the first African American U.S. secretary of transportation. James was released early to fly supplies, and this mobility enabled him to spread the word about the "Freeman Field Mutiny" to the black press. Although a few men were tried, most had the charges dropped.

In September 1949 James was sent to the Philippines as flight leader of the 12th Fighter Bomber Squadron. In July 1950, he was stationed in Korea where he flew 101 combat missions in F-51 and F-80 aircraft. He was promoted to captain in October. James's next assignment was at Otis Air Force Base (AFB), Massachusetts, and he was an all-weather jet fighter pilot with the 58th Fighter-Inceptor Squadron. He achieved the rank of major in June 1952, and he commanded both the 437th and 60th Fighter-Interceptor Squadrons, in April 1953 and August 1955, respectively. The Massachusetts Junior Chamber of Commerce named him "Young Man of the Year" in 1954 for his outstanding community relations efforts.

James rose steadily during his 35-year career in the U.S. Air Force, certainly following another of his mother's adages: "Don't stand there banging on the door of opportunity, then when someone opens it, you say, wait a minute, I got to get my bags. You be prepared with your bags of knowledge, your patriotism, your honor, and when somebody opens the door, you charge in." He was promoted to lieutenant colonel in 1956; colonel in 1964; brigadier general in 1970; major general in 1972; lieutenant general in 1973; and in September 1975 Daniel James Jr. became America's first black four-star general. During these years James served in commanding positions in Bentwaters, England (1960–1964); Arizona (1964–1966); Thailand in 1967; and Libya (1969–1970.) As a wing vice commander in Thailand, Colonel James flew 78 combat missions over North Vietnam.

In August 1969, he became commander of Wheelus AFB in Libya, the largest American air base outside the United States. His skilled participation in the negotiations with Libya to remove the base from its territory earned him the notice of Defense Secretary Melvin Laird, who appointed him deputy assistant secretary of defense for public affairs. In this position, which lasted from 1970 until 1974, General James defended the U.S. role in the Vietnam War to increasingly militant and hostile audiences, who not only reviled him as an Uncle Tom but who also threw snowballs and spat on him. His replies focused on his abilities, "I got here because I'm damned good," and his patriotism, "I couldn't live long enough to pay this country back what I owe it." He told his youthful critics to pick up a degree instead of a brick. In his talks James always praised the military, saying it had made more progress in providing equal opportunity than any other segment of society. He frequently quoted his mother who awaited a time when the activities of blacks would no longer be news, and there would be no more need for "firsts" and "onlys."

James's final and most important, position was as commander in chief of North American Air Defense Command (NORAD) and of U.S. Air Force Aerospace Defense Command (ADCOM). NORAD includes Canada and ADCOM is the U.S. component. NORAD is located in an underground tunnel dug through Cheyenne Mountain in Colorado, with 15 steel buildings of one-to three-stories, blast-proof doors and ventilation systems, among many other state-of-the-art accoutrements used to defend against air or nuclear attack. NORAD's budget at the time was $1.6 billion dollars and employed 58,000 people around the world. James was, according to an article in the *Wall Street Journal*, "the only U.S. military officer with authority to deploy nuclear weapons without presidential approval."

James retired on February 1, 1978, a few months earlier than he had planned, because of a heart attack he had suffered in the fall of 1977. His fatal heart attack came on February 25 in Colorado Springs where he had gone to address a convention of the American Trucking Association. His funeral, with more than 1,500 mourners present, was at Washington's National Shrine of the Immaculate Conception, and he was buried in Arlington National Cemetery.

## Sources

"Daniel James Jr." *Current Biography*. New York: Wilson Company, 1976; 196–198.

Grieder, William. "An American Success Story." *Washington Post* (July 21, 1975): 1, 16.

Huey, John. "Guarding the Skies." *Wall Street Journal* (November 23, 1976): 1, 34.

McGovern, James R. *Black Eagle: General Daniel "Chappie" James Jr.* Tuscaloosa: University of Alabama Press, 1985.

Phelps, J. Alfred. *Chappie: America's First Black Four-Star General—The Life and Times of Daniel James Jr.* Novato, CA: Presidio Press, 1991.

Smith, J.Y. "Tribute Paid to Gen. James." *Washington Post* (March 2, 1978): C1, 9.

Treaster, Joseph. "Gen. Daniel James Jr. Dies at 58; Black Led American Air Defense." *New York Times* (February 26, 1978).

Vroman, Mary Elizabeth. "Demonstrated Ability." *Ladies Home Journal* (February 1957): 149–157.

# Mae C. Jemison

Mae C. Jemison. Courtesy of NASA.

**Full Name at Birth:** Mae Carol Jemison

**Born:** October 17, 1956, Decatur, Alabama

**Education:** Morgan Park High School, Chicago, 1973; B.S. in chemical engineering and B.A. in African and Afro-American studies, Stanford University, Stanford, California, 1977; M.D., Cornell University Medical School, New York, 1981.

**Positions Held:** Area medical officer, Liberia and Sierra Leone, Peace Corps, 1983–1985; physician, CIGNA Health Plans, California, 1985–1987; astronaut, National Aeronautics and Space Administration (NASA), 1987–1993; founder, The Jemison Group, Houston, 1993– ; professor in Environmental Studies, Dartmouth College, Hanover, New Hampshire, 1993– ; director, the Jemison Institute for Advancing Technology in Developing Countries, Dartmouth College, 1994– ; Andrew D. White Professor-at-Large, Cornell University, Ithaca, N.Y., 1999–2005.

**Awards, Honors:** *Essence* Science and Technology Award, 1988; Gamma Sigma Woman of the Year, 1990; Ebony Black Achievement Award, 1992; Mae C. Jemison Academy, Detroit (MI) public schools, named 1992; Mae C. Jemison Science and Space Museum, Wilbur Wright Junior College, Chicago, dedicated 1992; Montgomery Fellow, Dartmouth University, 1993; Kilby Science Award 1993; inductee, National Women's Hall of Fame, Seneca Falls, New York, 1993; CORE Outstanding Achievement Award; National Medical Association Hall of Fame.

**Summary:** The first African American woman to go into space, Mae Jemison was an astronaut with NASA from 1987 to 1993. She was a mission specialist aboard the space shuttle *Endeavor* in September 1992. After her resignation from NASA in 1993, Dr. Jemison founded the Jemison Group, Inc., based in Houston, Texas. She is also a professor of environmental studies at Dartmouth College, Hanover, New Hampshire, as well as director of the Jemison Institute for Advancing Technology in Developing Countries, based at Dartmouth. Through these organizations, she works to bring advanced technology solutions to the aid of less developed nations and underserved populations.

## Early Years

Born in Decatur, Alabama, Mae Carol Jemison moved to Chicago with her family when she was three years old. Jemison's parents, Charlie and Dorothy Green Jemison, a maintenance supervisor and an elementary school teacher, moved the family north in order to enhance their children's educational opportunities. In addition to their youngest child's success as an astronaut, their son Charles became a real estate broker and their elder daughter, Ada, a child psychiatrist. In an *Ebony* interview (August 1989), Jemison said that whether it was science projects, dance lessons, or art classes, her parents "encouraged me to do it, and they would find the money, time, and energy to help me be involved." However, Jemison has also recalled in several interviews that when she told her kindergarten teacher "that when I grew up I wanted to be a scientist . . . the teacher asked me, 'Don't you mean a nurse?' "

Among her earliest passions were anthropology and archaeology, but Jemison always knew she would go into space someday. "I don't remember the time I said, 'I want to be an astronaut'; it's just always been there." While growing up in the 1960s, she avidly read science fiction, astronomy, and other science books, and watched the televised Gemini and Apollo space missions as well as the TV series *Star Trek*. When she finally realized her dream in 1992, Jemison began each shift with the words, "hailing frequencies open," the signature phrase of Lieutenant Uhura, the African American astronaut of the television series. Jemison later became friends with Nichelle Nichols, the actress who played Uhura.

A consistent honor roll student at Morgan Park High School in Chicago, Jemison was also a member of the pom-pom squad and the modern dance troupe. Her scientific ambitions were further inspired by a school visit that involved meeting a biomedical engineer. Jemison graduated in 1973, at the age of 16. Awarded a National Achievement Scholarship, she enrolled at Stanford University that fall.

## Higher Education

Jemison continued to develop two of her strengths at Stanford, majoring both in chemical engineering and in African and Afro-American studies. While at Stanford, Jemison danced and acted in university productions, explaining that while science is her primary passion, "you have to be well-rounded. One's love for science doesn't get rid of all the other areas. I feel someone truly interested in science is interested in understanding what's going on in the world. That means you have to find out about social science, art, and politics."

Following her graduation from Stanford in 1977, Jemison enrolled at Cornell Medical School in New York City. While a medical student, she traveled to Thailand and Kenya as part of programs to provide primary medical care. In 1979, Jemison also organized a citywide health and law fair in New York City as a representative of the National Student Medical Association.

## Career Highlights

After receiving her M.D. from Cornell in 1981, Jemison served her medical internship at the Los Angeles County/University of Southern California Medical Center. Her residency completed, in 1983 Jemison went overseas again, this time as a staff physician for the Peace Corps in Sierra Leone and Liberia. At the same time, as part of a project funded by the National Institutes of Health and the Centers for Disease Control, she conducted research on infectious diseases, including hepatitis B, schistosomiasis, and rabies.

Once she completed her Peace Corps tour of duty in 1985, Jemison returned to Los Angeles, where she worked as a primary care physician for the CIGNA health maintenance organization. After augmenting her education with night courses in engineering at the University of California, Los Angeles, Jemison first applied to NASA's astronaut training program in October 1985. As *Jet* later reported (September 14, 1992), Jemison was encouraged to apply to NASA by the successful 1983 flights of Sally Ride, the first American woman in space, and Colonel Guion S. Bluford Jr., the first African American in space, who were on the seventh and eighth shuttle missions, respectively. However, NASA suspended its astronaut program after the space shuttle *Challenger* disaster in January 1986, in which the black astronaut Dr. Ronald E. McNair was among those killed.

Jemison commented that the *Challenger* tragedy "was very sad because of the astronauts who were lost," but that it did not deter her from her ultimate goal. She applied again when NASA reinstated the program in late 1986, and in 1987 she was notified that she was among the 15 new astronaut candidates chosen from among some 2,000 applicants, and the first African American woman to be admitted into the training program.

Astronaut candidates must undergo a year of intense technical study and physical fitness testing. In 1988, Jemison completed her training and evaluation year and was qualified to serve as mission specialist on space shuttle flights. While waiting for her turn in space, she worked at the Johnson Space Center in Houston, Texas, primarily as a technical liaison between Johnson and the Kennedy Space Center in Cape Canaveral, Florida. She also was required to monitor shuttle and orbiter payloads, and to test shuttle software.

Jemison's chance to serve on a shuttle flight came in 1992, with a joint United States–Japan life science mission called STS-47 Spacelab J. "I'm extremely excited to be on the flight because it's something that I wanted to do since I was a small child," Jemison said at a NASA press briefing. She expressed mixed emotions at being considered a role model: "It's important not only for a little black girl growing up to know, yeah, you can become an astronaut because here's Mae Jemison," she told an Associated Press interviewer, "but it's also important for older white males who sometimes make decisions on those careers of those little black girls" (*New York Times*, September 13, 1992).

The mission was launched on September 12, 1992. As many astronauts did, Jemison took along several personal items, including art from West Africa, a signed poster from the Alvin Ailey American Dance Theater, the flag of the Organization of African Unity, and a banner from the Mae C. Jemison Academy, a science-oriented alternative school in Detroit named in her honor. While in orbit, Jemison was responsible for several biological experiments, including one that studied the effects of space flight on the fertilization and development of frog embryos.

After her successful space flight, Jemison found herself in demand as a speaker, which she enjoyed. "It's exciting to be able to share some of my experiences, and [to] let people know that space exploration is not something that's totally detached from them." Jemison encouraged audiences to reject the limitations imposed by others. Space exploration, she has said, "is a birthright of everyone who is on this planet."

Just six months after her shuttle mission, Jemison resigned from NASA, in March 1993. She wanted "to more actively encourage success from members of society who 'have traditionally been left out' of certain careers." She then founded the Jemison Group in Houston, Texas, to focus on projects that bring advanced technology solutions to underserved populations. One

Jemison Group project, Alafiya—the word means "good health" in the Yoruba language—was formed to develop satellite networks to improve health care delivery in West Africa and other less-developed regions. Other projects of the Jemison Group include the promotion of solar energy in new applications, science curriculum exchanges between the United States and South Africa, and The Earth We Share, an international youth camp devoted to increasing science and environmental awareness.

Jemison's early work with the Jemison Group led Dartmouth College to invite her, in 1993, to teach a course on space-age technology and developing countries. Jemison has since joined Dartmouth's environmental studies department, and is director of the Jemison Institute for Advancing Technology in Developing Countries, based at Dartmouth's campus in Hanover, New Hampshire. The Jemison Institute seeks to provide new solutions to problems in the developing world through the innovative use of science and technology, and also acts as an international clearing house for the exchange of information and training through its seminars, publications, and fellowship program.

Jemison continues to travel widely to promote science education and the development of advanced-technology strategies to assist emerging nations. She also participates in online group interviews with students across the nation as part of NASA's QuestChat program. In late 1998, Jemison was the only African American among the top seven nominees as possible future women to be president of the United States, according to a nationwide poll conducted by The White House Project, a public awareness campaign of Why Not A Woman, Inc., and she is among Cornell University's Andrew D. White Professors-at-Large for 1999–2005.

## Sources

"Dr. Mae Jemison Becomes First Black Woman in Space." *Jet* (September 14, 1992): 34.

"Dr. Mae Jemison Quits NASA: Has New Mission." *Jet* (March 29, 1993): 6.

Haynes, Karina A., and Marilyn Marshall. "Mae Jemison: Coming in from Outer Space." *Ebony* (December 1992): 118–121.

Jemison, Dr. Mae. *Find Where the Wind Goes: Moments from My Life*. New York: Scholastic Press, 2001.

"Jemison, Mae C." *Current Biography*. New York: H.W. Wilson, 1993; 277–281.

Leary, Warren E. "A Determined Breaker of Boundaries: Mae Carol Jemison." *New York Times* (September 13, 1992): 42.

"Mae Jemison." AppleMasters Program. Apple, Inc. 2000. Http://www.apple.com/applemasters/mae jemison/. Accessed February 5, 2000.

Marshall, Marilyn. "Child of the '60's Set to Become First Black Woman in Space." *Ebony* (August 1989): 50–55.

———. "Close-Up: A New Star in the Galaxy." *Ebony* (December 1992): 122.

National Aeronautics and Space Administration. Various pages. http://www.nasa.gov/. Accessed February 5, 2000.

Phelps, J. Alfred. *They Had a Dream: The Story of African American Astronauts*. Novato, CA: Presidio Press, 1994; 205–225.

The Jemison Institute. Dartmouth University. March 13, 1998. http://www.dartmouth.edu/jemison/. Accessed February 5, 2000.

# Willie "Suicide" Jones

**Full Name at Birth:** William or Willie Jones

**Born:** Between 1908 and 1911, Memphis, Tennessee, or possibly Mississippi

**Education:** Unknown

**Positions Held:** Professional parachute jumper and wing walker, traveling with more than 20 air circuses, 1923?–1950?, including the Orange Flying Circus, Fort Worth, Texas; pilot in the late 1930s–1940s; merchant seaman, possibly early 1940s; poultry house worker, late 1940s?.

**Summary:** A professional parachute jumper and wing walker from the 1920s until at least 1950, Willie "Suicide" Jones held the world record for a delayed parachute jump in 1939.

## Early Years

Although exact places and dates are difficult to determine, Willie Jones was born sometime between 1908 and 1911 either in Mississippi or in Memphis, Tennessee. In 1938, the *Chicago Defender* would refer to him as the son of Mrs. Rebecca Lang of Memphis, "who hoped," the paper reported, "that her boy would one day become an undertaker."

Jones began his flying career at a young age; stories vary as to exactly when and where. One story holds that he first flew while employed to do odd jobs for the family of a World War I veteran in Virginia, who took Jones up "just to frighten him." But his employer discovered that Jones had no fear of flying, and soon Jones was walking the wings and standing on his head while in flight. According to a *Chicago Defender* article, Jones joined his first air circus, the Orange Flying Circus of Fort Worth, Texas, in 1923. An *Ebony* article reports that he began flying in St. Louis at the age of 15 and took a walk out on the wing of a flying plane on his second plane ride at a Missouri fair in 1927.

In any case, "I've never had any fear in the air," Jones explained. "Doing tricks up there just seemed to come natural to me and gave me a big kick. So I . . . decided to stunt for a living."

## Career Highlights

Those were the early days of stunt flying: Jones performed a stunt in which he held onto a rope while the plane rolled in six loops. In another act, he climbed down a 30-foot rope ladder to change planes in mid-air. Later, Jones joined the Hollywood Flying Circus, whose members performed stunts in movies; with them, the *Defender* reported, Jones "averaged 50 leaps a day and went up with such expert stunt artists as Ace Corbin

and Speed Schuman." He would perform with more than 20 flying air circuses over the course of his career.

By 1939, Jones was the only African American parachute jumper in the world to participate in "more than six" U.S. Army air meets. In 1936, as the only African American entrant at an army air show at Boxdale Field, Shreveport, Louisiana, Jones won first prize over the other 12 entrants, all of whom were white.

One of Jones's "most thrilling" accomplishments, and the one that garnered him his nickname, was a night jump at Little Rock in 1938 on behalf of the government, which wanted to test the Arkansas National Guard Coast Artillery's searchlights, intended to locate enemy bombers in wartime. Jones jumped at over 10,000 feet: the searchlights sought to locate him as a target. Several times the lights caught his eyes, nearly blinding him; he landed by instinct, and took four days to recover his full sight. Six other (white) jumpers had refused offers to make the night jump, which was termed "suicide."

Jones arrived in the Chicago area fresh from a 27-state barnstorming tour with white stunt flyer Speed Schuman. In Chicago, he gained the interest and backing of Major Rupert A. Simmons, who had sponsored the first "colored" air show there in 1929. Under Major Simmons's sponsorship, Jones was the featured attraction at several air shows in the Chicago area, and eventually he became the world record-holder for the delayed parachute jump on March 2, 1939.

Jones had made two earlier attempts at the world record. The first, staged as the featured act of an air show at Markham Airfield in Harvey, Illinois, was made on August 28, 1938. He was attempting to beat an unofficial record claimed by a Russian who had jumped from 26,500 feet and who had opened his chute 650 feet from the ground. Jones jumped at 29,400 feet and fell approximately 27,000 feet before opening his chute. He had hoped to jump from 34,000 feet, but the Cessna plane in which he was flown aloft would climb no higher than 29,400.

Afterwards, Jones described the experience for a *Chicago Defender* reporter:

> I told you I'd put my feet on the ground and be all together.... It took me about two hours and a half to get up yonder, but when I leaped out from the 5½ miles distance, it required only about three minutes to come down to earth.
>
> It certainly was cold when [the test pilot] who carried me up told me that we were in 6 below zero weather, but I couldn't tell the difference in my warm electrical suit, only my face and nose got very chilly.... I guess I was coming down at the rate of about a mile and a half a minute. It felt like the first time you take a ride on an elevator and you get the creeps when it is descending, but I know my air, having made about 700 jumps from Cloudland, and I wasn't a bit disturbed. I was bumping the air so hard that it knocked my goggles off and twisted my suit a bit. Although I had my ear-drums packed with cotton, I thought they would burst from the terrific air pressure against them. I put my eyes right to the crowd and when it appeared to be getting plainer and I was about 2,400 feet from the earth, I pulled my ripcord and the umbrella opened. It gave me a terrible jerk that stunned me for awhile, but I happen to know 'my onions' in such situations, and knew when it straightened out. I was sailing to sweet Mother Earth whole and hearty.
>
> I am quite sure I set a world's record. However, I won't know definitely until my government instruments have been tested by the Department of Commerce. We, as a race, can do anything anybody else does if we have nerve enough to try.

The record was later ruled unofficial because Jones's instruments were not properly sealed.

Jones's second attempt at the world delayed parachute jump record took place on November 16, 1938. He bailed out of a plane at an estimated altitude between 29,000 and 30,000 feet, in a temperature of 25 degrees F. below zero. He opened his chute at 2,500 feet, but he landed unconscious in an empty lot at 167th and Wood Streets in Chicago. Rushed to a hospital, he was found to be suffering from exposure to cold temperatures.

On March 2, 1939, at the Municipal Airport in Chicago, Jones achieved an official air-leap record, jumping 24,468 feet as measured by an official barograph provided by the National Aeronautical Association and sealed under the direction of NAA officials.

Profiting from previous experience, Jones wore a face mask to overcome air pressure problems and taped his body to withstand abdominal expansion. For this flight, the plane was equipped with adequate oxygen and three heaters in its closed cabin; both pilot and jumper wore fur-lined suits and boots.

The *Chicago Defender* reported as follows:

> After soaring for three hours and ten minutes and gaining an altitude where the mercury registered a temperature of 45 degrees below zero, "Suicide" Jones was let out of the ship above the Dixie Airport near Harvey. He whirled through space 4 and one-half miles before opening the parachute. At 800 feet above the ground his trusted shute [sic] ballooned out and settled slowly to earth. He had the world's record.
>
> The U.S. Bureau of Standards report of the calibration of the barograph showed a maximum ceiling of 24,468 feet, thus establishing the first official American record—and also a world's mark—for an altitude delayed parachute leap.

Five months later, in August 1939, Jones was again in the news, planning to break Howard Hughes's long-distance record with a flight from New York to Seattle and back. He also was married, on the 25th of August, to Ruthygale Griffin, in Omaha, Nebraska.

His most "suicidal" jump came in 1939 or 1940, at an Arkansas air show. Ten years later *Ebony* recounted, "Jones had jumped with a single chute when the shroud line on his pack caught in a hook on his leather boots. He was sent hurtling down headfirst for more than a half mile to within 150 feet of the ground before his chute opened. 'I was really shaken up quite a bit and newspapers the next day headline a story which stated I was killed. Three days later I got scared,' recall[ed] Jones."

Then World War II intervened. A 1950 *Ebony* article referred to Jones as an "ex-merchant seaman," and it is likely that he took on that job during this period.

In May 1947, Jones announced his intention to fly around the world, relying on "God and tail winds" for assistance in beating a record set the previous month by Milton Reynolds's *Bombshell*. The newspaper account noted that Jones's Lockheed Lodestar twin-engine plane was more than 100 miles per hour slower than the *Bombshell*. "This will be the first time a Negro ever attempted to make such a flight around the world," Jones was reported to have said. (In fact, others—including both Thomas Cox Allen and Hubert Fauntleroy Julian—had announced global flights.)

Jones's featured participation in "Chicago's first major air show since long before the war" was announced in September 1948. At that show, held at the Chicagoland Airport, north of Wheeling, Illinois, September 10–12, Jones "whose fame as a daredevil pilot and parachutist is world-wide" was to attempt "to regain his crown" for the long-distance delayed parachute leap.

In 1950, an *Ebony* article would call him "ageless. . . . He admits to 37 but his old-time partner in air shows, Major Speed Chandler, swears that [Jones] was that age five years ago." By this time Jones's stunts included acts such as "turning upside down and putting his feet through the shroud lines while on his way down." He would tell a reporter that stunting was safer than it had been years before, when stuntmen did not carry an additional, safety chute. He added that he was "not nervous at the jump or in the fall before opening my chute . . . [But] my plague is nightmares which come to me as long as a year after I've had a narrow escape." To combat this he kept a full schedule, augmenting his air stunt activities with a job in a Chicago poultry house.

On July 22, 1980, Jones attended the ceremonies and luncheon in Chicago on Cornelius R. Coffey Day; a contemporary photograph shows Jones with pioneer aviator Coffey at that event.

## Sources

Harper, L.C. "Willie 'Suicide' Jones: The Man Who Likes Fresh Air and Goes for It in a Big Way." *Chicago Defender* (September 16, 1939): 13.

"Jones Leaps 29,400 Feet: New Record." *Chicago Defender* (September 3, 1939): 1–2.

"Leaping to Fame (exclusive interview): Willie 'Suicide' Jones Tells *Defender* Reporter How It Feels Dashing to Earth from 29,400 Feet in Cloudland." *Chicago Defender* (September 3, 1939): 1.

" 'Suicide' Jones: Veteran Stunt Man Has Made 375 Chute Leaps." *Ebony* (February 1950): 35–36.

" 'Suicide' Jones Out to Beat 'Bombshell.' " (May 16, 1947). No periodical title or page.

" 'Suicide' Jones Plans Record Hop." *Chicago Defender* (August 26, 1939): 1.

"Willie 'Suicide' Jones Sets U.S. Air Leap Record." *Chicago Defender* (May 13, 1939): 1.

# Hubert F. Julian

**Full Name at Birth:** Hubert Fauntleroy Julian

**Born:** September 20, 1897, Port of Spain, Trinidad

**Died:** February 19, 1983, Bronx, New York

**Education:** Educated in Trinidad, Britain, and Canada. First learned to fly in Canada, earning his pilot's license at the age of 19.

Hubert F. Julian. Courtesy of Betty Gubert Collection.

Received U.S. private pilot's license no. 21,512 on July 30, 1931.

**Positions Held:** Pilot, 1917–1940s; inventor of the *parachuttagravepreresistra*, an airplane safety device, 1920–1921; parachutist and barnstormer, 1922–early 1930s; member of Marcus Garvey's Universal Negro Improvement Association, 1923–1930(?); Colonel and Air Marshal, Ethiopian Imperial Air Force, 1930 and 1935; personal pilot and flight instructor to followers of religious leader Father Divine, 1932; foreign correspondent, *New York Amsterdam News*, 1939; motion picture producer, 1940; Captain, Finnish Aviation Regiment 2, 1940; U.S. Army, 1942–1943; administrator, Willow Run plant, Ford Motor Company, mid to late 1940s; president, Black Eagle Airlines, late 1940s; president, Black Eagle Enterprises, a registered munitions dealer, late 1940s to early 1970s?; chairman, Black Eagle Corporation, a sugar broker, mid-1970s.

**Awards, Honors:** Received Canadian and United States patents for an "airplane-safety appliance," 1921; Order of Menelik, Ethiopia's highest award for gallantry, 1930.

**Summary:** Called the "Black Eagle of Harlem," Hubert Fauntleroy Julian was criticized by some contemporaries for flamboyant self-promotion and sometimes quixotic ventures. His endeavors as an inventor, parachutist, and pilot contributed to the publicity of black aviation in the 1920s and 1930s. Julian maintained throughout his career that his enterprises were intended to advance the position of blacks in the world.

## Early Years

Born in 1897 in Port of Spain on the West Indian island of Trinidad, Hubert Fauntleroy Julian was the only child of Henry and Silvina (Lily) Hilaire Julian. When he was not yet a teenager, young Julian first saw an airplane and its pilot, whose dress and bearing impressed him as much as the plane itself. His subsequent sight of the pilot's fatal crash in 1911 did not alter his determination to become an aviator himself.

Educated at the Eastern Boys' School, the best private school on Trinidad, Julian excelled at sports. His tall figure and confident air attracted attention wherever he went. Julian's parents wanted him to be a doctor and, since his father managed a cocoa plantation, had the funds to send Julian to Britian for schooling when he was 14. However, when World War I broke out in 1914, Julian was sent to Canada and continued his studies at a Jesuit-run high school in Montreal, Quebec. There he spent much of his free time at St. Hubert, the Montreal airfield that was a major training base for the Royal Canadian Flying Corps. Canadian flying ace William A. "Billy" Bishop, returned from the European war front and an instructor at the field, began to teach him to fly. Julian obtained his Canadian pilot's license when he was 19.

## Career Highlights

Julian arrived in New York in the spring of 1921, to apply for a patent for an airplane safety invention he called a *parachuttagravepreresistra*. The device, already patented in Canada, was to be activated by the pilot if a plane developed trouble: At the flip of a switch, a horizontal blade much like a helicopter's would blow open a huge ribbed umbrella, capable of slowing a plane's emergency descent to 20 feet per second. In May 1921, the U.S. Patent Office issued Julian patent no. 1,379,264, for an "airplane-safety appliance." Julian sold the invention to a Canadian aircraft corporation. Later, he would assert that his invention provided inspiration for both the helicopter and the parachute device used to return space capsules to Earth.

After a brief return to Canada, Julian formally emigrated to the United States in July 1921, arriving with a chauffeured automobile, a snappy wardrobe, and a suitcase full of cash. He settled in jazz-age Harlem and began to cultivate an image as a playboy and "gentleman flyer." Julian broke onto the American air show scene as a parachutist, making his first jump at the Long Island Air Show in 1922. He went on to apprentice with noted barnstormer Clarence Chamberlin, who operated an air field in northeastern New Jersey and would cross the Atlantic with a passenger just two weeks after Charles Lindbergh's historic solo flight in 1927. On Julian's third jump with Chamberlin, he never let go of the wing strut and it tore away from the plane. With difficulty, Chamberlin landed the plane, one wing flapping. Julian still held the strut when he parachuted to the ground.

At that time, if a parachutist made a few jumps and survived, he was considered a vet-

eran. Julian announced his intention to parachute over Manhattan and targeted a vacant lot between 139th and 140th Streets and Seventh and Eighth Avenues. On April 23, 1923, he jumped from 3,500 feet, landing not in the vacant lot but on a post office roof nearby. The waiting crowds swarmed and Julian received a summons for inciting a riot. In court, Julian argued that he had "proved the worth of parachute troopers" and that he had applied for a permit before making the jump. The city confirmed that Julian had indeed applied for permission—but there was no ordinance addressing parachute jumping. The judge dismissed the case, ordering Julian not to jump over Manhattan for six months.

Julian hit the lecture circuit, telling crowds from Atlantic City to Detroit, "I want to prove that science and good will can go hand in hand and make the world a more fundamental place in which to live." He referred to himself as "Lieutenant Hubert Fauntleroy Julian, M.D." The initials stood for "Mechanical Designer."

Julian came to the attention of Marcus Garvey, a promoter of pan-Africanism who headed the Universal Negro Improvement Association. Julian became an officer in the UNIA's paramilitary African Legion and, under Garvey's influence, became interested in the ancient African empire of Ethiopia.

In late October 1923, six months and one day after his previous Manhattan jump, Julian parachuted into Harlem once again. Blown off course by a strong wind, Julian missed his target by six blocks and landed on the roof of the 123rd Street police precinct. "Negro in Parachute Hits Police Station," reported the *New York Times*. The *New York Telegram* bestowed on Julian the sobriquet that would remain with him for life: "The Black Eagle."

On January 10, 1924, Julian announced a new project: He would become the first man to make a solo flight to Africa. At that time, only six men had flown across the Atlantic, flying in pairs and making intermediate island stops. No one had crossed alone, and no one had attempted the longer, more dangerous route to a continent still unfamiliar to many in the Western world.

Julian planned a route south from New York to Florida and on to South America, crossing the Atlantic from Brazil to Liberia with a mid-ocean refueling on tiny St. Paul's Rock. In Africa, he intended to continue east to Ethiopia. His plane would be named the *Ethiopia I.*

The flight was much discussed, but skepticism ran high and donations comprised only a trickle of dollar bills and small change. Julian applied to the NAACP for support but was rejected: the organization was only incorporated to provide assistance to African Americans in court. The disappointed aviator launched a public subscription campaign, asking every black American to contribute one dollar for a "scientific undertaking."

Complaints outnumbered donations. The U.S. Post Office sent an African American agent to warn Julian that it was imperative that he make the flight; otherwise he faced penalties for collecting funds by mail with intent to defraud.

On July 4, 1924, still short of his fund-raising goal, Julian took off from the Harlem River, flying an overhauled World War I–era hydroplane. Less than five minutes later, at an altitude of 2,000 feet, the *Ethiopia I*'s right pontoon snapped off. Julian crashed into Flushing Bay. The U.S. Post Office, satisfied with Julian's intentions, concluded its fraud investigation.

Over the next few years, Julian continued to crisscross the country as a barnstormer and parachutist. In the spring of 1927, he married Essie Marie Gittens, whom he had known since their childhood in Port of Spain. He enlisted in an African American National Guard unit, the 369th Colored Infantry.

In his cross-country travels, he made contact with William J. Powell and the fledgling group of African American aviators based in Chicago. In 1928, he established the Julian Aeroplane Fund and announced another attempted Atlantic crossing for that summer.

He "appointed" Powell as "co-pilot and chief mechanic" for the flight; Powell declined the offer. However, since Julian had first announced his plans, four other aviators, including Amelia Earhart, had crossed the Atlantic. Julian's fund-raising efforts flagged once more and the flight was canceled.

In April 1930, when 10 percent of Americans were unemployed, Julian was approached by a representative of the prince regent of Ethiopia, Ras Tafari Makonnen. He was offered a chance to train recruits for the nascent Ethiopian Air Force to perform in November at the prince regent's coronation as Emperor Haile Selassie I. Julian sailed from New York six days later. Essie Julian stayed behind.

After a six-week, 7,000 mile journey, Julian arrived in Addis Ababa, Ethiopia's ancient capital. He found that the Imperial Air Force consisted of three planes: two German-made monoplanes and one British-made Gypsy Moth, a recent gift to the prince regent. The air force was run by two French pilots, paid by the French government, who viewed Julian's arrival with hostility. Soon after his arrival, Julian performed flying stunts for a huge crowd; then, with one of the French pilots at the controls, he parachuted from 5,000 feet to land 50 feet from the prince regent's viewing tent. He was awarded Ethiopia's highest award for gallantry, Ethiopian citizenship, and a commission as colonel in the air force.

Julian returned to New York that summer on an abortive mission intended to recruit African American technological skill to assist in the development of Ethiopia. Back in Addis Ababa as marshal of the Imperial Air Force, he busied himself training the Ethiopian flying cadets for the coronation. In late October, at an air show rehearsal shortly before the coronation, Julian took the prized, untried *Gypsy Moth* aloft in defiance of orders. The plane's engine died during a stunt and Julian crashed. The Imperial Air Force was reduced by one-third, and Julian was ordered out of the country.

Returning to North America, Julian briefly flew bootleg whiskey down from Canada. On July 30, 1931, he passed the Department of Commerce test and was awarded private license no. 21,512. On December 6, 1931, he performed in an all-black air show in Los Angeles, coordinated by William Powell, that showcased "the Black Eagle and the Five Blackbirds." It was the first time so many African American pilots had been in the air together.

Julian proposed several long-distance flights, which came to nothing. He worked for a time as Father Divine's personal pilot, when that religious leader made a barnstorming tour of America, and was also instructor to those of Father Divine's "angels" who wished to learn to fly.

Hearing rumors of a coming Italo-Ethiopian war, Julian returned to Ethiopia in 1935 to volunteer his services. He rejoined the imperial army and, in July, was once again granted Ethiopian citizenship. In August, it was reported that he again commanded the air corps. Soon, however, he was engaged in a public fight with Chicago aviator John C. Robinson. The government removed Julian from his command and transferred him to an administrative post at Ambo, about three days' journey from Addis Ababa. Robinson replaced Julian as commander of the air force.

By November, Julian had resigned his commission and left Ethiopia, voicing criticism of the country's vestiges of feudalism. In the United States, however, African Americans still supported the cause of Ethiopian independence. Sources with knowledge of Ethiopia's circumstances criticized Julian in turn, claiming that he misrepresented the situation there.

Finding himself discredited in the United States, Julian sailed for France in early 1936, having stated his intention either to resume his British citizenship or to apply for American citizenship. But once the Italians had captured Addis Ababa in June, Julian declared himself an Italian citizen "by conquest" and defected to Rome. There he adopted the name "Huberto Fauntleroyana Juliano." Later he would assert that his intention had been to assassinate Benito Mussolini to save Ethiopia, but that the plot had been foiled.

In the summer of 1939 Julian became an accredited foreign correspondent for the *New York Amsterdam News*, a leading African American newspaper. He sent dispatches from France until early September; once France declared war on Germany, the U.S. Embassy advised Americans to return home immediately. Julian, traveling on a League of Nations passport, returned to New York. Early in 1940 he announced, "I have accomplished what I set out to do in aviation," which was to "show the world that Negroes are capable flyers." Now he proposed to do the same for the motion picture industry. His debut effort was as "associate producer" of *The Notorious Elinor Lee*, produced and directed by Oscar Micheaux, which premiered on January 15, 1940.

Meanwhile the European war escalated on the Russo-Finnish front and Julian volunteered his services to the Finns; he served briefly as a captain in Finnish Aviation Regiment 2. Back in New York, he publicly challenged Nazi air marshal Hermann Goering to an aerial duel over the English Channel to avenge Hitler's insults to the black race in his manifesto *Mein Kampf*. Although the German embassy in Washington denied any acceptance of the challenge, Julian had galvanized patriotic support in the American press. "I am a man without a country," Julian proclaimed. "I fight and die for my race. . . ." But the British government would not allow the duel, despite Julian's laudable intentions, since the English Channel airspace was already crowded with the aerial war between the RAF and the Luftwaffe. Julian then volunteered for the Royal Canadian Air Force, determined to join the war. He passed the medical tests but not the flying exam. Realizing he was nearly too old for any military service, Julian turned to the U.S. Army, enlisting as an alien infantryman at Fort Jay, New Jersey, in July 1942. He at last became an American citizen on September 28, 1942, and the following May was honorably discharged at the age of 45. He served out the war as an administrator at Ford Motor's Willow Run aircraft plant, not far from Detroit.

After the war, Julian put his international contacts to work. He founded Black Eagle Airlines, Ltd., which chartered international freight flights and owned aircraft plants in several European countries. In 1949, Black Eagle Enterprises, Ltd. registered with the State Department as a munitions dealer and began to supply arms and materiel to client-nations—sometimes on both sides of a single dispute—around the globe. With minor interruptions for diplomatic reasons, such as a temporary revocation of his U.S. passport in 1954 over a Guatemalan incident, and a four-month imprisonment in 1964 during a rebellion in the Congo, Julian continued this occupation for many years.

By the early 1970s, Julian was operating a sugar brokerage from New York City, and in 1974, when the Ethiopian government imprisoned Haile Selassie I, Julian offered them $1.45 million for his release, saying, "I owe my prominence and stature to the benevolence of His Imperial Majesty."

Hubert and Essie Julian bought a duplex not far from Yankee Stadium in the early 1950s, and the Bronx remained their home until their deaths. Married to the Black Eagle for nearly 48 years, Essie Julian died on January 4, 1975. A daughter, Olga Vera Edmonds, was among her survivors. Julian later married Doreen Thompson, and they had a son, Mark Anthony Bernard. Julian himself died on February 19, 1983, at the Veterans' Hospital in the Bronx. He is buried in Calverton National Cemetery on Long Island.

## Sources

Gubert, Betty Kaplan. "Julian, Hubert Fauntleroy." *Encyclopedia of African American Culture and History*. New York: Macmillan, 1996. Vol. 3: 1514–1515.

Hart, Philip S. *Flying Free: America's First Black Aviators*. Minneapolis, MN: Lerner Publications, 1992; 40–45.

Julian, Hubert, as told to John Bulloch. *Black Eagle*. London: Jarrolds, 1964.

Lamparski, Richard. "Hubert F. Julian: The Black Eagle." *Whatever Became Of . . . ?* New York: Crown, 1967; 94–95.

Lewis, David Levering. *When Harlem Was in Vogue*. New York: Alfred A. Knopf, 1981; 111–112.

Nugent, John Peer. *The Black Eagle*. New York: Stein and Day, 1971.

Powell, William J. *Black Aviator: The Story of William J. Powell*. Washington: Smithsonian Institution Press, 1994; 22–28, 98–104. A new edition of Powell's *Black Wings*, first published in 1934.

Scott, William R. *The Sons of Sheba's Race: African Americans and the Italo-Ethiopian War, 1935–1941*. Bloomington: Indiana University Press, 1993; 81–95.

# K

## James B. Knighten

**Full Name at Birth:** James Bernard Knighten

**Born:** 1918, Tulsa, Oklahoma

**Died:** November 10, 2000, Las Vegas, Nevada

**Education:** Charles Sumner High School, St. Louis, Missouri; B.S. in social science, Dillard University, New Orleans, Louisiana [1940]; attended New York University Law School, 1946–(?).

**Positions Held:** Pilot, 99th Pursuit Squadron, 1941–1946; magazine publisher and editor, 1946–1947; pilot, U.S. Air Force, 1950–1968; operations inspector, Federal Aviation Administration (FAA), 1968–1988; stand-up comedian, Las Vegas, Nevada, 1989–2000.

**Awards, Honors:** Air Medal with two oak leaf clusters; European-Africa-Middle East Service Medal; service ribbons for North Africa, Sicily, and Italy; Nevada chapter of the Tuskegee Airmen Inc. was renamed the James B. Knighten Chapter, November 11, 1999.

**Summary:** James Bernard Knighten was one of the earliest graduates of the air school at the Tuskegee Institute in Alabama. He received his wings on May 20, 1942. A member of the 99th Pursuit Squadron, Knighten flew 81 missions in World War II. He later held positions as a magazine publisher, an air traffic controller, and an inspector for the Federal Aviation Administration. Retired from the Air Force as a lieutenant colonel in 1968, and from the FAA in 1988, Knighten, as Jay Bernard, chose the career of stand-up comedian in Las Vegas.

### Early Years

Born in Tulsa, in 1918, James Bernard Knighten moved to St. Louis with his family when he was 14 years old. His father was a bricklayer. Two of his classmates at Charles Sumner High School, Wendell O. Pruitt and Jim McCullin, also became Tuskegee Airmen. Knighten was close to Pruitt and dated one of his sisters. Pruitt, credited with the sinking of a German destroyer from the air, as well as with other "kills," crashed and died on a routine flight on April 15, 1945, near Tuskegee. McCullin became one of the 99th's first fatalities in combat, on July 2, 1943.

## Higher Education

Knighten graduated from Dillard University in New Orleans with a degree in social science, "and in football," according to Knighten. In the economically depressed, strictly segregated society of the late 1930s, Knighten could find work only as a waiter on the Santa Fe Railroad. His route was the Los Angeles-Chicago run. Sitting in a bar in Chicago, he heard over the radio that Negroes were going to be accepted into a new program for pilot cadets. The new opportunity, Civilian Pilot Training Program (CPTP), was established in 1939, and after much lobbying by civil rights groups and the black newspapers, Negroes were included. "I had never been in an airplane. I had never touched one and had no real desire to fly," Knighten said, but he applied anyway. At the same time, he applied to Howard University's Law School and to a theological seminary in Chicago. Knighten was accepted by both professional schools and by the CPTP. He chose to become a pilot, passed the physical test, and was sent to Tuskegee Army Air Field in Alabama. He earned his pilot's wings on May 20, 1942. His class of four graduates was the smallest class ever.

## Career Highlights

The 99th Pursuit Squadron was sent to North Africa in April 1943. Knighten flew missions there as well as over Sicily and Italy, totaling 81 missions by the time he was sent back to the United States in 1944. At about this time, he and Luana Robinson were married. Knighten's fellow pilots remembered him as: "a funny fellow, happy-go-lucky," (C.C. Robinson); "a brainy guy with good flying skills," (Clarence Jamison); and "Knighten was one of the hottest pilots we had. Everyone acknowledged that," (Charles Dryden). Knighten described one of his close calls. He started to follow Dryden toward home base after the two pilots had successfully eluded the Germans' machine gun fire, "but then I realized those German were coming back out of the sun, and I was their target! So I was sitting there with four German fighters shooting at me. All I could do was go into a right turn, count the Germans as they dove past me, and then turn back toward Africa and safety. But the Germans had other ideas. They climbed back up into the sun, and moments later they were coming down again, machine guns blazing, cannons flashing. How they missed me, I'll never know. So for me it was another tight, tight turn, tracer bullets streaking past me, and counting those swastikas on their planes as they went under my wing and back up into the sun. At this point they must have been out of bullets or low on gas, because they leveled off and headed north . . . Charlie [Dryden] was already safely home when I landed. Our months of fighter tactics training had paid off, with Lady Luck riding in both cockpits."

*The Eel* was the name of Knighten's plane and the nickname by which he was known. It referred to his slipperiness as a poker player—when down to his last dollar, he always found a way to bounce back.

After the war was over in 1945, Knighten realized he would not be able to fly for commercial airlines, as he had only 300 hours of flying time in twin-engine bombers. "There were thousands of white pilots with thousands of hours in the same type of airplanes the airlines were using. Why would they hire me and train me?" He went back to the railroads as a waiter until the fall of 1946, when he used the G.I. Bill to enter New York University Law School. To make ends meet, he waited tables at night in a Brooklyn restaurant. Knighten was also the editor and publisher of *Essence: The Magazine for Women*, and his wife was listed on the masthead as staff photographer. Only three issues were published, 1946 to 1947. There were articles on beauty, fashion, books, people of achievement, and fiction. Knighten contributed a story, "The Bridge of Decision," about a white major and a Negro lieutenant who had become good friends during the war overseas, but who could not remain so once they returned home.

Knighten returned to the U.S. Air Force around 1950, and retired in 1968 with the rank of lieutenant colonel. He spent his last eight years in the Military Air Transport Service flying passengers and cargo to and from the Far East. On September 23, 1956, Luana Knighten died suddenly of a heart attack, two days before she was to play Violet in the revival of *Take a Giant Step*, a 1953 Broadway production. They were the parents of two daughters, as was Barbara, the woman he later married.

At his retirement, Knighten went to work for the Federal Aviation Administration (FAA), as an operations inspector. For most of his 20-year career with FAA, he was stationed in New York. He was transferred to Los Angeles toward the end of that time, and in 1989, the Knightens moved to Las Vegas, where his third career, stand-up comic, began to take shape. He frequently appeared at the Debbie Reynolds Hotel and Casino, which closed in 1998.

Knighten always had in the back of his mind the idea of being a comedian. While at McGuire AFB, in New Jersey, Knighten played in clubs in New York City, and at resorts in the Catskill Mountains of New York and the Poconos Mountains of Pennsylvania. His first public performance was in a cabaret in New York in 1955. In the 1990s, Knighten, whose stage name was Jay Bernard, performed in nightclubs, in hotels, and at benefits, and he has acted in films as an extra. Knighten was not the only performer in the family. His daughter Kim Russell has written *Tuskegee Love Letters*, which is a one-act play based on the actual letters sent by her mother and father to his mother, her grandmother. She has also written, and performs in, the one-woman play, *Sojourner Truth: I Sell the Shadow*, a biographical study of the abolitionist.

Knighten was a founding member and past president of the Nevada chapter of the Tuskegee Airmen Inc., which was chartered on September 20, 1996. The chapter was renamed in his honor on November 11, 1999.

James B. Knighten died on November 10, 2000, and was buried on November 17 at the Southern Nevada Veterans Memorial Cemetery.

## Sources

"Comic Fixture at 'Jazz and Jokes' Knighten Dies at 80." *Las Vegas Review-Journal* (November 16, 2000). Online, http://www.vrj.com.

*Essence: The Magazine for Women* 1, 2 (Spring 1947). Issue at the Schomburg Center for Research in Black Culture, New York Public Library, in *Black and Third World Periodicals, Sample Issues, 1845–1963*. Microfilm RS 723, reel 2.

Holway, John B. *Red Tails Black Wings: The Men of America's Black Air Force*. Las Cruces, NM: Yucca Tree Press, 1997.

"James B. Knighten Chapter." May 22, 2000. Http://members.aol.com/vega104/index.htm.

Renzi, David. "Air Schtick." *Las Vegas Sun* (December 17, 1996): 1C, 4C.

Watson, George, New Jersey, to Betty Gubert, New York, telephone, May 4, 2001.

Zvosec, Carla J. "Celebrating Black History Month in Vegas." May 22, 2000. Http://lasvegas weekly.com/departments/02_10_99/lifestyle_history.html.

# L

## Roy E. LaGrone

**Full Name at Birth:** Roy Elmer LaGrone

**Born:** February 1, 1921, Pine Bluff, Arkansas

**Died:** December 8, 1993, Somerset, New Jersey

**Education:** Tuskegee Institute, Alabama [1942]; University of Florence, Italy, 1945–1946; Pratt Institute, Brooklyn, New York, 1949.

**Positions Held:** Flight Officer, 332nd Fighter Group, World War II; book jacket designer; art director for magazines and publishers; art director and graphics coordinator for the Robert Wood Johnson Medical School of Rutgers University, New Jersey, 1981–1991.

**Awards, Honors:** Artist-member, New York Society of Illustrators, 1961–1993. Paintings are held by numerous public buildings and museums.

**Summary:** Roy LaGrone, himself a Tuskegee Airman, has created a unique record of the men of America's black air force and their achievements. His medium has been paint on wood in hundreds of portraits of Tuskegee Airmen, as well as of African American pilots and astronauts who continued their legacy.

### Early Years

Roy Elmer LaGrone was born to Edward and Gussie LaGrone on February 1, 1921, in Pine Bluff, Arkansas. At his death, a brother, Edward Henry, of the same city, survived him. As a youngster, LaGrone read aviation magazines and drew pictures of pilots and planes. When a visiting barnstormer and stunt pilot came to Pine Bluff, offering plane rides, the teen-aged LaGrone paid his 50 cents, money he had earned by painting signs, drawing pictures for his teachers, and working in his father's grocery store. His first ride in the airplane, a Ford Trimotor, a plane that could carry 15 passengers, hooked him for life. "As soon as I got up there, I knew absolutely that this was what I wanted to do," LaGrone recalled years later.

### Higher Education

Although enrolled at Tuskegee Institute's art program, LaGrone was really intent on learning to fly. He served in the ROTC (Reserve Officers Training Corps) as a first sergeant. He learned to fly through Tuskegee's CPTP (Civilian Pilot Training Program) in 1942, and then he entered the military. When he was stationed in Italy in 1945, and the war ended, LaGrone was able to study art at the University of Florence. LaGrone continued to develop his skills in illustration at the Pratt Institute in Brooklyn, graduating in 1949.

## Career Highlights

After completing the CPTP, LaGrone was drafted into the U.S. Army Air Corps as a sergeant. The U.S. Air Force was then part of the army. LaGrone was stationed at Camp Robinson, Little Rock, Arkansas, before being assigned to the Chico Army Air Corps Flying School in California. When his training was successfully completed, LaGrone was transferred to Army Air Corps Administration School at Fort Logan, Colorado.

After his graduation in March 1943, he served with Special Services, 318th Air Base Squadron, at Tuskegee Army Air Field. Commissioned a Flight Officer, La Grone's next assignment took him to Caserta, Italy, with Allied Military Headquarters. In January 1946, LaGrone ended his stint in the military, and he started to pursue a career as an artist.

LaGrone began in 1949 as a designer and illustrator of book jackets for such New York publishers as Harper and Row, Scribner, Random House, and Macmillan. He planned layouts and mechanicals for magazines, *Family Circle* and *America*, among them. As an art director, he worked for both print and visual media: Avon Books, *Pageant* magazine, and CBS television.

In 1961, LaGrone was accepted for membership in the New York Society of Illustrators as a member artist. The society administers the Air Force's art program in the eastern United States. Artists are assigned to travel with air force units to document their missions. For 30 years, LaGrone traveled all over the world, covering such activities as the 1986 war games in Korea. One of LaGrone's last works, "Operation Provide Hope," depicts the 1992 food drop in Russia, and captures the moody light of a Siberian landscape. LaGrone created many paintings that are displayed at the Pentagon, Cape Kennedy, Wright-Patterson Air Force Museum in Ohio, and in other military buildings. With this program, LaGrone found the way to join his two passions: painting and the Tuskegee Airmen.

LaGrone first photographed his subjects. When he painted, he placed them in the foreground, and the planes they flew in the background. "I want the world to know that these were black men who flew these machines." LaGrone preferred to paint on wood for its solidity. "Canvas bothers me," he said. His favorite wood is called "doorskin," a type of Philippine mahogany.

He painted portraits of the pilots he had known, as well as of others, along with the planes they flew and with the insignia of their units merged into the total design of the painting. Many of the paintings employ multiple images and text, such as the portraits of the first class of five graduates. This painting also includes Noel Parrish, their white commanding officer, and the headquarters building at Tuskegee. At the bottom are the signatures of many Tuskegee Airmen with their graduation dates. (The signatures were obtained at an annual convention.) An individual portrait of Benjamin O. Davis also provides more than one image: Davis, as a young man in flight suit, as a bemedaled general, and with his men, is a sketch-like representation, while the others are in full color. LaGrone's portrayals have great storytelling aspects and are full of information, pictorial and textual. He has also depicted African American military pilots of the post-Tuskegee era, such as Lloyd "Fig" Newton, and some of the black astronauts.

In 1981, LaGrone became the art director and graphics coordinator for the Robert Wood Johnson Medical School of Rutgers University in New Jersey. He retired from that position in 1991. From his first marriage to Lynzine Haraway-LaGrone, LaGrone was the father of two daughters, Marilyn LaGrone-Amaral (or, Amaral-LaGrone) and Tania LaGrone. His second marriage, in 1979, was to a Finnish woman named Ester, whom he had met in 1975 in New York.

## Sources

Cooper, Charlie and Ann Cooper. *Tuskegee's Heroes: Featuring the Aviation Art of Roy LaGrone.* Osceola, WI: Motorbooks International, 1996.

Di Ionno, Mark. "An Airman's Legacy: Somerset Artist Leaves Painted Record of Tuskegee Unit." *Star-Ledger* (New Jersey) (December 12, 1993).

———. "Early Brush with Flying Launches an Aviation-Art Career of Renown." *Star-Ledger* (New Jersey) (December 17, 1992).

Elliott, Jack. "Artists at Front Put World War II in Perspective." *Star-Ledger* (New Jersey) (December 22, 1991).

Saxon, Wolfgang. "Roy E. LaGrone, 72, A Tuskegee Airman and Ex-Art Director." *New York Times* (December 14, 1993): B8.

# Robert H. Lawrence Jr.

Robert H. Lawrence Jr. Courtesy of NASA.

**Full Name at Birth:** Robert Henry Lawrence Jr.

**Born:** October 2, 1935, Chicago, Illinois

**Died:** December 8, 1967, Edwards Air Force Base, California

**Education:** Englewood High School, Chicago, 1952; B.S. in chemistry, Bradley University, Peoria, Illinois, 1956; Ph.D in chemistry, Ohio State University, 1965.

**Positions Held:** Major, U.S. Air Force; first African American astronaut, designated in 1967.

**Awards, Honors:** Air Force Commendation Medal; Air Force Outstanding Unit Award; a school in Chicago is named for him; Commemoration on The Space Mirror of the Astronauts Memorial Foundation, Florida, December 1997.

**Summary:** In June 1967, Major Lawrence became the first designated African American astronaut. He never traveled in space due to his untimely death in a training accident in December of the same year. There were no other African American astronauts until 1978 when Guion S. Bluford Jr., Frederick D. Gregory, and Ronald E. McNair were appointed.

## Early Years

Robert Henry Lawrence Jr. was one of two children born to Robert Henry and Gwendolyn Lawrence on October 2, 1935, in Chicago. Their parents were divorced when young Lawrence and his sister Barbara were preschoolers. Charles Duncan, their stepfather, was an underwriter for the Veterans Administration, and he later worked in the circulation departments of various magazines. Their mother worked for the civil service. Together, they provided the children a home rich in love and attention, if not in material things. Lawrence enjoyed swimming, baseball, football, and tennis. He loved track best of all, and he won city championships in both the mile and half-mile races. He learned to play chess from his stepfather, and both parents taught the children bridge and other games. Every Christmas brought him a new chemistry set, more advanced than last year's. The children spent summers with family friends in a country-like setting near St. Louis, Missouri, which was a treat for the city-bred children. Evening trips to see the airplanes at Lambert Field made these summers memorable as well. Back home, the family made weekend visits to the Adler Planetarium, the Art Institute, the Field Museum of Natural History, the Museum of Science and Industry, the Shedd Aquarium, or the Brookfield Zoo. Lawrence became proficient at playing the piano. He built model airplanes and gave his hamsters biblical names. While in high school, he received a scholarship to study painting at the School of the Art Institute. He was "scholarly and serious," recalled his father, a disabled veteran, "but I didn't consider him a precocious child." His teachers, however, found him exceptional and they encouraged him at every level of schooling.

## Higher Education

Lawrence earned a B.S. in chemistry in 1956 from Bradley University in Peoria, Illinois. While an undergraduate he enrolled in Air Force Reserve Officers Training Corps (ROTC). Upon graduation he entered the U.S. Air Force as a second lieutenant, and was assigned to flight training at Webb Air Force Base (AFB) in Big Spring, Texas, and later to flight instruction school at Craig AFB near Selma, Alabama. Lawrence was then sent to Fürstenfeldbruck AFB, near Munich, Germany, to train pilots in the German Air Force. After a fatal accident there, Lawrence recommended that the language of instruction be changed from English to German, which it was. Lawrence was fluent

in German, and the change earned him the esteem of both the students and the government.

While still abroad, Lawrence in 1958 married Barbara Cress, the daughter of a Chicago physician and high school teacher. Their son Tracey was born in 1960.

In 1961, Lawrence returned to the United States, where, through the Air Force Institute of Technology at Wright-Patterson AFB in Ohio, he enrolled at Ohio State University. His dissertation in nuclear chemistry, "The Mechanism of the Tritium Beta-Ray Induced Exchange Reactions of Deuterium with Methane and Ethane in the Gas Phase," earned Lawrence the Ph.D. in 1965.

## Career Highlights

Lawrence served as nuclear research officer at the Air Force Weapons Laboratory at Kirkland AFB in New Mexico. Lawrence had applied to NASA twice to join their astronaut program, but he had been turned down. In 1967, after logging more than 2,500 hours of jet flying time, Major Lawrence qualified for the Air Force's Manned Orbiting Laboratory (MOL) program at the Aerospace Research Pilot School at Edwards AFB in California. With this appointment, Lawrence became America's first African American astronaut designee and the only one with a Ph.D. at the time. The three other designees were Major Donald H. Peterson, Major James A. Abrahamson, and Lieutenant Colonel Robert T. Herres. The four of them, selected from a pool of 500 candidates, were to join 12 others. The Air Force's MOL program was independent of NASA, and it planned to orbit the earth for month-long periods with a two-man crew to conduct military surveillance.

At their press conference on June 30, 1967, a reporter asked Lawrence, "Do you yourself feel that this is a tremendous step forward in racial relations?" He replied, "No,

I don't think it is especially a tremendous step forward. I think it's just another one of the things that we look forward to in this country with respect to progress in civil rights. Nothing dramatic has happened. It's just a normal progression."

There had been an earlier African American astronaut candidate. Edward J. Dwight, an Air Force pilot, was selected as a candidate in 1962. He never was named an astronaut, and amid charges of racism, he resigned in 1966. After Lawrence's death in 1967, there were no other African American astronauts until 1978, when Guion S. Bluford Jr., Frederick D. Gregory, and Ronald E. McNair were appointed. In 1983, Bluford became the first African American to explore space.

Robert Lawrence's six-month career as an astronaut did not allow him to realize his dream of space flight. He was killed on December 8, 1967, in a simulated space ship landing at Edwards AFB. The F-104 Starfighter, a jet plane that can fly at twice the speed of sound, crashed during a training flight. His co-pilot survived. Lawrence's funeral was held at Chicago's First Unitarian Church, after which he was cremated. A scholarship in his memory was established at Bradley University for African American students of chemistry.

Because Lawrence never completed astronaut training and flew in space, his name was not etched into the black granite Space Mirror of the Astronauts Memorial Foundation at the Kennedy Space Center in Florida. Established in 1986 to honor all U.S. astronauts who lost their lives on missions or while training for missions, the foundation also maintains a Center for Space Education. After a six-year battle led by James Oberg, a space historian in Houston, Texas, and Lawrence's widow, Lawrence was officially declared an astronaut by the Air Force in January 1997. Induction ceremonies then took place in December 1997, the 30th anniversary of his death.

## Sources

Burns, Khephra, and William Miles. *Black Stars in Orbit*. New York: Harcourt Brace, 1995; 24–27.
*Florida Today Space Outline* "Lawrence Name Destined for Space Mirror, Finally." May 25, 1999. Http://www.flatoday.com/space/explore/stories/1997/012997d.htm.
Lawrence, Barbara. "A Tribute to Major Robert Lawrence, December 8, 1997." *The Syl Watkins Drum* (Orlando, Florida) (January 1998); 2–3; (February 1998): 1–3.
Llorens, David. "Farewell to an Astronaut." *Ebony* (February 1968): 90–92, 94.
"Our First Negro Astronaut." *Sepia* (September 1967): 76–79.

# Clarence D. Lester

**Full Name at Birth:** Clarence D. Lester

**Born:** February 8, 1923, Chicago, Illinois

**Died:** April, 1986, Richmond, Virginia

**Education:** Stanford University, Palo Alto California, B.A. in international relations.

**Awards, Honors:** Distinguished Flying Cross, Air Medal with 9 oak leaf clusters, 1944; Legion of Merit.

**Positions Held:** Tuskegee Airman, 1944, 1945; Air Force jet pilot, 1945–1969; associate director of social services, Montgomery County, Rockville, Maryland.

**Summary:** Clarence D. Lester was one of the Tuskegee Airmen, the first group of African American pilots ever to serve in the U.S. military. During World War II, Lester distinguished himself by shooting down three enemy planes on one mission. After the war, Lester remained in the military, retiring in 1969 as a colonel.

## Early Years

Clarence D. Lester Jr. was born in Chicago, Illinois and grew up on the South Side.

His father, Clarence D. Lester Sr., was a chef, and his mother, Lillian, was a nurse. One of his mother's close friends was Janet Harmon Waterford Bragg, also a nurse, and an early pioneer in Chicago's flourishing African American aviation scene.

## Higher Education

Lester attended West Virginia State College, a historically black college. He was good at sports in college: "I thought I was a hotshot football and basketball player in those days," said Lester in later life, in an interview which appeared in *Red Tails, Black Wings* by John B. Holway. After the Japanese bombed Pearl Harbor on December 7, 1941, the United States entered World War II, and Lester decided to apply for cadet training in the U.S. Army Air Corps, along with three other African Americans and 12 whites: "I was the only one fortunate enough to pass."

Having surmounted this hurdle, Lester was sent to the Tuskegee Army Air Field, where he successfully completed his flight training, receiving his wings on December 5, 1943.

## Career Highlights

In April 1944, Lester, having completed cadet training, was sent to Italy where he joined the 332nd Fighter Squadron. He soon earned the soubriquet of "Lucky." Lester explained the origin of the name: "One thing everybody asks me is, how did I get the name of Lucky? . . . I was 21 when I got overseas in April 1944. Most of the other fliers were three or four years older, and they all treated me like a kid. They called me Lucky because I was lucky at poker.

"The name carried over into flying. I flew a total of 90 to 95 missions, and I never got a bullet . . . and never had an accident. I did have a couple of close calls, however. I was just plain lucky."

He was assigned to pilot a P-47, a plane he was not familiar with. Instruction in flying new types of aircraft was rudimentary at best: "Those days weren't like it is today, where you . . . learn to fly [an unfamiliar aircraft] with the inspector in back with dual controls. . . . You memorized where all the instruments were, and the instructor gave you a written test. . . . Then they put you in a parachute and off you would go—it was sort of survival of the fittest. I'd never been in the P-47 before, had no idea what it was like, but away I went.

"I was doing pretty well until I tried to do 10 loops in a row. I executed about eight or nine loops, but when I tried to fly through the next one, I knew I wasn't going to make it. The airplane began to shudder going straight up and did a hammerhead stall . . . flipped over like a hammer striking a nail and started spinning upside down."

Standard operating procedure in a case like this was to bail out if the aircraft was below 5,000 feet and out of control. Lester attempted to follow the procedure, but could not get the canopy of the plane open. "I reached up to pull the T-handle, which was supposed to release the canopy . . . the T came off in my hand." Lester could not open the canopy wide enough to jump out of the airplane. "I was upside down, with everything spinning wildly, and I couldn't get the canopy open more than a couple of inches."

At that point, Lester realized that the plane was back under control: "I said to myself, 'Centrifugal force must be taking over.' The plane was in a tight spiral, but it was a controlled maneuver.

"I sat back down and started pulling the plane out of the spiral. I pulled out at about 500 feet off the ground . . . and came roaring across the runway at about 300 miles an hour. I pulled up, came around, and made a routine landing. . . . Later on I told my tentmate what had happened. He said, 'Boy, you're just as lucky as ever, aren't you?' "

On June 9, 1944, the 332nd flew its first top cover mission. The P-47s flew in very tight formation, in what was called a "four-finger pattern." The planes had no radar.

They had to maintain radio silence in order not to reveal their presence to the enemy. In bad weather, when visibility was poor, the group leader navigated for the group. The planes flew almost wingtip to wingtip. At times of no visibility, the group leader navigated by dead reckoning—using compass and speed readings to calculate direction.

In *Red Tails, Black Wings*, Lester discussed the problems they encountered: "Navigation was one of the big problems. I guess the biggest problems were, one, mechanical, two, weather, three, navigation, and four, the enemy. Only after you overcame the first three did you have to worry about the fourth.

"You started out on a correct heading as you entered the clouds, but if the wind was blowing, . . . you might be drifting. You might be flying a heading due north but actually going north-northwest. In the clouds you had no way to check visually . . . you had to fly formation, guiding on your leader only, wingtips almost touching. . . . It really took a strong heart to sit there."

Sometimes the planes would bounce around violently, and in the absence of any visual clues, the pilots did not know what was causing the turbulence. The temptation to panic was great: "[Y]ou began to wonder. What is it? Is it rough weather? Is the enemy shooting flak at me? Or is it the prop wash from another sixteen planes crossing through your flight? More than one time there were mid-air collisions. . . . That's where discipline was required. You just had to sit there and sweat it out. . . . It added years to your life. Those are the kinds of things you don't hear about in the movies."

Another factor that made their task more complicated was fuel consumption, which had to be closely calculated. The planes carried enough fuel to get them to their destination and back, with little to spare. On occasion, the fighters would accompany the bombers they were escorting beyond the point of no return, which caused them to run out of fuel on the way home. Their only option in that case was to bail out.

The pilots also suffered from the cold. The fighter pilots flew their planes at 25,000 feet or higher. At these altitudes, the temperature is extremely cold, no matter what the season. Various schemes were tried to combat the cold, such as fleece flying gear and electric suits. These were cumbersome in the cramped space of a fighter plane. The pilots coped by bundling themselves up. According to Woodrow W. Crockett, another member of the 332nd, "You wore thermals outside and dress uniform underneath. You had heavy gloves and fur-lined boots that you put your GI shoes in."

On July 19, 1944, Lester, flying the plane that he had christened *Miss Pelt*, managed to shoot down three German ME-109s on one mission, a record. He vividly recreated the scene: "It was a clear day in July 1944 when the P-51 Mustangs of the 332nd Fighter Group took off from our airfield at Ramitelli, Italy. Our mission was to rendezvous over Northern Italy's Po Valley at 25,000 feet with B-17 Flying Fortresses en route to bomb a German airfield in southern Germany. We had been given the task of escorting the bombers to the target and back.

"The rendezvous was made on time at 25,000 feet. . . . We were around 29,000 feet when bogeys [enemy aircraft] were spotted above us.

"We were flying a loose combat formation, 200 feet apart and zigzagging. . . . I saw a formation of Messerschmitt Bf 109s straight ahead but slightly lower: I dove in behind one plane as he flew level. He started maneuvering, . . . I started shooting, and the airplane started coming apart, . . . and he exploded. I was going so fast, I was sure I would hit some of the debris.

"As I dodged pieces of the aircraft, I saw this other plane all alone to my right. . . . I turned on my tail and came up behind him. . . . I closed to about two hundred feet and started over-running him and began firing. . . . His aircraft started to smoke and almost stopped. . . . I saw him climb out on the wing and bail out. I can still see him today with his blond hair, standing on the wing, just as plain as then. It was an amazing sight.

"Then I saw a third airplane down below me, and I took off after him. I picked him up pretty fast.... He started to dive.... When he got to about a thousand feet, he leveled ... and I was still peppering him. He was desperate by then, ... so he decided on a Split-S Maneuver.... it's a basic maneuver, but not at a thousand feet.... He never made it and went straight into the ground. ... Everything went just the same as in training except for the bullets—real bullets!

"All this took place in four or five minutes—six at the outside. On the return flight, it took a little while to realize what happened. Only then did the danger hit me."

For this heroism, Lester was awarded a Distinguished Flying Cross. During his time with the 332nd, Lester completed more than 90 missions and destroyed more aircraft on the ground.

Though their heroism was respected by white pilots, blacks and whites never socialized: "Like everything else then, it was separate but equal.... It wasn't always equal but it sure was separate.

"White pilots were replaced after 50 missions, but because we were segregated and didn't have other units to draw from, we had to fly 65 to 70 missions. That meant we got shot at 20 more times, which was sort of rough when you couldn't even go into the officers' club."

At the war's end Lester elected to stay in the Air Force. Posted to Germany, he was one of the first pilots to make the transition from propeller planes to jet planes. In 1951, flying in a ceremony over Paris, Lester's plane caught fire. "They have an ejection seat with a shell, which blows you out of the airplane. I was doing about 450 miles per hour at about 800 feet altitude. In those days the thought was that you should slow the airplane up before you ejected, but ... I didn't have time to slow it up. So I pushed the ejection button, and started looping through the air doing somersaults, still in my seat....

[T]he airplane turned straight down to the ground, and I saw it hit with a big explosion.

"After that the Air Force decided that maybe it wasn't a good idea to slow up before ejecting. Before this, they had encountered a lot of trouble with pilots hitting the airplane. Pilots had been decapitated, had their legs cut off.... But when nothing happened to me, they decided to try some tests. The results were, you were clear of the airplane a lot better the faster you go.... I like to believe my ejection started them thinking that faster is better." Freeing himself of the seat, Lester made a successful parachute landing, landing in a soft, newly plowed field: "All this sounds like it took a long time, but it was probably ... eight to ten seconds ... That was one of the luckiest things that happened to Lucky Lester."

After a variety of assignments, Lester's career culminated in an assignment to the Pentagon in the Office of the Secretary of Defense, Robert McNamara, working with the "Whiz Kids"—bright young associates with management training. "They were a bunch of bright kids, all right, just out of Harvard Business School. I was the 'Old Man.' I guess they needed a wiser, experienced head around to keep them on the right track."

In 1969, Lester retired as a full colonel. He was next appointed as associate director of social services, Montgomery County, Rockville, Maryland.

Despite the contribution the Tuskegee Airmen made to the war effort—they never lost a bomber—their exploits remained unknown and uncelebrated for many years. This point was driven home to Lester in 1975, when his daughter, Wanda, then a freshman at the University of Pennsylvania, was involved in an ugly incident. "It was a class in ethnics in work and she mentioned that I had been a pilot in the war. The teacher said, 'That can't be. There were no black pilots.' He practically called her a liar." Lester quickly dispatched newspaper clippings and photographs to his daughter:

"When she got them, she went to him and showed him all this stuff. You know, to this day, that man has never apologized to my daughter."

In April 1986, Lester succumbed to cancer. Surviving him were his wife, Maro Barnes Lester, his son, Clarence D. Lester III, his daughter, Wanda Felton, and his mother, Lillian T. Lester.

### Sources

Duggan, Dennis. "Spirits Soared Above Bias." *Newsday* (June 6, 1983).

Gleed, Edward C. "The Story of America's Black Air Force." *Tony Brown's Journal* (January–March 1983); 4–7.

Hochberg, Joshua E. "The Tuskegee Airmen: Courage on Two Fronts." *FAA Aviation News* (January–February 1993): 14–16.

Yancey, Matt. "Heroic Black Fliers Blazed Trail." *Atlanta Journal* (September 26, 1982).

# Neal V. Loving

Neal V. Loving. Courtesy of Clare T. Loving.

**Full Name at Birth:** Neal Vernon Loving

**Born:** February 4, 1916, Detroit, Michigan

**Died:** December 19, 1998, Springfield, Ohio

**Education:** Cass Technical High School, Detroit, 1934; engineering drafting course, Highland Park Junior College, Detroit, 1940; degree in aerospace engineering, Wayne State University, Detroit, 1961.

**Positions Held:** instructor, Detroit Department of Recreation, Works Progress Administration, 1936–1940; teacher, Aero Mechanics High School, Detroit, Michigan, 1941–1943; co-owner, Wayne Aircraft Company, 1941–1944; engine assembler, Ford Motor Company, 1943–1944; co-owner, Wayne School of Aeronautics, Detroit City Airport, 1946–1957; aerospace engineer, Wright-Patterson Air Force Base, Dayton, Ohio, 1961–1982.

**Awards, Honors:** More than 40 awards and honors, including Handicapped Federal Employee of the Year, United States Air Force, 1967; Meritorious Civilian Service Award, 1968; Distinguished Achievement Award, Organization of Black Airline Pilots, 1991; Major Achievement Award, Experimental Aircraft Association, 1995; honorary fellow, Society of Experimental Test Pilots, 1995; inductee, Michigan Aviation Hall of Fame, 1997.

**Summary:** Despite the loss of both legs in a glider crash in 1944, Neal Loving was a noted designer and builder of small powered aircraft and gliders, of which the most famous was a gull-winged midget racer known as *Loving's Love*, which he flew during the 1950s. He also founded the first African American aircraft factory, an all-black squadron of the Civil Air Patrol in Detroit during World War II, and a Detroit-based, integrated flight school. Loving went on to another career as a clear-air turbulence expert for the U.S. Air Force.

### Early Years

When Neal Loving saw the de Havilland DH-4 biplane that changed his life, he was arguing with his oldest brother about the placement of two competing radio antennae across their Detroit backyard. Just then the silver and blue biplane flew overhead. Seeing his younger brother's curiosity piqued by the sight, Loving's 14-year-old brother suggested to 10-year-old Neal that he take up aviation instead of radio.

Although Neal Loving had just found what would be a life-long passion, his family as a whole was not supportive. His father and his brothers, Barney and Robert, and his younger sister Ardine, were uninterested in his new obsession. His mother suggested that he go to the nearest branch of the Detroit Public Library. There, Loving found a trove of aviation magazines and aircraft books that he studied avidly. Dashing outside every time a plane flew over, Loving was soon able to identify aircraft simply by the sound of their engines.

Loving's parents, Hardin Clay Loving and Alma Loving, raised their four children in sometimes precarious financial circumstances. Loving's father studied optometry at the Columbia Optical College in St. Paul, Minnesota, graduating in 1924 while supporting his wife and four children with a full-time job as a conductor on the South Shore Railroad operating between Duluth and St. Paul. In 1925, he would be the first black to pass the Michigan State Board of Examiners in the practice of optometry. Loving later realized that his father, "a tall, fair-skinned man with gray eyes and dark wavy hair, must have been 'passing' for white as blacks were at that time restricted to more menial positions, such as Pullman porters."

Aviation in the late 1920s was still considered dangerous and was limited in its advancement opportunities for African Americans. Loving faced pressure from family and friends who felt that he shouldn't try to be "better than they were." Loving's father repeatedly told him to "stop playing . . . and learn something at which [he] could earn a living." A teacher suggested he get the application for the U.S. Air Corps, available at any post office. The 11-year-old did so, and was unfazed by the stipulation that the applicant be "a white, male citizen." "I threw the application blank away and continued to dream impossible dreams."

Loving saved up his daily lunch money and all his spending money to buy aviation magazines and model airplane material.

When he was 14, Loving saved up the $3 cost of an airplane ride. In the front seat of a Waco biplane, Loving was flown for the first time, from Detroit City Airport over downtown Detroit and up the Detroit River. The ride lasted about 15 minutes. Loving would recall it as "an unforgettable experience that lives in my mind. . . . Certainly my family thought I would never stop talking about it."

In January 1931, Loving entered Cass Technical High School, enrolling in the auto/aero department to specialize in aeronautics. Shortly after enrolling, Loving was called to the department head's office. "He felt obliged to inform me that there were no opportunities for Blacks like me in the aeronautical field. . . . He suggested I transfer to the auto department where my skills could be used to make a living among my own people." When Loving said that he "loved airplanes and . . . didn't care to be that practical," permission was granted, somewhat reluctantly, for Loving to remain in the aero program.

Many years later, when in his 50s, Neal Loving would remark, "I guess I have a history of people telling me what I can't do. So far they're all wrong."

Loving's application to join the Cass Aero Club was turned down; blacks were not eligible. Soon after, however, he met Don Pearl Simmons, founder of the all-black Ace Flying Club, which was committed to teaching young African Americans to fly. At his first meeting, Loving met the club's secretary, a tall young woman named Earsly Taylor. Although the Ace Flying Club would end when Simmons and his wife were killed in a crash a few months later, Loving and Taylor would be friends and business partners for many years.

## Career Highlights

Graduating from Cass Tech in January 1934, Loving went to work for the Detroit Welfare Department, cleaning streets. The resulting frostbite strengthened his resolution to pursue a career in aviation and not to make his living from manual labor outdoors. The following summer, he worked without pay for his former Cass Tech aero mechanics instructor, George Tabraham, gaining the experience necessary for an aircraft mechanic's license.

Inspired by articles in *Popular Mechanics* and *Modern Mechanix* magazines, Loving designed and built a ground trainer, a nonflying airplane for children, for which he received a "Project of the Month" award from *Mechanix Illustrated*. In 1935, the Junior Birdmen of America invited him to exhibit it at the Annual All-American Air Show at Detroit City Airport. Seven years after Loving had first visited the show at the age of 12, he was a full-fledged exhibitor.

He began to design a full-size glider in the fall of 1935, and, in order to raise money for materials, started to look for a better-paying job—a daunting task for an African American in the middle of the Great Depression. In 1936, he found a WPA-funded job teaching model airplane design and construction to youngsters at recreational facilities in Detroit.

Although he never flew the first glider, which had structural problems, Loving gained experience from it which he used in designing subsequent aircraft. He began taking flying lessons in 1938 and soloed for the first time in 1939. He and Earsly Taylor, who was also learning to fly, found their instruction hampered both by financial constraints and frequent restrictions against students of color. In 1939 Loving organized the St. Antoine YMCA Glider Club, open to boys at least 14 years old, the minimum govern-

mental age requirement for soloing a glider. They completed construction of the second glider, designated the Wayne S-1 and registered with the Department of Commerce as NX27775, before Loving's WPA job ended in 1940.

Loving then enrolled in a six-month accelerated course in engineering drafting at Highland Park Junior College, in order to hone his skills. He applied for a position with the Detroit Board of Education as an elementary drafting teacher and soon was called by George Tabraham, his Cass Tech mentor, who was now principal of the newly founded Aero Mechanics High School. In July 1941, Loving began work for Tabraham as an aircraft mechanics instructor, and he soon was one of the most popular instructors in the school.

NX27775 made its last glider flight of 1941 in late November. After the Japanese attacked Pearl Harbor a week later, war emergency rules and gasoline rationing effectively grounded most private aircraft. The Civil Aeronautics Administration (forerunner of the Federal Aviation Administration) contacted all owners of registered gliders, seeking to purchase aircraft for military purposes. Loving knew that the cockpit of NX27775 was too small to meet military standards, but he offered to build a larger version, designated the S-2, for the military and commercial markets. With Earsly Taylor, he formed the Wayne Aircraft Company. They were determined that theirs, the first black aircraft factory, would be a commercial success, even though work proceeded slowly since all the partners had other, full-time jobs.

With the S-2 glider and a Waco biplane available, Loving and Taylor applied to join the Civil Air Patrol (CAP), a volunteer civilian branch of the U.S. Army Air Force through which airplane owners provided preflight and premilitary training to young people, and were used for air-sea rescue missions. After they were turned down by the white squadrons in the Detroit area, they requested and were granted permission to form an all-black squadron, designated Squadron 639–5 (63rd Wing, Group 9, Squadron 5), with Taylor as commanding officer and Loving as executive officer. They had no trouble recruiting cadets; in addition to the standard preflight and premilitary training, they offered training in parachute jumping, and Squadron 639–5 became known informally as the Parachute Squadron.

In 1943, as the end of the war seemed near, wartime efforts began to be reduced or refocused, and Loving's position at Aero Mechanics High School was terminated. He applied to the Ford Motor Company for an engineering job; he was offered only an entry-level engine assembly position. Shortly thereafter, Loving received his draft notice. Certain he would be called to active duty, he increased his efforts to complete the design of the S-2 as soon as possible, while continuing his CAP duties and the seven-day-a-week job at Ford. The resultant long-term fatigue would eventually have disastrous consequences.

Called to the draft in February 1944, Loving passed all the examinations—except the cardiology exam. Even though Loving had his pilot's license and medical certificate in hand, the military physician stated adamantly that Loving's heart was bad, and classified him 4-F.

With no hope of military service, nor of an engineering position at Ford, Loving appealed to the War Manpower Commission for a Statement of Availability (SA) so that he might be able to use his drafting skills elsewhere. With the SA in hand, he planned to enroll at Wayne State University in the fall of 1944. In July, Loving took NX27775 out to practice for a flight demonstration.

On July 30, 1944, Loving was scheduled to hold a routine CAP training session. In addition to his long-term fatigue, he had only two hours sleep the night before. Loving put the glider in the air despite poor field conditions, the lack of a significant length of tow rope, and without noting either that his airspeed indicator was registering 10 mph higher than the actual airspeed or that the wind direction was perpendicular to the runaway, which would mean a loss of altitude.

As Loving prepared for landing, the glider stalled and crashed. Both of Loving's legs were crushed and required amputation. Released from the hospital early in 1945, within months Loving had acquired two artificial limbs and was walking, driving, and flying again.

Loving and Taylor had closed the Wayne Aircraft Company during Loving's long recovery in hospital. In 1946, they decided to form the Wayne School of Aeronautics. Many returning war veterans were learning to fly, and black veterans were routinely rejected by white schools. The Wayne School of Aeronautics began operation that summer, accepting students of all races.

By early 1947, the school was in full operation. Loving turned his attention once more to airplane design, specifically to midget-class racers, a new category intended to be affordable to builders and pilots with average incomes and without corporate sponsorship. He began work on the WR-1, his first powered aircraft, which became known as *Loving's Love*. The general design was approved by the Professional Racing Pilots Association (PRPA) in January 1948. Construction of the gull-winged WR-1 began in January 1949, and, now assigned CAA registration number N351C, was completed early in the summer of 1950. The plane's first test flight, on August 7, 1950, was nearly flawless. In the ensuing months the aircraft and its "black, legless designer/builder/pilot" attracted attention from aviators and news media wherever Loving flew.

In 1953–1954, he flew *Loving's Love* 4,800 miles round-trip between Detroit and Kingston, Jamaica, where Carl Barnett and Earsly Taylor Barnett had founded a flight school. At the second annual fly-in of the Experimental Aircraft Association (EAA) at Rockford, Illinois, in 1954, Loving won the "Most Outstanding Design" award for *Loving's Love*.

Loving married Carl Barnett's sister, Clare Thérèse, in 1955. They later adopted a son, Paul Leslie, born in 1958, and a daughter Michelle Stephanie, born in 1959. He began studying for an aeronautical engineering degree at Wayne State University in the fall of 1955. Two years later, he closed the Wayne School of Aeronautics and devoted himself full-time to his studies.

Graduating from Wayne State University in 1961, Loving went to work as an aeronautical engineer in the Flight Dynamics Laboratory at Wright-Patterson Air Force Base in Ohio. He became known for his work in clear-air turbulence measurement techniques and for his diplomatic skills. While project engineer for the Air Force's High Altitude Clear Air Turbulence Project, Loving traveled overseas to discuss potential turbulence problems which a supersonic transport (SST) might face, and coordinated agreements with other nations for worldwide operations bases for the Lockheed U-2 spy plane.

Loving retired in 1982 to devote his time to his family and to flying a "roadable" aircraft he kept in his garage in Yellow Springs, Ohio, where he and his wife continued to live in the house they had bought near Wright AFB in 1961. Loving stopped flying in 1991 when the FAA revoked his medical certificate because of an aneurysm in his lower aorta. He went on to write his autobiography, *Loving's Love*, published in 1994, and to become a motivational speaker. He died in 1998, at the age of 82.

## Sources

Duffy, Yvonne. "Disabled in America: Racism, Then Disability, Can't Ground Pilot." *Detroit News and Free Press* (July 17, 1994).

Hardesty, Von, and Dominick Pisano. *Black Wings: The American Black in Aviation*. Washington, DC: National Air and Space Museum, 1983; 71.

Loving, Neal V. *Loving's Love: A Black American's Experience in Aviation*. Washington, DC: Smithsonian Institution Press, 1994.

Luczak, Dennis. "Neal Loving: Heroic Airman and the Planes He Builds," *Tuesday* (August 1971): 6–8, 16.

"Obituaries—Neal V. Loving," *Yellow Springs News* (December 24, 1998).

Reich, David. "Eyes on the Skies." *Wayne State Magazine*. Spring 1998. Wayne State University. Http://www.alumni.wayne.edu/magazine/spring98.htm#Eyes. Accessed March 21, 2000.

# M

## Vance H. Marchbanks Jr.

**Full Name at Birth:** Vance Hunter Marchbanks Jr.

**Born:** January 12, 1905, Fort Washikie, Wyoming

**Died:** October 21, 1988, Hartford, Connecticut

**Education:** B.S., University of Arizona, 1931; M.D., Howard University Medical School, Washington, D.C., 1937.

**Positions Held:** Staff physician, Veterans Administration Hospital, Tuskegee, Alabama, 1939–1941; group surgeon, 332nd Fighter Group, Italy, World War II; senior flight surgeon, Korea, 1950–1953; deputy commander and chief, Air Force Hospital, Nagoya, Japan, 1954–1956; medical specialist on Project Mercury, NASA/USAF, 1960–1962; chief, environmental health services, Hamilton Standard, a division of United Aircraft Corporation, Windsor Locks, Connecticut, 1964–1986.

**Awards, Honors:** Bronze Star, World War II; Army Commendation Medal; Air Force Commendation Ribbon; Air Force Commendation Medal with an oak leaf cluster; William Alonzo Warfield Award, Howard University.

**Summary:** One of the earliest African American doctors to specialize in space medicine, Vance H. Marchbanks Jr. was part of the 11-man team of specialists who monitored the health condition of John Glenn as he orbited the earth on February 20, 1962, thereby becoming the first American to do so. Marchbanks, a Tuskegee Airman, contributed to the knowledge of the effects of space on the human body by his studies and designs.

### Early Years

Vance H. Marchbanks Jr. was born on January 12, 1905, the second child of Callie Hatton and Vance H. Marchbanks Sr. His father was a sergeant in the U.S. Tenth Cavalry stationed at Fort Washikie, when he was born. The unit was formed on September 21, 1866 at Fort Leavenworth, Kansas. It, along with the Ninth Cavalry, the 24th and 25th Infantry, were the first all-black regiments in the U.S. Army, although their officers were white. They served in the West and were named the "Buffalo Soldiers" by the Indians they fought.

"Born in the service" and raised in the atmosphere of a proud military tradition, young Marchbanks naturally wanted to be part of it. His aspiration was high—he wanted to go to the U.S. Military Academy at West Point, New York. The last African American to graduate from the Academy was Charles Young in 1889, becoming only the third to do so.

## Higher Education

In 1927, Sergeant Marchbanks was now a warrant officer and stationed at Fort Huachaca, Arizona. His son, while enrolled at the University of Arizona, had been designated as a competitor for the West Point examination by President Calvin Coolidge. In February 1927, when he took the test at Fort Bliss, Texas, he was rejected on the grounds of physical unfitness: his shoulders were "too narrow" (*Gary Sun*, May 13, 1927). There was not to be another African American graduate of West Point until 1936, when Benjamin O. Davis Jr. became the first black man in the twentieth century to achieve that goal.

Marchbanks graduated from the University of Arizona in 1931, and he went on to the Howard University Medical School in Washington, D.C., gaining his medical degree in 1937. At about this time he met Lois Gilkey, a Howard undergraduate, and they later married. The couple had two daughters, Roslyn Jeanne Robinson and Joy Marie Boddie, who were born about 1942 and 1944, respectively.

## Career Highlights

The new doctor began his career as the assistant resident physician at Freedman's Hospital in Washington, D.C. Marchbanks then joined the staff of the Veterans Administration Hospital in Tuskegee, Alabama, where plans were being made to establish the segregated Army Air Corps Flying School.

He was advised to apply for the extension course in aviation medicine that was offered through the School of Aviation Medicine (SAM) at Randolph Field, Texas. Marchbanks completed the course in December 1942, having entered the service on April 1, 1941, as a first lieutenant assigned to Fort Bragg, North Carolina.

With the rating of aviation medical examiner, Marchbanks was assigned "at last" in June 1943 to the station hospital at Tuskegee Army Air Field. In November 1943 he became the group flight surgeon for the 332nd Fighter Group at Selfridge Field, Michigan. When these Tuskegee Airmen, under the command of Benjamin O. Davis Jr. were sent to Italy, Marchbanks accompanied them as the flight surgeon. Before the war ended, Marchbanks had earned the Bronze Star for heroism, and he was promoted to major.

Marchbanks continued his military career at Lockbourne Army Air Force Base (AFB), Ohio, in 1946, and when integration became the rule for the armed services in 1949, he was assigned to March AFB, California. He became group surgeon of the 22nd Bombardment Group, serving with them on Okinawa, a Japanese island then under American control. During the Korean War, 1950–1953, Marchbanks became chief flight surgeon by amassing 1,500 hours in the air, which included three combat missions as the medical observer. He was then promoted to lieutenant colonel.

In January 1954, Marchbanks went to Nagoya, Japan, as the deputy commander and chief of the Air Force Hospital. With 400 beds, the hospital was the Air Force's largest in the Far East. Marchbanks was promoted to colonel in March 1955, and he became the Air Force surgeon on Okinawa. After about two years he was next assigned to Loring AFB, Maine, where the first B-52s had been assigned. While there in November 1957, he participated in Operation Long Legs, a nonstop flight of 22.5 hours and 10,600 miles. The flight, from Florida to Argentina to New York in a B-52 jet bomber, was designed to study crew comfort and the effects of fatigue on accidents. Marchbanks developed an index to measure hormone levels in blood and tissues that could presage an accident. He received an Air Force Commendation Medal for this study. Marchbanks received another medal for devising an oxygen mask tester, which also facilitated the cleaning of the mask.

In 1960, Marchbanks, the director of base medical services at the 831st Tactical Hospital, George AFB, California, received his history-making appointment. It was a direct result of his scientific studies during Operation Long Legs. He and 10 other specialists were selected to monitor the health status of John Glenn Jr., the first American to orbit the Earth. Project Mercury was launched on February 20, 1962, at Cape Canaveral, Florida. Glenn's ride lasted two minutes short of five hours as he circled the Earth three times, and landed in the Atlantic Ocean near the West Indies. Marchbanks headed the tracking station at Kano, Nigeria, one of 18 around the world. He monitored Glenn's heartbeat, respiration, pulse, and temperature on each of the three orbits. The remote control examination was possible through the use of electronic sensing devices, as Marchbanks's patient was in a 150-mile-high "bed," and traveling through space at 17,500 miles an hour.

Marchbanks retired from the Air Force in 1964 after 23 years of service. He settled in Hartford, Connecticut, and became the chief of environmental health services at Hamilton Standard, a division of United Aircraft Corporation. The company was later renamed United Technologies Corporation. The firm was contracted by NASA to develop a space suit and life support system for the Apollo moon project. Marchbanks headed a team that advised engineers on the physical and psychological factors to be considered in travel to the moon, as well as on the equipment and clothing needed. Marchbanks remained at Hamilton Standard until 1986.

Marchbanks wrote numerous articles on sickle cell anemia and aviation medicine for professional journals. Sickle cell anemia is a disorder that mainly affects African Americans, and is exacerbated while flying. His work has appeared in publications such as *Journal of the National Medical Association*, *Journal of Aviation Medicine*, *Journal of Aerospace Medicine*, and the *American Journal of Obstetrics and Gynecology*, among others. Professional organizations he belonged to include the American Board of Preventive Medicine, National Medical Association, Society of Flight Surgeons, the American College of Physicians, and the Hartford County Medical Association. He was a member of the board of directors of the Newington Children's Hospital. Marchbanks's fraternal associations include the Tuskegee Airmen, Inc., Kappa Alpha Psi and Sigma Pi Phi fraternities, and Howard University Medical Alumni Association.

In 1927, when the *Gary Sun* reported on the failure of Marchbanks to pass West Point's physical exam, it lamented that "another aspirant to the nation's great military academy must continue to plod the walk of obscurity unless some kind fate comes his way." Marchbanks, through his education, intelligence, and determination, stepped off the path of obscurity. The "fate" he created for himself increased our knowledge of the physiological effects of space and advanced methods required to deal with them.

## Sources

"Arizona Boy Loses Out in Army Exams." *Gary Sun* (May 13, 1927): 1.

"Aviation Physician Dies at 83." *Hartford Courant* (October 23, 1988): C1, 9.

Burns, Khephra and William Miles. *Black Stars in Orbit: NASA's African American Astronauts*. New York: Harcourt Brace, 1995; 28–29.

Harris, Jacquelyn. *The Tuskegee Airmen: Black Heroes of World War II*. Parsippany, NJ: Dillon Press, 1996; 109–114.

Marchbanks, Vance H. "The Black Physician and the USAF." *Journal of the National Medical Association* (January 1972); 73–74.

Mathes, Bernard. "Marchbanks: Man of Space." *Sepia* (December 1961): 32–34.

Proujan, Barbara. "Vance H. Marchbanks Jr." in Kristine Krapp, ed. *Notable Black American Scientists*. Detroit: Gale Research, 1999.

"Space Doctor for the Astronauts." *Ebony* (April 1962): 35–36, 38–39.

# August Martin

**Full Name at Birth:** August Harvey Martin

**Born:** August 31, 1919, Los Angeles, California

**Died:** June 30, 1968, Biafra, Nigeria

**Education:** DeWitt Clinton High School, Bronx, New York, 1938; courses at San Mateo Junior College and University of California.

**Positions Held:** Flight instructor for the U.S. Navy at Cornell University, 1942; Tuskegee Airman, 1943–1946; pilot, Seaboard World Airlines, 1955–1968.

**Awards, Honors:** The August Martin High School in Jamaica, New York, is named for him.

**Summary:** August H. Martin, a Tuskegee Airman, was the first African American to fly for a commercial airline, Seaboard World Airlines. In February 1967 Martin became one of the founding members of Negro Airmen International (NAI). He died in a plane crash while flying a mercy mission during the Nigerian civil war.

## Early Years

August Martin was born on August 31, 1919, in Los Angeles, California. He was educated at home by his mother, a licensed schoolteacher, until he was 12 years old. The family moved to New York, and Martin graduated from DeWitt Clinton High School in 1938. He then moved back to California and attended San Mateo Junior College. While at the college, he washed airplanes at the Oakland Flying Service to pay for flying lessons.

## Career Highlights

Martin made his solo flight on January 8, 1940, in a Fleet Model 2. He received further flight training at the federally sponsored Civilian Pilot Training Program (CPTP) at the University of California. By graduation he had earned his flight instructor rating.

Returning to New York State in 1942, Martin worked as a civilian inspector for the Navy V-12 program at Cornell University. In 1943, he joined the U.S. Army Air Corps and was sent to Tuskegee, Alabama, for training. Martin won his wings on September 8, 1945, but by the time his bombardment group was scheduled to go overseas, the war was over.

In 1946, Martin left military service to find a pilot's job in commercial aviation, but there were no such jobs for African Americans. He made do with work as an aircraft maintainer at Willis Air Service in Teterboro, New Jersey. From then until 1955, Martin flew part time for such airlines as Buffalo Skylines, El Al, and World Airways. To support his family, he even worked as a stevedore on New York City docks when he had no flying jobs.

In 1955, until his death in 1968, Martin was employed by Seaboard World Airlines, an American company that also had a base in Canada. Martin thus became the first African American captain of a U.S. scheduled air carrier. He flew several types of planes for Seaboard: the DC-3, DC-4, Lockheed Constellation, and Canadair CL 44. Along with Edward A. Gibbs and other African American pilots, Martin helped establish Negro Airmen International (NAI) in February 1967, a group that now has numerous chapters across the United States.

From June 1967 until January 1970, the country of Nigeria was engaged in a civil war. Its eastern region had declared itself independent, and named itself Biafra. Martin, while on vacation from Seaboard, volunteered to fly emergency relief supplies into Biafra for the International Red Cross. He died while attempting to land his plane, a Super Constellation, on a rainswept highway that was illuminated only by lanterns. Soon after his death, a high school in Jamaica, New York, which offered a specialization in aviation, was named the August Martin High School.

## Sources

*Blacks in Aviation 1996.* Miami, FL: Metro-Dade Aviation Department: 39–40.
*NAI News* [Hollis, New York] (December 1998): 2.

# Dorothy Layne McIntyre

Dorothy Layne McIntyre. Courtesy of Dorothy Layne McIntyre. Photograph by Holt.

**Full Name at Birth:** Dorothy Arline Layne

**Born:** January 27, 1917, LeRoy, New York

**Education:** LeRoy High School, 1936; B.S. in business administration, West Virginia State College, Institute, 1941; private pilot's license, February 23, 1940; additional courses at Kent State University and Cleveland State University.

**Positions Held:** Instructor, aircraft mechanics, War Production Training School No. 453, Baltimore, Maryland, 1942; secretary, Baltimore Urban League, 1942; public school teacher, Cleveland, Ohio, until 1979.

**Awards, Honors:** A dance, "Takeoff from a Forced Landing" was created in 1984 as a tribute to McIntyre; Bessie Coleman Award for "pioneering efforts on behalf of black aviators," February 4, 1994; included in International Women's Air and Space Museum, Burke Lakefront Airport, Cleveland, Ohio as well as in Cleveland's Historical Society and African American Museum.

**Summary:** Dorothy Layne McIntyre was an early African American woman pilot, earning her pilot's license in 1940. She also instructed employees in the aircraft industry during World War II.

## Early Years

Dorothy Arline Layne was born on January 27, 1917, in LeRoy, in western New York. Her parents, Lena Hart Layne and Clyde C. Layne, owned a large farm. Her interests at LeRoy High School, from which she graduated in 1936, included tennis, track, hunting, and swimming. The LeRoy Airport was nearby, and the family attended the annual air shows. Her siblings were Ruth L. Marshall, Clyde E., and Lewis Alexander, a stepbrother. Layne sometimes went up for airplane rides.

## Higher Education

Layne enrolled at West Virginia State College, in Institute. She majored in business administration and graduated in 1941. When the Civilian Aeronautics Authority (CAA) launched its program to train civilian pilots (CPTP), to have a ready supply of prepared pilots in the event of war, it included six, later 10, historically black colleges among the 200 colleges where training would take place. On September 11, 1939, West Virginia State became the first black college to be approved for the program. A favorable point in its selection was the proximity of Wertz Field, Charleston's airport, which adjoined the campus. Cooperation between the college and the airport had been active since 1930 and some students and instructors had been certified as pilots before the CAA program.

The CAA stipulated that one woman be admitted to each training group of 10 men. Dorothy Layne eagerly applied, confident that her strong skills in math and science would be an advantage. Her athletic prowess was a plus as well, because the physical test was "very strenuous, and you had to be insured by Lloyd's of London if you were accepted in the program." Flying was exhilarating for McIntyre: "It's such a peaceful feeling to be up there, especially when I'm alone. I say, 'Dorothy, this is the closest that you're going to get to heaven right now.'" She loved the speed of taking off as well as the effort required for a three-point landing. Then she could say, "I did it. Yes, I did it." Two other women in the classes at the college who became pilots at about the same time were Rose Agnes Rolls (Cousins) and Mary L. Parker. Parker soloed in a seaplane, and was the first African American woman to do so.

To earn her private pilot's license, Layne had to know civil air regulations, flight instruments, radio operation, airplane engines, parachuting, meteorology, and navigation. At least 35 hours in the air—solo and cross country—were required as well. She received her license on February 23, 1940. After McIntyre had her license, she responded to an ad in a Baltimore newspaper calling for licensed pilots who wanted to receive further training. When she telephoned, she received the enthusiastic response, "Where have you been? Come on down." In person, however, the recruiter looked at her and at the license in her hand, and said, "We're all filled up." McIntyre noted later in an interview, "In those days you heard a lot about 'we're all filled up.'"

McIntyre also has academic credit for courses she took at Kent State University and Cleveland State University after she moved to Ohio in 1942.

## Career Highlights

Graduating in 1941, Layne continued flying near Rochester, New York, and Cleveland, Ohio. In 1942, she taught aircraft mechanics at the War Production Training School in Baltimore, Maryland. The course was designed for those already in the aircraft industry who wanted to upgrade their skills as well as for those seeking to enter the industry. At the same time, Layne worked as a secretary in the industrial department of the Baltimore Urban League.

In 1942, she and Francis Benjamin McIntyre were married in Cleveland, Ohio, where they raised their two daughters, Dianne, a dancer and choreographer, and Donna Whyte, an administrator at Cleveland State University. McIntyre did not have a career in aviation, but she worked in other fields such as accounting, social work, and teaching. She retired from the Cleveland public school system in 1979. Her husband was a technical sergeant in World War II and he later retired as a supervisor from the U.S. Postal Service.

In 1984 McIntyre's role as a pioneer African American woman pilot received wider attention. It came from an unlikely source, the dance community. Her daughter, Dianne McIntyre, created "Takeoff from a Forced Landing," a dance to honor her mother's achievement. Founder of the modern dance company, Sounds in Motion, the younger

McIntyre presented the evening-length work on June 19, 1984, to the acclaim of dance critics. The composition included narration based on "Mrs. McIntyre's no-nonsense memories and crisp flight instruction [and other dialogue]." "The metaphor of the forced landing," which usually happens in a place not designed for landing, refers to successful struggles against setbacks. The pilot needs skill, common sense, ingenuity, and imagination to take the plane up again, as others do when they meet obstacles and disappointments. McIntyre remarked at opening night, "People who have always been on the ground would be surprised at what they don't know. It's only gravity that keeps us down, that pulls us to the Earth. But you know, I've always felt that if you could get a little air underneath your feet, you could just float."

In her retirement McIntyre remains active in church and civic organizations, and she enjoys swimming and travel, "especially on airlines, to get the enjoyable feel of flight."

## Sources

Baker, Rob. "Dianne McIntyre Takes off in Dance." *New York Daily News* (June 19, 1984): 43.

Dunning, Jennifer. "A Dance Troupe Takes Flight." *New York Times* (June 17, 1984): Sect. 2, 7, 11.

———. "Dance: Dianne McIntyre's Sounds in Motion." *New York Times* (June 20, 1984).

McIntyre, Dianne, correspondence to Betty K. Gubert, October 11, 2000.

Shapiro, Laura. "A Little Air Beneath Their Feet." *Newsweek* (August 2, 1993): 57.

Tapley, Mel. "Choreographer Dianne McIntyre has 'Flying' in her Blood." *New York Amsterdam News* (June 30, 1984).

"West Virginia State College First to Be Approved for Air Pilots." *Pittsburgh Courier* (June 1940).

"Who's Who." *Joyce Theater Edition of Playbill* (June 1984): 19–20.

"Woman Pilot to Teach Class in Aircraft." *Baltimore Afro-American* (January 1942).

# Ronald E. McNair

Ronald E. McNair. Courtesy National Aeronautics and Space Administration (NASA Photo No. 78-H-642) via National Air and Space Museum, Smithsonian Institution.

**Full Name at Birth:** Ronald Erwin McNair

**Born:** October 21, 1950, Lake City, South Carolina

**Died:** January 28, 1986, in the *Challenger* explosion

**Education:** B.S. in physics, North Carolina A&T State University, 1971; Ph.D., Massachusetts Institute of Technology (MIT), 1976.

**Positions Held:** Physicist, optical physics department, Hughes Research Laboratories, Malibu, California, conducting research on space communications; chosen as one of the first three black astronauts by the National Aeronautics and Space Administration (NASA) in January 1978; flew on *Challenger* Shuttle Mission STS-41-B, the second black American in space, February 3–11, 1984; mission specialist, *Challenger* space flight, 1986.

**Awards, Honors:** Presidential Scholar; Ford Foundation Fellow; Omega Psi Phi Scholar of the Year, honored as Distinguished National Scientist, National Society of Black Professional Engineers; the main street of his hometown, Lake City, South Carolina, was renamed for him, 1984; a building at the Massachusetts Institute of Technology was dedicated in his honor as the Ronald E. McNair Building, 1986; McNair Park, Crown Heights, Brooklyn, NY, dedicated 1994.

**Summary:** Ronald McNair, who grew up in South Carolina and attended segregated schools, received a Ph.D. from the Massachusetts Institute of Technology and was one of the first three African American astronauts. He died in the explosion of the *Challenger*.

## Early Years

Ronald Erwin McNair was born on October 21, 1950, in Lake City, South Carolina, the second son of Carl and Pearl McNair. His father was an automobile mechanic and his mother a schoolteacher. Lake City was a sleepy southern country town where segregation was still very much the rule. Black people went to segregated schools, could not use the public park or the library, and had to sit in the balcony at the movies. They were served at the local soda fountain, but they had to sit outside to consume their confections while whites sat comfortably at the counter.

The family put a strong emphasis on education; both his mother and his aunt were teachers, and his maternal grandmother went back to college late in life, graduating at the age of 65, at the same time McNair and his brother Carl received their college diplomas.

The McNair house overflowed with books, and the children were expected to do well in school. McNair learned to read at the age of three, and when he was four his father altered the date on his birth certificate and enrolled him in school with his brother Carl, who was a year older.

A childhood incident illustrates the tenacity of McNair's character. When he was about nine, his mother was summoned to the public library. She arrived to find the boy sitting on the charge desk. He wanted books, not trouble. McNair won a small victory—he was allowed to use the whites-only library from that time forward. The determination he demonstrated in this instance remained an integral part of his character for the rest of his life.

McNair was an excellent student in elementary school, and he was very involved in scouting, earning the title of Star Scout. A friend from Boy Scout days, Charles K. Wilson, recalls that, while other scouts sported Afro combs in their hip pockets, "Ron always had a slide rule . . . instead. . . . During Boy Scout camp, you'd see Ron off to himself, reading a book and thumbing a slide rule." In the summer, the McNair boys helped out the family finances by picking cotton and beans.

McNair attended Carver High School, a segregated institution. Although the faculty was excellent, the school was seriously underfunded and could not afford basic supplies. Nor did they offer the variety of courses available at the all-white high school. Nevertheless, McNair was a star student; a gifted athlete who participated in football, baseball, basketball, and track; and a talented musician. He played the saxophone in the high school band and was proficient at playing the clarinet. Although a serious student, he also enjoyed dating, had a warm circle of friends, and even played the occasional prank. Graduating at the top of his class, McNair's first career choice was music.

## Higher Education

He won a scholarship to North Carolina Agricultural & Technical University, which had excellent science programs. A guidance counselor encouraged him to switch his major to physics. Since his segregated high school had been deficient in some areas,

McNair had to work very hard to catch up, but catch up he did. In his junior year, he attended the Massachusetts Institute of Technology (MIT) under a North-South exchange program. This institution, located in Cambridge, Massachusetts, is one of the finest scientific and technical colleges in the country, if not the world. It was here, however, that McNair first encountered racial hostility, northern style. It came as something of a shock to find himself reviled and jostled by hostile whites. McNair, however, kept his focus on his reason for being at MIT—to take advantage of the magnificent educational opportunities offered.

He returned to A & T for his senior year and graduated at the top of his class in 1971. McNair applied for and was accepted in the graduate program at MIT. He had mixed feelings about the institution, where, according to him, "even the janitors had Master's degrees," and where he had encountered racial hostility. But McNair decided that the excellence of the educational opportunity offset the drawbacks. It was a courageous decision. He found that he was not adequately prepared for this elite institution, and he had to work extra hard to catch up. He failed at his first try at his qualifying exam, but was successful the second time. Again, his hard work and determination paid off, and he received his Ph.D. degree in 1976. Despite a very busy schedule, he kept up with his saxophone and taught karate in his spare time.

While at MIT, McNair performed original research on lasers, and after graduation wrote many papers and lectured on the subject. It was also while he was at MIT that he met his future wife, Cheryl Moore, a schoolteacher from New York City. They were married on June 27, 1976, shortly after his graduation.

## Career Highlights

McNair then accepted a position as staff physicist at Hughes Research Laboratories, in Malibu, California, and the young couple relocated to the west coast. His work at Hughes dealt with research on the use of lasers in satellite-to-satellite space communications. It was perhaps not a surprise, then, when, in 1977, he was invited to apply for the space program.

The U.S. space program began in response to the successful launching by the Soviet Union of *Sputnik I* in 1957. At the time, the United States and the Soviet Union were rival superpowers, each striving for dominance and world influence. Thus began the "space race." The Soviets put the first man into orbit on April 12, 1961. Eight years later, astronaut Neil Armstrong walked on the moon.

By the 1970s, NASA engineers began to plan for a reusable space shuttle. Previous spacecraft had been one-use vehicles. A reusable vehicle would not only be less expensive but also would have military and commercial applications. In January 1972, NASA announced readiness to develop a space shuttle, which would launch vertically but land back on Earth like a conventional airplane.

McNair sent in his application to NASA. In January 1978, he was informed that he had been chosen, along with 34 others, out of a pool of 10,000 applicants. He and his wife relocated to Houston, Texas, where he began the rigorous course of study required of astronaut candidates. He was one of three black men in the group, the first African Americans in the program. His studies involved advanced science and mathematics classes, as well as training in dealing with weightlessness and learning to manipulate the controls of the shuttle. Within a year, he was informed that he was eligible for a spot as a mission specialist in the space shuttle program.

It was during this rigorous astronaut training, six years of increasingly demanding work, that McNair and his wife became parents of a son, Reginald, in 1982, and a daughter, Joy, in 1984. They purchased a house in the suburbs and settled down in the Houston area.

On February 3, 1984, the dream was fulfilled. McNair took his first space flight, on Mission 41-B aboard the space shuttle *Challenger*. McNair was in charge of testing the Remote Manipulator Arm, an experiment with important implications. This device could be used for hauling a damaged satellite into the shuttle for repair, a use to which it was later successfully put. He conducted a series of other scientific experiments on the middeck as well. He also managed to smuggle his saxophone aboard and was the first man to play this instrument in space.

The spacecraft landed successfully on earth at the Kennedy Space Center, in Florida, on February 12. McNair was feted by his hometown, with both blacks and whites turning out to honor him, and the main street was renamed in his honor. This recognition must have been sweet to McNair, who as a boy was not allowed in the public library or the park. MIT invited him to lecture on his experience in space, and he spoke before the Massachusetts legislature as well, urging them to improve educational opportunities for inner-city black children.

His next mission would be almost two years in coming. The tenth *Challenger* flight, Mission 51-L, was originally scheduled for December 23, 1985, but was delayed several times and eventually was to take place on January 27, 1986. The publicity for this flight focused on Christa McAuliffe, who was to be "the first teacher in space." McNair's role in this flight involved the Remote Manipulator Arm, with which he was to release the *Spartan-Halley* satellite, which was to photograph Halley's Comet.

On the appointed day, there were problems with a bolt on the outside hatch, and by the time this was solved, a high wind had come up and the launch was rescheduled for the following day.

January 28 dawned as a beautiful sunny day, but unseasonably cold. Ice had to be cleared from the launch pad. Nevertheless, the crew of seven astronauts were confident and in high spirits. The shuttle was successfully launched, but a minute and a half into the flight, the craft exploded and hurtled into the ocean while the astronauts' families watched in horror. There were no survivors.

The president of the United States, Ronald Reagan, spoke at a memorial service for the *Challenger* crew, in which he said, "Your loved ones were daring and brave and had that special grace. . . . [They] honored us by the manner in which they lived their lives."

NASA ordered a salvage operation to trace the cause of the disaster; on March 8, the crew compartment was located, and the bodies were released to their families. McNair was buried in his home town.

A presidential commission that investigated the disaster located the cause of the disaster on faulty O-rings in the solid rocket booster. (Although engineers from Morton Thiokol, which built the boosters, had expressed doubt that the O-rings would work at low temperatures, they had been overruled by NASA and they had withdrawn their objections.)

In December 1986, a building at MIT was dedicated in his honor as the Ronald E. McNair Building. Speaking at the ceremony, Charles F. Bolden Jr., a fellow black astronaut, spoke of McNair's vision: "I see young men and young women coming to MIT and saying, 'I want to go where Ron McNair went . . . where Ron McNair chose to start his life taking risks.'" He concluded, "Ron was the best he could be."

## Sources

Atkinson, Joseph D., and Jay M. Shafritz. *The Real Stuff: A History of the NASA Astronaut Recruitment Program*. New York: Praeger, 1985.

Cohen, Daniel. *Heroes of the Challenger*. New York: Pocket Books, 1986.

Naden, Corinne. *Ronald McNair*. New York: Chelsea House, 1990.

"The Life of Ronald E. McNair, 1950–1986." Http:// www.acu.edu/academics/mcnair/aboutrem.html. Accessed November 6, 1998.

"National Aeronautics and Space Administration: The Crew of the Challenger Shuttle Mission in 1986." Http://www.hq.nasa.gov/office/pao/History/Biographies/challenger.html. Accessed October 16, 1998.

"The Seven Who Perished in the Explosion of the Challenger," *New York Times* (January 29, 1986): 9A.

Staff of the Washington Post. *Challengers: The Inspiring Life Stories of the Seven Brave Astronauts of Shuttle Mission 51-L.* New York: Pocket Books, 1986.

# Leslie A. Morris

Leslie A. Morris. Courtesy of National Air and Space Museum, Smithsonian Institution (SI Neg. No. 2001–1894).

**Born:** [1931], Harlem, New York

**Education:** Brooklyn Technical High School; B.S. in aeronautical engineering Pratt Institute, Brooklyn, New York; private pilot's license at Zahn's Airport, Long Island, New York.

**Positions Held:** Welder, Brooklyn Navy Yard; certified flight instructor, air traffic controller, full radar controller, Federal Aviation Administration, 1959–1965; second officer, November 1965–1968; first officer, 1968–1978; captain, 1978–1991, Eastern Airlines; chief pilot, Pan Am Shuttle, 1989–1991.

**Awards, Honors:** Professional Aviation Achievement Award, Negro Airmen International (NAI), 1992; National president of NAI for two terms, ending in 1992.

**Summary:** Leslie Morris has achieved a number of firsts in commercial aviation. Eastern Airlines hired him as their first African American pilot at the end of 1965. He became that airline's first black captain in 1978. In 1989, he was named chief pilot for the Pan Am Shuttle in New York. In addition, Morris established and directed a summer flight academy for more than 20 years as part of the NAI program of aviation education.

## Early Years

Born during the Great Depression, Leslie A. Morris and his sister were raised by their father in Harlem, sometimes called the "Capital of Black America." The children's mother died when Morris was two years old, about 1933. His interest in aviation began when he was a child, and his father fostered that interest. Morris attended and graduated from Brooklyn Technical High School, where he developed his knowledge of aviation by concentrating his studies on science and mathematics.

## Higher Education

Morris continued his education in Brooklyn, graduating from the Pratt Institute with a bachelor's degree in aeronautical engineering. While in college, Morris held a job as a welder at the Brooklyn Navy Yard. He earned his private pilot's license at Zahn's Airport on Long Island, and in 1957, joined the New York branch of the Air National

Guard. At their White Plains unit, he studied combat crew training and gunnery and rocketry, both air-to-air and air-to-ground. He learned to fly jet military aircraft such as the F-86-H and the T-33.

## Career Highlights

Morris went to work for the Federal Aviation Administration (FAA) in 1959 as a certified flight instructor. Still with the FAA, he became an air traffic controller and a full radar controller. He remained with the FAA until November 1965, when he left to become a pilot for Eastern Airlines.

Eastern's first African American pilot, Morris joined the company as second officer and he was assigned to flying the Constellation. In 1968, he was promoted to first officer, piloting such planes as the L-1011 wide body, the DC-8, and the Boeing-727. Ten years later, Morris achieved the rank of captain, again a first at Eastern. Six months after becoming captain, the FAA approved Morris as a check pilot, and he became a manager of flying, an administrative position that entailed the supervision of flight crews. Morris's log books showed over 8,000 hours of flying time. He had almost doubled that figure by 1991, the year he retired from Eastern Airlines.

Although Morris was successful at making a crack in the walls of color prejudice in commercial aviation, he was well aware that they were still high and thick enough to keep others out. He told *Everybody's* in 1985, "When I was growing up I never saw a black person in the cockpit. Now, we do have some but there are so few of us. We're spread fairly thin. I've been with the airline for 20 years now, and I still get these stares from both black and white passengers." Morris, in the same interview, thought one of the reasons for the scarcity of black pilots is that it is so expensive to learn to fly. "It would cost almost $8,000 to get a commercial license and that still doesn't qualify you—not even close—to become an airline pilot."

Near retirement in 1989, Morris signed on as chief pilot for the Pan Am Shuttle in New York. That put him in the position of being the first African American chief pilot of any major airline in the United States. After his retirement, he took on a job as a flight instructor on the Falcon 900, for Flight Safety, Inc.

Morris joined the Negro Airmen International (NAI) in 1969. He has held numerous offices in the organization, including the presidency of the New York chapter (Black Pilots of New York). He has also been national treasurer and operations officer. In 1992, NAI's 25th anniversary, Morris completed his second term as national president. During his years with NAI, Morris stimulated the growth of chapters around the country, and he had the operations of the organization computerized. From its inception in 1973 until at least 1992, Morris directed the NAI's Summer Flight Academy, a two-week program for teenagers, which is held on the campus of Tuskegee University in Alabama. He originated the idea to encourage youngsters who want to learn to fly. The courses cover not only the mechanics of aeronautics but also the history of black aviation pioneers, and the role that the Tuskegee Institute, its former name, played.

Morris and his wife, Virginia, live in New Jersey. In addition to the NAI, his memberships have included Aircraft Owners and Pilots Association (AOPA), Airline Pilots Association, Organization of Black Airline Pilots (OBAP), and the Ravens Flying Club, the New Jersey chapter of NAI.

## Sources

*Black Pilots of New York: 25th Anniversary Celebration.* Queens, New York, 1992; 11.

*Blacks in Aviation 1996: A Commemorative Brochure.* Miami, FL: Metro-Dade Aviation Department, 1996; 49.

McKenzie, Alecia, and Karen M. Turner. "The Father of Black Aviation [Albert E. Forsythe]." *Everybody's* (January–February 1985): 22, 24.

# N

## Grover C. Nash

Grover C. Nash. Courtesy of National Air and Space Museum, Smithsonian Institution (SI Neg. No. 99-15421).

**Born:** April 4, 1911, Dry Branch, Georgia

**Died:** August 1970, Macon, Georgia

**Education:** Master Mechanic, Curtiss-Wright Aeronautical University, Chicago, 1933; ground instructor in aviation.

**Positions Held:** Manager, service department of a parking lot chain, Chicago, 1938–(?); senior mechanical instructor, USA Aircraft Mechanical School, World War II; teacher of aviation mechanics, Dunbar Vocational High School, Chicago, 1947–(?).

**Awards, Honors:** Included in the exhibition, "Black Wings," National Air and Space Museum, Smithsonian Institution, Washington, D.C., 1982.

**Summary:** Grover C. Nash was the first African American pilot to fly the U.S. mail. On May 19, 1938, he flew from Chicago, in his own plane, to small towns in Illinois that had never received airmail service. Nash was a charter member of the Challenger Aero Club in 1931 and of the National Airmen's Association of America in 1937.

### Early Years

Grover C. Nash was born on April 4, 1911, in Dry Branch, Georgia, a small town 12 miles south of Macon. He was visiting his relatives on Route 4, Macon, when he died during the first week of August 1970. Among his survivors were two brothers and three sisters. Details of his early years, other than that the family's religion was Baptist, could not be determined. He tried to enroll at flying schools in Michigan, New York, and Pennsylvania, but he was refused at all of them because of his color. In 1931, Nash found a school in Chicago that would admit him, and he left to follow his interest in aviation.

## Higher Education

By 1933, Nash had earned a Master Mechanic's certificate from the Curtiss-Wright Aeronautical University in Chicago. He bought his own midwing monoplane, *The Little Annie*, that year as well, having completed his flight training in St. Louis, Missouri. His instructor there was the flamboyant Roscoe Turner, a pilot in World War I, and a prize-winning racing pilot from 1932 to 1939. Nash was also instructed by John C. Robinson, who with Cornelius R. Coffey, were the first African Americans to be admitted to Curtiss-Wright. Robinson was the founder of the Challenger Aero Club in 1931, a group of young black pilots.

Nash was also certified by the Civilian Aeronautics Administration to teach all ground subjects.

## Career Highlights

Nash remained in Chicago, where he found himself an integral member of the African American aviation community. As a charter member of the Challengers, he flew in their air shows, demonstrating flight techniques and performing stunts. Nash was also a lieutenant in the Military Order of Guards (Waterford, May 21, 1938). In August 1937 he was one of the founders of the National Airmen's Association of America. Accredited as an aircraft mechanic and certified as a ground instructor, he likely worked in these areas during the 1930s. But in 1938, he was in charge of the service department for a chain of parking lots in The Loop, Chicago's downtown business area. An obituary states that Nash had been a commercial pilot and a flight examiner, but no further details were given.

On May 19, 1938, during the celebration of National Air Mail Week, Nash became the first African American to fly the mail. He was one of 146 pilots who participated in the demonstration, whose purpose was to prove the practicality of flying mail between large cities and small towns that did not receive airmail.

Although airmail service had started in 1918, with U.S. army pilots as the personnel, it was neither on a regular schedule nor widespread. Only major cities were included. Night flights and transcontinental service did not become regular features until 1924. Flying the mail was considered a dangerous occupation because the pilots often flew in poor weather conditions, in light planes, at a time when flying was not a common means of transportation. The airmail service employed only white pilots, and the exclusion of black pilots began to emerge as a civil rights issue in President Roosevelt's first term, 1933–1937. The *Chicago Defender* (May 12, 1934) asked, "Why are there no black airmail pilots? What is there about this service that makes it all white. Dark men do just about everything else Americans do. Why can't they fly her mails?" This theme, that African Americans were not part of federal programs, to which they contributed money in taxes, was to be heard throughout the decade.

Nash flew a Davis high wing monoplane with an 85 horsepower Le Blonde engine during the demonstration. The plane's cruising speed was 90 miles an hour, and it was capable of 110 miles at top speed. He departed from Chicago for Mattoon, Charleston, Rantoul, and Kankakee, small towns in Illinois. At Mattoon, Nash was greeted by the postmaster, other city officials, and about 100 sightseers. He was given a tour of the city and dinner "at one of the leading cafes." At Charleston, beside the local officials, there was a band and a crowd of 8,000 to welcome the first airmail plane to come to the town. Nash did not expect such receptions, and he told Janet Waterford, a Chicago pilot and writer for the *Chicago*

*Defender*, that nowhere did anyone seem to notice his color.

According to Waterford, Nash made the longest flight of the day, and he carried more mail than any of the others. He was even asked to autograph the hundreds of letters he was carrying, which he did.

In response to the criticism of the white-only policy, postal officials commissioned another black man to participate in the celebration of National Air Mail Week. He was Theodore Cable, a dentist and an Indiana city councilman. The flights of Nash and Cable were symbolic, but the publicity surrounding the event highlighted the ability of African American pilots.

On October 31, 1938, Nash and Lillie Borras were married at Corpus Christi Catholic Church. The best man was Harold Hurd, another Chicago pilot.

During the years of World War II, 1942–1945, Nash was the senior mechanical instructor at USA Aircraft Mechanical School. By the end of his flying career, Nash had amassed over 8,000 hours of flying time. In 1947, he joined the faculty of Dunbar Vocational High School in Chicago, where he taught aviation mechanics and a course in preflight aeronautics. After he retired, Nash moved to Los Angeles. Besides his brothers and sisters, two children, Ralph and Linda, also survived him. His funeral service was held on August 10, 1970, at the White Springs Baptist Church, and he was buried in the church cemetery.

### Sources

"Aviator Chooses Bride." *Chicago Defender* (November 12, 1938): 14.

"Grover C. Nash." *Macon Telegraph* (August 10, 1970): 78.

Jakeman, Robert J. *The Divided Skies: Establishing Segregated Flight Training at Tuskegee, Alabama, 1934–1942.* Tuscaloosa: University of Alabama Press, 1992; 79–80.

"Pioneer Black Pilot Succumbs." *Chicago Daily Defender* (August 18, 1970): 5.

"Race Pilot Aids Uncle Sam during National Air Mail Week Celebration." *Chicago Defender* (May 28, 1938): 1.

Waterford, Janet. "First Race Pilot to Fly U.S. Mail Relates Experiences during Flight." *Chicago Defender* (May 28, 1938): 2.

———. "Race Aviator Flies U.S. Mail Route." *Chicago Defender* (May 21, 1938): 1.

# Lloyd W. "Fig" Newton

Lloyd W. "Fig" Newton. Courtesy of National Air and Space Museum, Smithsonian Institution (SI Neg. No. 99-15487).

**Full Name at Birth:** Lloyd W. Newton

**Born:** December 24, 1942, Ridgeland, South Carolina

**Education:** B.A. in aviation education, Tennessee State University, 1966; Armed Forces Staff College, Norfolk, Virginia, 1978; Industrial College of the Armed Forces, Washington, D.C., 1985; M.A. in public administration, George Washington University, Washington, D.C., 1985; National Security Senior Executives course, Harvard University, Cambridge, Massachusetts, 1987.

**Awards, Honors:** Distinguished Flying Cross, Air Medal with 16 oak leaf clusters; Air Force Commendation Medal; Vietnam

Service Medal; Republic of Vietnam Campaign Medal.

**Positions Held:** Combat pilot, Vietnam, 1968–1969; F-4 flight leader, 1969–1970; equal opportunities and treatment officer, Clark Air Force Base, 1970–1974; member of the Thunderbirds, 1974–1978; Air Force congressional liaison officer to the U.S. House of Representatives, 1978–1982; director of operations, J-3, United Special Operations Command, 1993–1995; commander of air education and training, Randolph Air Force Base, Texas, 1997.

**Summary:** Lloyd W. "Fig" Newton, a command pilot, achieved a place in aviation history when he became the first African American to be invited to join the Air Force's elite flying team, the Thunderbirds. Newton, now a general, flew 269 missions during the Vietnam War, and he has more than 4,000 flying miles to his credit.

## Early Years

Lloyd Newton was born in 1942, the fourth son of John H. and Annie Newton. The family eventually included six sons and a daughter. At a very early age, young Newton was fascinated by airplanes. "I remember when I was on my dad's farm, I would run out of the house to look overhead when I heard the sound of a plane. But I never thought that I'd actually get a chance to ever fly one."

Newton recalls being a "typical scrawny American kid," who was not particularly interested in participating in sports. At the age of 18 and about to graduate from Jasper High School, he considered volunteering for the Air Force. But his math teacher persuaded him to attend college.

## Higher Education

Newton graduated from Jasper High School in 1961, and in the same year he met Ruth Gadson, who was to become his wife.

He attended Tennessee State University in Nashville. It was at Tennessee State that he acquired the nickname "Fig," which has stuck to him ever since. His interest in flying revived during his college years, when he enrolled in the Air Force Reserve Officer Training Program (ROTC). "I went to Tennessee State as a mechanical engineering major but I ended up with a B.S. in aviation education," said Newton, quoted in an interview in *Ebony*.

In 1966, Newton graduated from college and was commissioned a second lieutenant in the Air Force. He was admitted to jet flight training at Williams Air Force Base, in Phoenix, Arizona. "Off I went," Newton is quoted as saying, "proud and scared." The transition was difficult. "From a small town, an all-black high school, to a 98 percent-black college, and then into a 99 percent-white class in pilot training, was quite an adjustment.... The nights were long and the days were hard, but it worked out fine."

Newton was inspired to persevere by the example of General Daniel "Chappie" James, whom he knew personally: "General James meant so much to me.... He was much more than a hero.... Men like him are responsible for guys like me getting to where we are. I'm just reaping the benefits of the sacrifices people like James made."

Flight school lasted 53 weeks. In 1967, after completing this training, the young pilot was assigned to George Air Force Base in California, where he received combat training in the F-4 Phantom. America was in the thick of the Vietnam War, and in 1968 Newton was transferred to Da Nang, in what was then South Vietnam, where he served as a combat pilot. He flew 269 combat missions, 79 over North Vietnam, in the F-4 Phantom II, in the course of one year, from April 1968 to April 1969.

It was a time of increasing protests in the United States against the Vietnam War. Newton disagreed with the antiwar movement which was growing in the United States. Despite the turmoil at home, he had no reservations about his Vietnam combat missions: "I don't think there's anyone who really wants to go to war. It's just one of those things—you got a job to do and you do it to the best of your ability."

His Vietnam stint ended, Newton was transferred to Clark Air Force Base in the Philippines in 1969. His first assignment at Clark was as an F-4 flight leader, leading a flight of four Phantoms. Promoted to captain in 1969, he was assigned as the equal opportunities and treatment officer and the base race relations officer, positions which normally went to men of higher rank. Newton was proud of his record in this challenging assignment: "There were 10,000 airmen at Clark at the time, with 19 percent of them a minority. I was lucky. With the outstanding staff I had to work with, we managed to enhance the racial harmony around the base. Communication and education is the key. We didn't solve all of the problems, but we sure made some steps in the right direction."

In 1972, Newton submitted his first application for a flying job with the Thunderbirds, an elite group of Air Force fliers whose precision flying is featured at air shows all over the United States and Canada. Officially known as "the United States Air Force Aerial Demonstration Squadron," they are masters of precision flying, whose daring maneuvers demand a high degree of skill. These maneuvers include loops, rolls, pitchups, and crossovers.

There are many applicants for the group, but only seven pilots are accepted each year. Though not chosen on this occasion, he applied again in 1973, and was again rejected, applied yet again in 1974, and was then accepted—the first African American ever to serve in the group.

Newton's first assignment, as newest member of the team, was as narrator and back-up pilot. It was his task to interpret to the spectators, sometimes numbering in the thousands, what was happening in the air. This was not his only responsibility—he also served as advance coordinator. Newton would arrive at each show site several hours before the rest of the team, along with the maintenance man. At the site, he made final arrangements for housing, transportation, parking, or whatever else was needed. "I also coordinate all the publicity and public relations when we're on the road. I'm known as the road public relations man for the team."

Being a narrator was not a simple assignment. The narrator had no radio contact with the pilots; his descriptions were based on what the aviators had done in rehearsal. When unforeseen circumstances arose, Newton had to improvise. He was helped by the logistics officer, who was in radio contact with the men in the air.

The following year found him flying with the team: "Flying is sort of a disease with me. . . . Once you do it a little while, you always want to do it." But even more important to Newton was communicating with people, explaining what the Air Force is about: "It's unfortunate that many people don't know what their Air Force is doing and what they're paying for. . . . That was one of my big reasons for wanting to come on the team."

Newton has successfully persuaded at least two persons of the importance of the Air Force. Two of his younger brothers, Lester and Donald, became career officers.

At the conclusion of his three-year assignment with the Thunderbirds, Newton was asked to extend his stay for another three-year term. This honor was unprecedented— he was the first man ever to be asked to return to the group.

From 1978 to 1982, Newton served as an Air Force congressional liaison officer to the U.S. House of Representatives. He has commanded three wings and an air division, and held numerous staff positions. From 1993 to 1995, he was director of operations, J-3, United States Special Operations Command. His latest position, which he assumed in March 1997, is as commander of air education and training, Randolph Air Force Base, Texas. In this capacity, he is responsible for the recruiting, training, and education of Air

Force personnel. His command consists of 13 bases, more than 43,000 active duty members and 14,000 civilians. He is also responsible for the Air Force Recruiting Service, two numbered air forces and Air University. On April 1, 1997, Newton, who has more than 4,000 flying hours to his credit, was appointed a general.

In 1975, *Ebony* magazine pictured Newton with his wife, Ruth Gadson, and their children, Lloyd Jr., Cheryl, and Lori. In his 1997 Air Force biography, his wife is identified as Elouise M. Morning, and the couple have five children.

### Sources

"A Jet Pilot's Dream Comes True." *Ebony* (May 1975): 82–84, 86, 88, 90.

"Lloyd 'Fig' Newton Play-by-Play Narrator for Air Force Thunderbirds." *Black Sports* 5, 3 (September 1975): 46–48.

"Major 'Fig' Newton a Thunderbird in the Sky." *Eagle & Swan* 1, 3 (June 1978): 28–29.

United States Air Force. *Biography: General Lloyd W. "Fig" Newton*. Information handout, 1997.

# Marcella A. Ng

Marcella A. Ng. Courtesy of Jackson Huang.

**Full Name at Birth:** Marcella Anne Hayes

**Born:** July 24, 1956, Mexico, Missouri

**Education:** David Hickman High School, Columbia, Missouri, 1974; B.S. in English, University of Wisconsin, Madison, 1978; U.S. Army transportation officer basic course, Fort Eustis, Virginia; U.S. Army Aviation Center, Fort Rucker, Alabama, helicopter pilot's license, 1979; U.S. Army aviation maintenance officer course, Fort Eustis, 1980; U.S. Army transportation officer advanced course, Fort Eustis, 1984; Combined Arms Services Staff School, Fort Leavenworth, Kansas, 1987; command and general staff officer course, Fort Leavenworth, 1993.

**Positions Held:** Company executive officer, adjutant, 394th Transportation Battalion, Nelligan Barracks, Stuttgart, Germany, 1980–(?); test officer, company commander, Training and Doctrine Command (TRADOC), Fort Hood, Texas; chief, movement region I, 25th Transportation Center, Seoul, Korea; movement control officer, brigade logistics officer, division transportation officer, 7th Infantry Division (Light), Fort Ord, California; chief Automation Logistics (Technology Division), battalion executive officer 24th Transportation Battalion, group operations officer 7th Transportation Group, Fort Eustis, Virginia, early 1990s; maintenance division chief, 19th Theater Army Area Command, Taegu, Korea, 1995; battalion commander, 49th Transportation Battalion, 1997–1999, inspector general, 13th Corps Support Command, Fort Hood, Texas, June 1999–September 2000.

**Awards, Honors:** Distinguished Military Graduate (DMG); Parachute Badge; both while in ROTC.

**Summary:** On November 27, 1979, Marcella A. Hayes became the 55th woman to receive her aviator's wings from the U.S. Army Aviation Center at Fort Rucker, Alabama. But more important from the standpoint of American military and aviation history, Hayes became the first African American woman pilot in the U.S. Armed Forces.

Making the army her career, Marcella A. Ng (her married name) advanced to the rank of lieutenant colonel in 1995.

## Early Years

Marcella Anne Hayes was born on July 24, 1956, in Mexico, Missouri, to Carrie A. Hayes Bradley and Andrew L. Hinch Jr. When Hayes was about eight years old, she and her younger sister, Ora Lynn, were formally adopted by her maternal grandparents, Howard and Ora Mildred Hayes, a mechanic and a nurse. Mr. and Mrs. Hayes, living in Centralia, Missouri, raised the children from birth in a stable home filled with love and a deep religious faith. They encouraged Hayes to do whatever made her happy. She was athletic and she was known as a tomboy, with a love of climbing trees and playing ball games. In her junior year in high school she was on the first girls' track team. As a senior, she was on the basketball team and was a member of the National Honor Society.

## Higher Education

After graduation from Hickman High School, Hayes enrolled at the University of Wisconsin at Madison. She graduated in 1978 with a bachelor's degree in English. During college Hayes joined the Reserve Officers Training Course (ROTC). Her cadre company commander during advanced camp training at Fort Riley, Kansas, an aviator, interested her in flying and Hayes began investigating the options open to personnel in the armed forces. She chose the transportation branch to assure herself a job in aviation maintenance, and, eventually, a chance to become a pilot. Following the stint at Fort Riley, Hayes was sent to Fort Benning, Georgia. Here she earned a paratrooper's badge after making five qualifying jumps at 1,250 feet in August 1977.

Hayes completed the request form, and before graduation, she received orders to attend the Transportation Officers Basic Course (TOBC) at the U.S. Transportation Center and School at Fort Eustis, Virginia. She took and easily passed the flight physical and the Flight Aptitude Selection Test (FAST). Entering the army in December 1978, Hayes completed the TOBC and was sent to Fort Rucker, Alabama, on March 22, 1979, for flight training. Of her rigorous training, Hayes recalled, "Every day was a challenge because there was always some new skill to master." After her first solo flight, she told an interviewer, "There's nothing like it. I wanted to cry out, 'Look Mom, I'm flying, and all by myself!' "

For instrument training, usually considered one of the hardest segments of flight training, her instructor was Robert Stamper. He wanted to fly "at least one female student . . . to take her through instruments. I wanted to find out whether a woman had any business in the cockpit." Hayes received an outstanding grade in the instruments course and she impressed Stamper with her intelligence and determination. Hayes believes the key to success is to stay motivated and confident that you will succeed.

## Career Highlights

On November 27, 1979, Second Lieutenant Marcella A. Hayes received her silver wings at Fort Rucker, Alabama, upon completion of her helicopter flight training. She thus stepped into the pages of history as the first African American woman pilot in the U.S. Armed Forces. She also was the 55th woman, out of a total of 48,000 officers, to graduate from the Army Aviation School. Her new assignment took her to the 394th Transportation Battalion at Nelligan Barracks, Stuttgart, Germany, where she had various duties. As the company executive officer she was responsible for the smooth processing of administrative matters, as well as the supervision of a dining facility for over 600 soldiers, and she was also motor officer for the unit's ground vehicles and equipment. Soon after arriving, Hayes and First Lieutenant Dennis K.C. Ng, whom she had met in flight school, were married on January 11, 1980. The couple have three children: a son, Kenika, who is serving in the Air Force, and two daughters, Kerri and Kadri, a high school senior and junior, respectively. Dennis Ng retired from the Army in 1996 with the rank of lieutenant colonel, after 23 years of service.

At Nelligan, Ng became assistant adjutant, and later adjutant, for supervision of all the phases involved in processing personnel actions. Ng's next assignment was at Fort Hood, Texas, as a test officer in the TRADOC (Training and Doctrine Command) Combined Arms Test Activity. She tested new equipment and concepts before they were accepted for implementation by the Army. Later, Ng became company commander for TRADOC, a position she held for two years before leaving for Seoul, Korea.

There, Ng became chief of movement, Region I, 25th Transportation Center. In this position, Ng coordinated common user transportation by rail, highway, or air throughout the northern half of South Korea, using seven geographically dispersed movement control offices. Returning to the United States, Ng was sent to Fort Ord, California, as the movement control officer, Division Support Command, 7th Infantry Division (Light), where her responsibilities included transportation and supply requirements for all units deployed and coordination of ground and air transport for returning units. Still with the 7th Infantry Division (Light), Ng was promoted to brigade logistics officer, Bayonet Combat Support Brigade. She was in charge of ensuring that subordinate battalions and separate companies received supply, maintenance, fiscal, and dining facility support. During the Desert Shield/Storm operation, which lasted from August 1990 until spring 1991 and involved 500,000 American

soldiers in the war between Kuwait and Iraq, Ng ensured that regularly assigned units, as well as units of the Reserves and the National Guard, met all logistical parameters prior to deployment overseas. Ng continued her duties at Fort Ord, but now as division transportation officer, which involved making sure the 7th Infantry Division could be rapidly deployed anywhere in the world, in whatever transportation mode was most effective.

Ng's next assignment was to Fort Eustis, Virginia, where she was promoted to major, approximately 1994 or earlier. She served as chief of the Automation Logistics Technology Division, whose mission was to identify appropriate automation technology for future use. Later she was the battalion executive officer of the 24th Transportation Battalion, serving as acting battalion commander in his absence. She was later group operations officer at Fort Eustis.

Returning to Korea about 1995, Ng achieved the rank of lieutenant colonel, and she became maintenance division chief, 19th Theater Army Area Command at Taegu, Korea. In this capacity, she developed policy and maintained oversight of the organization's force modernization and readiness. Support maintenance of ground and air equipment were under her authority as well. Once again returned to the United States, Ng was assigned to Fort Hood, near Killeen, Texas. This installation of 217,337 acres is the only American post capable of stationing and training two armored divisions.

Ng reported to duty as the battalion commander of the 49th Transportation Battalion (Movement Control). She remained in this position for two years (1997–1999). She led, guided, directed, and served as a mentor to soldiers in one of the most deployed units at Fort Hood. She was responsible for fulfilling movement control requirements in theaters of operation worldwide. In June 1999, she began a tour of duty as inspector general (IG) for the 13th Corps Support Command at

Fort Hood. An IG's responsibilities include inspecting, investigating, training, teaching, and mentoring at all levels, soldiers and leaders.

The Ng family is deeply religious, and they give credit to their Christian faith for sustaining them during their years of separation occasioned by their pursuit of their Army careers and education. Marcy Ng has continued to enjoy the outdoors, and through the years, has enjoyed mountain climbing, fishing, and skiing. Her indoor activities include racquetball, backgammon, sewing, and cooking. A few years ago, Ng and her husband became interested in motorcycling, and they are both actively involved with the Christian Motorcyclists Association, providing hospitality to bikers and nonbikers alike. Ng smiles when telling the story of the day that she, the battalion commander, rode her Harley Davidson Road King to work. Soldiers were aghast that someone would dare to park in the colonel's space. When the personnel on the base learned it was the commander herself, motorcycles of all types seemed to come out of the woodwork.

On September 1, 2000, Colonel Ng retired from the military. She is homeschooling her youngest daughter and thinking of gaining a teaching certificate. She serves as chaplain for the local chapter of the Christian Motorcyclists Association, and is active in her church.

## Sources

*Blacks in Aviation 1996.* Black History Month Brochure, Miami, FL: Metro-Dade Aviation Department; 74.

Ng, Marcella, Nolanville, Texas, to Betty K. Gubert, New York, e-mail, October–November 1999, January, April–May 2000, February–March, 2001.

Press Release, Public Affairs Office, U.S. Army Aviation Center, Fort Rucker, Alabama, November 27, 1979.

" 'Show Me State' Girl Shows the Way." *Ebony* (April 1980): p. 101–103.

# William R. Norwood

William R. Norwood. Courtesy of National Air and Space Museum, Smithsonian Institution (SI Neg. No. 2001–1896).

**Born:** February 14, 1936, Centralia, Illinois

**Education:** B.A. and private pilot's license, Southern Illinois University (SIU), Carbondale, 1959; MBA, University of Chicago, 1974.

**Positions Held:** Captain, U.S. Air Force, 1959–1965; second officer, 1965–1968, first officer, 1968–1983, captain, 1983–1996, United Airlines.

**Awards, Honors:** All-American football, SIU, 1958; included in the "Black Wings" exhibition of the National Air and Space Museum, Smithsonian Institution, 1982; President, Organization of Black Airline Pilots (OBAP), 1989; United Airlines Corporate Community Relations Award, 1991; O'Hare Airport, Chicago, Captain of the Year, 1995; Chicagoan of the Year, 1995; SIU Reunion Councils Founders Award, 1996; United Airlines Black Professionals

Organization's Outstanding Achievement and Leadership Award, 1996; Destiny Church Community Service Award, 1997.

**Summary:** William R. Norwood, in 1965, became the first African American pilot hired by United Airlines, and one of the three or four black commercial airline pilots then employed. In his more than 30 years in the airline industry, and as president of OBAP in 1989, Norwood has worked to increase the number of black pilots.

## Early Years

William R. Norwood was born on February 14, 1936, in Centralia, Illinois, to Allingal Humble Norwood and Sam Norwood, who was a carpenter. There was an older sister in the family and there may have been other children as well. The principal of Norwood's elementary school had been a member of the 99th Pursuit Squadron of the Tuskegee Airmen in World War II, and it was he who inspired young Norwood to think of flying as a career. Even as a youngster, he knew such a career would pose many challenges and that he would need to be a strong competitor. Sam Norwood always encouraged his son's love of sports, and William became the first African American quarterback on his high school's football team.

## Higher Education

While at Southern Illinois University in Carbondale, Norwood also played football and here too he was the team's first black quarterback. He even toyed with the idea of playing professionally for a Canadian team. But, worried that an old knee injury would become worse, and thus disqualify him as a pilot, Norwood gave up football for flying. His resolve was strengthened by a remark his sister heard at a football game, and then reported to him: "They have niggers playing quarterback—pretty soon they'll be flying airplanes." It became clear to Norwood that, as a black man, he would need to put in extra effort if he wanted to succeed.

Norwood received his private pilot's license in June 1959, from Southern Illinois University's flying school. That was at the same time as his graduation from SIU. In March 1974, Norwood obtained a Master's degree in Business Administration (MBA) from the University of Chicago.

## Career Highlights

Upon graduation, Norwood entered the U.S. Air Force and began his pilot training. In June 1960, he and Molly F. Cross were married in Birmingham, Alabama, where Norwood was in training at Craig Air Force Base. Their two sons, William R. and George A., were born in the early 1960s. During his six years in the air force, Norwood logged nearly 2,000 hours in the air as he piloted eight-jet B-52 bombers for the Strategic Air Command. Although Norwood had originally planned on a military career, he left the service in May 1965 after six years. He thought he was "going around in circles and getting nowhere fast."

At about this time, two of his friends in the Air Force left for employment at United Airlines, and they urged Norwood to do the same. But they were white, and Norwood was hesitant because of his color. He decided to apply after seeing United's advertisement that they were an "Equal Opportunity Employer." He was accepted and passed their training program doing, "one of the finest jobs of anybody to come through here," said one of his instructors.

Major scheduled airlines began hiring African Americans as pilots after the U.S. Supreme Court's April 1963 decision that racial discrimination by U.S. airlines was unconstitutional. This was the outcome of Marlon Green's battle, begun in 1957, to become a commercial airline pilot. Green, a captain in the air force for nine years, became the first black pilot to be hired by a major commercial airline, Continental. Soon after, David E. Harris and Jack A. Noel became the first black pilots at American Airlines and Norwood was employed as second officer at United. An article in *Ebony* (November 1965) regarded the newly hired black pilots as a hopeful sign of things to come. The writer duly noted, however, that they represented .0002 percent of the industry's 15,750 pilots. Norwood, writing in *Airline Pilot* (February 1989), gave these statistics: of the nation's 55,000 commercial airline pilots, 340 are African American, making them about half of one per cent of the total number.

As a second officer at United from 1965 until 1968, Norwood flew DC-6 propeller planes and later Caravelle jets. He became first officer in 1968 and was promoted to captain in 1983, holding this position until 1996 when he retired.

Norwood was one of the 30 founding members of the Organization of Black Airline Pilots (OBAP) in 1967. He has served as chairman of the board for the organization and was its president in 1989. He articulated OBAP's goals as follows: to motivate youth to become educationally prepared for life, to increase black participation in aviation, and to assist the black airline pilot with special needs and concerns. Over the years, they have included in their interests the need to document, preserve, and make known the history of African Americans in aviation. Norwood is also a life member of the NAACP, a member of the Airline Pilots Association, and United Airlines Speakers Panel, among other organizations. In 1974, Illinois governor Daniel Walker appointed him to the board of trustees of Southern Illinois University, a post he continues to hold. He often visits schools and civic groups as a motivational speaker in the causes of education and increased minority participation in the aviation industry. His advice is "work hard and success will come because now most things are possible. Aim for excellence and give your best to every job you attempt."

## Sources

"Breakthrough on the Airlines." *Ebony* (November 1965): 112–114, 116, 118–119.

Innis, Doris Funnye, and Juliana Wu. *Profiles in Black: Biographical Sketches of 100 Living Black Unsung Heroes*. New York: CORE Publications, 1976; 12–13.

Norwood, William R. "A Guiding Brotherhood." *Airline Pilot* (February 1989): 26–28.

White, Frank, III. "Spreading Their Wings." *Ebony* (February 1986): 75–76, 78, 82.

*Who's Who among African Americans*. New York: Gale Research, 1999.

# P

## James L.H. Peck

**Full Name at Birth:** James Lincoln Holt Peck

**Born:** September 8, 1912, Stoops Ferry, Pennsylvania

**Died:** February 6, 1996, El Cajon or San Diego, California

**Education:** Westinghouse High School, Pittsburgh; Peabody High School, Pittsburgh, 1928(?); University of Pittsburgh, 1928(?)–1930(?); Curtiss-Wright flight school, Bettis Field, Pittsburgh, 1930; Institute of Aviation, Cleveland, Ohio, 1931(?).

**Positions Held:** drummer, Alphonso Trent's Victor Recording Orchestra, 1931–1935; aviation journalist, 1937–1996; first lieutenant pursuit pilot, Republican Air Force, Spain, 1937; elevator operator, Pittsburgh, 1937–1940(?); aviation editor and syndicated columnist, Associated Negro Press, 1940(?)–1942; associate editor, *Air News*, 1942–1943; lieutenant, United States Merchant Marine, 1943–1945; correspondent, *Popular Science*, 1945–1947; Space Technology Laboratories, 1959(?); senior engineering writer, Aerospace Corp., 1959(?)–early 1960s; engineering, marketing and public relations writer,

TRW Systems, 196(?)–1971(?); B-1 bomber project, North American, 1972; retired from aerospace industry, 1981.

**Awards, Honors:** Spanish military honors, 1937; certificate of appreciation for contribution to Project Mercury, Aerospace Corporation, 1963.

**Summary:** The first African American "ace" pilot, James L.H. Peck flew with the Republican (Loyalist) Air Force during the Spanish Civil War in 1937. Subsequently, he became a leading aviation journalist. He was employed in the aerospace industry for many years and was the first African American to serve at Cape Canaveral in an engineering capacity.

### Early Years

The only son of James William and Clara Maria (Demmey) Peck, James "Jimmie" Lincoln Holt Peck was born in Stoops Ferry, Pennsylvania, a few miles from Pittsburgh. From a field near the Pecks' home, some World War I pilots flew passenger planes. "I guess this is where the flying bug bit me," Peck would recall. He was about nine years old.

Going on to high school in Pittsburgh,

Peck was known as a "better-than-average" trap drummer and "a first-class student."

## Higher Education

The "flying bug" stayed with him: after his high school graduation, Peck enrolled at the University of Pittsburgh, but he left after his sophomore year to enroll in the Curtiss-Wright flight school at Bettis Field. He earned his pilot's license at Bettis in 1930. Completing further studies at the Institute of Aviation in Cleveland, Ohio, Peck applied to the U.S. Army Air Corps and the Naval Air Service, but was rejected by both: the United States military air services were not open to African Americans in the early 1930s.

## Career Highlights

Peck became a drummer with Alphonso Trent's Victor Recording Orchestra, with which he toured the country from 1931 to 1935. Although he flew occasionally and continued his studies of aviation, he did not return to full-time research until 1936. His first aviation article, "Relation of the Human Element to Safe Flying," was published in *Aero Digest* in May 1937.

Also in 1936, the Spanish Civil War broke out. Many Americans and Britons volunteered to fight against General Francisco Franco, who was supported by Hitler and Mussolini. Peck and other Americans sailed to France in August 1937 and crossed the Pyrenees Mountains on foot to enter Valencia. There they witnessed and endured "the war's worst [air] raid up to that time, lasting three hours." Later, Peck wrote that the bombardment made the war become personal to him, not simply an opportunity to fly good planes.

As a lieutenant pursuit pilot in the Republican Air Force, Peck took part in "seven combats, 40 convoy missions, five strafing missions and 11 attacks on Italian and other Fascist vessels." He was credited with five victories against German and Italian fighters, including two Heinkel 51s and three Fiats, and thereby became America's first African American ace. Allen Herr in *American Aviation Historical Society Journal* (Fall 1977) writes that Peck's stories "are not corroborated by any known Spanish or American source on aviation in the Spanish Civil War." Honorably discharged in December 1937, Peck returned to the United States "with a full scrapbook, many tales, and pleasant memories of a France and Spain in which there exists little color discrimination." Late in his life, Peck referred to "the Spanish experience" as "a relatively short, hectic, interesting, and, of course, exciting part of my 'other life.'"

Peck viewed aviation journalism as his major contribution, and on his return from Spain, he devoted himself to becoming an expert in the field, supporting himself with a job as an elevator operator in a Pittsburgh department store. "Flying in the Spanish Air Force" appeared in *Sportsman Pilot* in February 1938.

A series of articles in the *Pittsburgh Courier* in July 1939 sounded the trumpet call: "Will Negro Aviators Ever Fly U.S. War Planes?" Peck discussed the training programs of the Army Air Corps and Civilian Aviation Authority and the difficulties inherent for African Americans, who were still barred from U.S. military aviation.

Peck also warned the U.S. Army Air Corps in 1939 that the German pursuit planes against which he had fought in Spain were notably better than the Curtiss P-40 fighters with which the Americans were preparing to enter the war. His concern fell on deaf ears.

His first full-length book, *Armies with Wings*, appeared in January 1940 and was hailed as "one of the better books on wartime flying." A later critic would describe Peck's style as "poetic" and liken him to French aviator/writer Antoine de Saint-Exupéry. Although the book comprised a discussion of contemporary military aviation in general, describing the construction of different types of aircraft and changes in military tactics and air power, Peck included material from his Spanish Civil War journal, since the Loyalist pilots flew many types of European airplanes.

Peck wrote prolifically, and his articles appeared in *Harper's* ("579 Miles an Hour, Vertical"), *Science Digest* ("Weapons of the War Planes," "Defense against Air Attack"), *The New York Times* ("Dogfight—A Lifetime in Forty Minutes") and *Scientific American* ("America's Winged Weapons") during 1939 and 1940. He married his first wife, Nellie Schorr, on October 16, 1940.

In December 1940 a pivotal article, "When Do *We* Fly?" appeared in *The Crisis*, the monthly magazine of the NAACP. Peck examined discrepancies regarding the Air Corps' stated intentions to enlist African Americans once the Civilian Aeronautics Administration and National Youth Administration had completed their training. Peck noted that many African American students had completed CAA training, yet they still were rejected by the Air Corps. Other newspapers also headlined the issue. The mounting outcry helped to influence the War Department and the Air Corps that more specific action toward the establishment of an African American flight squadron was necessary. The training program for the 99th Pursuit Squadron was established at Tuskegee in 1941.

Peck's syndicated column, *Plane Talk*, reached more than 100 newspapers through the Associated Negro Press, of which he was the aviation editor.

Peck's second book, *So You're Going to Fly*, appeared in 1941. Intended for young people interested in aviation, the book describes the successive stages of flight training, then discusses military and commercial aviation.

In 1942 he became associate editor of *Air News*, and co-authored the *Air News Yearbook* in 1943. He served also as a lieutenant in the U.S. Merchant Marine, having "de-

clined," according to author John Holway, "to submit to the prejudice in Alabama" by joining the Air Corps program at Tuskegee. His articles continued to appear in *Popular Science* ("How Aircraft Instruments Work," March 1944, "Tomorrow's Fighters?" April 1945) and *Air News* ("Warplanes in Peace," September 1944) throughout his Merchant Marine service.

Shortly after his discharge from the Merchant Marine, Peck broke the first story about radar, first as a broadcast report over CBS on August 14, 1945, then as a *Popular Science* article in September. On the occasion of Peck's appointment as aviation correspondent for *Popular Science* in 1945, he was complimented by a member of the Army Air Forces' planning staff, who had found Peck to be the "most-quoted aviation writer in the English language" and one whose work was reprinted in translation in technical and general aeronautical magazines "from the Dutch Netherlands to Latin America." Many years later, Peck would define his postwar magazine work as his "real contribution," both through his *Popular Science* articles and his freelance work.

Beginning with "Radar: Magic Eye That Sees the Invisible" in the September 1945 issue of *Popular Science*, articles on a range of aviation and aeronautical subjects appeared throughout the late 1940s and early 1950s. Peck chronicled the development of military aviation in the aftermath of World War II and during the years of the Korean conflict in pieces such as "Atomic Age Air Force" (*Air Trails*, December 1948), "Supersonic Combat: Today's Armament and Tactics Cannot Meet the Demands of Jet Aircraft" (*Ordnance*, March/April 1950), and a series of articles in *Flying*: "If War Comes" (December 1951, with C.H. Goodlin), "Stalin's New Storm Bomber" (February 1952), and "General Ike's Air Force" (March 1952). Advances in military and aviation technology were explained to the general reader in "Radar of the Deep, Sonar" (*Popular Science*, November 1945), "Underground Exploring by

Air" (*Popular Science*, August 1946), "They Call It Tac" (*Flying*, May 1952) and "Body Armor" (*New Frontiers*, Spring 1956). Peck also wrote pieces of a more general nature, such as "You Can Be Hypnotized" (*Our World*, September 1949) and "Tools—The Measure of Man's Progress" (*New Frontiers*, Spring 1957).

Peck then moved into a more corporate and technical realm—a "different and more important contribution," in his words—working in the aerospace industry from 1959 to 1981. Employed by Space Technology Laboratories (STL) in the late 1950s, Peck was, he later said, "the first—and for three years the only—black to serve at Cape Canaveral in any engineering capacity." While employed as senior engineering writer at Aerospace Corporation in El Segundo, California, in the early 1960s, Peck wrote and edited technical works under Air Force contracts, including *Trends and Future Developments in Aerospace Materials* (1961); *Range Data Books* for Pacific Missile Range and White Sands Missile Range (1962–1963). Peck would later recall that his most interesting assignment at Aerospace was as a member of the Booster Acceptance Team for the Mercury and Gemini manned space programs. "In this capacity I got to know all the original astronauts," he recalled. "I wrote comprehensive program reports [which were] all classified at the time. . . . highly technical, state-of-the-art documents."

Peck then spent 11 years with TRW Systems, based in California, serving in the "engineering, marketing (proposals) and public relations sides of the house." Peck noted a difference in his treatment, over time, on visits to the Cape Canaveral area: "When I first went there in late 1959 for STL I stayed at the Patrick Air Force Base Officers Quarters; couldn't stop at any motel in Cocoa Beach. When I returned there in 1966 as a TRW public relations rep, I had a suite at the Colony, the newest and best hotel there." One of his assignments for TRW was, in 1967, to head data management for the "Model 35"

spacecraft project, a spy satellite then in development. Peck also continued to write highly technical operating handbooks for projects such as a space simulation system.

By 1972, Peck had left Aerospace and was working on a B-1 bomber project at North American. He retired from the aerospace industry in 1981 but continued to write. Late in 1994, Peck and his wife, Dorothy, moved to El Cajon, California. At the time of his death in 1996, Peck was working on *Bomber One: The B-1 Story*, for Paragon House. It remains unpublished.

Peck was a member of the National Aeronautic Association, the Aircraft Owners and Pilots Association, the American Fighter Aces Association, the National Airmen's Association of America, the League of American Writers, and the Aviation Writers Association.

No obituary could be located.

## Sources

Holway, John B. *Red Tails Black Wings: The Men of America's Black Air Force*. Las Cruces, NM: Yucca Tree Press, 1997; 37–39, 50.

Jakeman, Robert J. *The Divided Skies: Establishing Segregated Flight Training at Tuskegee, Alabama, 1934–1942*. Tuscaloosa: University of Alabama Press, 1992; 191–193, 227.

Landis, Arthur H. "American Flyers in Spanish Skies." *Air Combat* (March 1975): 20–25, 72–74.

Peck, James L.H. *Armies with Wings*. New York: Dodd, Mead and Co., 1940.

Peck, James L.H. "Dogfight–A Lifetime in Forty Minutes." *New York Times Magazine* (May 26, 1940): 4, 20.

Peck, James L.H., El Cajon, California, to Betty Kaplan Gubert, New York, New York. December 15, 1994.

Peck, James L.H., San Diego, California, to Betty Kaplan Gubert, New York, New York. February 26, 1993; undated 1993.

Peck, James L.H. "When Do We Fly?" *The Crisis* (December 1940): 376–378, 388.

"Peck, James L(incoln) H(olt)." *Current Biography*. New York: H.W. Wilson, 1942; 653–655.

Sandler, Stanley. *Segregated Skies: All-Black Combat Squadrons of World War II*. Washington, DC: Smithsonian Institution Press, 1992; 1–3.

# Frank E. Petersen Jr.

Frank E. Petersen Jr. Courtesy of National Air and Space Museum, Smithsonian Institution (SI Neg. No. 99-40511).

**Full Name at Birth:** Frank Emmanuel Petersen Jr.

**Born:** March 2, 1932, Topeka, Kansas

**Education:** B.S., George Washington University, Washington, D.C., 1967; M.S. in international affairs; 1973; graduated from the National War College, 1973.

**Positions Held:** Marine pilot, Korea, 1953; squadron leader, VMFA-314, the Black Knights Squadron, 1968–1969; tactical air planner/programmer, Office of the Deputy Chief of Staff for Aviation, 1969–1971. Special adviser in charge of recruitment of African American officers, 1971–1975; group commander, Cherry Point, North Carolina; 1975–1979; deputy director for operations, Joint Chiefs of Staff, 1979–1982; commanding general, Marine Corps Development and Education Command, Quantico, Virginia;

retired 1988; vice-president, DuPont Facilities Services, 1988–1997.

**Awards, Honors:** Distinguished Flying Cross, 1953; Purple Heart, 1968; Air Medal, Navy Commendation Medal, Gray Eagle Award, U.S. Navy, 1988; Silver Hawk Award, U.S. Marines.

**Summary:** Frank E. Petersen Jr. was the first black Marine aviator, the first black squadron leader, the first black base commander, and the highest ranking black general in the Marine Corps. He was active in recruiting promising black candidates into the Marine Corps and fostering their careers. He retired in 1988 after 38 years in the Marine Corps.

## Early Years

Frank E. Petersen Jr. was born in Topeka, Kansas, on March 2, 1932, the second child of Frank E. Petersen Sr. and Edythe Southard. He had an older sister, Anne, and two younger brothers, William and Hans. The elder Petersen had emigrated to the United States from St. Croix, in the U.S. Virgin Islands, as a young man. Southard had grown up in the small town of Syracuse, Kansas, where she and her two sisters were the only black children in the local school.

At the time the young couple met, Petersen, by dint of hard work and perseverence, had worked his way up to freight car man for a railroad and Southard was attending the University of Kansas at Lawrence. Southard dropped out of school and they were married in December 1928. The Great Depression hit shortly afterward and Petersen was laid off. He took a correspondence course in repairing radios and started a successful radio repair business.

Both parents stressed the values of education and hard work. Petersen remembers his father as "a focused and aggressive man who took racial discrimination in stride and handled it by being independent and confident."

In the early years of their marriage, when finances were tight, Mrs. Petersen supplemented the family income by cooking and selling chicken dinners to neighbors. When the children were older, she completed her college education and became a teacher.

Young Petersen was fascinated by his father's work and soon mastered radio electronics under his tutelage. From his mother, he learned to enjoy reading and to use the public library, one of the institutions in Topeka that was not segregated.

Petersen worked during the summers, mowing lawns. He was also an avid reader and a Boy Scout. A gifted child, he was pulled from his segregated classroom and sent to an integrated "special school" for the academically talented at the start of junior high school. He resented this because it involved walking some five miles to school. Eventually he withdrew from this school and returned to the neighborhood school, disenchanted with the Topeka school system and the town generally.

His high school years added to the disillusionment. Though the school was "integrated," there were separate basketball teams for black and white players; separate proms, and two sets of homecoming kings and queens. Petersen's refuge from all this was St. John's AME Church, where he sang in the choir and participated in youth activities. Nevertheless, the young man wanted to get away from Topeka and decided to join the navy at 17, upon graduation from high school. He had a strong desire to "spread my wings . . . see the big world."

His parents refused to sign the papers that would enable him to enlist, and at their insistence, Petersen attended Washburn University, where, for a year, he says, "I just warmed the seat." He was determined to join the Navy, and when he turned 18, he enlisted. It was 1950, and the Korean War was just starting. Just two years earlier, President Truman had signed an executive order integrating the military.

Petersen passed the Navy entrance exam with the highest score ever recorded in that recruiting station—so high that the recruiting officer made him take it again, not believing that a black man could do so well. His score on retaking the test was even better. The recruiting officer then informed Petersen that he would make a "great steward."

Petersen reported this to his father, and though no one knows for sure what took place, in his next conversation with the recruiting officer he was offered placement at electronics technician school at Treasure Island, California.

## Career Highlights

It was at Treasure Island, after finishing boot camp, that Petersen heard of the death in Korea of Jesse Leroy Brown, the first black naval aviator, who had been killed in action. Though saddened by Brown's death, this news made him aware that a black man could aspire to be a pilot in the Navy, and he began to set his sights on flying. He applied for and was accepted for flight training.

Sent to the Naval Air Station in Pensacola, Florida, Petersen found himself the only black man in the program. He felt isolated, under constant scrutiny, and one of his instructors was abusive. He also encountered southern institutionalized racism—separate drinking fountains and rest rooms, seating in the back of buses, not being permitted to frequent restaurants and nightclubs where his white fellow cadets were welcome. Petersen mustered his resolve to succeed despite these circumstances. A chance encounter with Daniel "Chappie" James, a black Army Air Corps captain (later to become the first black four-star general) allowed him to share his fears and frustration and provided encouragement. He passed flight training successfully, was commissioned a second lieutenant, and became the nation's first black Marine aviator.

His troubles with racism were far from over. On reporting for duty, the sentry failed to salute him, and when he dropped by the officer's club he was arrested for impersonating an officer. These were but a few of the instances of racism, some petty, some deeply disturbing, which marred Petersen's early Marine career, but, encouraged by Chappie James and inspired by his father's example, he rose above these occurrences and forged ahead.

Petersen served a stint as a fighter pilot in Korea, flying 64 combat missions in 1953, for which he received six combat medals and the Distinguished Flying Cross. Rotated back to the United States, he served in a number of progressively more responsible assignments.

The year 1954 was a decisive one in Petersen's life. It was in that year that he received training as a jet pilot. He also applied for and received a transfer from the Marine reserves into the regular Marine Corps. On a more personal note, he met Eleanor Burton, who was to become his first wife. They were married on February 18, 1955, and they subsequently had five children.

In 1968, Petersen became the first black squadron commander in the Marine Corps and was assigned leadership of the VMFA-314, the celebrated Black Knights Squadron, a squadron with an illustrious record. He led this squadron in Vietnam, flying 290 missions between May 1968 and February 1969. He earned a reputation as an officer who encouraged his men, who listened to their complaints and was aware of their problems. He was particularly celebrated for counseling young African American men under his command, earning the affectionate soubriquet of "Godfather." Under his command, the squadron received an award as the top fighter squadron in the Corps. In August 1968, his plane caught fire after an enemy attack, and he was wounded, for which he received the Purple Heart.

In July 1969, he was assigned duty as a tactical air planner/programmer in the office of the deputy chief of staff for aviation, in Washington, D.C. In 1971, he became special adviser to the commandant in charge of the recruitment of African American officers. In this capacity, he joined a team led by Assistant Secretary of Defense Frank Render to tour military installations abroad and investigate race relations.

In this position, Petersen was highly visible and became a target for hostility from defenders of the status quo. In 1973, baseless charges were brought against him in an attempt to remove and silence him. Petersen fought back, and he was able to prove that these accusations were without foundation. However, by this time, his marriage, already stressed by his frequent absences, finally came apart.

In July 1975, Petersen was promoted to full colonel, and later that year he married Alicia Downes, adopting her small daughter, Monique. In October 1975, he became group commander of the Marine installation at Cherry Point, with responsibility for training pilots and crew members—another first. As Petersen was responsible for training Marines on the vertical takeoff Harrier aircraft, he had to learn to fly these new planes himself, which involved new flying skills. He was successful and ultimately qualified in carrier landings in the Harrier. This was yet another milestone.

In 1979, he was promoted to brigadier general, becoming the first black Marine to achieve flag rank. He was then assigned to the Pentagon as a deputy director for operations under the Joint Chiefs of Staff. It was while he was on this watch that the American embassy in Tehran, Iran, was taken over by militants who held 90 people hostage, 63 of them American. Petersen's assignment was to coordinate military and State Department activities surrounding this crisis. He received a Superior Service Medal for his handling of this matter.

After a stint back at Marine headquarters, his next assignment, in 1982, was as assistant wing commander of the First Marine Aircraft Wing, stationed in Okinawa. This was followed by a tour of duty as second in command at Headquarters, Fleet Marine Force Atlantic, in Alexandria, Virginia.

The culmination of his career arrived in 1986, when Petersen was promoted to lieutenant general and put in charge of Marine Corps Base in Quantico. As commanding general of the Marine Corps Development and Education Command, he had ultimate responsibility for the training of all Marine personnel.

While Petersen was on this assignment, he was the convening authority, responsible for investigating two high-profile court martial cases. The first was the retrial of a black corporal, Lindsay Scott, who was accused of raping a white woman. The second case involved Clayton Lonetree, a Native American Marine Corps sergeant accused of espionage. This case was potentially explosive and required tactful handling to ascertain the facts and attain a fair trial for Lonetree.

In 1988, after serving for 38 years, General Petersen retired from the military. Petersen summed up his career in the military to an interviewer from *Ebony* in 1986: "I would have to say . . . I had a hell of a lot of luck."

While still on active duty, he had been recruited by the DuPont Corporation. He joined the corporation upon leaving the military, becoming director of education and training. Eventually, Petersen was promoted to vice president, DuPont Facilities Services, Corporate Aviation. He retired from this position in 1997. He remains active, however, on the boards of many corporations and charitable organizations, including the National Aviation Research Foundation, Higher Education Assistance Foundation, Opportunity Skyway, and Business Executives for National Security.

## Sources

Fleming, Robert. "Col. Frank Petersen: The 'Godfather'—in Line for Star Rank." *Encore* (April 2, 1979): 22.

Huntington, Tom. "An Eagle's Wings." *Air and Space* (June–July 1988): 102–105.

Laluntus, N. "Col. Frank E. Petersen Becomes the First Black Marine Corps General." *Eagle & Swan* 2, 2 (May 1979): 44.

Petersen, Frank E. with J. Alfred Phelps. *Into the Tiger's Jaw: America's First Black Marine Aviator.* Novato, CA: Presidio Press, 1998.

"Top Man at Quantico." *Ebony* (December 1986): 140, 144, 146.

*Who's Who among African Americans, 1996–1997.* 9th ed. Detroit: Gale Research, 1996.

# James O. Plinton Jr.

James O. Plinton Jr. Courtesy of Photographs and Prints Division, Schomburg Center for Research in Black Culture, The New York Public Library. Astor, Lenox and Tilden Foundations.

**Full Name at Birth:** James O. Plinton Jr.

**Born:** July 22, 1914, Westfield, New Jersey

**Died:** July 4, 1996, Lake Wales, Florida

**Education:** B.S. in biology, Lincoln University, Lincoln, Pennsylvania, 1935; University of Newark's Department of Aeronautics,

Newark, New Jersey, commercial pilot's license and instructor's rating, 1940–1941.

**Positions Held:** Flight instructor, U.S. Army Air Corps, Tuskegee, Alabama, 1941–1944; co-founder of Ecuador's national airline, ANDESA, 1944; part owner and chief pilot for Quisqueya Ltd. (Haiti and Jamaica), 1946–1948; owner of Haitian-American Dry Cleaners and Laundry Services, 1948–1956; executive assistant to the director of personnel and industrial relations, Trans World Airlines (TWA), August 1957; vice president for special marketing affairs, Eastern Airlines, May 1971; vice president for marketing development, Eastern, 1976–1979.

**Awards, Honors:** National Order of Honor and Merit and National Order of Labor, Haiti, 1950s; Honorary Doctorate of Laws, Fisk University, Nashville, Tennessee, 1978; Honorary Doctorate in Aeronautical Science, Embry-Riddle Aeronautical Institute, Miami, Florida: Distinguished Service Award, Lincoln University; Outstanding Man of the Year Award in Marketing, Long Island University, Outstanding Achievement in Aviation, Negro Airmen International (NAI).

**Summary:** During his 40 years in aviation, James O. Plinton Jr. was often the first African American to break the field's color barriers. He was one of the first flight instructors at the Tuskegee Army Air Field during World War II. In 1957, he became the first black corporate executive in a major airline, TWA. In 1971 he achieved an even higher position, vice president, at Eastern Airlines, which made him the highest-ranking black in the airline industry. His efforts encouraged the airlines to open their ranks to other African Americans.

### Early Years

James O. Plinton Jr. born on July 22, 1914, in Westfield, New Jersey, one of four children of Mary E. Williams Plinton and James

O. Plinton Sr. Their father owned his own dental laboratory. He believed strongly in hard work, while their mother stressed the values of religion and education. "Mom taught us to love. Dad taught us to make wish conform to will, until wish and will became one," recalled Plinton (*Ebony* 1976). Plinton and his brother were often required to assist their father in his 12- to 14-hour workdays, six days a week. The habit of hard work remained with Plinton throughout his life. He considered it not only a gift from God but also the key factor in his success. "You accomplish things that way," was how Plinton put it at the end of his career (*Black Collegian* 1978). While still a youngster he was enthralled by the idea of flight, and he saw becoming a pilot as the answer to his longing to see far-away places.

### Higher Education

Plinton enrolled at Lincoln University, Lincoln, Pennsylvania, thinking of becoming a doctor, as his father wished. But Plinton always wanted to fly. "When I was at Lincoln, a big Saturday night would be a trip to the theater in a nearby town. As we all piled into a friend's car, most of the guys avoided the rumble seat because it was so windy back there. But I loved it, because I had bought a helmet and some goggles, and I would sit back there and pretend that I was flying." (*Ebony* 1976). (A rumble seat was recessed into the luggage area in the back of cars of the 1930s and 1940s, and its hinged cover became the seat back.) During his years at Lincoln, Plinton went out for varsity soccer, wrestling, tennis, and track. He belonged to the Dramatic Society, the glee club, and he was the president of the German Society.

Plinton graduated in 1935 with a degree in biology but he did not go on to medical school. He taught biology, chemistry, and English at Kimball High School in West Virginia for a short time. He served in the U.S. Merchant Marines, traveling to South America in 1936. The next year, he taught music and fencing in Plainfield, New Jersey, and in 1938, he was appointed to its post office. The University of Newark had a Civilian Pilot Training Program (CPTP) in which Plinton enrolled in 1939. The government had established the CPTP on college campuses to provide pilot manpower, as it was now almost certain that war was near. Plinton, the only African American in his class of 35 students, was warned how hard it would be to get through secondary training. He completed both parts, however, with honors. He then became one of the six men, out of 200 candidates, to receive further training as a flight instructor. He earned both his commercial pilot's license and flight instructor's rating from the University of Newark in 1940.

## Career Highlights

In February 1941, Plinton began what would be his 40-year career in aviation. He was sent to Tuskegee Army Air Field as one of the first black flight instructors. The others were C. Alfred Anderson, Fred Hutcherson, and Perry Young. There he trained 150 pilots, many of whom were part of the 99th Pursuit Squadron. This squadron, along with others, saw aerial combat in World War II, and were known as the Tuskegee Airmen. One of his students was Daniel "Chappie" James Jr., who became America's first African American four-star general. Plinton's leadership qualities were evident, and by the end of 1943, he was assistant director of Tuskegee's Division of Aeronautics, in charge of the War Training Service Program. He was also named manager of Tuskegee Airport no. 1. As the war began winding down, Plinton began thinking about a civilian career in aviation. He knew that opportunities would be limited in the United States, still a strictly segregated society, so he turned his sights to the Caribbean and South America.

In 1944, Plinton and a friend helped establish ANDESA, the national airline of Ecuador, by raising funds, purchasing planes, and training pilots. Invited in 1946 by the Haitian government to establish an air service, Plinton became part owner and chief pilot of Quisqueya (a Spanish-Indian term for Haiti) Ltd. Based in Kingston, Jamaica, Quisqueya began operations in June 1947, flying both passengers and cargo among the islands of the Caribbean.

Plinton, a man of great energy and devoted to hard work, found time for other entrepreneurial pursuits. In 1948, he opened the Haitian-American Dry Cleaners, the first such establishment in Haiti. A modern speedy laundry service was added, with equipment and parts flown in from the United States. The business grew to encompass 16 branches, and grossed about $250,000 annually. In 1952, he married Kathryn Hancock, who was working as a secretary to the consul general of the Netherlands. They had two children, James O. Norman, born about 1955, and Kathryn Ann, born about 1959. Mrs. Plinton died in 1993. On visits to the United States, Plinton gave enthusiastic speeches about business opportunities in Haiti, and he extolled the island as a tourist destination. For these efforts the Haitian government awarded him the National Order of Honor and Merit, equivalent to a knighthood, as well as the National Order of Labor.

After the Haitian army seized control of the government in 1956, the Plintons remained in the country for a few months before returning home. After 11 years abroad, and with over 5,000 miles of flying time, Plinton decided to try to break into commercial aviation. He contacted Robert Buck, a childhood friend who was then a captain for Trans World Airlines (TWA). Buck introduced him to Carter Burgess, TWA's president. After interviews and Plinton's successful participation in a problem-solving session, he was hired in August 1957 as executive assistant to the director of personnel and industrial relations. He thus became the first African American executive to work for a major airline in the United States. Plinton recalled, "I had to develop an image which would make it difficult, if not impossible, for an individual to say a black man could not hold an executive position with a major airline . . . I had to prove my ability to get the job done at that level."

Plinton's ability, attitude, and confidence assured his frequent promotions. He moved from working directly with the president of the company to working with the chairman of the board. He then became senior director of special marketing, which included the growing international markets. In 1964, Plinton achieved the considerable feat of gaining landing rights for TWA in the countries of the East African Federation: Kenya, Tanzania, and Uganda. His skills in diplomacy and negotiation captured the new market for TWA as it competed with Pan American Airways for the rights. Perhaps the presence of a highly placed black man helped complete the transaction. Knowledge of East Africa led Plinton to organize a big-game hunting safari, in 1968, with four friends. This first all-black safari was described in *Ebony*, February 1969. Plinton also traveled to Nigeria to assist with the development of the airport at Lagos. He established business ties between Lagos and Oklahoma City in a plan to encourage new and small businesses to expand their exports by using TWA for shipments and travel.

While still at TWA, Plinton devised a marketing plan he described as "a rifle-to-target approach instead of a shotgun approach." Air travel would be tailored to various economic levels, social interests, various professions, and ethnic groups. These segments could be further refined to suit foreign or domestic groups. But TWA rejected Plinton's plan and he was denied a promotion to a vice presidency position.

In May 1971, Plinton moved to Eastern Airlines, where he became vice president for Special Marketing Affairs, and saw his plan accepted. His position was then the highest ever achieved by an African American in the airline industry. *Black Enterprise*, September 1971, noted that of 3,182 senior officers and directors of the 50 largest companies in the United States, only 25 were black. Plinton rose at Eastern, too. In 1975, he became vice president for both urban and international affairs, a dual appointment, and in 1976, he was named vice president for marketing development. Here he reorganized Eastern's international division by consolidating the offices, then located in various cities, each headed by an individual executive. They were relocated to Eastern's headquarters in Miami, Florida, and placed under the supervision of a single executive. Plinton also increased opportunities for Caribbean travel, and he planned the company's three-year program to expand the number of pilots and flight personnel from East Africa. He retired from Eastern Airlines in 1979, but remained another year as special assistant, at the request of Frank Borman, Eastern's chairman and a former astronaut. Retired, Plinton became executive director of the Metropolitan Fellowship of Churches in Florida, and he also chaired the Tacolcy Economic Development Corporation, a nonprofit group of black business and professional leaders.

Plinton was an avid swimmer and jogger and was well known for his sense of humor. He was affiliated with many organizations as member or officer. Among them were: Negro Airmen International (1958–1996); Caribbean Tourism Association (director, 1972–1979); board member of Embry-Riddle Aeronautical University (1976–1996) and of the Miami Museum of Science and Space Transit (1988–1996). He was elected president of the national YMCA in 1973, and he held other positions in the organization until 1981. As a youth Plinton was denied membership in the Westfield YMCA because of his color, so it is fair to say this appointment was especially meaningful to him, and to American society as well. Plinton died of cancer on July 4, 1996.

## Sources

"Ex-GI Starts Haiti Airline." *Ebony* (February 1948): 28–30.

James, Dalton. "James O. Plinton Jr., Eastern Airlines." *Black Collegian* (March/April 1978): 47.

Johnson, Hershel. "Airline Pioneer." *Ebony* (November 1976): 103–104, 106, 108.

Salpukis, Agis. "James Plinton Jr., 81, Broke Color Barriers at U.S. Airlines." *New York Times* (July 14, 1996): 32.

Stuckey, Sheila A. "James O. Plinton Jr." in Jessie Carney Smith. *Notable Black American Men*. Detroit: Gale Research, 1999: 943–944.

Ward, Francis. "Jim Plinton's Flight to Corporate Success." *Black Enterprise* (September 1979): 59–60.

# William J. Powell

**Full Name at Birth:** William Jennifer

**Born:** July 1899, Henderson, Kentucky

**Died:** 1942, Sharon, Wyoming

**Education:** B.S. in electrical engineering, University of Illinois, Champaign, Illinois, 1922; Warren School of Aeronautics, Los Angeles, California, 1928.

**Positions Held:** Proprietor, automotive service stations, Chicago, Illinois, 1922–1928; founder and director, Bessie Coleman Aero Clubs, aviation pioneer, 1928–1938; founder and director, Craftsmen of Black Wings; editor and publisher, *Craftsman Aero-News*, Los Angeles, California, 1937–1938; film maker, Los Angeles California 1930s.

**Summary:** William J. Powell was a trailblazer in African American aviation. He devoted his productive years to encouraging black youth to become involved in aviation and related fields. He promoted African American involvement in aviation through establishing clubs, lecturing, staging air shows, and writing, including authorship of a book about his flying career, *Black Wings*.

## Early Years

William J. Powell was born in July 1899 in Henderson, Kentucky. Little is known of his early years, except that his surname was Jennifer. His father died when he was four years old, and his mother moved to Chicago, where she met and married a man named Powell. Powell, who is believed to have come originally from Arkansas, adopted William and his younger sister Edna.

Young Powell did very well in his new surroundings. He was bright and talented. He sang in the choir of the Ebenezer Baptist Church and learned to play the piano. He had a newspaper route as a youngster, impressing his customers with his punctuality. An excellent student, he received his elementary education at the Key School, and graduated from Wendell Phillips High School.

## Higher Education

Powell was accepted at the University of Illinois, Champaign, Illinois, but he interrupted his studies when the United States entered World War I in 1917. He volunteered for the army and was sent to Officers' Training School in Chillicothe, Ohio.

On completion of his training, he was assigned to the front lines in northern France. He served in the 317th Engineers and 365th Infantry Regiment. On the last day of the war, Powell was seriously injured in a poison gas attack. After a stay in the hospital, followed by a lengthy recovery period, he resumed his college career in Champaign. He financed the remainder of his schooling with money he had saved in the service.

His college years were very productive. He majored in electrical engineering, joined Alpha Phi Alpha fraternity, participated in the French Club, and started a student orchestra. He graduated in 1922, and he was the first black man appointed to the senior class alumni committee. It was at college that he met his future wife, Lucylle Hatchett, whom he married shortly after graduation.

## Career Highlights

Upon graduation, Powell returned to Chicago, where he soon became the successful proprietor of a gas station. By 1926, he is believed to have owned as many as six gas stations. Contemporary newspaper accounts inform us that he was among the first gas station owners to install hydraulic lifts. He was a member of the Masonic Lodge and sang in the choir of the Berean Baptist Church. Powell and his wife had two children, Bernardine, born in 1923, and William J. Powell Jr., born in 1927.

In August 1927, Powell traveled to Paris to attend the American Legion convention. Three months earlier, Lindbergh's solo flight across the Atlantic had caught the imagination of the world. Powell and a friend, Burrell Neely, visited the airfield at Le Bourget, where the historic flight had landed. The two men took their first airplane ride. In his autobiography, *Black Wings*, he says this was "the turning point" of his life. Powell had the vision to see that air travel was the wave of the future, and the foresight to want to open opportunities in this new enterprise for other African Americans.

Upon returning to Chicago, Powell sought to take flying lessons at a local flying school, but he was rejected on the grounds of race. Applying to the U.S. Army Air Corps, he was rejected again. Venturing further afield, he applied to several schools in different areas of the country by mail, clearly stating that he was African American. He was finally accepted at the Warren School in Los Angeles. He wound up his businesses in Chicago and moved to Los Angeles to enroll in the school in 1928.

Powell's plan, formulated with his friend Neely, was not just to become a flier himself but to create an organization that would train young black women and men for careers in aviation. In 1929, Neely joined Powell in California and together they formed the Bessie Coleman Aero Clubs, named after the charismatic Bessie Coleman. Coleman, popularly known as Queen Bess, was the first African American woman to gain a pilot's license. A woman famed for her daring, persistence, and skill, she had captured the imagination of African Americans, and had died in an aircraft accident at the height of her career. Perhaps because of the example of Coleman, throughout his whole life Powell was very supportive of women who wanted aviation careers.

James Herman Banning, a black aviator from Ames, Iowa, and, according to Powell's book, the first African American to become a licensed pilot, soon joined the group, as did several others who wished either to learn to fly or to pursue other careers in aviation.

The group rented office space, purchased a plane, and began training students immediately, but they soon encountered difficulties. Raising $10,000, the sum needed to become incorporated, was proving impossible. The small amounts they had been able to raise were dwindling rapidly. Then disaster struck. Their only plane was wrecked.

They managed to make a down payment on another plane, a Kinner Crown, which they proposed to fly to the Mississippi State Fair, in Jackson, where they had been guaranteed $2,500 to hold exhibitions. Banning and Powell set out, but they strayed off course and ended up in Mexico, out of gas, next to a body of water that they believed to be the Pacific Ocean.

Assuming their compass was in error, the two started trudging in the direction they believed was north. Their only provisions were two cans of tomatoes. The men spent four hours walking up the beach before they discovered that they were headed in the wrong direction. The two then headed back to the plane, where they spent the night in the cockpit. For four days they wandered without food or water. Their shoes were completely worn out, their provisions gone. At last,

Powell and Banning strayed into a small fishing village, San Felipe, where they were able to get help.

After many tribulations, Powell managed to organize the First All-Negro Air Show, on Labor Day, 1931, at the old East Side Los Angeles Airport. It was a roaring success, attended by 15,000 people. The profits were used to benefit the unemployed of the city.

On December 6, the group staged another air show at the East Side Airport, which was attended by 40,000 people. This day was memorable because it marked the first time seven African American pilots—the Blackbirds—were all in the air at one time. The seven, in order of takeoff, were Irvin Wells, Bill Aikens, Hubert Julian, William B. Johnson, Mathew J. Campana, Marie Dickerson, and Powell himself.

Powell next entered a National Air Derby, competing for the first time against white pilots, who were flying planes that were far superior to his. The race was from Los Angeles to Cleveland, but Powell and Irvin Wells, who was to join him in the flight, decided to proceed on to New York after the race. If successful, this venture would make them the first African American pilots to make a transcontinental flight.

The first lap of their flight went well, and they landed in Yuma, Arizona. The next morning, after repairing a broken gas line, they took off for Tucson, Arizona. On this leg of the flight, they had trouble gaining altitude, and one of the valves started to malfunction.

They managed to repair this and arrived in Tucson on schedule. But there was more trouble in Tucson; further repairs were needed, which delayed their departure to the next destination, El Paso. They did manage to leave eventually but did not arrive at El Paso that night, as they had no lights on the aircraft. After an emergency landing and more repairs, they slept in the plane, taking off the next morning. Gaining El Paso, they repaired more parts, and took off for the next lap, to Roswell, New Mexico.

They never made it. The motor failed as they went through the Sacramento Mountains, and they crash landed. Miraculously, both walked away without a scratch. Even the plane proved to be salvageable, although it had to be disassembled and hauled away.

Powell's next project involved a transcontinental race between two teams of black aviators, to be called the Negro Air Derby. The teams were to consist of Banning and Thomas C. Allen in the first plane and Powell and Wells in the second. Powell and Wells were to return to California, where the race was to commence. Unfortunately, Banning and Allen took advantage of the other men, leaving California while the two were en route from El Paso.

Banning and Allen, calling themselves the Flying Hoboes, successfully completed their flight. Three weeks after they had started, they arrived at Valley Stream, New York, on October 9, 1932, to a hero's welcome. The first African Americans to span the United States—actual flying time was 41 hours—decided to stage an exhibition tour of the United States. Their plans were shattered when they made a forced landing on the way to a show at Pittsburgh. They could not raise enough money to pay for repairs to the plane, and they returned to Los Angeles by bus.

Powell was chagrined that Banning and Allen had achieved the successful transcontinental flight he had always dreamed of making.

Several lucrative job offers were made to Powell, but he tenaciously clung to his idea of inspiring African American youth to explore the career possibilities of aviation. To this end, he and his group put on a play written by Powell, called *Ethiopia Spreads Her Wings*. It was a success and aroused great interest in flying among black people all over the United States.

Powell was a visionary. He had the imagination and foresight to see that aviation was in a formative stage and was going to grow exponentially. He saw a future for young African Americans that would include black-owned airlines and airfields—a network that would employ countless African American youths and open opportunities never before dreamed of. To this end, he wrote a book, *Black Wings*, which was published in 1934. The book, actually an autobiography although written in the third person as Bill Brown, chronicled his aviation experiences.

In *Black Wings*, Powell foresaw many future opportunities in aviation for African Americans. He exhorted black people to become aware of the opportunities awaiting them: "Negro leaders—why do you sleep? Black men and black women—arouse your imaginations. Act before it is too late. Do not let the aviation industry become completely monopolized . . . by other races who will only give you and me the most menial jobs . . . but get into aviation now while we have a chance to have black airplane manufacturers, black airplane designers, black airplane distributors, owners of black transport lines, and have thousands of black boys and black girls profitably employed in a great paying industry."

Powell made a documentary film, *Unemployment, the Negro and Aviation*, some time in the 1930s. He founded Craftsmen of Black Wings, under whose aegis he published the *Craftsman Aero-News*. This trade journal, which was published in 1937 and 1938, contained technical articles on flying and trends in aviation. But the emphasis was always on recruiting youth, and the journal featured articles of interest to young people. It also offered scholarships for free technical training for young African Americans.

In his effort to recruit young people, Powell endeavored to enlist rich and famous African Americans in his cause, among them Duke Ellington, the great jazz artist, and Joe Louis, then heavyweight champion of the world and a hero in the black community. He also spoke and lectured to black ministers and church leaders to persuade them that flying was not a frivolous hobby but the wave of the future.

Powell saw himself as a loyal American who had served his country, but he wanted the nation to abandon the discrimination and prejudice that kept African Americans poor and dependent. His solution was to train and recruit young people, and to build black-owned businesses that would employ them. This would lead to financial independence and eliminate the necessity of "continually begging the white people for jobs."

Intensely interested in civil rights issues, he became involved in the struggle of African American motion picture actors to improve their working conditions. He wrote several articles in the *Craftsman Aero-News* in support of this group. This may have led him to involve himself in the Negro Motion Picture Players Association, which he and eight others incorporated in the state of California in 1939.

After 1938, Powell disappeared from the public scene and little is known of his last years. His health failing, he was admitted to the Veterans Hospital in Sharon, Wyoming, and there he died, surrounded by his wife and children.

Powell did not see his plans come to fruition, but he lived to see the black pilots admitted to the U.S. Army Air Corps in 1941. A prophet ahead of his time, he wrote, in the preface to *Black Wings*: "Aviation is just beginning its period of growth and if we get into it now . . . we can grow as aviation grows." He confidently predicted, at the time the book was published in 1934, that "very soon air travel will be as common as railroad transportation is today."

## Sources

"Aviation." *Opportunity* (September 1932): 291.

"Aviation." *Opportunity* 15, 5 (May 1937): 156.

*Black Aviator: The Story of William J. Powell*. A new edition of William J. Powell's 1934 *Black Wings* with an introduction by Von Hardesty. Washington, DC: Smithsonian Institution Press. 1994.

Corn, Joseph J. *The Winged Gospel: America's Romance with Aviation 1900–1950*. New York: Oxford University Press, 1983.

"Two Negro Pilots Forced Down in Lower California." *Los Angeles Times* (November 2, 1929): 2, 10.

# Wendell O. Pruitt

**Full Name at Birth:** Wendell Oliver Pruitt

**Born:** June 20, 1920, St. Louis, Missouri

**Died:** April 15, 1945, Tuskegee, Alabama

**Education:** Charles Sumner High School, St. Louis, 1937; Stowe Teachers College, 1937–1938; Lincoln University, Jefferson City, Missouri, 1941; Advanced Flying School, U.S. Army Air Corps, Tuskegee, Alabama, December 13, 1942.

**Positions Held:** Commissioned lieutenant in U.S. Army Air Corps, December 13, 1942; captain, and combat pilot, 332nd Fighter Group, 302nd Squadron; flight instructor, Tuskegee Army Air Field.

**Awards, Honors:** Distinguished Flying Cross; Air Medal with six oak leaf clusters. Honored with Captain Wendell O. Pruitt Day, St. Louis, December 12, 1944; Wendell O. Pruitt Military Academy, St. Louis, opened 1984; Pruitt-Igoe housing project, St. Louis; Captain Wendell O. Pruitt Memorial American Veterans (AMVETS) Post no. 41, St. Louis.

**Summary:** One of the outstanding World War II combat pilots commissioned at Tuskegee, Pruitt saw action with the 332nd Fighter Group in the Mediterranean. He was credited with destroying three enemy planes in the air and eight on the ground. With another fighter pilot, Pruitt was credited with sinking a German destroyer, an action thought to be impossible for fighter planes.

## Early Years

The youngest of Elijah and Melanie Pruitt's 10 children, Wendell Oliver Pruitt attended Simmons and Marshall elementary schools in St. Louis. Mechanically inclined from an early age, Pruitt enjoyed building radios and repairing bicycles and, later, cars. As a student at Charles Sumner High School, he was active in the Spanish club and developed his musical and acting talents as a member of the a capella choir, the glee club, and the Robeson dramatic club. He graduated from Sumner in 1937.

## Higher Education

After studying at Stowe Teachers College for a year, Pruitt was matriculated at Lincoln University in Jefferson City, Missouri. Through the civil pilot training program at Lincoln, Pruitt received flight instruction at Jefferson City Airport and obtained his private pilot's license. He graduated from Lincoln in 1941 and was accepted into the U.S. Army Air Corps flying school at Tuskegee, Alabama. Training included several months each of preflight, primary flying, basic flying, advanced flying, and gunnery school.

Pruitt graduated from Tuskegee on December 13, 1942, and he was commissioned as a lieutenant in the U.S. Army Air Corps.

## Career Highlights

Pruitt was then assigned to the 332nd Fighter Group, stationed at Selfridge Air Base, Michigan. The 332nd conducted fighter training there until they were transferred to the Mediterranean theater in December 1943. They were assigned to coastal patrol and the support of ground troops, dive-bombing and strafing throughout the spring of 1944. At the end of May, the 332nd was transferred to the 15th Strategic Air Force and assigned to bomber escort duty, using new P-47 Thunderbolt fighter planes.

Pruitt's first victory occurred on June 9, 1944. Pruitt described the action as follows:

> We were assigned to fly top cover for heavy bombers. On approaching the Udine area [in northeastern Italy], a flock of Me-109's were observed mak-

ing attacks from 5 o'clock on a formation of B-24's. Each enemy aircraft
made a pass at the bombers and fell
into a left rolling turn. As the Jerries
[German planes] passed under me, I
rolled over, shoved everything forward
and closed in on one ME-109 at about
475 miles per hour. I gave him a short
burst of machine gun fire, found I was
giving him too much lead so I waited
as he shallowed out of a turn. Then I
gave two long two-second bursts. I saw
his left wing burst into flame. The
plane exploded and went straight into
the ground, but the pilot bailed out
safely.

In all, the group was credited with five victories during that mission.

A fellow pilot would remember Pruitt as
"daring, . . . [with] a little bit of the rogue in
him. He didn't mind breaking regulations
with his flying and did things the higher authorities didn't approve. He was the best we
had in the skies at that time. On the ground
Pruitt was a quiet, unassuming man. He just
flew loud."

Together with his wingman, Lee "Buddy"
Archer, Pruitt was known in the squadron as
"The Gruesome Twosome." Archer would
recall, "If there was any way we could fly to-
gether, we did. . . . We were the two 'Hip
Cats,' because we were both from big cities."

On June 25, 1944, Pruitt was one of a
flight whose mission was to strafe enemy
ground troops in Yugoslavia. The group of 12
planes were blown off course by strong winds
and split into two groups as they returned to
base. Captain Joseph Elsberry led a group of
six, which included Captain Pruitt and Lieutenant Gwynne Pierson. In Trieste harbor
they spotted an enemy destroyer. The ship
began a barrage and the flight moved in.
Pruitt, the fifth plane in the attack, scored a
direct hit that set the destroyer on fire. Pierson, following him, also made a direct hit
and the ship exploded. Because of the heavy
smoke in the area, the pilots made several
passes until they were able to see the ship
sink.

The common assumption was that fighters
could not sink destroyers, so there was great
skepticism when the action was reported.
The film from the group's wing-cameras was
scrutinized minutely before it was "conceded
that black fighter pilots had done the impossible, sunk a destroyer."

Captain Pruitt and Lieutenant Pierson
were awarded the Distinguished Flying Cross
for the action.

Soon after, the 332nd was issued P-51
Mustangs, faster and more powerful than the
P-47s. The men painted the tail assemblies a
distinctive red. Known to their German op-
ponents as *Schwarze Vogelmenschen* (Black
Birdmen), the 332nd were known to their
American comrades as "Red Tail Angels."
The 332nd never lost a single one of the
bombers under their protection.

Pruitt's fighter, a P-51B Mustang, was in-
scribed *Alice-Jo*, for the names of his fiancée
and that of his crew chief. Pruitt's fiancée,
Alice Charleton of Detroit, was also a pilot.

On October 12, 1944, during an attack
over Germany, the 332nd shot down nine
enemy aircraft and destroyed 26 more on the
ground. Pruitt received credit for two victories that day.

One of the first Tuskegee pilots to complete the 70 missions required for rotation
back to the States, Pruitt returned home in
late 1944. St. Louis welcomed him as a
hometown hero, honoring him with Captain
Wendell O. Pruitt Day on December 12,
1944.

Pruitt returned to Tuskegee as a flight instructor. He had already requested, and been
given, permission to rejoin the 332nd in Europe when, on April 15, 1945, he crashed
near Tuskegee while doing a low-altitude
slow roll with a student pilot. Both were
killed. Major Robert Pitts, an intelligence officer, would remember: "When the news was
heard in Italy, no one wanted to believe that
he was gone. There are many opinions as to
what happened, but I think most of the pilots
believe that for a second Pruitt forgot he was

flying one of those beat-up old trainers and not a P-51 when he did that roll."

Pruitt is interred at St. Peter's Cemetery in St. Louis.

The Wendell O. Pruitt Military Academy, a St. Louis public magnet school for students in grades 6–8, opened in 1984. It is the first and only public military middle school in Missouri. Its program incorporates military concepts such as self-discipline, leadership, and high standards of valued behavior into a standard middle school curriculum to prepare the uniformed students, known as "cadets," for success at the high school level.

Pruitt is depicted, with others, on the noteworthy "Black Americans in Flight" mural unveiled at the Lambert-St. Louis International Airport in 1990. He is also memorialized by the Pruitt-Igoe housing project and the Captain Wendell O. Pruitt Memorial American Veterans (AMVETS) Post no. 41, both in St. Louis.

### Sources

"Capt. Wendell Pruitt Killed in Plane Crash." *St. Louis Post Dispatch* (April 16, 1945).

Cooper, Charlie, and Ann Cooper: *Tuskegee's Heroes: Featuring the Aviation Art of Roy LaGrone.* Osceola, WI: Motorbooks International, 1996; 62–63.

Davis, Benjamin O. Jr. *Benjamin O. Davis Jr., American: An Autobiography.* Washington, DC: Smithsonian Institution Press, 1991; 128.

Francis, Charles E. *The Tuskegee Airmen: The Men Who Changed a Nation.* Fourth edition, revised and updated by Adolph Caso. Boston: Branden Publishing Co., 1997.

"Mayor Greets Negro Pilot Home on Leave." *St. Louis Post Dispatch* (November 28, 1944).

Motley, Mary Penick. *The Invisible Soldier: The Experience of the Black Soldier, World War II.* Detroit: Wayne State University Press, 1975; 206, 210.

Rose, Robert A. *Lonely Eagles: The Story of America's Black Air Force in World War II.* Los Angeles: Tuskegee Airmen Inc., Los Angeles Chapter, 1980; 5, 68–71.

Sandler, Stanley. *Segregated Skies: All-Black Combat Squadrons of World War II.* Washington, DC: Smithsonian Institution Press, 1992; 95–97, 110–111.

"Spotlight on Captain Wendell O. Pruitt." AmVets Post 41, St. Louis, Missouri. June 1, 1999. Http: www.angelfire.com/mo/AMVETSPOST41/. Accessed June 4, 2000.

# Louis R. Purnell

**Full Name at Birth:** Louis Rayfield Purnell

**Born:** April 5, 1921, Wilmington, Delaware

**Died:** August 10, 2001

**Education:** Lincoln University, Pennsylvania, 1939–1941; B.S., institution and date unknown.

**Positions Held:** Fighter pilot, 99th Pursuit Squadron and 332nd Fighter Group, 1941–1945; oceanographer, –1967; assistant curator, National Air and Space Museum, Smithsonian Institution, 1967–1990.

**Awards, Honors:** Distinguished Flying Cross, 1945; Air Medal with six oak leaf clusters, 1945.

**Summary:** Louis R. Purnell was one of the acclaimed Tuskegee Airmen, the first African American military pilots. He also had distinguished careers as an oceanographer and as an assistant curator at the National Air and Space Museum of the Smithsonian Institution, Washington, D.C.

## Early Years

Louis R. Purnell was born in Wilmington, Delaware, April 5, 1921. His mother was a teacher, and his father a school principal. According to Purnell, "We had a very strict household. . . . Maybe my dreams about flying were escapism." When he was six or seven years old, Purnell recalls, the black pilot Hubert Fauntleroy Julian was a hero to him. The flamboyant and legendary Julian, also known as the "Black Eagle," was, according to Purnell, "an elegant rogue with a haughty air. He impressed thousands with his black derby, monocle, wing collar, Prince Albert cutaway coat, striped trousers, and spats." Julian delivered a speech to the church that the Purnell family attended in Wilmington. The purpose of the speech was to raise money for an airplane Julian wished to buy for a nonstop flight from New York City to Rome.

Inspired by this romantic figure, the child dreamed of becoming a pilot. His family had other plans for him. They wanted him to become a doctor.

## Higher Education

Purnell attended Lincoln University in Chester County, Pennsylvania, from 1939 to 1941. Events in the world at large would cause him to abandon his college career, and he did not receive his degree at this time. After World War II, Purnell completed his B.S. degree and did graduate study in oceanography.

## Career Highlights

In 1939, the federal government came to a realization that the United States would likely be involved in the war that was beginning in Europe and Asia. The military would need pilots to pursue the war successfully, and there was a shortage of trained men. Furthermore, it was a time-consuming process to train a pilot properly, a process that took months. Pilot training was expensive as well, and many of those who might be interested could not afford the cost. To get around these difficulties, the Civilian Pilot Training Program was established. At first, participation was limited to white men, but under intense political pressure from civil rights leaders, the black press, and members of Congress, the government relented and set up separate programs for African Americans.

Purnell was one of the African Americans who were part of the project. He finished his primary flight training while at Lincoln, and then, in the summer of 1941, proceeded to Tuskegee Institute, in Tuskegee, Alabama,

for advanced training. As Purnell remembers: "I finished the course in September, but my color prevented me from going any further: blacks were not accepted as aviation cadets."

Fortuitously, in January 1941, a Howard University student, Yancey Williams, aided by the NAACP, initiated a lawsuit against the Air Corps demanding admission to the military training program. Purnell was unaware of this lawsuit, and was about to initiate one of his own, when the government relented and allowed Williams to enter the program. Both suits were dismissed, and the Air Corps began to admit African Americans to a segregated training program.

On December 7, 1941, the Japanese attacked Pearl Harbor, and the United States declared war against the Axis forces. In January 1942, two weeks after Pearl Harbor, Purnell left Lincoln University and reported to Tuskegee Army Air Field as an aviation cadet.

"The washout rate there [at Tuskegee] was exceptionally high compared with the percentage of failures at Maxwell Field in Montgomery, where white pilots were trained. It appeared . . . that those in power were trying to limit the number of black graduates. Still, those of us who managed to graduate against the odds had the feeling that we had what it took."

There was reluctance on the part of the high command to use these men in battle. "We were undoubtedly the most highly trained squadron in the U.S.; the Air Corps brass couldn't decide what to do with us, so we flew and flew for nearly a whole year to maintain our proficiency."

At last, on April 15, 1943, the African Americans trained at Tuskegee were sent to North Africa as the 99th Pursuit Squadron and began flying missions. Some of the white pilots undoubtedly resented these men, but "we found that a strong feeling of camaraderie usually prevailed among fighter pilots regardless of their race." This esprit de corps was demonstrated when his plane engine started to emit smoke and his squadron left him behind. Purnell saw the approach of four planes, which he thought were enemy aircraft. "I was one happy soul when I recognized that the four planes were not Hitler's boys but from the white squadron based near us. They stayed with me until I was over land."

By July of that year, the 99th had been increasingly employed on ground attack: dive-bombing and strafing. "Although we thought of it as dirty work, we had become dive-bombing experts, and I considered dive-bombing and strafing my specialties."

The Tuskegee program produced almost a thousand pilots, 450 of whom served in combat as the 99th Fighter Squadron and later as the 332nd Fighter Group. In the course of 1,578 missions, the Tuskegee Airmen shot down 111 airborne craft, destroyed 150 on the ground, and damaged 25 airborne and 123 ground-bound transports. They are the only group that never lost any bombers to enemy fighters while flying as escorts. Known as the Red Tail Angels, because of the markings on their planes, the Squadron was noted for sticking to the bombers they were protecting, and even for escorting crippled bombers to safety. Purnell received many grateful letters after the war from men whose lives he had helped save.

Upon completion of 50 missions, Purnell's tour of duty ended and he was sent home on leave to the United States. Disembarking at Fort Dix, New Jersey, he then went to New York, where he stayed in the Theresa Hotel in Harlem, one of the few hotels that would accommodate African Americans. While there, he encountered his old hero, Hubert Julian. It was the only time the two met. As Purnell related: "I received a call from the front desk informing me that I had a visitor." Purnell took the elevator to the lobby. "The elevator doors opened and there stood Hubert Fauntleroy Julian, looking much as he had when I was an impressionable seven-year-old. He went into his act immediately. Strolling up and down the lobby with one eye on a small audience, he said in a loud

voice, 'Is this any way to treat a returning hero? He should be out on the town. Give him the keys to the city . . . Here are the keys to my car. Return the car whenever you wish. . . . It's right outside.'

"I felt like two cents, being put on display like this. . . . But I thanked him and set out to identify the car. I found it quickly enough: a big black Cadillac with a ticket on the windshield parked beside a fire hydrant. I . . . got in, turned the ignition—and saw that the gas gauge registered empty. . . . I drove the car around the block, parked it in the space where I had found it, . . . and returned to the hotel to give Julian the keys. . . . [H]e berated me . . . telling me I didn't know how to accept things graciously."

When his leave ended, in October 1943, Purnell was sent to Tuskegee Army Air Field, where he served as an instructor. Purnell explained why he did not enjoy this assignment: one student "froze at the controls while I was teaching him to recover from spins. . . . Deciding that combat might be a little safer, I requested permission to join the 332nd Fighter Group." The 332nd was formed by combining the original four black squadrons, headed for combat under the leadership of Colonel Benjamin O. Davis Jr.

The group embarked on a month-long cruise on a Liberty Ship that eventually delivered them to Taranto, Italy. "The airplanes we flew . . . were hand-me-downs, but our linemen did an excellent job of keeping them airworthy." Eventually, however, these planes were replaced by newer aircraft. Purnell loved the new planes. "The Mustang was a real sweetheart. Had it been a woman, I would not have hesitated to marry it."

By winter 1944, the men of the 332nd were escorting B-24s and B-17s as they bombed targets in Germany, Austria, and Czechoslovakia. The group had an enviable record: they never lost a bomber to enemy fighters. Nevertheless, there were those who would disparage them. A white bomber pilot, temporarily residing at the 332nd's base camp, wrote a letter that Purnell had to read as one of his duties as censor. It read: "[I]t's bad enough I'm not on my own base. I'm stranded at a nigger base, eating nigger food, and sleeping in a nigger bed." The author of the letter, Purnell found, was a Sergeant Schwartz.

"The next day, as the crews began to assemble for takeoff, I located Schwartz.... 'Sergeant Schwartz,' I said, 'it wasn't so bad sleeping in nigger beds and eating nigger food, especially when we protect you in flight.'" Having made his point, Purnell walked away, leaving the flabbergasted Schwartz speechless.

Purnell managed to survive the war unscathed; the nearest he came to disaster was when one of the cooks, attempting to teach himself to drive, drove a jeep into his tent. Fighter pilots ordinarily do not see the victims of war, as they fly so high. But on one occasion Purnell was appalled to discover, stuck to his plane, the remnants of another human being whom he had killed. The event made a strong impression on him.

In 1945, with the war successfully concluded, Purnell sought new challenges. Completing graduate courses in oceanography, he became an oceanographer. "It was a special area of paleontology. We surveyed the mid-Atlantic ridge, we went to the Pacific, we went all over the world."

Nevertheless, the pull of aviation was strong, and in 1967 he became an assistant curator in the National Air and Space Museum of the Smithsonian Institution. According to an interview, Purnell "wanted to be around flying again." His duties involved the acquisition and care of spacecraft. "We had spacecraft from every mission.... I became a specialist in spacesuits, too, and food—all the things that went on a mission."

Purnell retired from the Smithsonian in 1990 to pursue other interests. He is interested in locksmithing, and has a museum-quality collection of locks; he also enjoys making picture frames for the art works of his wife, JoAnn. Still interested in aviation, he continues to fly and to give speeches and interviews about his experiences as a Tuskegee Airman. In doing this, he hopes to encourage young African Americans to pursue careers in aviation and space flight.

## Sources

Crowley, Susan. "On a Silver, Satin Road." *AARP Bulletin* (March 1991): 16.

McKissack, Patricia, and Fredrick McKissack. *Red-Tail Angels: The Story of the Tuskegee Airmen of World War II*. New York: Walker and Co., 1995.

Pierce, Fred. "Tuskegee Airman, Parnell [*sic*], Speaks at College Park." *Atlantic Flyer* (Bedford, Massachusetts) (March 1993): B21–24.

Purnell, Louis E. "The Flight of the Bumblebee." *Air & Space* (October–November 1989): 33–40.

"Reader Forum." *AARP Bulletin* (May 1991): 15.

# R

## George S. Roberts Sr.

**Full Name at Birth:** George Spencer Roberts

**Born:** September 24, 1918, Fairmount, West Virginia

**Died:** March 1984, Sacramento, California

**Education:** West Virginia State College, Institute [1940]; Army Command and General Staff College, Fort Leavenworth, Kansas [1950s].

**Positions Held:** Operations officer, 99th Pursuit Squadron, 1943; Commander, 99th Pursuit Squadron, 1943; Commander, 332nd Fighter Group, 1944–1945; professor, air science and tactics, Tuskegee Institute, Alabama, 1945–1946; Commander, USAF unit, Langley AFB, Virginia, 1950; various assignments in Korea, Japan, Vietnam, and the United States; banker, Sacramento, California, 1968–1981.

**Awards, Honors:** Distinguished Flying Cross; Air Medal; seven Commendation Medals, each with three to nine oak leaf clusters; honored as a pioneer at the "Black Wings" exhibition, National Air and Space Museum, 1982; Sacramento chapter of the Tuskegee Airmen, Inc. renamed the George S. Spanky Roberts Chapter, 1984, posthumously.

**Summary:** George "Spanky" Roberts was one of Tuskegee's first class of five graduates on March 7, 1942. The others were Benjamin O. Davis Jr., Lemuel R. Custis, Mac Ross, and Charles H. DeBow Jr. Roberts served as commander of the 99th Pursuit Squadron in Italy in 1943, and he retired from the military in 1968 with the rank of colonel.

### Early Years

George Spencer Roberts was born in Fairmount, West Virginia, on September 24, 1918. He described himself as, "Indian, black, Caucasian, a little Jewish." His father, from Kentucky, had been a jockey and a baseball pitcher. He volunteered to be in the combat engineers in World War I, but his services were refused because of his color. Later he was drafted and became a first sergeant. Young Roberts was a baseball fan, and he loved flying all his life. "When I was junior high school age, my parents dug up the money from someplace to take a hop in a four-seater aircraft. The pilot asked me if I'd like to fly it. I had to stand up to reach the pedals, but I flew the airplane for probably 20 minutes." This experience, coupled with living fairly near the airport, where he could watch planes often, helped plant the idea of flying in Roberts's mind.

## Higher Education

At West Virginia State College, a historically black college, Roberts studied psychology, sociology, and engineering. It was here that he got his nickname of "Spanky." During hazing episodes by upperclassmen, he told them he would spank them if they didn't let him alone. Because of his small size and youth, the older students just laughed, and gave him the nickname that "followed me all the years of my life."

In 1939, West Virginia State College became the first of the six black colleges and universities selected for inclusion in the Civilian Pilot Training Program (CPTP). A federal program administered by the Civil Aeronautics Administration (CAA), it was designed to develop a ready group of pilots in the event of war. Roberts learned to fly in the CPTP, and he was also enrolled in the college's ROTC (Reserve Officers Training Corps). Roberts "had been haunting the hell out of the Air Corps" to let him enroll. He finally received word from the War Department that the Air Corps was to be opened to African Americans, or to Negroes, the term then in use. At the end of November 1940, Roberts passed the written and physical exams, thus becoming the first Negro cadet accepted for training in the U.S. Army Air Corps.

That first class was trained at Tuskegee Army Air Field, in what was called either "The Tuskegee Experiment" or "The Noble Experiment." Members of the military, and indeed of civilian society as well, were not sure that people of color had the requisite intelligence, physical stamina, and courage for flying airplanes. The first class began with 13 cadets, but only five remained to graduate in March 1942. They won their silver wings

and were commissioned as second lieutenants. The next class had only three graduates, but after that, more and more cadets successfully completed the courses. Eventually, close to 1,000 pilots were trained at Tuskegee Air Field.

## Career Highlights

The 99th Pursuit Squadron, commanded by Lieutenant Colonel Benjamin O. Davis Jr., was sent to North Africa in April 1943. Roberts, who had been promoted to captain, was the operations officer of the squadron. They had been kept out of combat and given no chance to demonstrate their skills. Later sent to Italy, they flew in combat missions. In September 1943 Roberts took over as commander of the 99th in Italy, when Davis was assigned elsewhere. Promoted to major, Roberts was a pilot of great skill, and he led 64 planes as cover for heavy bombers and on strafing missions. He eventually flew 78 missions with the squadron and amassed 6,000 flying hours.

In 1944, he became, first, deputy, then commander, of the 332nd Fighter Group, which consisted of four squadrons: the 99th, the 100th, the 301st, and the 302nd. He remained in this position until the war ended in 1945. Roberts then went to Tuskegee Institute, where he held the position of professor of air science and tactics.

After the armed forces were integrated in 1948 by President Harry Truman's executive order, Roberts in 1950, became the first black commander of any integrated U.S. Air Force unit. The unit was at Langley Air Force Base (AFB), Virginia. Roberts later graduated from Army Command and General Staff College at Fort Leavenworth, Kansas. In 1952, the Roberts family became the first blacks to live at the Fort, which was founded 125 years earlier. Roberts was also assigned to Suwan AFB, Korea; Chanute AFB; Okinawa, Japan; and Griffiss AFB, New York. He served as director of support for all fighter planes in Vietnam, and he directed the

F-104 program for 18 allied nations and ground radar at McClellan AFB, California.

Roberts retired with the rank of colonel in February 1968 after 27 years of active duty. He and his wife, the former Edith McMillan, whom he had married on the same day he received his pilot's wings, then took up residence in Sacramento, where Roberts was a banker for 13 years. They had four children: George Spencer Jr., Edith Lanelle Brent, Michalyn Ann Green, and Lee Roberts Cavier. From his retirement until his death in early March 1984, Roberts actively helped develop a network of Tuskegee Airmen living in California. He was active in the local chapter, addressing community organizations, school children, and members of the military on black military history, among other subjects. A strong feature of the Tuskegee Airmen, Inc. (TAI) is their scholarship program. It makes grants without regard to racial groups or gender. "We are against segregation in any form," Roberts wrote. After his death, the Sacramento chapter of TAI was renamed in his honor.

As a banker, he helped senior citizens who were without relatives to manage their estates. He served on the board of directors of Meals a la Cart, an organization that delivered nutritious meals to the homebound, and of the Metropolitan Industry and Education Council, which helped high school graduates in their job searches. In addition, he volunteered at the Computer Learning Center. After Roberts had had both his hips replaced, he helped form an organization called Hipsters, a support group for people facing such operations.

George "Spanky" Roberts was buried at Mt. Vernon Memorial Park on Greenback Lane in Citrus Heights, California, on March 12, 1984.

### Sources

"Col. 'Spanky' Roberts Dies." No source, no date. Reprinted in Hayden C. Johnson, *The Fighting 99th Air Squadron, 1941–1945*. New York: Vantage Press, 1987.

Cooper, Charlie, and Ann Cooper. *Tuskegee's Heroes: Featuring the Aviation Art of Roy LaGrone*. Osceola, WI: Motorbooks International, 1996.

Holway, John B. *Red Tails Black Wings: The Men of America's Black Air Force*. Las Cruces, NM: Yucca Tree Press, 1997.

# Brenda E. Robinson

**Born:** [1957], Philadelphia, Pennsylvania

**Education:** North Penn High School, Lansdale, Pennsylvania; B.S. in aeronautics, Dowling College, Oakdale, New York; [1978].

**Positions Held:** Transport pilot, Fleet Logistics Support Squadron Forty, Norfolk, Virginia, 1980– .

**Summary:** On June 6, 1980, Brenda E. Robinson became the first black woman pilot in the history of the U.S. Navy. Only 41 women before her had received the Navy's gold wings and the commission of ensign.

### Early Years

Brenda E. Robinson was born to Susan and Edward G. Robinson in Philadelphia, Pennsylvania about 1957. Almost no information about Robinson's childhood or family background was available, but she did tell a reporter, "All I ever wanted to do was fly." She graduated from North Penn High School in Lansdale, in the mid-1970s.

### Higher Education

Robinson completed her studies for a bachelor's degree in aeronautics at Dowling College in Oakdale, New York, on Long Island, about 1978. She was one of only five women to major in aeronautics at Dowling. When she graduated, she had also obtained her private pilot's license, after soloing successfully.

She enlisted in the Navy in November 1978, her first choice, because she could go directly into flight training while the Air Force required two years of service before admission to flight school. Before she chose the Navy, Robinson also learned, that if she completed flight training successfully, she would be the Navy's only black woman pilot. "I knew I was doing something unique and realized I would be a pioneer, but I didn't go around telling others I'd be the first black woman pilot," she said. On March 23, 1979, Robinson began Aviation Officers Candidate School in Pensacola, Florida.

The 16-week course was rough. "The first week was miserable. I had trouble eating. On many occasions, I asked myself what I was doing here," Robinson recalled in an interview for *Eagle & Swan*, a periodical aimed at black military personnel. In fact, the attrition rate for both men and women candidates was high. The primary training course took place at Whiting Field in Milton, Florida. The advanced training was held at Corpus Christi, Texas, where Ensign Robinson received her gold wings, pinned on by her mother, on June 6, 1980. She thus became the first African American woman to complete pilot training in the U.S. Navy. An earlier candidate, Jill E. Brown in 1974, would have been the first, had she not left the Navy after six months.

## Career Highlights

Robinson's first assignment was in Norfolk, Virginia, with the Fleet Logistics Support Squadron Forty, where she flew the C-1A "Tracker" aircraft to transport cargo and personnel.

She believes that women should speak up, and she supports the Equal Rights Amendment (ERA) for women. She gives credit to the women's movement for making "it possible for me to get into military aviation." By law she, as a woman, is prevented from engaging in combat operations on ships or in aviation squadrons that will fight. These assignments are desirable because they usually act as stepping stones for promotion to higher ranks with greater responsibility. Although this was the situation Robinson encountered when she earned her wings, she nevertheless took training to enable her to land the C-1A on the flight deck of an aircraft carrier. Landing on, or taking off from, a ship is one of the most difficult challenges a Navy pilot can face. It requires great skill and daring, as the "airstrip" (the ship) can be moving at up to 35 miles an hour. There are only 200 yards of landing space. Many other factors need to be taken into account by the pilot during these landings and take-offs, but Robinson knows her confidence and skill will see her through.

## Sources

"Brenda Robinson: Flying High." *Eagle & Swan* (December 1980): 25–26.

Martinez, Manny. "Ensign Brenda E. Robinson: Aviator, a Navy First." *Eagle & Swan* (November 1980): 28–29.

# John C. Robinson

**Full Name at Birth:** John Charles Robinson

**Born:** November 26, 1903, Carabelle, Florida

**Died:** March 27, 1954, Addis Ababa, Ethiopia

**Education:** Degree in automotive mechanics, Tuskegee Institute, Alabama, 1924; graduate, Curtiss-Wright Aeronautical Institute, Chicago, 1931; U.S. Dept of Commerce, private pilot's license no. 26,042, by 1932; transport pilot's license by 1935.

**Positions Held:** auto mechanic, Detroit, mid 1920s; mechanic, Yellow Cab Company, Chicago, mid 1920s; auto repair garage owner, Chicago, late 1920s–late 1930s(?); instructor, Curtiss-Wright Institute, Chicago 1931–(?); organizer, Brown Eagle Aero Club and Challenger Air Pilots Association, early 1930s; Ethiopian Air Force, 1935–1936; founder and head, John C. Robinson Na-

John C. Robinson. Courtesy of National Air and Space Museum, Smithsonian Institution (SI Neg. No. 87-15491).

tional Air College, Chicago, 1936–1944(?); instructor, Chanute Air Base, Rantoul, Illinois, early 1940s(?); Ethiopian Air Force, 1945(?)–1948(?); operator, Sultan Airlines, Ltd., 1948–(?).

**Summary:** Robinson was instrumental in the early African American aviation community in Chicago and an early influence on the foundation of an aviation program at Tuskegee Institute. He succeeded Hubert F. Julian as air marshal in Ethiopia and became known as the "Brown Condor." Active in aviation education in the Chicago area through the 1930s and early 1940s, Robinson returned to Ethiopia in 1944 to continue development of the Ethiopian Air Force. He died from injuries suffered in a plane crash in Ethiopia in 1954.

## Early Years

John Robinson first saw an airplane when he was a seven-year-old boy in Gulfport, Mississippi. Born in Carabelle, Florida, in November 1903, Robinson had moved to Gulfport with his mother, Celeste, after the death of his father. In the booming new town on the Gulf of Mexico, Celeste Robinson ran a boarding house and remarried, to Charles Cobb, a mechanic with the Gulf and Ship Island Railroad. They had a daughter, Bertha. The family was close, and Robinson considered Charles Cobb his father.

Throughout his childhood Robinson held onto his dream of flying someday. His parents' goal was to help him to go to college, to Tuskegee Institute, but they tried to make Robinson understand that—just as Charles Cobb had to settle for working on locomotives rather than being an engineer—black men didn't fly planes any more than they ran trains.

At 14, Robinson began working as a delivery and stock boy for a local department store.

## Higher Education

In 1920, he left home for Tuskegee, where he majored in automotive mechanics. His grades were average in English and math, but he had high marks in mechanical science. Tall, quiet, and serious, he had a natural ability for all things mechanical. His classmates also remembered his natural ability on the dance floor. After graduation in 1924, Robinson moved north to Detroit, where he went to work as an auto mechanic. Soon he found a flying field on the outskirts of the city. By helping a pilot with a mechanical problem on his plane, Robinson wangled his first airplane ride. He also met another African American auto mechanic with an interest in aviation, Cornelius Coffey.

## Career Highlights

Robinson moved on to Chicago, which was more "air minded" than Detroit at that time. He went to work as a mechanic for the Yellow Cab Company, but soon realized that, in a white-owned company, an African American could only advance so far. In the late 1920s, Robinson left Yellow Cab and, with his wife, Earnize, opened an auto repair shop. The Robinsons would operate the concern together for many years.

Robinson pursued his interest in aviation. He applied to the Curtiss-Wright Aviation School, but he was turned down. Undeterred, Robinson got a night job sweeping classrooms at the school. Finishing work at his own shop, he would hurry to Curtiss-Wright and quickly clean all the rooms except the one in which the evening aviation ground school was held. Then he would spend the class period sweeping and dusting at the back of that classroom. When the class took breaks, Robinson would copy the drawings and equations from the blackboard.

He founded an Aero Study Club, whose members were friends from Tuskegee and other aviation enthusiasts. When the club met on Sundays, he would share the information he had gathered in the Curtiss-Wright classroom. Cornelius Coffey commuted from Detroit to Chicago to talk with Robinson about aviation; the two pooled their resources to purchase a used motorcycle engine and an airplane kit, which the Aero Club constructed. Robinson persuaded the Curtiss-Wright night school instructor to inspect the finished aircraft, which turned out to be airworthy.

The Curtiss-Wright staff became aware of the intelligence and skills of their African American maintenance worker and finally admitted him into the program. Robinson graduated from Curtiss-Wright in 1931, its first African American graduate. The institution soon hired Robinson as its first African American instructor, and Willa Brown, Janet Waterford, Cornelius Coffey, and other early members of Chicago's African American aviation community were soon enrolled as Curtiss-Wright students.

The group had difficulty finding flying facilities, since many airfields continued to be segregated. Robinson was instrumental in organizing the Brown Eagle Aero Club, subsequently reorganized as the Challenger Air Pilots' Association. It was the first African American flying club in the Chicago area. With business partners, Robinson financed the construction of a private airstrip in nearby Robbins, Illinois, an all-black community, in 1933. The field was the first Department of Commerce-accredited airfield in the United States that was African American owned and operated. When a windstorm destroyed the hanger at the Robbins airstrip soon after it opened, the club moved to facilities at Harlem Airport.

In May 1934, on the occasion of his Tuskegee Institute class's 10th-year reunion, Robinson landed a small plane in a field at Tuskegee, intending to encourage the Institute to build an airfield and begin an aeronautics program.

By the time Tuskegee offered him a position as an aviation instructor, however, Robinson had volunteered his services to Haile Selassie, the emperor of Ethiopia, who was fighting off an imminent invasion by the forces of Italian dictator Benito Mussolini. Offered a commission in the Ethiopian army, Robinson sailed for Africa in May 1935. In the aftermath of a public dispute with Hubert Fauntleroy Julian, Robinson became the commander of Ethiopia's tiny air force, with the rank of colonel.

After the Italians invaded on October 3, 1935, it quickly became clear that the Ethiopian military was not equipped to withstand the Italians' state-of-the-art firepower. The Ethiopian air force numbered approximately 20 planes, which, according to Robinson, were all unarmed. To the surprise of many, including Robinson, Italy's bombers were able to carry out successful bombing raids over the mountainous terrain from altitudes of over 6,000 feet. Despite these distinct drawbacks, Robinson repeatedly eluded the Italian fighters through skilled flight maneuvers and strategic use of the rough terrain and frequent cloud cover, as he flew courier and reconnaissance missions between the emperor's capital at Addis Ababa and the forces fighting in the north. The press dubbed Robinson "the Brown Condor" for his exploits.

After Italy captured Addis Ababa in May 1936, Emperor Haile Selassie sailed into exile. John Robinson returned to the United States.

Robinson received a hero's welcome in New York and Chicago; the only American volunteer in the late Ethiopian conflict, he spoke in several cities on behalf of "United Aid for Ethiopia." In late June, he traveled to Tuskegee to negotiate the establishment of an aviation program at the Institute. However, in early July negotiations collapsed; apparently, Robinson sought more autonomy— and an eponymous aviation school—than the Institute, advocating a more conservative approach, was willing to accord him.

Back in partnership with Cornelius Coffey, Robinson opened the John C. Robinson National Air College and School of Automotive Engineering at Poro College on South Parkway in Chicago on September 28, 1936. By the following summer, 50 students were enrolled, of whom 10 were African Americans. Coffey later left the partnership to found a flying school of his own.

Concluding from news reports that war was inevitable, Robinson, Coffey, and other members of the Chicago aviation community encouraged the U.S. government to admit African Americans to the Civilian Pilot Training Program (CPTP), which helped to train civilian pilots for emergency duty during wartime. With the support of other groups, such as the NAACP, their efforts were successful, and the CPTP was opened up to African Americans in 1939. Under the auspices of CPTP, the Tuskegee Institute developed a viable aeronautics aviation program. Robinson, committed both to his own Air College in Chicago and to the exiled government of Ethiopia, did not play a direct role in the Tuskegee program, which was headed by C. Alfred "Chief" Anderson.

During World War II, Robinson acted as aviation consultant to the National Aviation Administration (NYA), supervising the NYA's mechanical school locations in Illinois and continuing to operate his own school on South Parkway. Although Robinson had, at some point, parted company with Coffey, Willa Brown and the National Airmen's Association, he continued to lobby for the enrollment of African Americans as flying cadets in the Chicago School of Aeronautics, which held a U.S. Army training contract. Although now too old himself to be considered for active duty in the U.S. Army or Army Air Corps, Robinson toured air bases in 1940 and 1941, at the request of the War Department, to describe his Ethiopian combat experience and the Italians' use of strategic formation bombing. He may also have served as an instructor at Chanute Air Base at Rantoul, Illinois, south of Chicago.

In 1943, the British drove Mussolini's forces from Ethiopia, and Haile Selassie returned from exile. The following year, the emperor invited Robinson to assist in the redevelopment of Ethiopia's military and civil air strength. Taking with him a small group of African American flight instructors and mechanics, Robinson returned to Ethiopia in 1944. Aircraft were acquired through a U.S. lend-lease arrangement. Robinson's aviation specialists started a comprehensive training program, which was the forerunner of the later development of the Imperial Ethiopian Air Force and a commercial airline.

The American specialists returned to the United States in 1946 at the completion of their assignment. Robinson, however, settled permanently in Ethiopia. The Ethiopian Supreme Court sentenced Robinson to a three-month jail term in 1947 on the charge of assaulting Count Gustaf Von Rosen, also a senior officer in the Ethiopian Air Force. Robinson claimed he had struck the count in self-defense after Von Rosen supposedly called him a "low Chicago gangster" and attempted to draw a gun on him.

Robinson subsequently left the Ethiopian Air Force. He was appointed principal instructor at the aviation school sponsored by Haile Selassie's grandson, the popular Duke of Harar, and served as Harar's private pilot. In 1948, with the duke's support, Robinson organized Sultan Airways, Ltd., which handled both passenger and cargo flights.

In March 1954, a training plane that Robinson was flying crashed at an Addis Ababa airfield. Robinson died from burns two weeks later and was buried with military honors at Gulele cemetery in Addis Ababa.

## Sources

"Ethiopia Honors Dead U.S. Flier." *New York Amsterdam News* (April 3, 1954): 1, 2.

Hardesty, Von, and Dominick Pisano. *Black Wings: The American Black in Aviation*. Washington, DC: National Air and Space Museum, 1983; 12, 14.

Jakeman, Robert J. *The Divided Skies: Establishing Segregated Flight Training at Tuskegee, Alabama, 1934–1942*. Tuscaloosa: University of Alabama Press, 1992; 1–2, 21–32, 63–64.

Scott, William R. *The Sons of Sheba's Race: African Americans and the Italo-Ethiopian War, 1935–1941*. Bloomington: Indiana University Press, 1993; 69–80.

Simmons, Thomas E. *The Brown Condor: The True Adventures of John C. Robinson*. Silver Spring, MD: Bartleby Press, 1988.

# Ted W. Robinson

**Full Name at Birth:** Theodore Wesley Robinson

**Born:** [1924], [Chicago, Illinois]

**Education:** Pilot's license, Tuskegee, Alabama, November 20, 1945; University of Illinois, 1948; pilots' licenses and ratings for transport, instructor, instrument, and glider rating and instruction.

**Positions Held:** Street car motorman, Chicago Transit Authority; flight instructor, Harlem Airport, Chicago; Captain, U.S. Air Force Reserve; mechanical engineer, Wright-Patterson AFB, Dayton, Ohio, 1957–1962; research engineer, Federal Aviation Administration (FAA), 1962–1966; general aviation inspector, FAA, 1966–mid-1980s; consultant and historian, National Air and Space Museum, Washington, D.C.

**Summary:** Theodore W. Robinson has followed many paths in the field of aviation. In 1966, he became the first African American general aviation inspector for the Federal Aviation Administration (FAA). Robinson has been pilot, instructor, administrator, and historian. In 1979, he acted as curatorial consultant for the landmark exhibition, "Black Wings: The American Black in Aviation." Mounted by the Smithsonian's National Air and Space Museum in 1982, it became a permanent exhibition, and the catalyst for the blossoming of studies of the role of African Americans in aviation.

## Early Years

Robinson's interest in flying was sparked when he found a blue toy airplane in his aunt's basement in Chicago. As a youngster growing up during the 1930s, the Great Depression years, Robinson used whatever change he could earn to buy magazines about aviation, which he eagerly read. He also built model airplanes. He learned about the Coffey School of Aeronautics, at Chicago's Harlem Airport, from articles in the *Chicago Defender*, a leading African American newspaper. The newspaper was supportive of the young aviators in its city, and its coverage helped to make Chicago the center of black aviation.

Pictures of the student pilots with the school's directors, Cornelius Coffey and Willa Brown, led Robinson to the school and to a world where black people flew. At the age of 18, Robinson joined the U.S. Army Air Corps, and he was sent for flight training to Tuskegee Army Air Field in Alabama. By the time he graduated as a second lieutenant in November 1945, World War II had ended. But Robinson "had at least achieved the dream of learning to fly."

## Career Highlights

Eager to have a career in civilian aviation, Robinson came up against race prejudice so severe that he likened it to running into a stone wall. Applying to TWA in 1946, he was told he had to belong to the Air Line Pilots Association. The ALPA then told him he had to be an airline pilot before he could join the organization.

In 1948 while he was a student at the University of Illinois, Robinson was asked by the operator of a flight school in Springfield to be an instructor there. It seems that the school had recruited a group of black veterans, to profit from the G.I. Bill of Rights, which provided education and training at government expense, among other benefits. "G.I." refers to members of the army and stands for "general issue," a term for the clothing and equipment used by army personnel. Robinson and another Tuskegee Airman, both accredited flight instructors, were hired because the all-white staff would not teach the African American veterans. The job did not last long because of the hostile atmosphere and the danger posed by the inferior and damaged aircraft they were expected to train on.

Unable to find full-time work, Robinson worked for the Chicago Transit Authority as a streetcar motorman, and he was a part-time flight instructor at Harlem Airport. To keep up his flying skills, Robinson joined the U.S. Air Force Reserve, where he rose to the rank of captain. His pilot licenses include the transport license with ratings for large aircraft, instructor rating for both single- and multiengine airplanes, instrument instruction, and ratings for glider flight and instruction.

Still hoping to break into commercial aviation, Robinson applied to United Airlines in 1954. After taking a test he was told he didn't have the "right personality" to be a pilot. No other African American had the required personality either, until 1963, when the U.S. Supreme Court declared discrimination in the airline industry to be unconstitutional. Major airlines then began hiring at least one African American. The only pilot who was hired earlier than 1963 was Perry H. Young, a helicopter pilot. Young was hired in December 1956 by New York Airways, a helicopter service only.

From 1957 until 1962 Robinson worked as a mechanical engineer in the design section at Wright-Patterson Air Force Base, Dayton, Ohio. He then joined the FAA as a research engineer in Atlantic City, New Jersey. Robinson became the FAA's first black general aviation inspector in 1966, and he continued working for the FAA, in other capacities, until the mid-1980s when he retired.

When he consulted for the exhibition, "Black Wings," Robinson was particularly interested in showing that "Blacks were trying to learn a new technology and trying to break in, but they were also fighting racial barriers that were well entrenched in the society." Now living in Maryland, Robinson is well positioned to devote much of his time to the National Air and Space Museum in Washington, D.C., as a volunteer. He is one of the editors of the Smithsonian Institution Press's series of biographies of black pioneer pilots. Robinson flies as often as he can, in his Mooney four-seater plane, and he works with young people who are interested in flying.

## Sources

Drew-Holland, Carol. "People & Places." *New York Voice* (October 22, 1983): 10.

Kisor, Henry. *Flight of the Gin Fizz: Midlife at 4,500 Feet.* New York: Basic Books, 1997.

# Mac Ross

**Full Name at Birth:** Mac Ross

**Born:** Dayton, Ohio

**Died:** July 10, 1944, Italy

**Education:** Roosevelt High School, Dayton, Ohio; B.S. in mechanical arts, West Virginia State College, Institute, 1941; Private pilot's license, 1941.

**Positions Held:** Inspector, GHR Foundry (steel mill), Dayton, before 1941; Commanding Officer, 100th Fighter Squadron, August 1942.

**Awards, Honors:** Distinguished Flying Cross, Legion of Merit, Purple Heart, other campaign medals; Mac Ross chapter of the Tuskegee Airmen at Wright-Patterson Air Force Base (AFB), Ohio; Mac Ross Memorial Philatelic Room, Main Post Office, Dayton, June 27, 1989.

**Summary:** Mac Ross was one of Tuskegee's first class of five graduates on March 7, 1942. The others were Benjamin O. Davis Jr., Lemuel R. Custis, George S. Roberts Sr., and Charles H. DeBow Jr. Ross commanded the 100th Fighter Squadron in Italy, 1942–1943.

## Early Years

Mac Ross was one of 10 children of Willie and Samuel Ross. His father was employed by the post office in Dayton. Interviewed in 1989, his older sister Suretha Brooks, said that, as a child, he loved airplanes, and had always wanted to be a pilot. Ross was also interested in photography and printing. He graduated from Roosevelt High School, and at one time, he was a pitcher for the Dayton Silver Leaf Club, a black baseball team. Ross was a member of the segregated Fifth Street YMCA's basketball team as well.

## Higher Education

Ross went to West Virginia State College, where he earned a bachelor's degree in mechanical arts around 1941. Since West Virginia State became the first black college to be chosen as a site for the Civilian Pilot Training Program (CPTP), Ross was able to realize his childhood ambition to become a pilot. The CPTP was established by the federal government to train civilians as pilots, thereby insuring a ready supply of trained men in case of war. By 1939, the possibility of a war that would involve the United States began to seem likely. Ross earned his private pilot's license in 1941. He then enlisted in the U.S. Army Air Corps, which for the first time in its history began accepting African American men as aviation cadets.

He was assigned to Oxnard AFB, in California, but four days later he was transferred to Tuskegee Army Air Field (TAAF) in Alabama. Tuskegee became the location for training black pilots and ground crew because military services were strictly segregated by color, as was every other area in American society. Ross's sister Suretha often visited him while he was a cadet at Tuskegee. She was treated to a demonstration of her brother's flying skills, as he was proud of his ability to maneuver a plane. Ross was in the first class of 13 aviation cadets at TAAF. On graduation day, March 7, 1942, he was one of the five who remained to receive their silver wings, designating them as pilots with the rank of second lieutenant.

## Career Highlights

But unforeseen events occur, and several weeks after winning his wings, Ross had to bail out of his plane when it caught fire. He told the investigative committee, "I was at 6,000 feet when I noticed the temperature gauge was above the red line. I threw my cowl flaps wide open to cool the engine. When the heat continued to climb I called the field and told them I was coming in for a forced landing. Then there was a noise like a small explosion. . . . Fire came from the exhaust and from under the engine. I rode the ship down to 4,000, but it was too late. I put it in a stall position then, and when the nose went up I stood up in the cockpit and jumped out over the back of the tail fin. They dug up the airplane parts the next day."

The committee officials decided that there

had been no pilot error and that Ross had demonstrated the ability to act coolly under extreme pressure. Ross, however, worried that the destruction of the P-40 combat plane would end the Tuskegee "Experiment." He said, "I've wrecked a ship worth thousands of dollars. Maybe they'll start saying that Negroes can't fly after all!"

When Ross parachuted from his plane and landed safely in an Alabama cotton field, he became the first African American member of the Caterpillar Club. This group was made up of pilots who had used their parachutes to save their lives.

The Tuskegee program continued, and in August 1942, Ross was named commanding officer of the 100th Fighter Squadron, which was formed when there were enough pilots for a second squadron. In December 1943, they were sent into overseas combat in Italy. Ross flew more than 50 missions in World War II. At some point during the time in Italy, Colonel Davis replaced Ross with another officer. With the introduction of a new type of plane, the P-51 Mustang Fighter, the men had to be retrained. The plane's oxygen tube automatically increased the oxygen as the altitude increased. Sometimes the tube became blocked, without the pilot realizing he wasn't getting enough oxygen. He could lose consciousness in short order, and crash. That may have been the cause of Mac Ross's death on July 10, 1944. Author John Holway

writes, however, that the accident report called it a suicide, and Holway speculates that Ross was despondent because he had been replaced. On the same day, however, another pilot, Leon Roberts of the 99th, died in France after bombing German shipyards, and his friends believed his plane crashed because Roberts blacked out from the lack of oxygen.

On June 27, 1989, the U.S. Postal Service in Dayton dedicated the Mac Ross Memorial Philatelic Room at the main branch. His widow, remarried and living in Los Angeles, Abbie Ross DeVerges, spoke of his quiet but confident manner, and of his love of life and people.

## Sources

Cooper, Charlie, and Ann Cooper. *Tuskegee's Heroes: Featuring the Aviation Art of Roy LaGrone.* Osceola, WI: Motorbooks International, 1996; 84.

"14 Dayton and Valley Men Reported War Casualties." *Dayton Journal* (August 1, 1944): 12.

Holway, John. *Red Tails Black Wings : The Men of America's Black Air Force.* Las Cruces, NM: Yucca Tree Press, 1997.

Madison, Nathaniel. "Philatelic Room to Honor Tuskegee Unit Flyer." *Dayton Daily News* (June 26, 1989): 1A, 5A.

Rankin, Allen C. "How a Man Gets His Wings at Tuskegee." No source [1942], Clipping File: U.S. Army-Air Force-99th Pursuit Squadron, at Schomburg Center for Research in Black Culture, New York Public Library.

# S

## Ida Van Smith-Dunn

Ida Van Smith-Dunn. Courtesy of National Air and Space Museum, Smithsonian Institution (SI Neg. No. 91-6590).

**Full Name at Birth:** Ida Van Larkin

**Born:** March 21, 1917, Lumberton, North Carolina

**Education:** Redstone Academy, valedictorian, 1934; Barber Scotia Junior College, Concord, North Carolina; bachelor's degree in education; Shaw University, Raleigh, North Carolina; M.S., Queens College, 1964; private pilot's license, 1967; instrument rating and ground instructor certification.

**Positions Held:** Schoolteacher, North Carolina, late 1930s; schoolteacher, New York City, 1940(?)–1977; aviation instructor, York College, CUNY, mid-1970s(?); founder and president, Ida Van Smith Flight Club, Inc., 1967–  .

**Awards, Honors:** World Aerospace Education Award, 1978; Bishop Wright Air Industry Award, 1979; Ninety-Nines Award of Achievement, 1998.

**Summary:** Learning to fly at the age of 50, Ida Van Smith-Dunn founded the Ida Van Smith Flying Clubs in 1967, to expose young people to aviation. Her students have gone into a wide range of aviation careers, and she has received many awards for her promotion of aviation education.

### Early Years

From the age of three, Ida Van Larkin was often taken by her father to their hometown airfield in Lumberton, North Carolina. In the 1920s, barnstormers were the rage, and the Larkins never missed an air show.

Ida Van and her older brother and sister were brought up in a supportive and religious household. Years later, Ida Van Smith-Dunn recalled that her father tried to find someone to teach her to fly. "They said that they didn't have any instructors. But the planes were there. . . . I knew then that even if they had instructors, that they weren't going to teach any black people to fly. I didn't cry about it because I was really involved with my studies in high school. I knew that somewhere along the line, if I continued to be interested, I would learn to fly."

## Higher Education

Graduating from Redstone Academy as valedictorian in 1934, Smith-Dunn studied at Barber Scotia Junior College in Concord, North Carolina. She went on to study at Shaw University in Raleigh, from which she would graduate with a major in education and a minor in mathematics.

## Career Highlights

After graduating from Shaw, she taught school in North Carolina. After two years, she married Edward D. Smith. Moving to Queens, New York, Smith-Dunn taught history and special education in the New York City public school system and raised four children, Jacquelyn, William, Sy Oliver, and Carleton. She earned her masters' degree from Queens College in 1964.

Smith-Dunn was studying for a doctorate at New York University when, one day in 1967, she drove to La Guardia Airport and had her first flight lesson. "Nobody at my house knew where I was," Smith-Dunn remembered, "nobody in the world knew where I was, none of my acquaintances. So the flight instructor and I flew over the Hudson River, around, and he showed me differ-

ent maneuvers and everything. I was just—talking about *in* air, then I was *on* air. . . . I had been wanting to do that for so long." She completed her flight training at Fayetteville, North Carolina, close to her parents' home, and there realized the intense interest young people had about flying. "The kids heard there was a black woman out at [the] airport, . . . and they would come to watch. When I would land the plane and start to my car . . . they would waylay me. . . . I always stopped and talked to them, and they would ask me so many questions. Some of them I didn't even know the answer yet." But she promised to find out for them. "You really have to be honest with kids. . . . I spent a lot of time with them. Every day. . . . So that's how the flight clubs started."

Smith-Dunn earned her private pilot's license that year, and also received her instrument rating, which qualified her to fly during bad weather, as well as certification as a ground instructor. She founded the first Ida Van Smith Flight Club in Jamaica, New York, and began by using a stationary aircraft instrument panel set up in her living room. The program was expanded into the public schools, and Smith-Dunn also started an aviation career exposure program at York College, City University of New York.

Soon there were flight club chapters in Lumberton, North Carolina, Fort Worth, Texas, and on the Caribbean island of St. Lucia. Eventually, nearly a dozen chapters of the Ida Van Smith Flight Club were established. Experts from many areas of aviation volunteer to show the students and their parents around airports and different aircraft. The students visit aerospace museums and air traffic control centers, and have opportunities to learn about aircraft instruments and the aerodynamics of flight.

Each club has, on average, 20 members, ranging in age from 19 to as young as three. "Anything that a child does very young, he will probably be able to learn better and feel more at ease than if he waited until he was my age to begin," Smith-Dunn has explained:

> Nothing about managing . . . and flying a plane [was] too difficult, too heavy, in any way that [the students] couldn't handle. . . . All they needed was the brainpower. There were some from affluent families, but some of the kids I had in the classes came from very, very poor, poor homes in Queens, and they had almost nothing. But I talked to the parents and encouraged them to make certain that the kids didn't stay out of school for any reason whatsoever. . . . [M]ention aviation and one kid would say, "I've taken aviation." Another kid will want it, see, and it just goes around. To them, it . . . meant prestige, you see, because it was so new to them.
>
> When I met the kids, I always said to them, we're not trying to make pilots out of everyone, but we want you to know that you can be a pilot if you want to be, or whatever else you want to pursue in life, you can do it.

Over the years, more than 6,000 young people have been involved with Smith-Dunn's program; many have become military, commercial, or private pilots, aeronautical engineers, submarine navigators, and air traffic controllers.

Smith-Dunn also produced and hosted a cable television program associated with the Ida Van Smith Flight Club, and was a columnist for Long Island newspapers, writing about aviation. She retired from public school teaching in 1977 and devoted herself to the flight clubs, which are now headquartered in Lumberton, North Carolina. In 1978, she was awarded the World Aerospace Education Organization Award by the International Women's Conference held in Nairobi, Kenya. Along with Jerrie Cobb, who in 1960 was the first American woman to qualify as an astronaut, Smith-Dunn was awarded the prestigious Bishop Wright Air Industry Award in 1979.

Smith-Dunn is a member of Negro Airmen International and of the International Ninety-Nines, an international organization of women pilots co-founded by Amelia Earhart. In 1984, she was the first African American woman inducted into the International Forest of Friendship, in Atchison, Kansas. The forest, a bicentennial gift from the Ninety-Nines to the United States, consists of trees from all 50 states as well as the territories and countries that represent the worldwide locations of more than 6,000 members. Since her own induction, Smith-Dunn has sponsored the induction of other African American aviators and military figures, including Janet Harmon Bragg, Dr. Roscoe C. Brown, Bessie Coleman, Dr. Mae Jemison, and General Colin Powell.

The Ida Van Smith Flight Clubs and Smith-Dunn herself were honored as part of the "Women and Flight" exhibition at the National Air and Space Museum in Washington in 1997; Smith-Dunn is also honored in the International Women's Air and Space Museum in Dayton, Ohio. In 1998, Smith-Dunn received the Ninety-Nines' Award of Achievement for her outstanding contribution to aviation education.

Smith-Dunn's second husband is Benjamin E. Dunn.

## Sources

"Aviation's Pied Piper." *Ebony* (November 1978): 106–108, 110.

"Flight Instructor: Ida Van Smith." *Profiles in Black: Biographical Sketches of 100 Living Black Unsung Heroes.* Ed. Doris Funnye Innis and Juliana Wu. New York: CORE Publications, 1976; 138–139.

Freydberg, Elizabeth Hadley. "Smith, Ida Van." *Black Women in America: An Historical Encyclopedia.* Ed. Darlene Clark Hine. Brooklyn, NY: Carlson Publishing, 1993; 1079–1080.

"Pioneers of Flight: Ida Van Smith." National Air and Space Museum, Smithsonian Institution, Washington, D.C. Http://www.nasm.edu/nasm/aero/women_aviators/ida_van_smith.htm. December 15, 1999. Accessed June 4, 2000.

Russo, Carolyn. "Ida Van Smith-Dunn." *Women and Flight: Portraits of Contemporary Women Pilots.* New York: National Air and Space Museum,

Smithsonian Institution/Little, Brown, 1997; 102–105.

Smith, Ida Van. *Fly with Me Coloring Book (A True Story)*. Rochdale Village, NY: Keith Publishers, Inc., 1988.

# Chauncey Spencer

Chauncey Spencer. Courtesy of Chauncey Spencer.

**Full Name at Birth:** Chauncey Edward Spencer

**Born:** November 5, 1906, Lynchburg, Virginia

**Education:** Dunbar High School, Lynchburg, Virginia; B.A. in sociology, Virginia Theological Seminary and College, Lynchburg, Virginia, 1930; Coffey School of Aeronautics, Chicago, Illinois, pilot's license, 1936–1938.

**Positions Held:** Employees relations officer, USAF, Wright-Patterson AFB, 1941–1956, and at Norton AFB, 1956–1959; police commissioner, San Bernardino, California, 1962–1970; deputy administrator, Highland Park, Michigan, 1970–1979.

**Awards, Honors:** Dwight H. Green Trophy, NAAA, 1938; citation and medal, Mayor LaGuardia, New York, 1939; Exceptional Civilian Service Award, USAF, 1948; honored as a pioneer at the "Black Wings" exhibition, National Air and Space Museum, 1982; inducted into the Hall of Fame of the Aeronautical Historical Museum, Richmond, Virginia, 1983; honored by the city of Lynchburg, 1986, Lynchburg College, 1987, and the Michigan State Legislature, March 1992; Recognition Award, National Air and Space Museum, February 15, 1994; Chauncey E. Spencer Day, Dayton, Ohio, June 23, 1995; Award, Tuskegee Airmen Museum and Detroit chapter, October 15, 1999.

**Summary:** Chauncey E. Spencer advanced the integration of African Americans into U.S. military aviation as a private pilot during the 1930s. A founding member of the National Airmen's Association of America in 1937, he flew to Washington, D.C., in 1939 to lobby for the inclusion of African Americans into the government-financed Civilian Pilot Training Program. Although in his 90s at the time this book is being compiled, Spencer continues to offer his sharp recall of events, as well as generous access to his archives, to filmmakers, journalists, and researchers.

## Early Years

Chauncey Edward Spencer was born on November 5, 1906, to Edward A. Spencer and Anne Bethel Bannister Spencer in Lynchburg, Virginia. His older sisters, Bethel and Alroy, were born in 1901 and 1903, respectively. Edward Spencer owned a grocery store with his brother and he later worked at the post office. He invested widely in real estate and he founded Spencer Place, a private housing development of 14 homes. Anne Spencer (1882–1975) was the valedictorian of her class of 1899 at Virginia Theological Seminary. She was a teacher and librarian at Dunbar High School, the founder of the local chapter of the National Association for the Advancement of Colored People (NAACP), and a poet whose work was widely admired by the writers of the Harlem Renaissance. The Spencer home was open to visits by distinguished African Americans of the time. James Weldon Johnson, poet, novelist, and civil rights activist, George Washington Carver, scientist, and the singers Marian Anderson, Roland Hayes, and Paul Robeson were some of the guests. Literary visitors included Langston Hughes and Claude McKay. Thurgood Marshall, then head of the NAACP's Legal Defense Fund, W.E.B. Du Bois, and Mary McLeod Bethune also visited the Spencers.

But it was the sight of an airplane "cutting through the feathery clouds like a knife slicing bread," in 1917, that influenced Chauncey Spencer's life more than the prominent visitors did. The next day he built his own "plane" with a barrel, a wagon, and old sheets. Too young to fly, Spencer pursued other daring activities such as climbing up on construction sites high above the ground and walking around the edges. At age 13 he was selling chicken giblets, obtained free from the cook at Randolph Macon College who was throwing them away. At 14, he delivered medicine for a pharmacy and worked as a hotel bell hop. On a visit to his sisters, who were attending Hunter College in New York, Spencer experienced sharper discrimination than he had in the South. But he also heard a speech by Marcus Garvey, the founder of the Universal Negro Improvement Association. Garvey's famous exhortation, "Up, you mighty race, you can accomplish what you will," was an effective antidote. It built upon his mother's activism and her determination not to be swallowed up by racial injustice.

Spencer's last year at the all-Negro Dunbar High School was stormy. The superintendent of city schools ordered the black high schools to end 15 minutes later than the white high schools, to avoid fights that might occur if the students left at the same time. Spencer refused to comply with this order that he felt was insulting and discriminatory. Despite intervention by his parents he was suspended, and then expelled.

## Higher Education

Spencer completed his last year of high school at Virginia Theological Seminary and College, from which he graduated in 1930 with a B.A. in sociology. The Lynchburg institution had a reputation for seeking independence from its white sponsor, the American Baptist Home Mission Society. An early president was a staunch advocate of racial independence, going so far as to refuse financial assistance from the society. The next president, R.C. Woods (1910–1926) oversaw the construction of three new campus buildings and the accreditation of the seminary as a college. In June 1927, Spencer entered into a brief marriage with Elvira Jackson.

From 1936 to 1938, Spencer pursued flying lessons at the Coffey School of Aeronautics in Chicago, where Cornelius Coffey, the director, was his instructor.

## Career Highlights

There were not many job opportunities when Spencer graduated at the beginning of the Great Depression. He washed dishes in Chicago and then managed a movie theater in Gary, Indiana. Moving back to Chicago, Spencer was employed by the Works Project Administration (WPA), a government program, from 1933 to 1935. He was a researcher for *Black Metropolis: A Study of Negro Life in a Northern City* by St. Clair Drake and Horace Cayton. This study of Chicago, published in 1945, became a classic of sociological investigation. Spencer then worked for the U.S. Postal Service until 1941.

Spencer's lifelong passion for aviation changed his life, and the lives of many other

African Americans who wanted to fly. In the mid-1930s, Spencer began taking flying lessons at the Coffey School of Aeronautics at Harlem Airport. Air-minded blacks tended to gravitate to Chicago, and to a lesser degree, Los Angeles. The pilots and aviation enthusiasts Spencer met there became the legendary pioneers who flew airplanes despite strong barriers of economic and racial discrimination. The core group in Chicago included Willa Brown, Cornelius Coffey, Grover C. Nash, Marie St. Clair, Janet Waterford, and Dale White. They incorporated themselves as the National Airmen's Association of America (NAAA) on August 16, 1937. Their main goal was to increase the number of African Americans who would enter the new field of aviation, and to provide a clearinghouse to exchange information. They needed money and publicity.

At an airshow in October 1938 before more than 25,000 spectators, some of the NAAA pilots flew their planes through loops, wing-overs, barrel rolls, and spirals. Spencer cut such a dashing figure that he was nicknamed "Clark Gable," after the screen idol who starred in the 1938 film, *Test Pilot*. Spencer's specialty was daring parachute jumps, either not opening his parachute until barely 1,200 feet from the ground or tossing it away all together. Of course Spencer had a concealed parachute and when he finally would pull the rip cord the crowd gasped and cheered. One of these exploits resulted in a 10-day paralysis for Spencer, but he and his colleagues were buoyed by their successes, and they ignored such setbacks.

Spencer's most important flight began on May 9, 1939, when he and Dale L. White set out from Chicago to fly to Washington, D.C. They were enacting a plan by the NAAA to urge Congress to include Negro pilots in the new Civilian Pilot Training Program (CPTP), created to provide a reserve of pilots if war were to come. Their plane was a cream-and-red Lincoln-Paige biplane that, Spencer wrote, "literally flew backwards whenever we met a heavy wind." Financing

the flight was shaky too, pieced together from such sources as Spencer's savings from his WPA job; contributions from his mother; and additional contributions from the Jones brothers, department store owners, and Chicago's leading black numbers racketeers.

Forced down by a broken crankshaft, they landed in a farmer's field in Sherwood, Ohio, where they waited two days for the damage to be repaired. In Washington, they were met by Edgar G. Brown, the major lobbyist for Negro causes and head of the Negro Federal Employees Union. As they were getting off the electric underground train that connects the Capitol and congressional offices, Brown introduced them to Senator Harry S Truman, who was passing by. Truman was surprised to learn they were barred from joining the U.S. Army Air Corps. According to Spencer, Truman asked many questions and went out to see the plane, although he refused a ride. He then said that "if we had guts enough to fly this thing to Washington, he'd have guts enough to back us." Truman, from Missouri, and Everett Dirksen, the senator from the NAAA's home state, Illinois, were strong supporters of legislation to include Negroes in the CPTP. In June 1939 the legislation was enacted that opened the way for African Americans to be trained as pilots. Significant as this event was, it had a greater future impact. In 1945, Truman succeeded Roosevelt as president, and on July 26, 1948, he issued Executive Order No. 9981, which ended racial discrimination and segregation in the U.S. armed forces.

On August 18, 1940, Spencer and Anne Howard were married at the clubhouse at Harlem Airport. Eight children were born to them from 1943 to 1963: Edward, Carol, Michael, LuJuan, Chauncey II, Joel, Shaun, and Kyle.

Spencer enlisted in the Army in March 1941, hoping to become a cadet at Tuskegee. But a few months later the age limit was set at 28 years and Spencer, then 35 years old, became a civilian employee at Wright-Patterson AFB near Dayton, Ohio. He was assigned to undercover work as an aircraft mechanic at Tuskegee Army Air Field to insure compliance with President Roosevelt's Executive Order No. 8802. This directive prohibited discrimination in all federal installations. Spencer's report included enough evidence of unequal treatment so that several months later the top command was replaced by Colonel Noel Parrish. Parrish treated the men with dignity; his most famous quote is "There is no colored way to fly."

Returning to Wright-Patterson as employee relations officer, a black supervisor of whites, Spencer was charged with making sure all personnel were treated fairly. He was told to go slow by some and called a Communist and an Uncle Tom by others. His ability to implement equal opportunity was noted by Cleveland's *Call and Post* (December 23, 1944) as it wrote of "Spencer's heroic accomplishments . . . in 1940, there were 23 janitors at Patterson Field. In 1944, there are 600 Negroes working in all capacities." By March 1947 that figure rose to nearly 9,000 African Americans employed at the air base. In 1948, Spencer received the Air Force's highest civilian honor, the Exceptional Civilian Service Award for "outstanding achievements in racial relations . . . and establishment of public good will."

Despite this honor, Spencer was accused of being a security risk in September 1953. He was suspended from his job and his annual income dropped from $6,400 to $187. His family suffered harassment such as late-night telephone calls, garbage thrown on their lawn, and shunning by neighbors and the children's classmates. Spencer's defense costs were $18,000, and in June 1954, he was completely exonerated of all charges, with the Air Force finding that his continued "employment was clearly consistent with the interests of national security." But the harassment continued, and in 1956, the Spencers moved to San Bernardino, California. Spencer became employee relations officer at nearby Norton AFB until 1959, when he retired from the Air Force.

In 1962, Spencer became the security officer at San Bernardino High School, a position that included involvement in policy meetings and covering classes for absent teachers. He was also the president of the local NAACP chapter. In 1965, he was appointed police commissioner by the newly elected mayor of San Bernardino. He remained in this position until 1970 when he was offered the job of deputy administrator for Highland Park, near Detroit, Michigan. On his first day, July 13, with the mayor out of town, Spencer had to quell a full-scale riot, which erupted when a white bar owner shot and killed a black customer. The following years were less dramatic, and Spencer remained until 1976. Two years earlier he had donated his papers to the Bentley Historical Library of the University of Michigan, and he continued to add to the collection over the next 22 years.

Planning to return to California, he stopped at his birth place, Lynchburg, Virginia, for 60 days at the invitation of the city administration. He acted as consultant during the creation of the Anne Spencer Memorial Foundation, now a Virginia Historic Landmark and on the National Register of Historic Places. Restoring his parental home, his mother's studio cottage, and her extensive garden was to take years, and the Spencers decided to remain in Lynchburg. Spencer was variously president, chairman, and board member of the foundation.

Many honors came to Spencer in his later years. Perhaps the most fulfilling was his role as consultant to and his inclusion in "Black Wings: The American Black in Aviation." This landmark exhibition at the Smithsonian Institution's National Air and Space Museum in 1982 became a permanent exhibition and did much to make new information available. Spencer, with his vivid recall of events and his ebullient personality, was much in demand as a speaker throughout the decade. In 1992, Governor Douglas L.

Wilder invited him to represent the Commonwealth of Virginia at the air convention in Oshkosh, Wisconsin, the largest annual convention of aviation enthusiasts.

## Sources

"Goodwill Flyers End 3,000-Mile Epoch Hop." *Chicago Defender* (May 27, 1939): 4, 11.

Spencer, Chauncey E., Lynchburg, Virginia, to Betty K. Gubert, New York, personal interview, June 3, 1995; correspondence, clippings, telephone interviews, 1999.

Spencer, Chauncey E. *Who Is Chauncey Spencer?* Detroit, MI: Broadside Press, 1975.

"Spencer Thrills Crowd in Two-Mile Air Leap." *Chicago Defender* (October 1, 1938): 1, 2.

Waters, Enoch P. *American Diary: A Personal History of the Black Press.* Chicago: Path Press, 1987.

Wimer, Robert. "A True Pioneer in Aviation History." *The News and Advance*, (Lynchburg, VA) (March 5, 1995): F4.

# Emmett Stovall

**Full Name at Birth:** Emmett Luster Stovall

**Born:** [1925, Seale], Alabama

**Education:** Wendell Phillips High School, Chicago, one year; high school completion test; Dunbar Vocational School, aircraft mechanics certificate, 1944; Johnson's Flying School, Chicago, private pilot's license, 1944; Lewis Lockport College, commercial pilot's license, multiengine rating, instrument rating.

**Positions Held:** Welder, International Harvest Tractor Works, 1949 to 1964; owner, National Air, Inc., 1964–   .

**Summary:** When, as a child, Emmett Stovall decided to become a pilot, he didn't know there would be three strikes against him: poverty, little education, and a black skin in a society that was strictly segregated by color. Through determination, intelligence, and skill, Stovall overcame these obstacles to become not only a pilot but also the owner of an air service. In addition, Stovall trained other pilots, both black and white, in a school he established.

## Early Years

Emmett Stovall was born about 1925, and he grew up in Seale, Alabama, near the airfield at Fort Benning, Georgia. The Stovalls were farmers, but with 10 children, five boys and five girls, they had to augment their income with other jobs. Mr. Stovall cut wood to sell and Mrs. Stovall took in washing. Young Stovall had many chores: cutting wood; feeding the pigs, cows, horses, and mules; babysitting for two younger sisters; and picking the cotton his father planted. The family's other crops were corn, peanuts, sorghum, soybeans, and several kinds of vegetables.

One day when he was eight years old and picking cotton, Stovall looked up to see a small plane, "dipping and climbing, looping the loop, and flying upside down." He saw himself in the cockpit, and from then on, his mind was on flying, not farming. This brought him into conflict with his father, who told him flying was for white folks, not for him. His mother, however, supported his dream by buying him flying magazines and admiring the model planes he made. She also convinced her husband that he should permit Emmett to go to the airfield on Sundays, and that's where he spent his spare time between the ages of 10 and 12.

When Stovall was 12, his mother died in childbirth. Two years later his father married a woman who took Stovall's model planes and used them for firewood. Saying he was 16, Stovall worked summers at Fort Benning. He carried water to the prisoners in the stockade, washed the airplanes, and swept the floors. When he really was 16, his stepmother took his paycheck. It was then he decided to run away to an aunt living in Chicago. Stovall attended Wendell Phillips High School, but left at 17 to join the U.S. Army Air Corps with an affidavit, signed by his sister Cleo, saying he was 18.

Sent to basic training at Fort Maxey, Texas, Stovall was assigned to motor transport training. Men without some college education were not assigned to flight training. For six months, Stovall drove trucks, chauffeured officers, and finished his high school courses. When the army found out he was underage, he was discharged.

## Higher Education

Back in Chicago, Stovall could find work only at the stockyards, slaughtering hogs. At the same time, he enrolled at Dunbar Vocational School where he earned an airplane mechanic's certificate in 1944. He also signed up for flying lessons at Johnson's Flying School, an integrated group at Chicago's Harlem Airport, receiving his private pilot's license in 1944 as well. Stovall wrote in his autobiography, "By the time it was all over, I could outfly any student in the place without really working at it." Of his first solo flight, he exulted, "I was all alone up there in the cool blue, no one telling me what to do. The plane was all mine, and the moves were as I wanted them to be."

When the stockyards closed in 1945, Stovall began work at the Curtis Candy Company. As at the stockyards, he continued his aviation education. He enrolled at the Lewis Lockport College to study navigation and meteorology, the only African American in his classes. On December 22, 1945, Stovall and Orlee Wafer, a sister of one of his fellow workers, were married. He continued working at the candy factory until 1947, when he was severely burned by a vat of hot syrup. His recovery took five months.

## Career Highlights

Stovall then pumped gas and drove a cab until he became a welder with the International Harvester Tractor Works. He remained in this position for 15 years, all the while gaining flying hours and earning advanced licenses. But even though Stovall was qualified to be an airline pilot, with instrument rating, no airline would hire him. He then decided to start his own airline because, as he said, "I can't spend the rest of my life as a welder who gets turned down by the airlines."

Stovall bought a used plane, a BT-13 Trainer, and started National Air, Inc. At first it was a weekend business, flying freight and charter passengers, but by 1969, the business had grown so much that Stovall had to hire other pilots. There were four planes, with two regularly scheduled air-freight flights every day. He became the first black Beechcraft dealer in the Midwest. He opened a school, and demanded the same rigorous training that was demanded of him. His instructors had to have 2,500 hours of flying time, and experience with multiengine planes, with instrument flying, and flight time in thunderstorms.

Stovall's clients have included Chrysler Corporation and Buick Motors. Distinguished passengers who have used Stovall's air service include Reverend Jesse Jackson, senators Paul Douglas and Robert F. Kennedy, and Martin Luther King Jr. The Stovalls have one daughter, Gloria Jean, who was born around 1954.

## Sources

"Black Pilot Finds Reward in Operating His Own School." *Chicago Defender* (April 2, 1969).

"The Sky's No Limit for Black Airplane Whiz Emmit [*sic*] Stovall." *Chicago Defender* (October 20, 1969).

Stovall, Emmett. *In the Face of the Sun*. Chicago: Children's Press, 1970.

# T

## Carol Taylor

Carol Taylor. Courtesy of Carol Taylor.

**Full Name at Birth:** Ruth Carol Taylor

**Born:** December 27, 1931, Boston, Massachusetts

**Education:** Elmira College, Bellevue School of Nursing, RN, 1955.

**Positions Held:** Flight attendant, Mohawk Airlines, 1958; registered nurse, 1955–1977; journalist, civil rights activist, public speaker, 1977– .

**Awards, Honors:** Awarded a plaque honoring her achievement, Organization of Black Airline Pilots (OBAP), 1998.

**Summary:** Carol Taylor, professional nurse, author, and activist, made aviation history when she became the first African American airline stewardess in 1958. She continues to write and speak out for civil rights causes.

### Early Years

Ruth Carol Taylor was born in Boston, Massachusetts, on December 27, 1931, to Ruth Irene Powell and William Edison "Shaw" Taylor. She was always known as Carol. Her father, a farmer and a barber, received his nickname as a tribute to his football prowess at Shaw University in Raleigh, North Carolina. Her mother was a registered nurse. She has one brother, Shaw Powell Taylor.

The family lived in Cambridge, Massachusetts, for two years, then relocated to New York City. After a few years, her parents bought a farm in upstate New York and the Taylors moved there. Mrs. Taylor, who was white, made all the arrangements to purchase the property, and when the rest of the family showed up, the sellers tried to cancel the transaction. Despite this rocky beginning, the family stayed put.

Taylor and her brother enjoyed living and working on the farm. Attending the all-white high school was another matter. According to an interview, "The first kind of fights I had were for my own human rights. In high school I was the only black African student and I got it all."

## Higher Education

After graduation from Trumansburg High School, Taylor applied to Cornell University, where she was refused admission because of her race. She attended Elmira College for six months, the third black student to be admitted. Then her father died, and she left the area to attend Bellevue School of Nursing in New York City. She graduated as a registered nurse in 1955.

## Career Highlights

The 1950s are generally remembered as a tranquil decade, but it was during this period that the first stirrings of the civil rights movement took place. The Supreme Court decision in *Brown v. Board of Education* in 1954 removed the legal justification for "separate but equal" education in public schools. Encouraged by this, other African Americans refused to sit back and accept being treated as second-class citizens. They began to demand access to the same jobs, facilities, and housing that white Americans enjoyed.

Equal access to jobs was a very important step toward full equality. The airline industry, which was expanding and showed promise of future growth, had great but as yet untapped potential as an employer of qualified black men and women. No African American was currently—in the mid-1950s—employed in flight, as a pilot or flight attendant, though some were employed in a service capacity.

These in-flight jobs paid well, had prestige and glamour, and were considered highly desirable. Accordingly, the Urban League of Greater New York, where many airlines had corporate headquarters, decided to pressure the airlines to hire qualified men as pilots and women as flight attendants. In this, they were aided by the New York State Commission against Discrimination (SCAD), which investigated the matter. The cases of Carol Taylor and Dorothy Franklin, who applied as stewardesses to TWA, and Perry Young, an experienced pilot, were among those considered.

In the mid-1950s, flight attendants—then known as stewardesses or hostesses—were all young, unmarried women, chosen largely on the basis of physical attractiveness. There were stringent height and weight requirements women had to meet; in addition, they had to conform to prevalent standards of beauty. And they were all white. But things were beginning to change, driven by the nascent civil rights movement. Taylor, ever the activist, decided to help them along.

Having practiced her profession of nursing for a number of years, she applied to Trans World Airlines (TWA), a major U.S. carrier, for a stewardess job and was turned down. Taylor filed a complaint with the New York State Commission on Discrimination. But before this matter could be adjudicated, she became aware that Mohawk Airlines, a regional airline in upstate New York, was seeking a qualified Negro woman to serve as the first black flight attendant.

Taylor was one of 800 African American women who applied. She was chosen for the position, she believes, because "I answered the questions about race . . . in the way I knew they wanted them answered . . . and . . . my accent didn't ring of the deep south."

Taylor dropped her case against TWA when she went to work for Mohawk. The case of Dorothy Franklin, an employee of the New York Public Library, was successfully concluded when TWA was judged to have discriminated against her on the basis of race and not because, as they had claimed, her legs were "not shapely." In February 1958, she dropped her suit when TWA agreed to hire "a Negro girl"—not necessarily Franklin—within 90 days.

In May 1958, Margaret Grant, a psychology major at Hunter College, New York, was hired by TWA, becoming the first African American hostess on an international airline. By June, Grant had to leave the training program when it was discovered that she had a medical condition that would be exacerbated by air travel.

Taylor's appointment to the position was accompanied by a barrage of publicity. Articles about her appeared in the *Time* and *Newsweek* issues of January 6, 1958. "Stories about me had gone all over the world. I was in *Jet, Ebony*, . . . Six months was all I could take. I figured it was an upstairs maid job."

Taylor, who began working for Mohawk in early 1958, had no illusions about the job. "It wasn't something that I had wanted to do all my life," she stated in an interview with *Jet* in 1997. "But it irked me that people were not allowing people of color to apply. . . . Anything like that sets my teeth to grinding." In an interview with the *New York Amsterdam News*, she stated, "I just wanted to make a point."

Her point made, after six months of employment with Mohawk, Taylor resigned to marry Rex Legall, a Trinidadian cricket star. The couple relocated to the British West Indies. In 1960, she and her husband moved to London, where she worked for a time at a theatrical company and became a columnist for *Flamingo*, an African-Caribbean magazine.

Taylor's daughter Cindy was born in London shortly after the couple moved there.

Her marriage to Legall broke up soon afterward. She returned to the United States in the early 1960s, just in time to be involved in the civil rights movement. She was founder-president of a group called Negro Women on the March and participated in the 1963 March on Washington.

After the assassination of President John F. Kennedy, Taylor was disillusioned, losing faith in the momentum of civil rights in the United States. She moved to Barbados, where she worked as a journalist. While there, she founded Barbados's first professional nursing journal. True to form, Taylor was active in community work, receiving an award from the Boy Scouts Association for her volunteerism. An ardent defender of consumer rights, she was elected to the presidency of the Bajan Consumer League. She also became coordinator of the Committee on Human Rights of a women's organization, WOW (the Working Organization for Women). Her son Larry was born in Barbados in 1969.

In 1977, she moved back to New York City and was dismayed to discover that "racism was as alive and well as it had ever been. . . . I asked myself, 'What can one person do?' Fortunately, I have always believed that one person can make a difference. . . . No matter how hard the road, you continue chipping away. . . . I can hang in there like a pit bull."

Taylor was working as a private duty nurse when she got the idea for the Racism Quotient Test to be administered to white people. The test, known as RQ and somewhat analogous to the IQ test, was designed to reveal unexamined racist attitudes. Working with Dr. Mari Saunders, a psychologist, she developed a 20-question test. Taylor and Saunders formed the Institute for Inter Racial Harmony, under whose auspices they administered the test to members of corporations and educational institutions. They found at least one third of the individuals tested to be "dysfunctional racists." The group also held educational seminars to raise the public's awareness of racism.

In 1985, fearing for her teenage son's safety in a hostile environment, Taylor wrote *The Little Black Book*, a set of practical rules to improve the odds for survival of young urban black men. Among her rules: "When you are approached by police, do not . . . try to prove your manhood," and, "Learn to read, write . . . and to speak English correctly." Her book has sold over 200,000 copies to date, according to Taylor.

At present, Taylor, now retired from nursing and living in Brooklyn, New York, is an activist. She writes and speaks to interested groups. She can be found protesting in the streets whenever she finds evidence of racism, particularly police brutality She considers herself a "Peoplist," one who considers all people to be equal. She is also a feminist and a strong pro-choice advocate. Taylor often works with the Reverend Al Sharpton, a prominent New York activist, but will protest by herself if she feels it is in the interest of justice. "When I'm in a protest, it does not matter if I'm the only one. I feel I'm in the only place I have to and want to be."

## Sources

Alim, Fahizah. "A Survival Message for Black Males." *Sacramento Bee* (July 5, 1992): C1.

Cadogan, Glenda. "What Makes Carol Taylor Tick?" *Daily Challenge* (March 29, 1999): 2.

Kaplan, Fred. "Attack Backs Her 30 Rules." *Boston Globe* (August 16, 1997): A5, A6.

Price, Jo-ann. "TWA to Hire Negro Air Hostess." *New York Herald-Tribune* (February 10, 1958).

Rorty, James. "The First Colored Air Hostess." *Crisis* (June–July 1958): 339–342.

"Ruth Taylor Quietly Makes History." *Ithaca* (New York) *Journal*, February 10, 1958.

"TWA Hires a Negro Student to Become Flight Stewardess." *New York Times* (May 12, 1958).

"TWA Hires First Negro Stewardess." *Pittsburgh Courier* (May 17, 1958): 3, 4.

Witkin, Richard. "Aviation: Stewardess." *New York Times* (December 24, 1957).

# Roger C. Terry

**Full Name at Birth:** Roger C. Terry

**Born:** 1921, Los Angeles, California

**Education:** B.A. in political science, University of California at Los Angeles, 1940; J.D., Southwestern School of Law; flight instructor training, Tuskegee Army Air Field, Tuskegee, Alabama, 1942.

**Positions Held:** Pilot, U.S. Army Air Corps (now the Air Force) 1943–1945; assistant district attorney and probation officer, Los Angeles County, Los Angeles, California, 1950–1980; national president, Tuskegee Airmen, Inc. (TAI), president, Los Angeles chapter, TAI.

**Summary:** Roger C. Terry was one of the original Tuskegee Airmen, the first aviators to serve as pilots in the U.S. Army during World War II. Terry was among a group of African American officers stationed at Freeman Field, Indiana, who protested their exclusion from the base officers club in 1945, contrary to army regulations. Many of the men who participated in this protest were arrested, but charges were dropped against all but three of them. Of the three, only Terry was convicted. His conviction was overturned 50 years later, in 1994.

## Early Years

Roger C. Terry was born in Los Angeles in 1921. He attended local public schools in Los Angeles and in Compton, California.

## Higher Education

Terry attended junior college in Los Angeles and then transferred to the University of California at Los Angeles (UCLA) for his last two years. In *Red Tails, Black Wings,* Terry explains why: "Tuition at the university was 50 dollars a semester—that was a lot of money—but only five dollars at the junior college level." Terry was active in athletics in college, playing varsity basketball: "Jackie Robinson and I were teammates. We were the first two blacks to play basketball in the Pacific coast conference—that was before they knew Negroes could play basketball. . . . He was a forward and the top scorer in the PCC. I played everything."

Upon graduation, in 1940, Terry took the test for the Army Air Corps. He was among the 250–300 men who passed the test, out of thousands who applied. Upon reading about his admission, the colonel was dismayed to find that Terry was an African American: "I was already sworn in, but I got a letter saying I was too tall and weighed too much. . . . Bull! . . . Ben Davis was six-foot-one!" (Ben Davis Jr. was another of the Tuskegee fliers.)

Terry was sent to Moton Air Field, in Tuskegee, Alabama, where the army had set up a segregated training site for African American aviators. The instructors were civilian pilots, many of them black. C. Alfred "Chief" Anderson, one of the first African Americans to get a pilot's license, was in charge of instructors.

Charles M. Bussey, one of the original Tuskegee Airmen, described conditions at Tuskegee in an interview published in the *Los Angeles Times*: "It was an ugly place to be. . . . The barracks had never been finished. We had for the most part deep southern instructors, some of whom were very rabid in their hatred of black folks."

Bussey stressed the point that the pilots were not given survival training: "The lack of that survival skill, specifically swimming, caused an awful lot of deaths. . . . [W]e lost many, many, fine pilots."

After completing flight training and receiving their wings, the Tuskegee men were sent to Italy, where the group were assigned to escorting bombers on their missions under the command of Benjamin O. Davis Jr. Their superb teamwork and discipline caused them to excel in this function, and the group could boast that they never lost a bomber to enemy fire. Known as the "Red Tails" because of the

distinctive markings on their planes, the unit flew 1,500 sorties in Italy, and downed 111 enemy aircraft, as well as sinking one German navy destroyer. Sixty-six members of the group were killed in action.

This creditable showing did not prevent the men from being treated as second-class citizens. They had to eat in segregated dining halls, and they had to suffer the humiliation of observing German prisoners of war being fed in white dining halls.

On January 15, 1944, the 477th Bombardment Group was formed. Terry was assigned to this group, which began its training at Selfridge Field, Michigan. Upon their assignment to training, General Hunter, their commanding officer, briefed the men: "The War Department is not ready to recognize blacks on the level of social equal to white men. This is not the time for blacks to fight for equal rights. . . . They should prove themselves in combat first. There will be no race problem here, for I will not tolerate any mixing of the races. Anyone who protests will be classed as an agitator, sought out, and dealt with accordingly. This is my base and, as long as I am in command, there will be no social mixing of the white and colored officers. The single Officers Club on base will be used solely by white officers. You colored officers will have to wait until an Officers Club is built for your use."

The 477th was moved to Godman Field, Kentucky, on May 5, 1944. On March 1, 1945, they were moved to Freeman Field, as the facilities at Godman were inadequate. Before the move, Colonel Selway, the base commander, met with the African American officers and notified them that there would be two separate but equal officers clubs, one for supervisors and trainers (all of whom were white) and the other for trainees (all of them black).

Club no. 2, to be used by the white officers, had a large fireplace and a game room with table tennis, billiard tables, and card tables. It was attached to the officers' mess hall and a guest house. Club no. 1 was a shabby room heated by two coal stoves, with no amenities except a bar and a few card tables. The men quickly dubbed it "Uncle Tom's Cabin" and refused to use it.

The men of the 477th decided to protest the situation. They held several strategy sessions to plan their course of action. The officers were aware of their limits under the Articles of War. They agreed not to disobey direct orders to leave the club. They determined either to gain peaceful admittance to the club or to be given an explanation of why the base commander, Colonel Selway, insisted on violating army regulations regarding officer access to recreational facilities.

On March 8, 1945, three black officers peacefully entered the club and seated themselves. When they requested service, however, Major A.W. White, the officer in charge of the club, ordered them out. When the African Americans questioned him, Major White stated that, by order of Colonel Selway, no black officers would be admitted. The black officers left and later reported the incident to the rest of the group.

The next evening, Lieutenant William Parks attempted to enter the club. He was prevented by Major White. The next move by the black officers was a letter, written by Parks, requesting clarification of the policies regarding Officers Club no. 2. The African American officers were aware of army regulation 210–10, that forbade discrimination on the basis of race in the use of base recreational facilities. Parks mentioned this regulation in his letter.

The letter alarmed the authorities, and Colonel Thomas Keach, the executive officer of the 477th, met with Parks and warned him that his letter could jeopardize his career and was dangerous to the existence of the 477th. Subsequent to this, Keach arranged a meeting with the black officers. Colonel John B. Patterson, deputy commander, presided. Patterson informed the group that regulation 210–10 did not apply to Freeman Field, as it was a training facility. Patterson then read a letter, reportedly from General Hunter, that

designated all supervisory, command, and instructional personnel by title. The group complained that none of the titles named were held by black men. Patterson informed the group that any officer of the Overseas Training Group (OTU) who set foot in the club would be tried for insubordination.

Between April 1 and April 5, African American officers of the OTU and Reserve Training Unit (RTU) from other sites were sent to Freeman Field, some of them combat veterans. These officers supported the actions already taken. It was decided as a matter of strategy that the protest would be carried on by these new arrivals, who could be presumed not to have knowledge of Patterson's orders.

The African Americans, wishing to assert their rights in as nonconfrontational a manner as possible, decided to approach the officers' club in small groups of no more than five men. What these officers could not know was that someone had warned Major Joseph A. Murphy, commander of C Squadron, 118th Air Force Base Unit, of the actions that were planned. To thwart the African Americans' plans, the assistant provost marshal was stationed at the front entrance of the club, and all other doors were locked.

On April 5, the first group of officers from the 477th arrived at the club. They encountered a single white officer, Lieutenant J.D. Rogers, armed and wearing the brassard that identified him as Officer of the Day, representing the commanding officer. His only responsibility was to bar black officers from the club. When the first of the black officers, Lieutenant Marsden A. Thompson, attempted to enter, Rogers stopped him just inside the door. While Rogers was engaged with Thompson, two other black officers entered the club and requested service.

The club officer, Major White, then appeared and warned the group that they would be placed under arrest if they did not leave. When they did not comply, White took everyone's name and placed them under arrest in quarters. The officers then left and returned to quarters peacefully, as ordered.

Shortly after, however, another 14 African American officers entered the club. White took their names and ordered them under arrest in quarters. Meanwhile, White was joined by Captain Anthony Chiappe, commander of the 118th Base Squadron, who ordered the men assembled. He then told them that if they had any complaints, they should take them up with him the next day, and, as their commanding officer, he would see what he could do. This group of officers departed from the club.

Immediately after this incident, three more African American officers attempted to enter the club. Lieutenant Terry was one of these three. Rogers confronted the officers and tried to prevent them from entering. A scuffle ensued. Rogers later claimed that Terry had shoved him aside.

The post provost marshal then turned up and refused entry to an additional three black officers. By the time the evening ended, 36 African American officers had been placed under arrest. At that time, Major White closed the club for the night.

Selway, confident that the arrested officers were a small group of "agitators," reopened the club the next day. A total of 25 black officers, in three groups, entered the club that evening. White intercepted all three groups, took their names, placed them under arrest in quarters, and ordered them to leave. With arrests of black officers now totaling 61, Selway again ordered the club closed.

Selway then sought advice from two officers from the Judge Advocate's Office. They counseled him to release all the officers except the three who had reportedly jostled Rogers. They further suggested that Selway issue a new base regulation, which Selway accordingly did. Base Regulation 85–2, entitled "Assignment of Housing," designated mess and recreational facilities for all officers. The regulation classified all black officers in Combat Command Training Squadrons as trainees. However, the white officers of the

all-black 387th Service Group were not affected by the order. Selway ordered all the officers to sign an endorsement to the regulation, indicating that they had read and understood it.

A large majority of the men refused to sign, even when directly ordered to do so by Chiappe. All were arrested. One hundred and one officers were secretly flown to Godman Field on April 13, 1945, under the guise of temporary duty. Confined to barracks, guarded by sentries, and surrounded by barbed wire, the African Americans had leisure to contemplate the relative freedom of German prisoners of war who were also quartered at the base.

The case was starting to generate negative publicity. The Washington chapter of the National Association for the Advancement of Colored People (NAACP) attempted to investigate, but they were not allowed to interview the officers. Nevertheless, news of this action was getting out, and pressure from civil rights organizations, the press, and congressman began to mount. Under this pressure, the men were given administrative reprimands—all except Terry, Clinton, and Thompson.

In May 1945, the War Department's McCloy Committee conducted an investigation into the events at Freeman Field. On May 18, the committee reported that Selway's actions violated Army Regulation 210–10, and recommended that his actions be brought to the attention of General Arnold, chief of Army Air Forces. Charges against all the men in the so-called Freeman Field Mutiny were dropped, with the exception of Clinton, Thompson, and Terry, who had been involved in the altercation with Rogers. These three were accused of jostling Rogers after having been given a direct order.

The three men had been held under arrest for 87 days without being formally charged. They were confined to quarters and not permitted to perform their duties as officers. Terry recalled the ordeal: "I spent three months by myself. Nobody could speak to me. I had to knock on the door and ask the corporal of the guard to get the officer of the guard to take me to the bathroom. On the hour, every hour, they asked who you were." At last, the three were formally charged. Clinton and Thompson were tried separately, on July 2, 1945, and were acquitted. Terry's trial started on the next day, July 3.

The prosecution presented testimony by Rogers, who stated that Terry had pushed him. Several other witnesses backed up his story. Terry was found guilty of offering violence to a superior officer when given an order and ordered to pay a fine of $150. He refused to appeal the decision, considering it a "red badge of courage."

The action at Freeman Field led to an order by Secretary of War Henry L. Stimson that the policy of the War Department "does not permit the exclusion, on the basis of race and color, of any member of the military [to facilities, including] membership in officers clubs, messes, or similar social organizations." Thus, through their activities, the men of Freeman Field destroyed the justification for racist and exclusionary policies, paving the way for the future integration of the armed forces.

Terry returned to civilian life shortly after these events. He went on to receive his law degree, and he spent 35 years in law enforcement, including service with the Los Angeles County District Attorney's office and the Los Angeles County Probation Department. In 1980, Terry retired.

Terry was active in the Tuskegee Airmen, serving as president of the Los Angeles chapter of the organization and as national president. As a member of the group, Terry made a point of reaching out to minority youth, speaking to groups of school children about his experiences and exhorting them to make the best of their opportunities, which had been so dearly bought.

Terry reminisced about his involvement in the Freeman Field Mutiny in 1992, in *USA Today*: "I did it because I was annoyed. . . . They had sent us to war and we had done our duty, but when we came back we could only go to certain places and ride in the back of the bus. There comes a time when you have to take a stand."

On August 12, 1995, at the Tuskegee Airmen's annual dinner in Atlanta, Georgia, the Air Force formally vindicated all the men who had protested the order at Freeman Field, including Terry. Rodney A. Coleman, assistant secretary of the Air Force, restored all the "rights, privileges, and property" Terry had lost due to his conviction. Terry described his reaction: "I jumped up, spilling water over the Chief of Staff. . . . My speech was short. For the first time in my life, I was speechless. I didn't have a damn thing to say."

## Sources

"Afro-American Almanac: Historic Events." Http://www.toptags.com/aama/events/fmutiny.htm>. July 2, 2001.

Harney, James. "Tuskegee Pilots: Men on a Mission." *USA Today* (July 30, 1992): 6.

Holway, John B. *Red Tails, Black Wings: the Men of America's Black Air Force*. Las Cruces, NM: Yucca Tree Press, 1997.

Millican, Anthony. "Spreading Their Wings: Black WW II Airmen's New Mission Is to Inspire and Motivate Youths." *Los Angeles Times* (July 12, 1992): B1, 5.

Scott, Lawrence P. *Double V: The Civil Rights Struggle of the Tuskegee Airmen*. East Lansing: Michigan State University Press, 1994.

Warren, James C. *The Freeman Field Mutiny*. Vacaville, CA: Conyers Publishing, 1995.

# James A. Tilmon Sr.

**Full Name at Birth:** James Alphonso Tilmon

**Born:** July 31, 1934, Hominy, or, Guthrie, Oklahoma

**Education:** Attended Howard University, Washington, D.C., 1951–1953; Tennessee A&I State University, Nashville; Maryland

State College, Princess Anne; B.A. in music, Lincoln University, Jefferson City, Missouri, 1957.

**Positions Held:** Captain, U.S. Army Corps of Engineers, 1957–1965; captain, American Airlines, 1965–[1990]; television host and weather forecaster, WMAQ-TV, Chicago, 1968–1994; president, Tilmon Productions, Inc., 1970–(?); [weather forecaster], WFLD-TV, Chicago, December, 1994–(?).

**Awards, Honors:** Army Commendation Medal; Captain's Chair Award, American Airlines, 1969; Number One Award, Chicago West Side Organization, 1974; Black Achievers Award, YMCA, 1974; Emmy Award, Ebony Fashion Fair, 1975.

**Summary:** James A. Tilmon Sr., one of the first African Americans to become a pilot for American Airlines when commercial aviation opened its doors to people of color, has also been a pioneer in both the educational and commercial sides of the television industry. Tilmon was the nation's first black talk show host, for a 1968 Chicago program called *Our People.* In 1974, he became Chicago's first black weatherman, while still working full time for American Airlines. A talented clarinetist as well, Tilmon has played with several orchestras in Illinois.

## Early Years

James Alphonso Tilmon, was born in Hominy, or, Guthrie, Oklahoma, on July 31, 1934, the second of two sons. His father, George Tilmon, was the principal of the town's Carver elementary school, and his mother was a teacher in the primary grades. Tilmon saw his first airplane when he was eight years old. His father had to explain to him that it wasn't a silver bird, but was a machine, and a man was flying it. The eight-year-old Tilmon decided then that, when he was grown, that would be his job. That early ambition led him to pioneering careers in commercial aviation and in television as well.

About two years later, the family moved to Boley, an all-black town so George Tilmon could become superintendent of schools there. Another move occurred in 1948, to Sand Springs, where Tilmon's father became principal of the high school. Young Tilmon continued to build ever-more-complex model airplanes, and he read everything he could find on aviation. He was captain of the Sand Springs High School's basketball team, but only for one game. His father, convinced that his son had a heart murmur, forbade any more play after that first game. But not wanting to leave him with nothing, the elder Tilmon bought his son a clarinet and provided lessons.

## Higher Education

After completing his elementary and high school education in Oklahoma, Tilmon entered Howard University in Washington, D.C., in 1951, planning to major in chemistry. He had thought of becoming a doctor. Two years later he decided to study music instead, and he enrolled at Tennessee A&I State University in Nashville. While there, Tilmon joined the Reserve Officers Training Corps (ROTC). He later attended Maryland State College in Princess Anne County for one semester. A professor of military science at the college thought he lacked the aptitude for aviation, and he noted that on his record.

Tilmon then enrolled at Lincoln University in Jefferson City, Missouri, where he received a bachelor's degree in music in 1957. Despite the damaging note on his college record, Tilmon's interest in aviation was unabated. At Lincoln, he also joined ROTC, and although he was a music major, he included studies in engineering as well.

## Career Highlights

Upon graduation in 1957, Tilmon joined the U.S. Army Corps of Engineers because he had heard it provided an excellent background for flight school. Tilmon spent eight years in the Corps, and his postings, both domestic and overseas, were numerous. Among his many assignments were Fort Leonard, Missouri; San Marcos, Texas, where he received primary flight training; and in 1959, Fort Rucker, Alabama. Tilmon took his advanced flight training here, which included instrument flying. In 1961, he was sent to Mineral Wells, Texas, where he received training in flying helicopters. Further assignments took him to Honau, Germany, where he flew small planes for the 37th Engineer Group. His stays in Germany and France provided Tilmon with respites from American racism and served to broaden his horizons. Tilmon married, and he and his wife Louise had three children, James Alphonso Jr., another son, and a daughter.

Although Tilmon was now a captain, he felt a lack of opportunity for personal growth. He sought the advice of Colonel John C.H. Lee, his commanding officer in Germany, and a direct descendent of Robert E. Lee, the Confederate general. Tilmon considered him to be the epitome of an army officer. With no hesitation, Lee advised Tilmon to leave the army to live his own life, and to work for civil rights for other African Americans. Tilmon began applying to the airlines, and in 1965, American Airlines offered him the position of flight engineer on jet planes. Tilmon thus became the third African American to be hired by the airline, after David E. Harris and Jack A. Noel in 1964. This opening of opportunities for black pilots came on the heels of the U.S. Supreme Court's decision in April 1963 that racial discrimination by U.S. airlines was unconstitutional. Tilmon worked out of Chicago for American, and the family moved to the mostly white suburb of Highland Park, where Louise Tilmon taught mathematics at the local high school. There, Tilmon found much to engage his energy, in the form of new interests and careers to explore, while still maintaining a full schedule as a pilot for American Airlines.

Tilmon believes that it is archaic for an individual to think he has capabilities in one or two areas only. He normally worked about 18 to 20 hours a day and he stated, "Man is like a computer. If you own a computer you don't want any down time." Perhaps his brother's sudden death in 1973 made him subscribe to the idea that "although a man's life is limited quantitatively it is not qualitatively . . . I don't want to waste time."

Still working for American, Tilmon began his television career in 1968 with a talk show, *Our People*, on Chicago's educational channel, WTTW-TV. It grew out of his work as a consultant with the Chicago Board of Education, and the need to make known the opinions and aspirations of African Americans. *Our People* was broadcast live, and it made Tilmon the nation's first black talk show host on television. The show was on the air until February 1972. Later that year, in June, *Tilmon Tempo* premiered on the NBC affiliate, WMAQ-TV. The viewpoint now was international and multicultural and featured such guests as a rabbi and a jazz musician, and subjects as diverse as Japanese music and Hungarian needlework. Tilmon now felt that African Americans no longer needed to "remain on our turf . . . we will have a much stronger base of operation when we can align ourselves with others who share our common problems."

While *Our People* was still on the air, and Tilmon continued to work full time as a co-pilot, he incorporated Tilmon Productions, Inc., in Highland Park. He was the president and his father was vice president. Partners in the company were his co-pilot at American, Captain Richard Ortman, and the flight engineer, Eugene Shea. Tilmon founded the multimedia company to bridge the gap in communications among ethnic groups. It produced videotapes, reel-to-reel and cassette audio tapes, slide presentations, and motion pictures for industry, government agencies, and departments of education. Some of the firm's clients were the Federal Aviation Administration (FAA) and the U.S. Department of Health, Education, and Welfare (HEW). *Brother*, a feature film about equal opportunity in the FAA, won four industrial film awards. A multimedia production called *Black Man in America* was also successful in its depiction of the variety of black men across the country.

Having begun clarinet lessons in high school, Tilmon became proficient enough to play with such groups as the Evanston Symphony in 1969, the Highland Park Symphony Orchestra in 1973, and the Lake Forest Symphony Orchestra in 1975. Despite the hours needed for rehearsal and performance, Tilmon always enjoyed music for the break it provided him from the demands of the many careers he followed, all at the same time. He told *Ebony* (April 1973) that, "When I have that horn in my hand, I'm a musician—and nothing else."

In the fall of 1974, Tilmon began yet another career, that of a television weather forecaster. He was already known to NBC's local channel, WMAQ-TV, as an experienced television personality when they were conducting a nationwide search for a qualified and effective commentator on the weather. The station realized that although Tilmon ran a variety show, his knowledge of weather was profound. He himself pointed out, "In flying, weather is survival." He considered his new position as a further development in his life as a flyer, and not as an unrelated venture. While flying for American, his flight plans took him around the country, where he could see cloud patterns and their movements for himself and interpret their meanings. By the early evening time of the first of his two television weather reports, he had a very good handle on the country's weather. He enjoyed seeing how accurate his forecasts turned out to be. Although Tilmon could actually see the weather from his plane, he also used the services of meteorologists who checked maps and other data. Tilmon continued his weather re-

ports until 1988. He resumed them in 1990 and continued as the channel's science and aviation specialist until December 1994, when he left for a FOX station, WFLD-TV. *EM—Ebony Man* (January 1991) refers to Tilmon as a former pilot for American Airlines, but whether he retired or left for other reasons could not be determined. Pilots are required to retire at age 60. In 1986, Tilmon was on medical leave from the airline (*Ebony*, February 1986).

Tilmon's time away from work is spent on the tennis court or at the swimming pool. He is a Trustee at Kendall College. He is often asked to speak to community groups and at schools and colleges. As he pursued his careers, Tilmon was always concerned for those who would come after him. He told *Jet* (July 24, 1975), "For too long, young ghetto kids have thought that all of their values centered around their immediate area. I want to expose all kinds of people to roles of life they are not familiar with."

Fifteen years later, in an interview with *EM—Ebony Man* (April 1990), Tilmon was disappointed by the dwindling number of black aviators entering the field. By then a captain with American for 25 years, Tilmon blamed less government support for equal opportunity, and the black community for not encouraging its youngsters to break into nontraditional fields. He worried that, "aviation will be yet another one of those careers where you just don't see us."

## Sources

Anderson, Monroe. "Jim Tilmon: Jet Age Renaissance Man." *Ebony* (April 1973): 56–58, 60–62.

"Black Weathermen: The New Stars of Television." *EM—Ebony Man* (January 1991): 52–53.

"Chicago Weatherman has Resolve for Job Madness." *Jet* (July 24, 1975): 20–22.

Drotning, Phillip T. *Up from the Ghetto.* New York: Cowles Book Co., 1970; 58–74.

Harmon, George. "Restless Black Pilot Eyes Better Skies for 'Brothers.'" *Cincinnati Enquirer* (April 13, 1969). This article may have also appeared in Chicago papers.

Innis, Doris Funnye, and Juliana Wu. *Profiles in Black: Biographical Sketches of 100 Living Black Unsung Heroes.* New York: CORE Publications, 1976; 30–31.

"James Tilmon: Meteorologist and Pilot." Http://www.lib.lsu.edu/edu/lib/chem/display/tilmon.html. Accessed February 14, 1999.

Neimark, Paul. "TV Weatherman in the Skies." *Sepia* (December 1975): 56–61.

"New Firm to Bridge Communication Gap." *Jet* (May 7, 1970): 56.

White, Frank, III. "Spreading Their Wings." *Ebony* (February 1986): 75–76, 78, 82.

"Wings of Progress." *EM—Ebony Man* (April 1990): 54–55.

# Shirley Tyus

**Born:** [1950]

**Education:** Professional Flight School, Friendly, Maryland, 1977–1979.

**Positions Held:** Model; bookkeeper; flight attendant, United Airlines, 1971 or 1972–(?); pilot, Wheeler Airlines, North Carolina; second officer, United Airlines, 1987–  .

**Summary:** Shirley Tyus, who began her career in the aviation industry as a flight attendant in 1972 for United Airlines, became that company's first African American woman pilot in 1987.

## Career Highlights

When Shirley Tyus went to work for United Airlines as a flight attendant, she was the mother of a small child, André, who was born around 1969. Her previous employment had included part-time modeling and bookkeeping. At United, Tyus became interested in the mechanics of flight, and she began to see a future as a pilot. She queried the pilots about the kind of training that was needed and she sought their opinions on the merits of various flight schools. After five years as a flight attendant, she enrolled at the Professional Flight School in Friendly, Maryland, and she earned her private pilot's license in 1979. During this time Tyus had married a Ghanaian artist named Kofi. He was the owner of a greeting card business, which he had started in 1971, and he ran it from home. He was thus able to manage the domestic duties as well.

Tyus estimates that her aviation education cost $30,000, and she noted that she sometimes had to struggle against the resentment from some instructors and students. But, "I'm a bear to live with at times. To attain what I have attained, I have had to be single minded and focused."

To be a pilot for United Airlines, one needed at least 350 hours of logged flight time. Tyus pursued this goal by becoming a pilot for Wheeler Airlines, based in Raleigh, North Carolina. She flew for the black-owned airline on her days off and during her vacations, while continuing to work as a flight attendant for United. Selena Warren Wheeler, the airline's administrative assistant, and the mother of the owner, Warren H. Wheeler, recalled Tyus. "Shirley was a very hard worker . . . she would fly during the day, then she would get up at two or three in the morning and fly all night." She sometimes slept at the Wheeler home between assignments. Flying this way, in her "spare time," she eventually logged over 2,000 hours of flight time, and she joined the many other African American pilots who were trained at Wheeler Airlines.

In 1986, Tyus attempted to become a pilot for United. She took the tests and was interviewed. Not accepted by the airline then, she tried again the following year. This time she was successful, and she became United's first African American woman pilot. Her comments about her setback reveal an indomitable spirit. She said, "One of the most difficult things to do when you are trying to reach your goal is to raise your head once it's been bowed by defeat. I knew that I would eventually make it, so I refused to let anyone or anything stand in my way." According to *Ebony* (April 1991), Tyus was one of four black women pilots out of United's total of 7,000 pilots.

Beginning as a second officer, or the third person in the cockpit of the Boeing 727, Tyus was responsible for a wide range of logistical information, such as maintenance of cabin pressure, navigation, and evaluation of changing weather conditions. Careful monitoring of the computer and the instrument panel were her responsibilities as well.

Tyus and her husband are the parents of two daughters, as well as of her son, André. They are Akosua, born about 1984, and Ofusua, born about 1988, and the family lives in Washington, D.C.

## Sources

Elder, Charles. "Flight Attendant to Pilot's Seat." *Washington Post* (March 9, 1989): C11, D1.

"Flying the Friendly Skies." *Ebony* (April 1991): 62, 64, 66.

# W

## Patrice Clarke Washington

**Full Name at Birth:** Patrice Clarke

**Born:** September 11, 1961, Nassau, Bahamas

**Education:** B.S. in Aeronautical Science, Embry-Riddle Aeronautical University, Daytona Beach, Florida; commercial pilot's license, 1983.

**Positions Held:** Pilot, Trans Island Airways, 1983–1984; pilot, Bahamasair, 1984–1988; flight engineer (1988), first officer (1990), captain (1994–   ), United Parcel Service Airlines (UPS).

**Summary:** In 1988, Clarke Washington became the first black woman pilot hired by UPS, a major U.S. airline. In November 1994, she became the first black woman captain. A pilot since 1983, she has been the first in almost all her positions. She was the first woman to fly for Trans Island Airways and Bahamasair, airlines in the Caribbean.

### Early Years

Born in Nassau on September 11, 1961, Patrice Clarke (some sources use "Clark") grew up with her two sisters and her mother, who was divorced. Mrs. Clarke worked at two jobs, six days a week to support the family. Although there was no male role model, Clarke Washington later recalled it served as an advantage, "because I didn't have the stereotypes . . . boys do certain things and girls do certain other things. I always thought if somebody could do it, I could too."

Five-year old Clarke's first plane ride was to Miami to visit family and friends. Subsequent trips each summer awoke her interest in geography and flight and she was inspired enough to want to become a pilot. When she revealed that she wanted to fly airplanes at a Career Day program at her junior high school, her classmates laughed. Not discouraged by the incident, she pursued her goal of flight. By the year 2000, she had spent nearly 8,000 hours in the air.

### Higher Education

Clarke Washington took her bachelor's degree in aeronautical science from Embry-Riddle University in Daytona Beach in 1983. She also earned a commercial pilot's license at the same time. She was the only black person enrolled in the flight program and thus she became the first black woman to become a graduate of Embry-Riddle.

## Career Highlights

Trans Island Airways, a Bahamian charter company, hired the newly graduated pilot. It was a small company flying passengers throughout the Bahamas, the northern Caribbean, and south Florida. They used twin-engine Piper Aztecs and Navahos and paid $10 an hour. Clarke Washington continued her flight training to prepare herself to fly larger airplanes. In 1984, she became a first officer for Bahamasair, flying the considerably larger Boeing 748 and 737 planes, carrying as many as 120 passengers.

As a black woman pilot, Clarke Washington has received some startled and disturbed looks from passengers who couldn't believe she was going to fly the plane. One passenger even refused to fly with her. But Clarke Washington kept her spirits up by thinking of the greater obstacles faced by such pioneering pilots as Bessie Coleman, Willa Brown, and Eugene Bullard.

When she joined UPS in 1988 as a flight engineer, the funny looks became a thing of the past. With headquarters in Louisville, Kentucky, UPS flies not people but documents and packages throughout the world. She was promoted to first officer in 1990, and in November 1994, Clarke Washington became the first black woman captain of a major airline. She remained the only one until Melissa Ward was named captain at United Airlines, a passenger airline, in 1999.

Patrice Clarke and Ray Washington met at a pilot's convention and were married in 1994. A former B-52 pilot, Washington holds the rank of captain as well, but he flies for American Airlines. Clarke Washington often thinks of the young people coming behind her, and her message to them is, "Dream good dreams for yourself, work hard, persevere, surround yourself with positive people, and know that one day your dreams too will come true."

## Sources

Boyd, Charles. "In Search of the Marine Corps 1st African American Female Pilot." Http://www.black-collegian.com/Feb97/1stFemPi.html. Accessed June 24 1998.

Kiser, Henry. *Flight of the Gin Fizz—My Life at 4,500 Feet.* New York: Basic Books, 1997; 233–235.

"Pilot Flies Where No Other Black Woman Has Flown Before." *Emerge* (May 1995): 11.

"Soaring to New Heights." *Ebony* (July 1995): 74,76,78.

Welch, Rosanne. *Encyclopedia of Women in Aviation and Space.* Santa Barbara, CA: ABC-CLIO, 1998.

# Douglas C. Watson

Douglas C. Watson. Courtesy of Barbara W. Watson.

**Full Name at Birth:** Douglas Courtenay Watson

**Born:** June 21, 1920, New York, New York

**Died:** May 30, 1993, Jamaica, New York

**Education:** B.S. in aeronautical engineering, New York University (NYU), New York, 1941, M.S. in aeronautical engineering, 1949; Massachusetts Institute of Technology, advanced studies in aircraft operations research, 1959.

**Positions Held:** Aeronautics designer, AGA Company (Aircraft, Glider, and Autogiro),

Willow Grove, Pennsylvania, 1941 to [1944]; chief of requirements and planning—systems effectiveness group, Fairchild Republic Aviation Corporation, Farmingdale, New York, 1951–1978; president and founder, Sabre Research Corporation, 1978–1993.

**Awards, Honors:** Chance-Vought Memorial Prize for excellence in design, NYU, 1941; Douglas C. Watson Scholarship Award Program, Aviation/Aerospace Education Foundation, Dowling College, Oakdale, New York, 1998.

**Summary:** Douglas C. Watson distinguished himself by becoming the first African American aeronautical engineer. Watson worked on the design of the F-105 and F-84 jet fighters. He played a major role in the development of the long-range P-47N, a bomber escort, and he considered that his most important contribution to aviation. Watson's talent and generosity to other members of minorities helped diversify aeronautical engineering.

### Early Years

Douglas Courtenay Watson was born in Manhattan to James S. and Violet Mae Lopez Watson on June 21, 1920. He had an older sister, Barbara Mae (1918–1983), and there were to be two more children, James Lopez, born in 1922, and Grace E. Both parents were born in Jamaica in the West Indies, and in June 1905 James S. Watson emigrated to New York. He attended evening high school until 1910 when he enrolled at City College's evening division and at New York Law School, graduating in 1913. He and Violet Lopez were married in 1917. In 1930, he was elected to New York's municipal court, becoming the first black judge to serve on that body and he was reelected in 1940 for another 10-year term.

The parents urged their children to "look to the world," and to imagine a future with-

out limits. On Wednesday evenings, the family met in the library of their home at 117 W. 120th Street in Harlem for discussions. On occasion, prominent visitors joined them and the children were expected to take part in the conversations that ensued. Among their guests were James Weldon Johnson, the poet and novelist, and Kwame Nkrumah and Nnamdi Azikiwe, who later became presidents of their respective countries, Ghana and Nigeria. Barbara and James became lawyers, while Douglas Watson's bent was for engineering and mechanics. (In 1977, Barbara M. Watson became the first woman and the first African American to become assistant secretary of state in charge of consular affairs. She was appointed ambassador to Malaysia in 1981 by President Carter. James L. Watson fought in World War II, and his career includes service as a New York state senator from the 21st district, and as a civil court judge. He later became the senior judge on the U.S. Court of International Trade. Grace E. Watson worked in Washington for the Department of Health, Education, and Welfare in various executive positions for such organizations as Volunteers for Education and the Horace Mann Learning Center.)

Young Douglas Watson's interest lay in machines, and particularly those in aircraft. He pored over the articles on aviation and mechanics in the encyclopedia and he subscribed to *Model Aviation News*, the issues of which he kept as a reference collection. He built model planes impressive enough to win citywide competitions in 1934 and 1935.

### Higher Education

After graduating from Hunter College Model Elementary School and Townsend Harris High School, Watson entered New York University's Guggenheim School of Engineering in September 1937. As a freshman he joined the football team, but he dropped the sport to concentrate on his studies. Watson enjoyed reading poetry and the works of Antoine de Saint-Exupéry, the aviator-philosopher.

Ranked third among the graduating engineers of his class of 1941, Watson also won the Chance-Vought Memorial Prize Competition. His winning entry was a design for an eight-place, twin-engine transport plane. Despite his academic distinction and the enthusiastic recommendations of his professors, Watson was the only one of his class who was not offered a job. His applications to aircraft manufacturers were rejected, even though the aeronautical industry was then expanding rapidly to meet the needs of the approaching war. Watson pursued his studies and earned a master's degree in aeronautical engineering from NYU in 1949. He continued advanced studies in aircraft survivability systems at the Massachusetts Institute of Technology in 1959.

## Career Highlights

In 1941, Watson began his career as an aeronautics engineer and designer at the AGA corporation (Aircraft, Glider, and Autogiro) of Willow Grove, Pennsylvania. The president of the new company, Virgil H. Frazier, although a southerner, hired Watson. He agreed with his former professors, Alexander Klemin and Frederick K. Teichmann, that Watson had unusual talent and creativity. He worked as an assistant to Bernard Sznycer, an immigrant Polish aeronautical engineer, to design a new kind of aircraft for military use. They were given only 35 days to complete the job, even though AGA was counting on the new design to land them a large contract from the U.S. Army. Eventually the two-person team expanded to 14 people, and the task was completed on time. Watson remained at AGA until 1944. He maintained a life-long friendship with Sznycer and his wife, a ballerina. Other African American aeronautical engineering students

at NYU were inspired by Watson's achievements. William Simpson and Oswald Williams joined him at AGA and Fairchild Republic for distinguished careers of their own.

After Watson and Sznycer left AGA, they worked for a Canadian company. They were part of the team that designed a helicopter called *The Prelude*. After Igor Sikorsky built the first practical single-rotor helicopter in 1939, which the government ordered in large quantities throughout World War II, the race was on to develop and produce new types of helicopters.

Watson and Barbara Margetson, the daughter of Rose and Edward Margetson, were married on April 8, 1947. Her father was a composer, choir director, and organist for the Church of the Crucifixion in Manhattan, where they were married. Margetson was also the founder of the Schubert Music Society. Mrs. Watson, with a 1955 master's degree in psychology from Hunter College, worked in social services for United Cerebral Palsy in Queens, and in children's services at Brooklyn Home for Children, and at St. Vincent's Children's Services, also in Brooklyn, until her retirement in 1989. They had two sons, Marc C., born February 28, 1948, and Craig M., born November 26, 1951. Marc Watson is now a vascular surgeon in Montclair, New Jersey, and he is the president of Horizon Health Systems, an industrial screening corporation. Craig Watson is a vice president and chief information officer for FMC Corporation in Chicago.

In 1951, Watson joined Fairchild Republic Aviation Corporation in Farmingdale on Long Island, New York. He held various positions here, including principal systems design engineer. During his tenure at Republic, he helped develop the F-105 and F-84 jet fighters. Watson considered his role in the design of the long-range P-47N, a bomber escort, to be his major contribution to aviation. He left Republic in 1978 to establish his own company, Sabre Research Corporation. Watson was president of this firm as well as its consulting engineer. His sons served as directors. He specialized in aircraft analytical techniques, conducted seminars in related fields, and designed spaces in hotels, such as offices, as well as private homes. Watson also enjoyed inventing. One of his inventions is the Ice-Skateboard, an attachment that converts skateboards for use on ice.

Watson earned a pilot's license around 1964, and he flew a Cessna-182. He painted landscapes and abstractions for pleasure. He also enjoyed sailing, carpentry, concert going, travelling, and collecting books on aircraft and architectural design. Some of the organizations he belonged to were: American Institute of Aeronautics and Astronautics, American Aviation Historical Society, and Experimental Aircraft Association. He worked with his neighborhood association, the Boy Scouts, and he often spoke to youth groups and college students. Watson had an affinity for the young. He even compared the design of an airplane to the birth and raising of a child, likening the camaraderie, joys, and problems of the two ventures. And finally, the pride in seeing the design in flight, and the sadness that it has come to an end.

In 1998, the Aviation/Aerospace Foundation (AAEF) established an endowed scholarship at Dowling College's School of Aviation and Transportation, Oakdale, New York. It is called the AAEF—Douglas C. Watson Scholarship Award.

Although Watson suffered from emphysema, he died of a silent heart attack in his sleep at home. He donated his body to the NYU Medical School. After that Watson's ashes were scattered over Oak Beach, New York.

## Sources

Archives at the Schomburg Center for Research in Black Culture, New York Public Library, house the papers of James S. Watson and Barbara M. Watson, his father and sister.

Bontemps, Arna. *We Have Tomorrow*. Boston: Houghton Mifflin, 1945; 68–78.

"Douglas Watson, First Black Aeronautical Engineer Dies." *New York Amsterdam News* (June 12, 1993): 44.

Hevesi, Dennis. "Douglas C. Watson, Design Engineer, 73, in Military Aviation." *New York Times* (June 3, 1993): D23.

Nicholson, Dolores. "Barbara Watson," in *Notable Black American Women, Book II*. Detroit: Gale Research, 1996; 691–693.

Watson, Barbara, Jamaica, New York; Watson, Craig, Chicago, Illinois; Watson, Marc, Montclair, New Jersey, to Betty K. Gubert, New York, telephone interviews, correspondence, September–December 1999.

# George Watson Sr.

George Watson Sr. Courtesy of George Watson Sr.

**Full Name at Birth:** George Watson

**Born:** August 10, 1920, Wildwood, New Jersey

**Education:** Lakewood High School, New Jersey, 1941; attended Ohio State University, 1948; Ricker College, 1959; Air University (Extension Course Institute), courses in guided missiles, 1957, 1961; Ocean County College, 1982.

**Positions Held:** Stock control chief and unit supervisor, 366th Air Service Squadron of the 96th Air Service Group (Tuskegee Airmen ground support), World War II, Italy;

first African American recruiter for the Army and Air Force, Trenton, Asbury Park, and Lakewood, New Jersey, 1951–1955; retired as technical sergeant, 1969; Installer and frameman, New Jersey Bell Telephone Company, 1970–1986.

**Awards, Honors:** Air Force Outstanding Unit Award, Air Force Good Conduct Medal, both with bronze oak leaf cluster; European-African-Middle Eastern Campaign Medal with two bronze service stars; National Defense Service Medal with one bronze service star; Air Force Commendation Medal; Sharp Shooter Medal; Key to the City, Tuskegee, Alabama; special commendation to Watson from the state of New Jersey on Tuskegee Airmen Day, July 9, 1994; inducted into the Lakewood High School Hall of Fame, May 1999; New Jersey Distinguished Service Medal, March 8, 2001.

**Summary:** George Watson Sr., trained at the Tuskegee Army Flying Field and served as a member of the ground support for the black pilots who flew during World War II. It was estimated that 10 men of the ground crew were needed for every flyer. After 26 years in the U.S. Air Force, Watson retired in 1969. He tirelessly promotes the history of the Tuskegee Airmen and works as the historian of the Hannibal M. "Killer" Cox Jr. chapter of the Tuskegee Airmen, Inc., located at McGuire Air Force Base, New Jersey.

### Early Years

George Watson was born on August 10, 1920, in Wildwood to William "Jack" Watson, a carpenter, and Anna Hughes Watson, who was born in the Charlottesville–Gordonsville area of Virginia. There were already two children when he was born, a son Robert Newman from an earlier marriage, and a daughter Hazel, who died at a young age. Two more sons were born, William Jr. and Harry, and the family lived in Asbury Park and Neptune, New Jersey. With such a large family, money was always scarce, and when William Watson Sr. died in 1930, their economic conditions worsened. Soon after his father's death, Watson contracted typhoid fever, and the doctor recommended a dryer climate. In 1933, the family moved to Lakewood, which was known for its dry, pine-scented air. Beginning in his childhood, and continuing throughout his life, Watson kept scrapbooks on topics that interested him, one of which was musical entertainers. He was very aware of the entertainment scene because his brothers Harry and William were professional tap dancers. Harry was nicknamed "Feets" and both brothers performed at the Apollo Theater in New York. Watson recovered from his childhood ailments well enough to become a star football player at Lakewood High School, graduating in 1941. In 1938, he made the all-star county second team as end and tackle; in 1940, he made the team as quarterback.

After his graduation in June, Watson worked for eight months in a drug store as a "jack of all trades—drug clerk, soda jerk, window washer, janitor, and all-around handy man . . . I was so bored at the job and the lack of excitement in the small town that I decided to volunteer for the service."

### Higher Education

Watson did not earn a college degree but he pursued higher education throughout his life. During his 26-year military career he attended the Air Force Senior Non-Commissioned Officers' Academy and the Army and Air Force Recruiters' School, as well as civilian institutions such as Ohio State University and Ricker College in Maine. Through the Air Force's Air University's Extension Course Institute at Gunter AFB, Alabama, Watson earned diplomas in the principles of guided missiles in 1957, and in aircraft and missile electrical mechanics in 1961. He also took courses at Ocean County College, New Jersey, in 1982.

## Career Highlights

Watson volunteered for the U.S. Army in February 1942, just months after war had been declared. Early in March, his segregated group of soldiers traveled by train from Fort Dix, New Jersey, to Tuskegee Army Air Field in Alabama. At that time, the Air Force was still part of the Army, and was known as the Army Air Corps. Watson was assigned to the 96th Service Group of the 366th Service Squadron, and they were assigned to the 100th Pursuit Squadron of flyers. The 96th was a ground crew, the support service that was required to keep the pilots flying. More than 900 black pilots were trained, and of those, 450 flew in combat. Watson's promotions were rapid. He became a sergeant on September 1, 1942; staff sergeant on September 24, 1942; and technical sergeant on February 1, 1943. But two months later, on April 1, an order came through demoting him to private, and then promoting him back to staff sergeant. This seesaw in rank was in the same order. It completely mystified Watson, who had an unblemished record. He was never able to discover who wrote the order or why, despite the inquiries he directed to Washington.

Later that April, the group was sent first to Selfridge Field, then to Oscoda Army Air Base, both in Michigan, where they felled trees to construct a rifle range. In October, Watson traveled to Detroit to take the aviation cadet examination, but he never learned if he passed or failed. In late December, they left Oscoda for Norfolk, Virginia, a point of embarkation for Europe. After 26 days on the ocean, they reached Bari, in southern Italy, on January 29, 1944, and then traveled to Capodichino, arriving a month later. They set up 30 tents for the enlisted men, three for the officers, one for the kitchen, and one as dispensary. A drainage system was constructed and the men dug foxholes. Other jobs included wiring the tents for electricity and repairing and maintaining the planes, parachutes, and machine guns.

Watson, as stock control chief and unit supervisor, "was responsible for the smallest nut on such aircraft as the P-47 Thunderbolt to ensuring the fastest propeller-driven aircraft, the P-51 Mustang, was safely delivered in its entirety." His job was to make sure there were adequate supplies and that all classes of supplies and equipment were properly receipted, stored, and issued. Watson remained in this position in Italy until 1945, when World War II ended.

Before he went overseas, Watson and Louise Juanita Jackson, of Prattville, Alabama, were married on June 4, 1943. They met in Montgomery, where Jackson was a beautician. She later became an instructor in the field of beauty culture. Their children, George Jr. and Tina Ann, became educators, while Maurice Allen is employed by New Jersey Bell Telephone Company. Watson has two grandsons; George Bryce Watson III, is employed as a pilot by United Airlines and Mark Watson is a lawyer.

On November 30, 1948, Watson regained his rank of technical sergeant while stationed at Lockbourne AFB in Ohio. From 1951 through 1955, he was a recruiter for the Army and Air Force in Trenton, Lakewood, and Asbury Park. Watson was the first African American to hold this position. Watson remained in the Air Force as an aircraft and missile technician until his retirement in 1969. Lockbourne AFB is remembered as the last base where the Tuskegee airmen were stationed before the military integrated its personnel. The African American forces were then integrated into white units. Aside from Italy, the foreign countries Watson served in were Germany, Britain, Turkey, and Iran. Service in the United States took him to Colorado, Florida, Illinois, Maine, New York, and Texas.

In 1970 Watson went to work for the New Jersey Bell Telephone Company as a frameman and telephone installer. Retired from his second career in 1986, Watson did not remain idle. He turned to two of his greatest interests, the scrapbooks he kept all of his life and the history of the Tuskegee Airmen, America's black air force. Using these scrapbooks and the diaries he wrote during the war, Watson published a book, *Memorable Memoirs* in 1987. It covers his early life in New Jersey, and his wartime experiences in Alabama, Michigan, and Italy. Once the book was published, Watson turned his attention to Greenwood Cemetery in Lakewood, which the state had closed in 1985 for faulty record keeping and lack of maintenance. He, with a corps of volunteers, cleared up records, started a fund for maintenance and preservation, raised sinking tombstones, and obtained insurance. The cemetery reopened on December 9, 1987, largely due to Watson's energetic efforts. Greenwood, set aside for the burial of blacks in the days when segregation continued even after death, was of particular interest to the African American community.

Watson is one of the original members of Tuskegee Airmen, Inc. (TAI), founded in 1972 as an organization of the all-black Army Air Corps veterans of World War II. When they decided to open their membership to aviation enthusiasts, regardless of race, gender, or military service, Watson supported the action. He was criticized for it, but replied, "After being on the receiving end of bigotry, I would not wish it on anyone else." He is also on the board of governors of the Tuskegee Airmen National Museum in Detroit.

Watson is the historian for the Hannibal M. Cox chapter of the TAI based at McGuire AFB. Colonel Cox (1923–1988) fought in World War II, the Korean War, and the Vietnamese War. He earned a Ph.D. and he was a vice president at Eastern Airlines. The chapter named for him promotes talks to schools and to community organizations, provides scholarships, and sponsors exhibitions and film showings. The chapter succeeded in having a street at McGuire AFB renamed Tuskegee Airmen Avenue on June 19, 1988. Watson is in frequent demand as a speaker in schools, churches, community groups, hospitals, and state prisons. His appearance at a bookstore in Freehold, New Jersey, drew 100 listeners. He has received numerous honors and awards from veterans' and community groups. The NAACP and the TAI have given him lifetime achievement awards, and the mayors of Lakewood and Newark (March 20, 1997) have honored his work.

Watson received special commendation from the New Jersey Senate and General Assembly on July 9, 1994, which they designated Tuskegee Airmen Day. The resolution read, "in recognition of his devotion to preserving the memory of the exploits of these pioneering African Americans."

Watson went to Kuwait in October 1999 with Lieutenant Colonel Lee A. Archer and Lieutenant Colonel Herbert E. Carter, both retired black pilots of World War II. They traveled to Ahmed Al Jaber Air Base to dedicate Tuskegee Airmen Heritage Hall, and to witness the ceremony renaming the 4406th Operations Group to the 332nd Air Expeditionary Group. The new number recalls the 332nd Fighter Group, which comprised the four squadrons trained at Tuskegee.

## Sources

"Cemetery Restoration His Goal." *Asbury Park Press* or *Ocean County Observer* (July 11, 1988).

Fisher, Joseph. "His Scrapbooks Source of Memorable Material." *Asbury Park Press* (December 13, 1987): F8.

Harris, Jacqueline. *The Tuskegee Airmen: Black Heroes of World War II.* Parsippany, NJ: Dillon Press, 1996; 82–85.

Reininger, Stuart. "Black History Month: Education Helps Fight Bigotry." *Ocean County Observer* (February 12, 1990): A8.

Voorhis, Mark T. "The Legend Continues." *Sword Point* [332d Air Expeditionary Group, Kuwait] (October 13, 1999): 1, 4–5.

Watson, George, Sr., Lakewood, New Jersey to Betty K. Gubert, New York, telephone interviews, correspondence, and clippings, March–April 2000.

Watson, George, Sr. *Memorable Memoirs*. New York: Carlton Press, 1987.

Williams, Carol Gorga. "Tuskegee Airman Flies Again." *Asbury Park Press* (November 17, 1991): 1, 17.

# Warren H. Wheeler

**Full Name at Birth:** Warren Hervey Wheeler

**Born:** October 1, 1943, Durham, North Carolina

**Education:** Attended North Carolina Agricultural and Technical University for one year, 1961, American Flyers School, Oklahoma City, Oklahoma, 1962.

**Positions Held:** Flight instructor; pilot, Piedmont Airlines, 1966–1986; owner and president of Wheeler Flying Service, 1969–1986; pilot, US Air, 1986–1995.

**Summary:** Warren Wheeler was a pilot and entrepreneur who founded and ran a successful regional airline, Wheeler Flying Service, the nation's first African American scheduled airline, serving the Raleigh-Durham, North Carolina, area. He was also responsible for training more than 100 pilots, black and white.

## Early Years

Warren Wheeler was born on October 1, 1943, in Durham, North Carolina. He had an older sister, Julia. His father, John H. Wheeler, headed a family business, the Mechanics and Farmers Bank, the fourth largest African American bank in the country, and was a prominent citizen of the community. His mother, Selena Warren Wheeler, was a librarian.

Mrs. Wheeler achieved local renown when, while still attending college, her father, Dr. Stanford Warren, president of the Board of Trustees of the Durham Colored Library, asked her to act as library director. Although she had originally planned to attend law school, she remained at the library until her retirement in 1945. Under her direction, the library flourished, becoming the center of the African American community. She also began to collect and catalog books of African American interest. This collection, which now has 6,868 volumes, was named the Selena Warren Wheeler Collection in her honor.

According to Mrs. Wheeler, Durham provided a hospitable climate for black enterprises, including the library that she directed. "Durham has always been a little bit better. I think that all the black businesses had a lot to do with it. There was a lot of communication between the leaders of the [black and white] communities. These people talked together. They couldn't help but do it." The business climate favorable to African American enterprise that Mrs. Wheeler found in Durham was to be of inestimable help to her son when he founded a business.

It was his sister who first stimulated young Wheeler's interest in flying. She was taking flying lessons and took him for an airplane ride. The young man decided to take lessons as well and received his private pilot's license at 15. He was immediately focused on flying as a career, despite his father's wish that he go into the banking business.

## Higher Education

Wheeler attended North Carolina Agricultural and Technical University for a year, but he decided his interests lay elsewhere. He is quoted as saying, "I didn't know what I wanted to do, but I knew I was no banker." Dropping out of college, he enrolled in the American Flyers School in Oklahoma City, Oklahoma. Having successfully completed this course at 19, Wheeler was fully rated to fly multiengine planes and to teach others to fly.

## Career Highlights

In 1962, the civil rights movement was underway and picking up momentum. Segregation was still a fact of life, particularly in the South. No airline would hire Wheeler as a pilot, even though he was fully qualified. Part of the problem was his youth and inexperience, but a larger part of it was due to prejudice. At that time, there were no African Americans employed as pilots by major commercial airlines. Most white Americans believed that no black man could be a pilot, whatever his credentials. Things, however, were beginning to change.

Wheeler opened his own flight school and charter service in an effort to get more flying hours. "The whole idea of the school was to get enough flight hours to get hired by an airline." In this he was successful, and at the age of 22 Wheeler was hired as a pilot by Piedmont Airlines in 1965. He was Piedmont's first black pilot, and the youngest person in his training class. He was also among the first 10 black commercial pilots in the United States.

In 1969, while still employed by Piedmont, where he was now a captain, Wheeler took the first steps toward opening his own regional flying service. He took a leave of absence from his job, and, borrowing $36,000 from the Small Business Administration, started Wheeler Flying Service. He also received assistance from the Coastal Plains Regional Commission, which wanted to promote air transportation on the regional level in North Carolina. The business started modestly, with one airplane and one employee—Wheeler.

According to Wheeler, "At first, people were reluctant to try us. We were a new business, and, quite naturally, they were skeptical; they didn't think we'd be around long." However, Wheeler Airlines obviously filled a need, and by 1976 the company's fleet consisted of three Cessna-402 planes used for scheduled commuter service and another eight planes, which were used for charter flights. The company employed 27 persons, including 12 pilots, and was earning revenues in excess of $20,000 a month, according to an article in *Sepia* in 1976. About 80 percent of Wheeler's business consisted of white businessmen. Many of these were employed by Burroughs Wellcome, a major pharmaceutical firm with headquarters in Durham and a factory in Greenville, 100 miles away. The U.S. Postal Service and courier services for banks made up the balance.

Wheeler retained his connection with Piedmont, flying 65 hours a month for them. According to Wheeler, "Some people think I'm trying to get inside information about Piedmont by flying for them.... Actually, Piedmont doesn't see me as being in competition with them, and neither do I. My airline fills in gaps in their schedule, and all they ask is that I keep them informed of what I'm up to." Wheeler Flying Service also served as a feeder airline for Piedmont and other national air carriers. On occasion, the large carriers asked Wheeler to delay their flights for a few minutes so that their passengers could make connections to their final destinations in rural North Carolina.

Work at Wheeler Flying Service was demanding. All employees, including pilots, had to pitch in and help with chores like ticket selling and baggage handling. Nighttime phone calls about schedules and charters were forwarded to staffers' home telephones on a rotation basis. But none of the employees worked harder than Wheeler, who found it necessary to maintain two apartments—in Durham and in Norfolk, Virginia—in order to keep up his hectic schedule.

As a black-owned airline, Wheeler Flying Service was able to offer opportunities to young African American pilots. Warren Wheeler was cognizant of his responsibilities to offer a helping hand to other black people. According to Wheeler, "I always have in the back of my mind that I want to hire blacks. ... Fortunately, more blacks are becoming competent pilots, but I can't hire someone who is not the most qualified applicant because of color. . . . I believe in hiring people on merit, though anyone who pretends not to be prejudiced in favor of his own race is kidding himself."

Among African Americans who have been given an opportunity by Wheeler is Jill Brown, who in 1974 became the first black woman accepted by the U.S. Navy to train as a pilot. Shirley Tyus, now a pilot at United Airlines, also flew for Wheeler Airlines. In 1980, a federally subsidized employment program, CETA (named after the Comprehensive Employment and Training Act passed by Congress), allowed Wheeler to hire 12 black candidates for flight training. Wheeler is credited with having trained more than 100 pilots, black and white.

In 1986, the airline business had changed. Large and commuter airlines were merging, and larger carriers were looking to take over lucrative routes formerly serviced by local carriers. Wheeler Flying Service was a victim of these trends. Wheeler was forced to file for Chapter 11 bankruptcy proceedings in 1986, ceasing operations shortly thereafter. Warren Wheeler became a pilot with US Air, from which he retired in 1995.

In 1992, Wheeler was nominated to the board of directors of Opportunity Skyway and was unanimously elected for a two-year term. Opportunity Skyway, a nonprofit corporation based in Maryland, was dedicated to keeping teenagers in school, and encouraging them to work hard and prepare for successful careers. Wheeler was chosen because of his abiding interest in giving minority and disadvantaged youths an opportunity to choose careers in aviation.

## Sources

"First Black Airline Gets Off the Ground." *Ebony* (April 1976): 44–52.

Glassner, Barry. "Nation's Only Black Scheduled Airline." *Sepia* (April 1976): 18–23.

Holahan, Sharon. "Black Pilots Breaching Corporate Cockpit Barriers." *Aviation Convention News* (September 1, 1980): 74.

"Spreading Their Wings." *Ebony* (February 1986): 76, 78.

# John L. Whitehead Jr.

**Born:** [1924], Lawrenceville, Virginia

**Died:** Sacramento, California

**Education:** Pilot's wings, Tuskegee, Alabama, 1944; B.S. in industrial engineering, West Virginia State College, 1948; U.S. Air Force Experimental Test Pilots School, 1958; Sacramento, California, A.A. in electronics, 1984.

**Positions Held:** Pilot, 332nd Fighter Squadron, World War II; instructor of jet pilots, Williams Air Force Base, Arizona [1949 to 1951]; pilot, Korean War, early 1950s; Air Force liaison with Boeing Aircraft Corporation and Northrop Aircraft Corporation; chief of quality analysis division and test pilot, Hill AFB, Utah; pilot, Vietnamese War, 1960s; chief of standardization and evaluation division; deputy group commander of the maintenance and supply group, Edwards AFB, California, at retirement [1974].

**Awards, Honors:** Distinguished Flying Cross with three oak leaf clusters; Air Medal with seven oak leaf clusters; Army Commendation Medal; Air Force Commendation Medal.

**Summary:** John L. Whitehead Jr., a Tuskegee Airman, was at the forefront of military integration in 1948, and was a pioneer in the change from piston-engined fighter planes to jet-powered aircraft. He was the first African American pilot to graduate from the U.S. Air Force Experimental Test Pilots School, the first African American instructor of jet pilots, and the first African American pilot to fly the B-47 jet bomber.

## Early Years

Born in Lawrenceville, Virginia, about 1924, Whitehead's love of aviation began when he was a teenager. In 1942, he got a job as a line boy at Charleston Airport, near his hometown, and he joined the Enlisted Reserve Corps. When he turned 19 the following year, the minimum age at which one could volunteer for the military, he left his job and enlisted in the U.S. Army Air Corps. He was assigned to Tuskegee Army Air Field in Alabama.

## Higher Education

On September 8, 1944, Whitehead received his pilot's wings and was commissioned a second lieutenant. Whitehead left the military in 1947 to pursue his studies at West Virginia State College, where he completed a bachelor's degree in industrial engineering in 1948. Whitehead was recalled to active duty in August of that year. His next advanced educational experience was his selection for the U.S. Air Force Experimental Test Pilots School at Edwards Air Force Base in California. Graduating in January 1958, he became the first black experimental test pilot in the Air Force. During his retirement in Sacramento, California, Whitehead earned an A.A. degree in electronics in 1984.

## Career Highlights

Whitehead was a member of the 301st Fighter Squadron, one of the four black squadrons that made up the 332nd Fighter Group. Assigned to combat in Foggia, Italy, in March 1945, Whitehead was able to fly 19 missions before the war in Europe ended on May 8 of the same year. It was in Italy that Whitehead was given his nickname of "Mr. Death," which referred to his slender frame, and not to any ferocity of personality.

When the operations officer, Captain Robert J. Friend, saw the five-foot, six-inch, 121-pound lieutenant, he exploded, "My Gawd! What have they sent us now as replacement—Mr. Death?" Whitehead liked the name so much that he had it painted on his plane, a Mustang, and it became his nickname for life.

During combat Whitehead had two extremely close calls. One was in a brief battle with 33 German planes. Two American pilots lost their lives that day, and he barely missed being the third. The other skirmish found him separated from his wingman, and flying alone over enemy territory. German radar-directed antiaircraft guns were firing at him, front and back. With Whitehead looking at holes in his wings and his engine "running rough," he later told *Ebony*, "I talked to that engine like it was a baby all the way home, and I was sure hoping it understood me." When he returned to home base he saw that a piece of metal had gone through his parachute to nearly a quarter inch of his body.

Returning to the United States in the fall of 1945, he was assigned to Tuskegee Army Air Field, and then transferred to Lockbourne Army Air Base in Ohio. He left the service in January 1947 to obtain a degree in industrial engineering from West Virginia State College in 1948. He briefly returned to the 332nd Fighter Group at Lockbourne in August, until the group's dispersal about 1949. President Truman had issued Executive Order 9981 in 1948, integrating all branches of the armed forces. African American military personnel were now absorbed into units that had previously been all white.

Whitehead was sent to Williams Air Force Base (AFB) in Arizona as their first black jet pilot instructor in [June 1949]. He was respected and well liked because of his teaching skills and patience. He worked hard to break down the fear his students felt at piloting planes that flew 600 miles an hour, burning 400 gallons of fuel an hour. Popular at the AFB, Whitehead wrote a gossip column and enjoyed playing pinball. Not a reckless pilot, Whitehead never had an accident, and he didn't fly when weather conditions were unfavorable. "I try to remember that Mother Nature still runs this earth," was his comment to *Ebony*. Although Whitehead was the first black jet instructor, there were three other former Tuskegee pilots at the base with Whitehead in the position of instructor. They were Vernon Vincent Haywood, Henry B. Perry, and Lewis Lynch.

Whitehead then served as the training command representative on the B-47 aircraft at the Boeing Aircraft Corporation. During the Korean War, June 1950 to July 1953, he again saw combat, this time flying 104 missions. The Air Force later assigned him to Northrop Aircraft Corporation as chief production test pilot, and as a test pilot at Hill AFB in Utah in 1956. At Hill, he was also named chief of the quality analysis division. Whitehead, during his career, was also stationed in France and California.

With increased American participation in the Vietnam War in the 1960s, Whitehead served in a third war, flying combat missions in Southeast Asia. He returned to Edwards AFB in California, where he held such positions as chief of standardization and evaluation division, maintenance squadron commander, and at his retirement after 30 years, deputy group commander of the maintenance and supply group. Retired with the rank of lieutenant colonel, Whitehead had amassed 9,500 hours of flight time, with more than 5,000 hours in jets. He flew in 40 different types of airplanes, testifying to his skill and versatility as a pilot.

Whitehead died in Sacramento, California.

## Sources

Cooper, Charlie, and Ann Cooper. *Tuskegee's Heroes: Featuring the Aviation Art of Roy LaGrone.* Osceola, WI: Motorbooks International, 1996; 106, 120.

"Mr. Death." *Ebony* (January 1951): 28–30, 32–34.

# Oswald S. Williams Jr.

Oswald S. Williams Jr. Courtesy of O.S. Williams Jr.

**Full Name at Birth:** Oswald Sparrow Williams Jr.

**Born:** September 2, 1921, Washington, D.C.

**Education:** Boys' High School, Brooklyn, New York, 1938; B.S. in aeronautical engineering, New York University (NYU), 1942; M.S. in aeronautical engineering, NYU, 1947; M.B.A., St John's University, Jamaica, New York, 1981.

**Positions Held:** Engineer, Pitcairn Autogiro Company, Willow Grove, Pennsylvania, 1942; Republic Aviation Corporation, Farmingdale, New York, December 1942–July 1947; Greer Hydraulics, Inc., Brooklyn, May 1951–September 1956; Thiokol Chemical Corporation (Reaction Motors Division), Denville, New Jersey, 1956–1961; Grumman Aerospace Corporation, Bethpage, New York, 1961–1972; vice president (Marketing), Grumman International, Inc. 1973–1986; professor of marketing, St John's

University, College of Business, Jamaica, New York, 1986–   .

**Awards, Honors:** Associate Fellow of American Institute of Aeronautics and Astronautics.

**Summary:** Oswald S. Williams Jr., the second African American aeronautical engineer, made his greatest contribution to space science in 1970, when he headed the team that designed the 16-rocket steering system of the Lunar Module (LM) that would permit the Apollo astronauts to land on the moon. In the ill-fated Apollo 13 mission, when explosions disabled the main ship, the Command/Service Module (CSM), the LM, because of its design, was able to effect the return of the three astronauts to Earth, thus saving their lives. In 1974, Williams became the first black vice president at Grumman International, Inc.

## Early Years

Oswald Sparrow Williams Jr. and Donnell Glass Williams, born in 1921 and 1925, respectively, were the two sons of Marie Madden Williams and O.S. Williams Sr. Their father studied to become a pharmacist, but he had to take work as a waiter on the railroad. When post office employment became available to people of color in Washington, D.C., Williams Sr. worked there. The family moved to the Bedford-Stuyvesant section of Brooklyn when the children were still young. Ozzie, as he was known, later attended Boys' High School, graduating in 1938. He enjoyed building model airplanes and he became interested in many scientific and cultural subjects, including Egyptian hieroglyphics. A favorite outing for him and a friend was a visit to Central Park in Manhattan. There they could see the Egyptian obelisk called Cleopatra's Needle and study the hieroglyphics carved on it.

## Higher Education

Williams enrolled at New York University's School of Engineering in September 1938. An assistant dean of engineering tried to dissuade him, pointing out that there would be no jobs for him because of his race. That just made him more determined to become an aeronautical engineer. He did, graduating in 1942, one year after his friend and mentor, Douglas C. Watson. Watson and Williams were the first two African American aeronautical engineers. Worse than the initial discouragement was the blatant insult Williams's English teacher dealt him during the first class. To illustrate the concept of a mixed metaphor, the instructor looked straight at him, the only black in the room, and said, "There's a nigger in the woodpile and we're going to nip him in the bud." So searing was this moment, that Williams after more than 60 years, plans to title the autobiography he is writing, *Up from the Woodpile.*

In 1943, he and Doris Louise Reid were married. She, with degrees from Hunter College and Teachers' College, taught mentally handicapped children for 35 years. They had three children: Gregory Reid (1946–1982), who held a doctoral degree in experimental psychology, and who died of asthma; Bruce Goodwin, born 1951, an engineer; and Meredith Marie, born 1957, a software designer in the nuclear physics department of Cornell University. Williams earned a master's degree in aeronautical engineering from NYU in 1947, making him the first African American with two degrees in the subject. In 1981, Williams earned an MBA from St. John's University.

## Career Highlights

Oswald Williams likes to divide the 56 years of his working life into three parts. He was an aeronautical engineer for the first 30, then a marketing executive for 14 years, specializing in Africa, and finally, a professor at St. John's University for 12 years. Throughout the three careers Williams faced the challenges of racism, but he was able to rise above them by the quality of his performance.

After graduation, Williams went to work in 1942 at Pitcairn Autogiro Company (also called AGA for aircraft, glider, and autogiro) in Willow Grove, Pennsylvania. Douglas C. Watson had been hired by the company's owner, Virgil H. Frazier, a white southerner, and Watson helped Williams to get the job. Although World War II was in full swing and aeronautical engineers were scarce, both men were unable to find positions with large companies because of their color. Williams designed glider aircraft to rescue American troops in the Pacific. At the end of 1942, he moved to Republic Aviation Corporation in Farmingdale, New York. He was Republic's first black engineer, and he got the job by bluffing his way into an interview with the chief engineer. Just 21 years old, Williams talked his way through several armed security checkpoints. He told the engineer's secretary he was there to discuss her boss's "engineering employment problems." Intrigued, the chief engineer, a Russian emigré, gave him a job. He remained until July 1947, working first in the drafting department, designing minor parts for the plane he had been dreaming about, the P-47 "Thunderbolt." This plane was the one flown by the Tuskegee Airmen as they escorted the B-17 "Flying Fortresses." He later became a senior aerodynamicist, working on design studies of rocket-powered missiles and satellites. This pioneering work occurred 10 years before the Soviet Union launched its satellite, *Sputnik*.

After some unsatisfying employment due to the postwar recession, Williams worked at Greer Hydraulics, Inc., in Brooklyn, where he again was the first black engineer. At Greer from May 1951 until September 1956, Williams headed a project for the Air Force to develop an airborne radio for locating aircraft that had crashed. At the completion of the beacon project, Williams received the honor of associate fellowship in the American Institute of Aeronautics and Astronautics. His next employer was Thiokol Chemical Corporation, in Denville, New Jersey, from 1956 to 1961. He did pioneer tests on small liquid-fueled rocket engines, proving they could be used to steer spacecraft. William's 34-page paper, "Performance and Reliability of Attitude Control Rocket Systems," was published in 1959 by the American Rocket Society, of which he was a member. It was later translated into Russian.

The most significant part of Williams's first career, as an aeronautical engineer was to come at Grumman Aerospace Corporation in Bethpage, New York, where he was employed from 1961 until 1986. He conducted studies of steering rocket requirements for the Gemini and Apollo projects, and, in 1962, was a member of the Grumman team that negotiated the $1.75 billion contract to make the Apollo Lunar Modules for NASA. In Houston for the three weeks of negotiations, Williams and another black team member were denied a room at the Grumman team's official hotel. The team then found a new hotel, which had just announced a desegregation policy. When Williams visited Houston again in the 1970s, segregation was a thing of the past. "It shows you how much things can change," he said. Williams had a leading role in Vice President Hubert Humphrey's program on youth motivation, "Plans for Progress," in 1966. He headed a task force of black professional employees from various corporations in visits to southern minority colleges. Their mission was to motivate undergraduates to select courses that would prepare them for technical or business careers in the corporate world.

Williams's most important contribution to space exploration came when he was appointed manager of the three engineering groups who designed, tested, and installed the 16 small rocket engines, called "thrusters," that steered and stabilized each Apollo lunar module (LM) built for moon landings and takeoffs. This eight-year effort included responsibility for over $40 million in subcontracts alone.

But in April 1970, when the Apollo 13 mission was on its way to the moon, several oxygen tanks exploded and left the main ship (Command/Service Module) incapacitated. The lives of the astronauts, James A. Lovell Jr., Fred W. Haise Jr., and John L. Swigert Jr., were in extreme danger. The chief source of propulsion was gone and power for their life-support systems was dwindling. The *World Almanac* wrote, "The world marveled as the crew used the systems of the lunar landing module to transport them safely to earth." Lovell called the LM their "lifeboat." Williams said the fuel tanks for the 16 thrusters were "over designed," that is, built to handle much more than they needed to. Their extra capacity enabled the astronauts to reenter the Earth's atmosphere at a safe angle. They came to Grumman the following month to personally shake hands and thank its managers for having designed "the little engines that could," and for saving their lives. Williams, although deeply touched by the event, recently said jokingly, "I haven't washed that hand for 30 years."

Williams's second career, international business executive, began in 1973, when he moved over to Grumman International, Inc. He was appointed vice president of marketing in 1974, becoming the company's first black vice president. Holding this position until 1986, Williams made nearly 30 trips to 17 African countries to establish business ventures. In addition to product sales, he conducted extensive market surveys and research projects. With four Nigerian partners, he set up Nigeria Vanguard Industries to manufacture fiberglass products. He also organized the export of Grumman truck body kits, which were assembled in Nigeria, easing unemployment and providing workers with marketable skills. Williams was later invited to conduct seminars on marketing to Africa in London, Paris, and Stockholm, and, sponsored by the U.S. Information Service

(USIS), he lectured on technology acquisition in many Asian and African nations, such as Bangladesh, Indonesia, Nepal, Pakistan, Somalia, Sudan, and Thailand. Williams became a member of the Nigerian-American Chamber of Commerce, the American Management Association, and the American Marketing Association. He also wrote several articles on technology transfer to underdeveloped countries.

Traveling in so many African countries, Williams grew to admire and collect the art works of the many ethnic groups of the continent. He is a knowledgeable collector, and he has appeared on Queens television to share his enthusiasm and pleasure in collecting African art. Williams himself is an amateur sculptor in terra cotta and he has written many lyric poems, of which several have been published. He belongs to the New York Poets' Cooperative. He considers these artistic activities as "antidotes" to his technical and business careers.

When Williams retired from Grumman in 1986, he started his third career, as a tenured professor in the Department of Marketing at St. John's University in Jamaica, New York. As well as teaching undergraduate courses the elements of marketing, Williams developed a new graduate course in comparative marketing systems, including those in developing countries, and he served on the dean's advisory committee to develop an African American studies program. He received a student award for "Best Marketing Professor, and the Most Caring."

William's interests—aerodynamics, marketing, and civil rights—have led him to join many organizations and pursue many activities. Besides the arts, his hobbies include photography, bowling, swimming, and saltwater fishing. Williams and his family have been lifelong supporters of the NAACP and participants in career workshops. After the death of their son, they established the Dr. Gregory R. Williams Memorial Scholarship Fund. Administered by the United Negro

College Fund, family contributions, up to 1999, have totaled $85,000.

## Sources

*African Americans: Voices of Triumph. Leadership.* Vol. 2. Alexandria, VA: Time-Life Books, 1993; 60.

"Elect Williams VP at GII; To Set up African Office." [Grumman publication] (September 27, 1974).

*The Ida Van Smith Flight Clubs Historical Review.* Queens, New York, 1977, cover and eight pages of text and photographs.

Innis, Doris F. *Profiles in Black: Biographical Sketches of 100 Living Black Unsung Heroes.* New York: CORE Publications, 1976; 84–85.

Kempf, Debra. "Engineer, Marketer, Poet & Humanitarian Joins SJU." [St. John's University newspaper] (November 24, 1986): 14.

"Making Friends in Africa." *Black Careers* (July–August 1980): 18–23.

Poinsett, Alex. "Ozzie Williams: Our Man in Africa." *Grumman World* (Summer 1982): 4–5.

*A Three Career Man: Prof. O.S. Williams.* Director/Producer K.J. Prestwidge, Queens Public Access Television, Flushing, NY, 1991.

Williams, O.S. Jr., clippings and interview with Betty K. Gubert, New York, February 4, 2000.

# Y

## Perry H. Young Jr.

Perry H. Young Jr. Courtesy of Shakeh Young.

**Full Name at Birth:** Perry Henry Young Jr.

**Born:** March 12, 1919, Orangeburg, South Carolina

**Died:** November 8, 1998, Middletown, New York

**Education:** Oberlin High School, 1937; Oberlin College, Oberlin, Ohio, 1938–1940; private pilot's license, 1939; Lewis School of Aeronautics, Chicago, commercial pilot's license, 1940; New England Helicopters, New Bedford, Massachusetts, helicopter pilot's license, 1954; American Flyers, Fort Worth, Texas, airline transport rating, 1955.

**Positions Held:** Flight and ground instructor, U.S. Army Air Corps, Tuskegee Army Air Field, 1942–December 19, 1945; owner/operator, Port-au-Prince Flying Service, October 1946–October 1948; pilot and supervisor of maintenance, Société Haitienne-Américaine de Développement Agricole (SHADA), October 1948–February 1953; pilot, Puerto Rico Water Resources Authority, February 1953–October 1955; flight mechanic, Seaboard World Airlines, Canada, October 1955–June 1956; captain and line pilot, New York Airways, December 17, 1956–May 18, 1979; captain and line pilot, Island Helicopter Corporation, September 15, 1980–May 1981; chief pilot, New York Helicopter Corporation, May 19, 1981–March 14, 1986; operations administrator, Island Helicopter Corporation, March 17, 1986–May 1, 1987.

**Awards, Honors:** Honored as a pioneer at the "Black Wings" exhibition, National Air and Space Museum, 1982; Pilot Safety Award, Helicopter Association International, 1982; Pilot of the Year, 1984, Award for Outstanding Service, 1986, Island Helicopter Corporation.

**Summary:** Both an airplane and helicopter pilot, Perry H. Young Jr. made aviation history in December 1956. He became the first African American to be hired as a pilot by a regularly scheduled passenger airline, New York Airways, a helicopter service. He achieved another first in February 1957 when he was promoted to captain. Young's pioneering appointment was the wedge, however narrow, that opened the airline industry to African Americans as pilots, stewards, mechanics, and other positions.

## Early Years

Perry Henry Young Jr., was born on March 12, 1919, in Orangeburg, South Carolina, to Perry Henry Young Sr. and Edith Lucille Motte Young, the first of their four children. Mrs. Young was one of the 22 student founders of Delta Sigma Theta at Howard University in January 1913. The sorority now counts more than 125,000 members in 750 chapters in the United States, Africa, and the Caribbean. Before her marriage Mrs. Young taught French and literature at Howard University. Mr. Young owned a dry cleaning store and several garages, where his sons learned to work with motors. Everyone in the family played musical instruments: Mr. Young and the elder sister Farra played the cello; Mrs. Young played the piano; the younger sister Birneisis and William, the fourth child, played the violin. Beside the flute and piccolo, Perry Young also played the violin well enough to place first and sec-

ond in two of the music school's annual violin contests. The youngster also had time for the usual childhood pursuits, such as climbing trees. When he was 12, a local newspaper in Oberlin reported he broke his leg doing just that.

In 1929, the family moved to Oberlin because of Mrs. Young's wish to live in a town that housed not only a respected college but also the renowned Oberlin Conservatory of Music. Both his sisters graduated from the conservatory. His brother William was a cadet at Tuskegee, and he earned his pilot's wings in 1945. In high school, Young played the flute in the orchestra and he also won a letter in football as a guard and halfback. He graduated in June 1937.

## Higher Education

Despite winning a four-year scholarship in violin from the Oberlin Conservatory of Music, Young decided to enroll in Oberlin College to study chemistry and premedical courses in 1938. Right after graduation from high school, Young took a plane ride at a local airport, and from then on he could think of nothing else. He washed cars at a filling station, earning $9 a week to pay for lessons that cost $5.20 for 20 minutes. He took his first solo flight on Christmas Day 1937, little realizing that for an African American, a pilot's career was all but nonexistent. Twenty years later, Young would say, "Flying is my whole life. I love it." He continued flying lessons while he was in college, earning a private pilot's license on August 14, 1939. When the first national air conference for blacks was held in Chicago less than two weeks later, Young flew to it. His instructor, Ray McClenaghan, the manager of the airport at Lorain, Ohio, lent him his own plane, a Piper Cub, as a reward. The sponsor of the meeting, the National Airmen's Association of America, noted that Young, at 19, was the youngest pilot in attendance. Bitten by the flying bug and buoyed up by meeting other black flyers, Young left Oberlin College in 1940 to pursue aviation as a career.

## Career Highlights

Offered a job as instructor at the Coffey School of Aeronautics in Chicago, which had just begun its Civilian Pilot Training Program (CPTP) on a government contract, Young worked there from 1940 to 1941. During World War II Young was a civilian flight instructor at Tuskegee Army Air Field in Alabama. The army would not induct him because of his experience as an instructor, which was more useful to them. He trained more than 150 members of the 99th Pursuit Squadron to fly combat missions against enemy targets. One of his students was Clifton R. Wharton Jr., who became president of the largely white Michigan State University in 1969, and in 1989 became the chief executive officer of TIAA-CREF, the country's largest private pension fund. Wharton remembered his instructor as "extremely able and patient." The squadron became part of the Tuskegee Airmen and was highly decorated. When the war ended in 1945 Young applied to numerous airlines with the hope of employment as a commercial pilot. When no job offers materialized, Young briefly attended Howard University in Washington, D.C., at night, while working for the Public Buildings Administration's trucking service during the day. He also taught at Fisk University, Nashville, Tennessee, in the department of aviation education.

Finally disgusted with the lack of opportunity to fly in the United States, Young and two friends decided to try their luck abroad in 1946. His partners were James O. Plinton Jr., who later became vice president in charge of personnel for Trans World Airlines (TWA), and Fred Hutcherson Jr., who had flown for the Royal Canadian Air Force, and later began his own air service in Chicago,

after flying for the Colombian national airline. With the support of wealthy backers, they drew up a proposal for Haitian National Airlines, which was to fly from Liberia to Haiti to New York. But just before the papers were to be signed, the Haitian government changed hands, and the new regime demanded a 51 percent share. The sponsors withdrew. Young remained in Haiti and managed to buy two airplanes and start his own company, Port-au-Prince Flying Service. "It took me about two years to go broke," recalled Young. When the business failed in October 1948, Young sold his planes to the Société Haitienne-Américaine de Développement Agricole (SHADA), and went to work for them as a pilot and supervisor of maintenance until February 1953. SHADA developed industries such as lumber, and the farming of sisal, an important crop in the world market. Young married a Haitian woman and they had three children: Melitta, born in 1950, and who died in her 20s; Perry III, born in 1952; and Linda Ribeiro, born in 1953, and who married a Ghanaian, and is now a teacher in Accra.

In 1953, Young and his family left Haiti for Puerto Rico, where he held the position of executive pilot for Puerto Rico Water Resources Authority until October 1955. During this time Young was able to travel to New Bedford, Massachusetts, where he earned his helicopter license from New England Helicopters in 1954. In 1955, he gained his Airline Transport Rating from American Flyers in Fort Worth, Texas. Young began to feel homesick after having been out of the country for about 10 years and he returned to the United States and filed several job applications with different airlines.

While waiting for a response, he became a flight mechanic for Seaboard World Airlines, based in Canada. The company already had one black pilot, August Martin, so Young settled for the mechanic's position. Seaboard operated the Distant Early Warning (DEW) radar system against enemy attack. After flying in climates so cold he suffered a mild case of frostbite, he returned to the Caribbean. He flew passengers for KLM, the Dutch airline, between the Virgin Islands and the Dutch islands from August to December 1956. At this time Young had logged 13,000 hours of flying time, 200 of them in helicopters.

In December 1956 Young was interviewed by New York Airways, a regularly scheduled helicopter service flying between Newark Airport, New Jersey, and New York's airports, LaGuardia and Idlewild, the former name of Kennedy Airport. Young was offered the position of helicopter pilot. When he accepted, he and New York Airways made history. It was the first time that an African American pilot had been hired by a commercial airline with regularly scheduled passenger flights. In an interview with Sidney Fields (*New York Daily Mirror*, February 14, 1957), Young mused that his appointment was "The end of a long road and the start of another. The end of looking and the start of making sure I make good. I want that door open for the others."

Young had been considered before by this airline, but had been rejected because it was decided he did not have enough helicopter experience. What made him eligible now was the recent ruling by the Civil Aeronautics Board (CAB) that the new 12-passenger B-58 helicopters required co-pilots. Another element was the pressure brought by the State Commission against Discrimination (SCAD) on the airlines to cease discrimination in hiring. Chaired by Charles Abrams, SCAD had been successful in getting 18 airlines in New York State to subscribe to a policy of nondiscrimination in all hiring.

Hired on December 17, 1956, Young made his historic flight as co-pilot on February 5, 1957, from LaGuardia to Idlewild. In the same month, he was promoted to captain, having logged the required additional hours. Young remained with the company until May 18, 1979, when it declared bankruptcy. Young's long experience as a helicopter pilot then came into play as he helped develop

Virgin Island Airways, a helicopter airline in St. Thomas. From May 1979 to February 1980, Young, as director of operations, developed an operations manual for the fledgling airline. He did the same for another new helicopter service, Air Trans New York, until September 10, 1980.

Five days later, Young joined Island Helicopter Corporation (IHC), a sightseeing service in Manhattan. In a few months, he was appointed to captain and line pilot. In May 1981 he was appointed chief pilot, a position he held until his retirement on March 14, 1986. New York Helicopter Corporation, a subsidiary of IHC, was being formed as a scheduled passenger airline that would fly between Manhattan and the three local airports—Newark, LaGuardia, and Kennedy—and Young assisted in writing the operations manual. He then stayed on as operations administrator of IHC until May 1, 1987.

Perry Young and Shakeh Dildabanian, a real estate property manager, were married on May 22, 1971. Their home in Pine Bush, New York, is called Malgré Tout, French for "in spite of all." When he wasn't flying, and, after his retirement, Young enjoyed reading, tending his large vegetable garden, and landscaping his property with decorative stone walls. He was a long-time member of such professional organizations as the Air Line Pilots Association, American Helicopter Society, National Airmen's Association of America, Negro Airmen International, Organization of Black Airline Pilots, and Tuskegee Airmen International.

## Sources

"Aviators from Six States Hold Chicago Meet." *Chicago Defender* (September 2, 1939): 3.

Fields, Sidney. "Only Human." *New York Daily Mirror* (February 14, 1957).

"First Negro Airline Captain Will Spend Ground Time on L.I." *Long Island Sunday Press* (April 21, 1957): 17.

LeDuff, Charlie. "Perry H. Young Jr., 79, Pioneering

Pilot, Dies." *New York Times* (November 19, 1998): B13.

Lucas, Bob. "America's Only Negro Whirly-Bird Pilot." *Sepia* (April 1960): 37–40.

"Passenger Helicopter Pilot." *Ebony* (June 1957): 128–130.

Witkin, Richard. "First Negro Airline Pilot Hired; He Will Fly Helicopters Here." *New York Times* (December 14, 1956): 32.

Young, Shakeh, Pine Bush, New York, to Betty K. Gubert, New York, correspondence, personal and telephone interviews, clippings, April 1999–January 2000.

# Bibliography

## Selected Books

Biggs, Bradley. *The Triple Nickles: America's First All-Black Paratroop Unit.* Hamden, CT: Archon Books, 1986. Paper edition, 1994.

Bragg, Janet Harmon. *Soaring Above Setbacks: The Autobiography of Janet Harmon Bragg, American Aviator.* As told to Marjorie M. Kriz. Washington, DC: Smithsonian Institution Press, 1996.

Burns, Khephra, and William Miles. *Black Stars in Orbit: NASA's African American Astronauts.* New York: Harcourt Brace and Co., 1995.

Carisella, P.J. and James W. Ryan. *The Black Swallow of Death; The Incredible Story of Eugene Jacques Bullard, the World's First Black Combat Aviator.* New York: Van Nostrand Reinhold, 1972.

Cooper, Charlie and Ann. *Tuskegee's Heroes: Featuring the Aviation Art of Roy LaGrone.* Osceola, WI: Motorbooks International, 1996.

Davis, Benjamin O., Jr. *Benjamin O. Davis, Jr., American.* Washington, DC: Smithsonian Institution Press, 1991.

Dryden, Charles W. *A-Train: Memoirs of a Tuskegee Airman.* Tuscaloosa, AL: University of Alabama Press, 1997.

Fisher, Lillian M. *Brave Bessie: Flying Free.* Dallas, TX: Hendrick-Long Publishing Co., 1995.

Francis, Charles E. *The Tuskegee Airmen: The Men Who Changed a Nation.* Boston, MA: Branden Publishing Co., 1997. 4th edition, edited, revised, updated, and enlarged by Adolph Caso.

Gubert, Betty K. *Invisible Wings: An Annotated Bibliography on Blacks in Aviation, 1916–1993.* Westport, CT: Greenwood Press, 1994.

Hardesty, Von, and Dominick Pisano. *Black Wings: The American Black in Aviation.* Washington, DC: Smithsonian Institution Press, 1983.

Harris, Jacqueline. *The Tuskegee Airmen: Black Heroes of World War II.* Parsippany, NJ: Dillon Press, 1996.

Hart, Philip S. *Flying Free: America's First Black Aviators.* Minneapolis, MN: Lerner Publications, 1992.

———. *Up in the Air: The Story of Bessie Coleman.* Minneapolis, MN: Carolrhoda Books, 1996.

Haskins, James. *Black Eagles: African Americans in Aviation.* New York: Scholastic Press, 1995.

———. *Space Challenger: The Story of Guion Bluford.* Minneapolis, MN: Carolrhoda Books, 1984.

Holway, John B. *Red Tails, Black Wings: The Men of America's Black Air Force.* Las Cruces, NM: Yucca Tree Press, 1997.

Jakeman, Robert J. *The Divided Skies: Establishing Segregated Flight Training at Tuskegee, Alabama, 1934–1942.* Tuscaloosa: University of Alabama Press, 1992.

Jemison, Mae. *Find Where the Wind Goes: Moments from My Life.* New York: Scholastic Press, 2001.

Joseph, Lynn. *Fly, Bessie, Fly.* New York: Simon and Schuster, 1998.

Julian, Hubert F. *Black Eagle.* As told to John Bulloch. London: Jarrolds, 1964; London: The Adventurers Club, 1965.

Lindbergh, Reeve. *Nobody Owns the Sky: The Story of "Brave Bessie" Coleman.* Cambridge, MA: Candlewick Press, 1996.

Lloyd, Craig. *Eugene Bullard, Black Expatriate in Jazz Age Paris: The First African-American Combat Pilot.* Athens: University of Georgia Press, 2000.

Loving, Neal V. *Loving's Love: A Black American's*

*Experience in Aviation.* Washington, DC: Smithsonian Institution Press, 1994.

Lynn, Jack. *The Hallelujah Flight.* London: Robson Books, 1989; New York: St. Martin's Press, 1989. [Thomas C. Allen and J. Herman Banning]

McGovern, James R. *Black Eagle: General Daniel "Chappie" James, Jr.* Tuscaloosa: University of Alabama Press, 1985.

Naden, Corinne. *Ronald McNair, Astronaut.* New York: Chelsea House, 1991.

Nugent, John Peer. *The Black Eagle.* New York: Stein and Day, 1971. [Hubert F. Julian]

Petersen, Frank E. *Into the Tiger's Jaw: America's First Black Marine Aviator.* With J. Alfred Phelps. Novato, CA: Presidio Press, 1998.

Phelps, J. Alfred. *Chappie: America's First Black Four Star General, the Life and Times of Daniel James, Jr.* Novato, CA: Presidio Press, 1991.

———. *They Had a Dream: The Story of African-American Astronauts.* Novato, CA: Presidio Press, 1994.

Powell, William J. *Black Aviator: The Story of William J. Powell: A New Edition of William J. Powell's Black Wings,* with an introduction by Von Hardesty. Washington, DC: Smithsonian Institution Press, 1994.

Rich, Doris L. *Queen Bess: Daredevil Aviator.* Washington, DC: Smithsonian Institution Press, 1993. [Bessie Coleman]

Sandler, Stanley. *Segregated Skies: All-Black Combat Squadrons of WW II.* Washington, DC: Smithsonian Institution Press, 1992.

Scott, Lawrence P. *Double V: The Civil Rights Struggle of the Tuskegee Airmen.* East Lansing, MI: Michigan State University Press, 1993.

Scott, William R. *The Sons of Sheba's Race: African Americans and the Italo-Ethiopian War, 1935–1941.* Bloomington: Indiana University Press, 1993. [Chapters on Hubert F. Julian and John C. Robinson]

Simmons, Thomas E. *The Brown Condor: The True Adventures of John C. Robinson.* Silver Spring, MD: Bartleby Press, 1988.

Smith, Charlene E. McGee. *Tuskegee Airman: The Biography of Charles E. McGee.* Boston, MA: Branden Publishing Co., 1999.

Spencer, Chauncey E. *Who Is Chauncey Spencer?* Detroit, MI: Broadside Press, 1975.

Taylor, Theodore. *The Flight of Jesse Leroy Brown.* New York: Avon Books, 1998.

Warren, James C. *The Freeman Field Mutiny.* San Rafael, CA: Donna Ewald, 1995.

## Selected Videos

*Black Aviators: Flying Free.* The History Channel, March 2001.

*Black Stars in Orbit: NASA's African-American Astronauts.* Khephra Burns, writer; PBS Video, 1990.

*Flyers in Search of a Dream.* Philip S. Hart, writer; PBS Video, 1993.

*Nightfighters: The True Story of the 332nd Fighter Group, The Tuskegee Airmen.* Xenon Entertainment Group, Santa Monica, California, 1994.

*Willa Beatrice Brown: An American Aviator.* Severo Perez, writer; California Department of Education, 1999.

# Index

## About the Authors

BETTY KAPLAN GUBERT is the compiler of *Invisible Wings: An Annotated Bibliography on Blacks in Aviation, 1916–1993* (Greenwood 1994), among other bibliographies. Formerly head of reference services at the Schomburg Center for Research in Black Culture, New York Public Library, for 21 years, she is the subject specialist in art for *MultiCultural Review*, and has had several articles published in such journals as *African Arts, American Libraries, Judaica Librarianship*, and in scholarly reference works such as *American National Biography, Encarta Africana*, and the *Encyclopedia of New York City*.

MIRIAM SAWYER is director of the Rutherford Public Library, Rutherford, NJ. She received her B.A. from Ohio University and her MLS from State University of New York at Albany. She has written numerous articles for library publications, and was editor of *New Jersey Libraries*, the official publication of the New Jersey Library Association, 1994–1996. At present she is a regular reviewer for *MultiCultural Review*, a periodical published by Greenwood.

CAROLINE M. FANNIN is a writer and library administrator. She received a bachelor's degree in writing and literature from Wheaton College, and a master's degree in library service from Rutgers University. Her previous collaborations have covered topics ranging from abortion and capital punishment to the works of Flannery O'Connor.